EDUCATING WOMEN

Educating Women

Schooling and Identity in England and France,
1800–1867

CHRISTINA DE BELLAIGUE

OXFORD

UNIVERSITY PRESS

OXFORD
UNIVERSITY PRESS

Great Clarendon Street, Oxford OX2 6DP

Oxford University Press is a department of the University of Oxford.
It furthers the University's objective of excellence in research, scholarship,
and education by publishing worldwide in

Oxford New York

Auckland Cape Town Dar es Salaam Hong Kong Karachi
Kuala Lumpur Madrid Melbourne Mexico City Nairobi
New Delhi Shanghai Taipei Toronto

With offices in

Argentina Austria Brazil Chile Czech Republic France Greece
Guatemala Hungary Italy Japan Poland Portugal Singapore
South Korea Switzerland Thailand Turkey Ukraine Vietnam

Oxford is a registered trade mark of Oxford University Press
in the UK and in certain other countries

Published in the United States
by Oxford University Press Inc., New York

© Christina de Bellaigue 2007

British Library Cataloguing in Publication Data

Data available

Library of Congress Cataloging-in-Publication Data

De Bellaigue, Christina.
Educating women : schooling and identity in England and France, 1800-1867 / Christina de Bellaigue.
p. cm.
Includes bibliographical references and index.
ISBN 978-0-19-928998-1 (alk. paper)
1. Women--Education--England--History--19th century. 2. Women--Education--France--History--19th
century. I. Title.
LC2052.D4 2007
371.8220973'09034--dc22
2007013461

Typeset by Laserwords Private Limited, Chennai, India
Printed in Great Britain
on acid-free paper by
Biddles Ltd., King's Lynn, Norfolk

ISBN 978–0–19–928998–1

1 3 5 7 9 10 8 6 4 2

For Ben
Et pour mes parents

Acknowledgements

I have incurred many debts in working on this book. My research was generously supported by the Arts and Humanities Research Board, and by the Warden and Fellows of Merton College, Oxford. I am grateful to the Spencer Foundation and the American National Academy of Education for the generous Post-Doctoral Fellowship that enabled me to spend a productive year at the Stanford Institute for Research on Women and Gender.

My heartfelt thanks are due to Gillian Sutherland, who has guided me throughout my research and whose intellectual rigour and wisdom have been unfailing. Jean-Noël Luc fostered the early stages of my work and has continued to offer guidance and support. Many other friends and colleagues have given generously of their time and advice, particularly Susan Groag Bell, Elvire de Coëtlogon, Kathryn Gleadle, Gabrielle Houbre, Olwen Hufton, Joanna Innes, Hazel Mills, and Karen Offen. I am indebted to Rebecca Rogers for her encouragement and for allowing me to read her manuscript before it was published. Michèle Cohen, Gillian Dow, Maroussia Raveaud, and William Whyte also shared their unpublished work. Michèle Cohen, Gillian Dow, Celina Fox, Robert Gildea, Janet Howarth, Alison Kay, Diana Selig, and Robert Tombs have all kindly read and provided constructive comments on all or parts of the draft. I am grateful to the readers for Oxford University Press for their thoughtful and careful commentaries, and to Rupert Cousens, Anne Gelling, and Alice Jacobs for their patience and guidance. I am entirely responsible for any errors and flaws that remain.

For permission to make use of the copyright material in their charge I am indebted to the British and Foreign School Society (BFSS) Archive, Brunel University, to the College of Preceptors Archive at the Institute of Education Archives, to the Mistress and Fellows of Girton College, Cambridge, to the Governesses' Benevolent Institution, to the Principal and Fellows of Harris Manchester College, Oxford, to the Lilly Library, Indiana University, Bloomington, Indiana, to North London Collegiate School Library, to the Angus Library, Regent's Park College, Oxford for permission to use material left to the college by Marjorie Reeves, to the Society of Authors as agent for the Provost and Scholars of King's College, Cambridge, to the Special Collections Department of the University of Sheffield Library, to the Trustees of the Wedgwood Museum, Barlaston, Stoke-on-Trent, Staffordshire, and to Whitelands College, Roehampton University. Charmian Snowden and the late Nanette Godfrey very kindly invited me to Tudor Hall School to see their archival material. I am very grateful to the many archivists and librarians who have provided expert advice.

Particular thanks are due to Sue Mills at the Angus Library, Kate Perry at Girton College, Agnès Varia at the Archives Municipales de Bordeaux, and Brian York at the BFSS Archives Centre. Parts of Chapter 4 appeared in an article in *The Historical Journal* in 2001 and are reprinted with permission from Cambridge University Press. Parts of Chapters 4 and 5 appeared in an article in *Paedagogica Historica* and are reprinted with permission from Taylor and Francis Publishing (http://www.tandf.co.uk).

None of this would have seen the light of day without the help of my husband and family, who provided much-appreciated help with statistics, with references, with drafting, and with proof-reading. Their unfailing encouragement and support has sustained and inspired me.

Contents

Abbreviations

AD Gironde	Archives Départementales de la Gironde, Bordeaux
AD Nord	Archives Départementales du Nord, Lille
AD Seine	Archives Départementales de la Seine, Paris
AM Bordeaux	Archives Municipales de Bordeaux
AM Douai	Archives Municipales de Douai
AN	Archives Nationales de France, Paris
BFSS	British and Foreign Schools Society Archive, Brunel University
GBI	Governesses' Benevolent Institution
GPDSC	Girls' Public Day School Company
HCSS	Home and Colonial School Society
HMCO	Harris Manchester College, Oxford
JJ Coll.	John Johnson Collection of Printed Ephemera, Bodleian Library, Oxford
KUL	Keele University Library, Special Collections and Archives
LLIB	Lilly Library, Indiana University, Bloomington
LSM	London Association of Schoolmistresses
NLC	North London Collegiate School Archives, London
REF	*Revue de l'Enseignement des Femmes*
SIC	Schools Inquiry Commission
SIC	*Parliamentary Papers, XXVIII: Reports of the Schools Inquiry Commission*
SIE	*Société pour l'Instruction Élémentaire*

List of Illustrations

List of Figures

Introduction

In 1841, the school inspection committee of the first *arrondissement* in Paris reported that a Mlle Bray, an English schoolmistress, had infringed the regulations governing girls' boarding-schools in Paris. Mlle Bray's school had been founded by her mother in 1819; it had generally received good reports from the inspectors: they commented on its cleanliness, the large number of English boarders, and noted (without further comment) that the food was prepared 'after the fashion of the English'. However, contrary to the provisions of a prefectoral ruling of 1810, Mlle Bray had failed to put up a sign indicating her name and the nature of her establishment at the entrance to her school. The committee warned that unless the requisite sign was displayed, she would no longer be authorized to keep a school. Mlle Bray protested in terms that hint at deep-seated differences between the practices of girls' education in England and France. She argued that 'in her own country, this was not done', and that 'to conform to the ruling would be to dishonour her establishment'.[1]

Many of Mlle Bray's contemporaries might have shared this sense that her position would have been different in England. Nineteenth-century observers frequently commented on the marked contrasts they saw between the lives of women on either side of the Channel.[2] In 1832, the economist Adolphe Blanqui argued that 'the ideal, for a woman, would be to become an adult in France, having been a girl in England'. He contended that when they married, French women left 'the kind of slavery' of their previous existence and discovered a new freedom. For English women, however, the reverse was true; they enjoyed such liberty only before marriage.[3] The author Hubert Jerningham captured this apparent contrast succinctly: 'in France, marriage is the establishment of

---

[1] Note de Zoë Hubert, *c.*1846; Inspection pension Bray, 1838, 1840, 1841; Procès verbaux du Comité de Surveillance du 1er arrdt., 13 May 1841, AD Seine, VD⁶ 158–3. All translations from the French are my own, except where a translator is named. I have aimed to convey the meaning of the French as closely as possible, rather than to translate elegantly. When the precise wording is difficult to render exactly, the French is given in italics in the notes.

[2] See below and, for example, the chapters on women in F. Trollope, *Paris and the Parisians in 1835*, 2 vols. (London, 1836) and F. Tristan, *Promenades dans Londres*, 2nd edn. (Paris, 1978); G. Eliot, 'Woman in France: Madame de Sablé', *Westminster Review*, 91 (1854), 448–73; C. de Sault (pseud. of C. de Charnacé), 'Les femmes dans la société anglaise', *Revue Européenne,* 8 (1860), 299–331; J. Boucherett, 'The condition of women in France', *Contemporary Review*, 5 (1867), 98–113.

[3] Blanqui (aîné), 'Des demoiselles et des dames en France et en Angleterre', *Journal des Femmes*, 1 (1832), 246.

woman's freedom; in England, that of woman's dependence'.[4] Such ideas were reiterated throughout the period by commentators on both sides of the Channel, and echoed long-standing ideas about differences between French and English society. In the eyes of some observers, France was the pinnacle of polite society, where men and women mixed freely and women exerted a cultured and civilizing influence through the *salons*. In England, it was claimed, women lived apart from men, and were subordinated to them. Other observers saw English society as the model: there, they felt, men occupied themselves with serious public matters, while women eschewed French frivolity and display, and cultivated the private domestic virtues 'which give the tone to English character'.[5]

Yet despite these perceived differences, in the first half of the nineteenth century both countries witnessed a parallel development of interest in the question of female education, reflected in the proliferation of treatises that sought to define the role of women and delineate notions of ideal womanly behaviour. And on both sides of the Channel, the dominant conception of the purpose of female education was broadly the same. In England, the educationist Hannah More argued that 'the profession of ladies, to which the bent of their instruction should be turned is that of daughters, wives, mothers and mistresses of families', while in France a ministerial ruling of 1820 stressed that 'the sole purpose' of female education was to educate girls for 'their natural and respectable vocation' as mothers.[6] In both countries, numerous authors expounded upon the notion that whereas men should be prepared for the masculine sphere of politics and business, women should be educated for motherhood and domesticity. Partly in response to such arguments, boarding-schools for girl were multiplying.

This book tracks the parallel development of schooling for girls in England and France in the period 1800 to 1867. Comparison sheds light on the experiences of young girls and adult women in the two countries, while at the same time offering an opportunity to uncover and explore the differences that lay behind Mlle Bray's predicament. As I demonstrate in the chapters that follow, such differences reflected and reinforced contrasts between the experience of French and English women. Uncovering these overlapping differences offers new insights into the complex interaction of the different cultural, political, economic, and religious forces that affected the lives of women in the first part of the nineteenth century.

---

[4] H. Jerningham, *Life in a French chateau* (London, 1867), 196.

[5] S. Ellis, *The women of England, their social duties and domestic habits* (London, 1839), 37; M. Cohen, 'Manliness, effeminacy and the French: gender and the construction of national character in eighteenth century England', in M. Cohen and T. Hitchcock (eds.), *English masculinities, 1660–1800* (London, 1999), 44–61; For a wide-ranging study of relations between Britain and France in this period, see R. and I. Tombs, *That sweet enemy: the French and the British from the Sun King to the present* (London, 2006).

[6] H. More, *Strictures on the modern system of female education with a view of the principles and conduct prevalent among women of rank and fortune* (London, 1826), i. 109–10; Instruction du ministre relative aux maisons d'éducation des filles, le 19 juin 1820, cited in *Revue de l'Enseignement des Femmes* (hereafter *REF*), 2 (Feb. 1845), 17.

The comparative perspective also provides an opportunity to explore contrasts between the lives of French and English women identified by contemporary observers, and to engage with questions about national differences in conceptions of femininity. Such questions have recently been the subject of considerable debate, a debate that intensified following the publication of Mona Ozouf's *Les mots des femmes* (1995). In *Les mots des femmes*, Ozouf argues that examining the work of French women writers reveals a 'French singularity' in gender relations. Echoing earlier commentators, she contends that patterns of sociability, inherited from the *salons* of the *Ancien Régime*, mean that women in France are less excluded from circles of influence than their British or American counterparts. In Ozouf's analysis, three factors—this social mixing, France's Revolutionary heritage (in the shape of a radical conception of universal equality), and an ideal of complementarity between the sexes elaborated at the beginning of the nineteenth century—all combine to produce a distinctive understanding of femininity, and harmonious relations between the sexes in France. This 'French singularity', she argues, explains the contrast between the tranquillity and measured tones of French feminism and the 'aggressive individualism' of British and American feminism.[7]

Les mots des femmes has been the subject of considerable controversy. With justification, the book has been criticized for playing down the constraints and exclusions to which French women have been subject, and for underestimating the degree to which gender has been a site of struggle in France.[8] Nonetheless, at least for the nineteenth century, I would argue that Ozouf is right to maintain that there were differences between the pattern of gender relations in France and Britain. But by explaining contrasts between the experiences of French women and those of British and American women with reference to an idea of 'French singularity', she does little to disentangle the knot of gendered assumptions and associations that inform notions of national character.[9] More damagingly, her analysis neglects the social, political, economic, legal, and religious forces which had an influence on women's lives, and overlooks the ways in which patterns of gender relations were challenged and reconfigured through the agency of individual men and women. Questions about how far, and for what reasons, the daily lives of French and English women differed are left unanswered.

In order to answer these questions, I adopt a more empirical approach, responding both to the challenge posed by Ozouf's view of national differences in ideas of femininity, and to calls in the British historiography for an analysis

---

[7] M. Ozouf, *Les mots des femmes* (Paris, 1995).

[8] Her caricature of Anglo-American feminism has also come in for justified criticism. See 'Femmes: une singularité française?', *Le Débat,* 87 (Nov.–Dec. 1995), 118–46; E. Fassin, 'The purloined gender: American feminism in a French mirror', *French Historical Studies,* 22 (1999), 113–39.

[9] M. Perrot, 'Une histoire sans affrontements', *Le Débat,* 87 (Nov.–Dec. 1995), 130–4.

which relates prescription to practice.[10] Rather than focusing on the literature that sought to prescribe the way women should behave, I examine how idealized conceptions of femininity influenced the lives of those French and English women to whom such prescriptions were addressed. The detailed comparative study of boarding-schools for girls permits a case-study of national differences in these conceptions. It provides an opportunity to unpick notions of national character and to set the differences in gender relations perceived by both contemporary observers and historians in their cultural, social, economic, religious, and political context. The case-study looks beyond the prescriptive literature to explore how individual women might be constrained or empowered by the theoretical conceptions of femininity current in society. It offers insights into the ways in which women responded to and helped articulate rhetorical ideas of domesticity, motherhood, and femininity, and provides an opportunity to examine how such ideas might be undermined, challenged, or reinforced in the practice of every day life. At the same time, it uncovers the ways in which developments in girls' education influenced contemporary understandings of gender.

Focusing more particularly on private lay boarding-schools, private school-mistresses, and their pupils provides a constructive opportunity to develop this kind of approach. Debates about the nature and role of women crystallized around the question of education. In both countries it was emphasized that girls were best educated by their mothers in the family home, yet growing numbers were being sent away to school, growing up in non-familial environments and experiencing the kind of group socialization deemed essential to the development of young men destined for public life, but inimical to the ideal of private and domestic female virtue.[11] Lay schoolmistresses, by their very existence, undermined ideals of domestic womanhood. Many were unmarried and childless, when the accepted destiny of women was to be wives and mothers, and by their work they subverted the proposition that the female sphere was purely domestic. They could not conform to prevailing notions of femininity without a certain degree of ambiguity. Nor could lay schoolmistresses align themselves unequivocally with the model of the teacher developed by women religious. And while they might have more autonomy than their religious counterparts, they could not rely on the material and institutional backing that a religious order or *congrégation* might provide. Examining the experiences of lay teachers uncovers the ways in which women were able to operate as independent agents, as businesswomen,

---

[10] A. Vickery, 'Golden age to separate spheres? A review of the categories and chronology of English women's history', *Historical Journal*, 36 (1993), 383–414; K. Wilson, *Island Race: Englishness, empire and gender in the eighteenth century* (London, 2003), 4. See also L. Kerber, 'Separate spheres, female worlds, woman's place: the rhetoric of women's history', *Journal of American history*, 75 (1988), 9–39.

[11] M. Cohen, 'Gender and the public/private debate on education in the long eighteenth century', in R. Aldrich (ed.), *Public or private education? Lessons from history* (London, 2004), 15–35.

and as professionals, without the support or controlling influence of religious organizations. At the same time, focusing on the experiences of lay women provides an insight into the impact of religious affiliation on women's lives beyond the convent. It sheds light on the relationship between religion, gender, and national identity. Private schools, established by middle-class women and run for profit, give a particular insight into the possibilities and constraints of women's lives on either side of the Channel.[12]

Studying private boarding-schools also uncovers the experiences of that section of society which was likely to have been most affected by national differences in perceptions of femininity and which was also a dynamic force in the history of girls' education. It was to 'the estimable class of female who might be more specifically denominated *women*, and who yet enjoy the privilege of liberal education, with exemption from the pecuniary necessities of labour' that authors seeking to define an ideal of womanhood addressed their efforts.[13] It was middle-class women whose circumstances attracted the attention of observers on either side of the Channel. Middle-class women were at the core of the women's movement which at mid-century sought to influence the development of female education and to expand the opportunities available to women. And it was these middle-class girls and women who populated private lay boarding-schools. In the nineteenth century, the distinction between elementary and secondary education did not imply an age-related progression through a hierarchy of schools. The key distinction between the two was that of social class, dividing the elementary schools offering basic instruction to working-class children from the secondary establishments that catered for middle-class children and proposed a more expanded curriculum.[14] Private boarding-schools for girls, adding literature, history, geography, and sometimes scientific instruction to the basic instruction offered by the elementary schools, were secondary establishments, both in terms of their curriculum, but more especially in terms of their middle-class clientele and personnel.

Focusing on the period 1800 to 1867 uncovers both the rise of this distinctive, and neglected, form of female schooling, and the first signs of its gradual eclipse as new forms of government-sponsored institution began to supplant private

---

[12] Marie-Madeleine Compère argues that the study of educational provision across national boundaries must be based on an analysis of comparable institutions (M.-M. Compère, *Histoire de l'éducation en Europe. Essai comparatif sur la façon dont elle s'écrit* (Paris, 1995), 269). However, as the discussion above indicates, my decision to focus on lay schools in the French context rests on the sense that the position of lay schoolmistresses is more revealing of the place of middle-class women in society than that of women religious. At the same time, my research suggests that distinctions between religious and secular establishments were less significant than might be expected to many contemporaries, particularly with reference to girls' education. As will be shown in the following chapters, lay establishments were heavily influenced by religious models, and teachers and pupils often moved from lay schools to convent schools and vice versa. Focusing on lay establishments thus offers insights into the educational landscape as a whole.

[13] Ellis, *Women of England*, Preface.

[14] G. Sutherland, ' "Secondary education", the education of the middle classes', in G. Sutherland (ed.), *Education in Britain* (Dublin, 1997), 138–49.

establishments in the provision of secondary education for girls. In France, although Republican educational reformers tended to suggest that in the first half of the century girls' education was the exclusive preserve of religious orders, private lay boarding-schools or *pensions* dominated the supply of secondary schooling for girls and outnumbered convent schools until the 1860s. In England, aside from a handful of proprietary schools established by joint committees of shareholders in the 1840s, and from the convent schools which began to appear at mid-century, these private establishments were the only institutions offering secondary instruction to girls.[15] On both sides of the Channel, private boarding-schools were thus a key form of schooling for middle-class girls in the first part of the nineteenth century.

By the 1860s, however, a growing number of voices in both countries were calling for the extension of girls' education, and this period saw the first efforts to mobilize resources nationally for the development of secondary instruction for girls. In 1867, Victor Duruy sponsored the creation of *cours secondaires*—lecture courses given by *lycée* professors that aimed to offer a secondary education to middle-class girls.[16] The following year saw the publication of the multi-volume report produced by the Schools Inquiry Commission (SIC) on secondary education in England. As a result of public pressure from schoolmistresses and feminists, it included within its scope the first official investigation of female education. Building on its findings, the Endowed Schools Act of 1869 included provision for the redistribution of endowments to create secondary schools for girls.[17] Although in both England and France, private boarding-schools continued to cater for considerable numbers of girls, in the second half of the century it was the new high schools and *lycées* that led the way in female education.

The historiography of girls' education has a somewhat different focus on either side of the Channel. English studies tend to privilege the role of individuals rather than policy in examining the evolution of girls' education. Many concentrate on the role of key figures in the mid-century reform of women's education. Moreover, partly as a result of the links between these individuals and the early history of the women's movement, and partly because of a stronger tradition of women's history in Britain, the English historiography is often underwritten by

[15] On the development of other forms of schooling for girls, see notes 18 and 19 below. On convent schools in England, see W. J. Battersby, 'Educational work of the religious orders of women; 1850–1950', in G. Beck (ed.), *The English Catholics* (London, 1950), 337–54; S. O'Brien, 'French nuns in nineteenth century England', *Past and Present*, 154 (1997), 142–81; R. Kollar, 'Foreign and Catholic: a plea to Protestant parents on the dangers of convent education in Victorian England', *History of Education*, 31 (2002), 335–50.

[16] S. Horvath, 'Victor Duruy and the controversy over secondary education for girls', *French Historical Studies*, 9 (1975), 83–102; F. Mayeur, *L'éducation des filles en France au XIXe siècle* (Paris, 1979), ch. 5.

[17] *Parliamentary Papers, XXVIII: Reports of the Schools Inquiry Commission* (London, 1868) (hereafter, *SIC*); G. Sutherland, ' "Secondary education" '; L. Goldman, *Science, reform and politics in Victorian Britain* (Cambridge, 2002), ch. 8; S. Fletcher, *Feminists and bureaucrats: a study in the development of girls' education in the nineteenth century* (Cambridge, 1980).

an interest in the history of feminism.[18] In France, historians have been more concerned with examining the development of schooling for girls as an aspect of the history of educational policy and schooling provision.[19] This difference both reflects and has substantial roots in differences in the sources available to historians on either side of the Channel. In France the early development of an administrative framework to supervise private boarding-schools generated official regulations, inspection reports, and personnel records which are the key sources for historians of secular education. In England, the lack of government involvement in girls' secondary education before the 1860s means that historians are heavily dependent on correspondence, memoirs, and biographies in researching the history of girls' schooling. The nature of the sources has thus influenced the focus of national historical accounts.

I have sought to offset this influence by drawing on a wide range of sources, and using them to shed light on questions not fully addressed in the national historiographies. In France, the volume of inspection reports, dossiers on individual schoolmistresses, official rulings, and official correspondence imposes a narrowed geographical range. I have drawn particularly on material from the departments of the Seine, the Nord, and the Gironde. This selection cannot be representative of France as a whole, but nevertheless offers a good cross-section of French society.[20] On the other side of the Channel, my research has focused on England,

[18] S. Burstall, *Retrospect and prospect: sixty years of women's education* (London, 1933); J. Kamm, *How different from us: a biography of Miss Buss and Miss Beale* (London, 1958); J. Kamm, *Hope deferred: girls' education in English history* (London, 1965); J. Kamm, *Indicative past: a hundred years of the Girls' Public Day School Trust* (London, 1971); C. Dyhouse, *Girls growing up in late Victorian and Edwardian England* (London, 1981); M. Vicinus, *Independent women: work and community for single women, 1850–1920* (London, 1985), ch. 5; J. S. Pedersen, *The reform of girls' secondary education in Victorian England: a study of elites and educational change* (New York, 1987); S. Skedd, 'The education of women in Hanoverian Britain, c.1760–1820', D.Phil. thesis (Oxford, 1996); On the important contribution of Nonconformists, see C. Binfield, *Belmont's Portias: Victorian non-conformists and middle class education for girls* (London, 1981); R. Watts, 'The Unitarian contribution to education in England from the late eighteenth century to 1853', Ph.D. thesis (Birmingham, 1980); R. Watts, 'The Unitarian contribution to the development of female education, 1790–1850', *History of Education*, 9/4 (1980), 273–86; M. Reeves, *Pursuing the muses: female education and Non-Conformist culture, 1700–1900* (Leicester, 1997).

[19] O. Gréard, *L'enseignement secondaire des jeunes filles*, 3rd edn. (Paris, 1883); F. Mayeur, *L'enseignement secondaire des jeunes filles sous la Troisième République* (Paris, 1977); Mayeur, *L'éducation des filles;* K. Offen, 'The second sex and the Baccalauréat in Republican France, 1880–1924', *French Historical Studies*, 13 (1983), 252–86; J. Burr Margadant, *Madame le Professeur: women educators in the Third Republic* (Princeton, 1990); Rebecca Rogers' work provides the most recent and comprehensive study of private schools for girls: 'Competing visions of girls' secondary education in post-Revolutionary France', *History of Education Quarterly*, 34 (1994), 147–70; 'Boarding schools, women teachers and domesticity: reforming girls' secondary education in the first half of the nineteenth century', *French Historical Studies*, 19 (1995), 153–83; 'Schools, discipline and community: diary-writing and schoolgirl culture in late nineteenth century France', *Women's History Review*, 4/4 (1995), 526–55; *From the Salon to the schoolroom: educating bourgeois girls in nineteenth-century France* (Philadelphia, 2005).

[20] Paris had the largest concentration of private boarding-schools for girls throughout the period. It was in the Seine that a supervisory framework was developed which would provide a model

the educational histories of Wales, Scotland, and Ireland having their own par-
ticularities.[21] Within England, the geographical dispersal of the sources available
means that the regional focus adopted for France is inappropriate. Moreover,
evidence from the one official inspection of girls' schools—the SIC—reveals a
significant degree of consistency in the structure and content of girls' schools
throughout the country. For both countries, I have used evidence from memoirs,
biographies, and correspondence to build up biographical samples documenting
the lives of schoolmistresses and pupils. This approach offers insights into the
experiences of individuals, whilst also permitting me to uncover general trends
and to place experiences in context. Working comparatively underlines the
national peculiarities of the history, while the application of insights drawn from
the French historiographical tradition to the English context, and vice versa,
sheds new light on the evolution of women's education in the two countries.

The very unevenness of the sources, however, illustrates a contrast in the history
of girls' education on either side of the Channel. While girls' schools in England
developed independently of government supervision, their French counterparts
were contained within a regulatory system that shaped their development and
imbued them with a public character that English schools were far from sharing.
Moreover, despite the chronological symmetry of the history of girls' education
in the two countries, and despite the shared conception of female education
as a preparation for domestic life, closer examination of the development of
girls' boarding-schools in England and France uncovers significant contrasts
between the institutions established on either side of the Channel. English
schools tended to be small, emphasizing their familial atmosphere and domestic
setting; French schools, by contrast, were often much larger and more public in
orientation. Whereas English schoolmistresses sought to present themselves as
'schoolmothers', their French counterparts elaborated a conception of their role
that had a different resonance. At the same time, while English schoolgirls might

---

for the administration of *pensions* or boarding-schools throughout the country. The cosmopolitan
Parisian context contrasts with the Nord, dominated by an increasingly prosperous industrial and
entrepreneurial bourgeoisie, and with the Gironde, dominated by an established commercial middle
class. See A. Daumard, *La bourgeoisie parisienne de 1815 à 1848*, (Paris, 1996); D. Garrioch, *The
formation of the Parisian bourgeoisie, 1690–1830* (Cambridge Mass., 1996); A. Jardin and A. J.
Tudescq, *La France des notables (1815–1848): la vie de la nation* (Paris, 1973); L. Trenard, *Histoire
de Lille: l'ère des révolutions (1715–1851)* (Toulouse, 1991); B. Smith, *Ladies of the leisure class: the
bourgeoises of Northern France in the nineteenth century* (Princeton, 1981); R. Gildea, *Education in
provincial France, 1800–1914: a study of three departments* (Oxford, 1983); L. Desgraves and G.
Dupeux (eds.), *Bordeaux au XIXe siècle* (Bordeaux, 1969); P. Guillaume, *La population de Bordeaux
au XIXe siècle: essai d'histoire sociale* (Paris, 1972).

[21] On other parts of the British Isles, see A. V. O'Connor, 'Influences affecting girls' secondary
education in Ireland, 1860–1910', *Archivium Hibernicum*, 41 (1986) 83–98; J. McDermid, *The
schooling of working-class girls in Victorian Scotland: gender, education and identity* (London, 2005),
and 'Handmaiden to a patriarchal tradition? The schoolmistress in Victorian Scotland', *Études
Écossaises*, 9 (2003–4) 43–57; W. Gareth Evans, *Education and female emancipation: the Welsh
experience, 1846–1914* (Cardiff, 1990).

emphasize the sense of freedom and autonomy they enjoyed at school, French pupils tended to focus on the restrictions and constraint of school life. There was of course more variation in individual cases than these generalizations might suggest. Nevertheless, the disparities revealed by the study of girls' boarding-schools in France and England hint at the differences between the situation of women in the two countries observed by contemporaries and discussed by Ozouf. Exploring these contrasts in context demonstrates that one cannot make sense of them by reference to ideals of femininity and notions of sociability alone. Differences between girls' schools in France and England reflect the interaction of gender with pre-existing patterns of educational provision and expectations, with the roles of church and state in the two societies, and with the differing rhythms and patterns of economic growth. Contrasts observed by contemporaries between the situations of women on either side of the Channel were rooted in the complex and mutually reinforcing effects of all these factors.

By exploring the emergence and expansion of private schooling for girls, looking at the recruitment and training of schoolmistresses; the strategies involved in establishing a school and claiming professional standing; the lives of schoolgirls and the instruction they received; and the experiences of pupils and teachers who crossed the Channel, this book illuminates unexplored areas of the history of women and of education. Boarding-schools offer a framework through which to explore women's lives in England and France. The case-study permits an analysis which does not confine individual women within categories of 'French femininity', or 'English womanhood', and which at the same time allows us to understand the actions and representations of pupils and teachers in the context of the structures and constraints surrounding them.[22] Exploring the experiences of schoolmistresses and their charges provides an insight into the ways in which girls and women constructed, were affected by, and responded to discourses of femininity in their daily lives. It highlights the degree to which these ideals were modified and undermined in practice. As suggested above, notions of domestic femininity emphasizing motherhood and women's role in the home were gaining increasing currency in both countries at the beginning of the nineteenth century. Comparison reveals that in both countries such ideals had a powerful impact on the development of girls' schooling, and on the experiences of teachers and pupils. But examining the lives of the women and girls to whom prescriptions concerning womanhood were addressed reveals that in different cultural, social, political, and religious contexts, notions of domesticity resonated differently and played themselves out in different ways. The comparative study of boarding-schools and their inhabitants uncovers the interaction of the forces shaping women's lives in the first half of the nineteenth century.

---

[22] I am influenced by Nancy Green's view of the social historian's role, 'Classe et ethnicité, des catégories caduques de l'histoire sociale?', in B. Lepetit (ed.), *Les formes de l'expérience: une autre histoire sociale* (Paris, 1995), 165.

1

The Development of Schooling for Girls in England and France

In the 1860s the governments of France and England each dispatched observers to record the situation of boys' secondary education on the opposite side of the Channel. To Matthew Arnold, sent to the Continent on behalf of the SIC, and to his counterparts Joseph Demogeot and Henry Montucci, sent to England and Scotland by the *Ministre de l'Instruction Publique*, the contrasts between the two countries were marked. The disparities they observed related both to the degree of public involvement in schooling and to the establishments providing it. In England, Demogeot and Montucci were struck by the lack of system in the provision of secondary education, and the fact that it was 'completely abandoned to individual initiative with the public authorities abstaining completely from any involvement'.[1] By contrast, Arnold praised the degree to which middle-class education in France was 'treated as a matter of national concern', and applauded the 'serious effort' made to provide good-quality schooling for those who needed it.[2] Considering the schools themselves, both Arnold and his French counterparts were struck by the difference between the domestic atmosphere of English schools and the more institutional character of French establishments. To Demogeot and Montucci, 'the English school is a family, a private house . . . Our schools, are in general large halls of residence . . . The French *collège* is a regiment.'[3] Both reports were being used to prove a point: Arnold referred to the French example to argue for the creation of a state system of secondary education in England; Demogeot and Montucci used their report to criticize the over-centralization of the French system. Even allowing for exaggeration, however, their accounts point to profound differences in the conception of boys' education and schooling on either side of the Channel in the nineteenth century.

Neither Matthew Arnold nor his French counterparts visited girls' schools, nor did they consider the question of female education. Yet, as we have seen, the subject was attracting considerable interest in both England and France in

---

[1] J. Demogeot and H. Montucci, *De l'enseignement secondaire en Angleterre et en Écosse* (Paris, 1868), pp. iii–iv.

[2] M. Arnold, 'A French Eton or democratic education and the state' (1864), ed. R. H. Super, *The complete prose works of Matthew Arnold* (Ann Arbor, 1962), ii. 264.

[3] Demogeot and Montucci, *De l'enseignement secondaire*, 593. Arnold, 'A French Eton', 297.

this period, and, on both sides of the Channel, idealized notions of domesticity, which emphasized the importance of preparing girls for motherhood and home duties, fuelled the expansion of schooling for girls. By the 1860s, contemporary observers in both countries were criticizing girls' schools in very similar terms. The SIC felt that female establishments in England were characterized by 'want of thoroughness and foundation, want of system; slovenliness and showy super-ficiality; inattention to rudiments [and] undue time given to accomplishments'. The previous year Jules Simon had complained that, in France, 'girls, even in the best boarding-schools, receive a futile, incomplete education, entirely taken up with accomplishments, including nothing serious or edifying'.[4] Yet this apparent symmetry is belied by closer examination of girls' schools in the first part of the nineteenth century. Differences between female establishments in England and France echoed, but were not identical to, the contrasts remarked by contemporary observers of boys' education. At the same time, the criticisms of girls' schools made by the SIC and Jules Simon underestimated both the diversity and the importance of female schooling before 1860.

ENGLAND—THE EMERGENCE OF A DOMESTIC MODEL OF SCHOOLING

The Development of Schooling for Girls

In 1792, Clara Reeve observed that 'in every town you go through, you may see written in letters of gold, "A Boarding-school for Young Ladies" '.[5] Schools for girls were proliferating. In the sixteenth century aristocratic families had sent their daughters away to be educated in the households of godparents or family members. Some were sent to convent schools.[6] The dissolution of the monasteries, and the closure of convent schools, saw the development of other strategies for female education, further stimulated by the Civil War, which disrupted early modern familial arrangements. There were already so many girls' schools in Hackney in the 1630s that the area was known as 'the ladies' university of female arts', and all over the country the number of schools for girls continued to grow throughout the second half of the seventeenth century.[7]

These establishments catered mainly for the nobility and gentry. However, rising levels of female literacy point to increasing interest in female instruction

---

[4] 'Report of the Commissioners', *SIC* i. 548; Jules Simon, speech to the Corps Législatif, 2 Mar. 1867, quoted in F. Buisson (ed.), *Dictionnaire pédagogique* (Paris, 1914), i. 1022–3.

[5] C. Reeve, *Plans of education with remarks on the systems of other writers* (1792; New York, 1974), 111.

[6] M. Bryant, *The London experience of secondary education* (London, 1986), 70; K. Charlton, *Women, religion and education in Early Modern England* (London, 1999), 126–30.

[7] D. Gardiner, *English girlhood at school* (Oxford, 1929), 211.

in the middle ranks of society. By 1714 the proportion of women able to read had risen, very approximately, to 25%, and it rose again to 40% by 1750.[8] This increase was part of a general trend, fostered by the Reformation emphasis on reading the scripture and by the demand for literacy in an increasingly mercantile society. The group most affected was the growing professional and commercial class, and writing and arithmetic schools emerged to provide the training their sons required.[9] Although for their daughters education at home and informal instruction continued to be the norm, demand for girls' schools was also increasing. A study of 120 prominent women born in the eighteenth century, of whom the majority were drawn from the professional and merchant class, reveals that twenty-four (20%) had been educated in boarding-schools.[10] By the end of the eighteenth century, as Clara Reeve observed, girls' schools catering to the middle classes were multiplying. The number of private establishments for girls in Islington, Putney, Chelsea, and other outlying (as they were then) areas of the capital continued to grow. In Oxfordshire in the 1760s thirty-one schools for girls were advertising in *Jackson's Oxford Journal*; by the 1810s, their number had doubled.[11]

In the nineteenth century the number of boarding-schools for girls continued to increase. The nature of these establishments, however, makes this increase difficult to quantify precisely. Boarding-schools were private commercial ventures and rarely established with a view to institutional permanence. Moreover, building on early modern practices of household education rather than being formally constituted institutions, many private schools had simply developed from family schoolrooms. For example, the school kept by the Unitarian sisters Helen and Emily Higginson in Derby in the 1820s had grown from their taking in outside pupils to educate with their younger sister Isabella.[12] This pattern of establishment continued to be common throughout the century. Thus, in the 1870s, the London schoolmistress Mrs Herschell replied to a father's enquiry about her establishment by saying that 'I am educating my younger daughter at home, with a few girls of good family'.[13] Even where there was no such familial basis, future schoolmistresses sometimes began simply by taking pupils into their own homes. Hannah Pipe, a successful London schoolmistress in the 1850s, had started by teaching in her mother's home in Manchester.[14] For others, the first

---

[8] O. Hufton, *The prospect before her: a history of women in Western Europe* (London, 1995), 424.

[9] L. Stone, 'Literacy and education in England, 1640–1900', *Past and Present*, 42 (1969), 130–1; Bryant, *London experience*, 57–70.

[10] N. Hans, *New trends in education in the eighteenth century* (London, 1951), 195–8.

[11] Bryant, *London experience*, 14–9; S. Skedd, 'Women teachers and the expansion of girls' schooling in England, c.1760–1820', in H. Barker and E. Chalus (eds.), *Gender in eighteenth century England* (London, 1997), 104–5.

[12] Letters of Helen Martineau, Oxford, Harris Manchester College, Oxford (hereafter HMCO), MS J. Martineau 8.

[13] G. M. Herschell to Gill, 20 Dec. 1878, Lilly Library, University of Indiana, Bloomington (hereafter LLIB), Gill MSS.

[14] A. Stoddart, *Life and letters of Hannah E. Pipe* (London, 1908), 38.

step in establishing a school was to seek out and rent an appropriate site, as was the case for the Byerley sisters, who kept a successful establishment in the 1810s and 1820s. In 1810 they rented a town house in Warwick in which to begin their school and moved to progressively larger premises as it expanded.[15] Some establishments, like the Byerleys', which continued to operate as a school until about 1860, endured over several decades, often being transferred to new owners. Despite their casual beginnings, private schools for girls might develop a certain institutional solidity. Nevertheless, the informality of the arrangements involved in opening a school, their vulnerability to market forces, and the absence of any kind of administrative control over private education, meant that many girls' schools were relatively short-lived, disappearing as rapidly as they appeared. In Salford, only eight of the twenty private girls' schools in existence in 1835 had been established before 1830.[16] This transience and the fluidity of the boundaries between the family schoolroom and the school means that it is difficult to determine exactly how many schools for girls were in operation at any one time.

Yet evidence from commercial directories and educational surveys does give some idea of the numerical weight of girls' boarding-schools in the first half of the nineteenth century. By 1828 one London directory was listing 289 schools in the outskirts of London, and sixty peppered throughout the city.[17] Census returns reveal that London schools recruited pupils both from the capital and from farther afield. Most of the twenty-eight pupils at Eliza Payne's school in Lambeth in 1841 were not born in Middlesex. The same was true of pupils at the Miss Brownings' school in Blackheath in the same year.

Although schools in the capital benefited from the prestige of being able to advertise 'the best London masters', the proliferation of female establishments was very much a national phenomenon. In the eighteenth century, girls' schools tended to cluster in well-established market towns, rather than the newer industrial cities.[18]To a certain extent this pattern endured in the nineteenth century. Even towns as small as Melton Mowbray, which had a population of only 776 in 1831, managed to support one boarding-school and four private day-schools for girls. Similarly, Stratford-upon-Avon, with a population of 5,171 in 1831, had two boarding-schools and two schools for 'ladies' in 1835.[19] Spa resorts and coastal cities were also popular locations, combining the advantages of 'good air' and fashionable society. There were eight boarding-schools and six private schools for girls in Leamington Spa (with a population of 6,209

[15] P. D. Hicks, *A quest of ladies: the story of a Warwickshire school* (London, 1949), 19.

[16] *Report of the Manchester Statistical Society on the state of education in the borough of Salford* (Manchester, 1835), 11.

[17] G. B. Whittaker, *Boarding school and London masters directory* (London, 1828), 1–27.

[18] J. H. Plumb, 'The new world of children in eighteenth century England', *Past and Present*, 67 (1974), 72.

[19] Pigot and Co., *National and provincial directory for Herefordshire, Leicestershire, Monmouthshire, Rutlandshire, Staffordshire, Warwickshire, Worcestershire, North Wales and South Wales* (Manchester, 1835), 74, 332.

in 1831) in 1835.[20] Bristol and Clifton were particularly well supplied, with forty-five ladies' boarding-schools in 1821, when the population was 95,758.[21] But in the nineteenth century, schools also began to appear in industrial and commercial cities. There were forty-five ladies' boarding-schools listed in the Liverpool directory of 1828–9 and thirty-two in Birmingham (including Aston and Edgbaston) in 1836.[22] By 1861 *Crockford's Scholastic Directory* included sixty-two pages listing 'private schools for ladies'—approximately 8,060 establishments distributed throughout cities and towns all over the country.[23] *Crockford's* list included private day-schools for girls as well as boarding-schools and thus incorporated institutions that were closer to elementary schools than to secondary establishments catering exclusively for middle-class girls. Nonetheless, the directory clearly demonstrates that by the 1860s secondary schools for girls were ubiquitous.

It is more difficult to assess what proportion of the population made use of these schools. Susan Skedd estimates that in Oxfordshire in 1821, only 4% of girls aged 5–15 attended private schools, a figure which points to the elite nature of these establishments.[24] In Manchester, only 3% of the female school-age population were pupils at private schools.[25] It is only possible to estimate very roughly how these local studies relate to the national picture, but relating the number of schools listed in *Crockford's* directory to the figures calculated by William Farr for the SIC, which put the number of middle-class girls aged between 10 and 20 at 306,807, suggests that at mid-century at least half of all middle-class girls were attending a private school of some sort.[26]

Ideas of Domesticity and Female Education

To many contemporaries, the proliferation of 'ladies' academies' was explained by the pretensions of middle-class parents who sought to provide an aristocratic education for their daughters.[27] Historians have tended to concur, emphasizing

---

[20] Ibid. 318.

[21] Pigot and Co., *National and provincial directory for Berkshire, Buckinghamshire, Gloucestershire, Hampshire, Oxfordshire* (Manchester, 1830), 93–4.

[22] Pigot and Co., *National and provincial directory for Cumberland, Lancashire, Westmoreland* (Manchester, 1828–9), 133.

[23] *Crockford's Scholastic Directory for 1861* (London, 1861).

[24] Skedd, 'Education of women', 175.

[25] D. Chadwick, 'On the social and educational statistics of Manchester and Salford', *Transactions of the Manchester Statistical Society* (1861), 30.

[26] William Farr's figure was calculated for the benefit of the SIC, cited in J. Roach, *A history of secondary education in England, 1800–1870* (London, 1986), 4. There were approximately 8,060 private schools for girls listed in *Crockford's* in 1861. The average number of pupils in private girls' boarding-schools in this period was 19.7 (based on a sample of 56 establishments opened by schoolmistresses active between 1800 and 1867). Using this figure to calculate the number of girls who could have been accommodated in *Crockford's* 8,060 schools suggests that around 158,782 of the 306,807 middle-class girls identified by Farr could have been attending a private school in 1865.

[27] Reeve, *Plans*, 60–1; More, *Strictures*, i. 71–6.

the social aspirations that motivated parents to send their daughters to school.[28] The story behind parents' decisions to send their children to boarding-school was often more complex than this narrative suggests, even if growing demand for girls' schooling does seem to have been motivated in part by the same impulses which pushed parents to seek out public-school education for their sons, namely 'to dignify a process of upward mobility'.[29] But the rapid expansion of schooling for middle-class girls at the end of the eighteenth century and in the early years of the nineteenth century also owed much to the growing influence of notions of domestic femininity that stimulated interest in female education.

At the end of the eighteenth century, as Leonore Davidoff and Catherine Hall have demonstrated, authors like Hannah More and William Cowper were contributing to the elaboration of a rhetoric of domesticity that was a core element in the self-definition of a growing middle class. Drawing on Protestant Evangelical notions emphasizing the holiness of the family, these writers idealized the comforts of the home as a sanctuary from the world of business and portrayed the women whose role it was to maintain that sanctuary as naturally loving, pious, and retiring. In this discourse, femininity was increasingly tied to the idealized private domestic sphere, and middle-class status increasingly seen to depend on men's ability to provide for their women through work in a public arena characterized as male.[30] According to Hannah More, it was women's 'profession' to be 'the daughters, wives, mothers and mistresses of families'. She contended that 'a woman sees the world, as it were, from a little elevation in her own garden, whence she takes not in that wider range of distant prospects, which he who stands on a loftier eminence, commands'. Women were 'the lawful possessors of a lesser domestic territory', and should not aspire to be 'the turbulent usurpers of a wider foreign empire'.[31] Although this trend built on long-standing patterns of gender relations, and although in practice the frontiers between such territories were more permeable than the language of spheres suggests, the concurrence of Evangelical ideas, middle-class aspirations, and economic changes leading to a growing separation between home and work, infused ideals of domesticity and the concept of 'separate spheres' with a new energy and force.

The influence of these ideas on the development of girls' education was considerable. One reason for the proliferation of girls' boarding-schools was that

[28] P. J. Miller, 'Women's education, "self-improvement" and social mobility—a late eighteenth century debate' *British Journal of Educational Studies*, 20 (1972), 302–14; Pedersen, *Reform*, ch. 1.

[29] J. R. de Honey, *Tom Brown's universe: the development of the public school in the nineteenth century* (London, 1977), 124.

[30] L. Davidoff and C. Hall, *Family fortunes: men and women of the English middle class, 1780–1850*, rev. edn. (London, 2002).

[31] More, *Strictures*, i. 109–10, ii. 29–30. First published in 1799, *Strictures* had gone through thirteen editions by 1826.

in a context in which work for pay was constructed as a male prerogative and femininity predicated on domesticity, teaching—as an extension of the maternal role—was the only occupation a middle-class woman could undertake without losing caste. More positively, underlining the importance of women's duties also justified the extension of female education.[32] By the 1780s a growing number of authors were arguing that in order to fulfil their domestic role women needed a rational intellectual education. Pedagogues like Maria Edgeworth emphasized the importance of educating girls who could 'sympathise in all their [husband's] thoughts and feelings, who can converse with them as equals, and live with them as friends; who can assist them in the important and delightful duty of educating their children; who can make their family their most agreeable society and their home the attractive centre of happiness'.[33] Hannah More called for girls to be given a solid intellectual education as preparation for their future 'profession'. Similarly, Anna Laetitia Barbauld underlined that a girl's destiny was 'to be a wife, a mother, a mistress of a family', and argued that 'the knowledge belonging to these duties is your professional knowledge, the want of which nothing will excuse'. This 'professional knowledge' was best acquired through a rational education.[34] Nineteenth-century authors like the Unitarian J. O. Squier argued that women needed a 'solid and substantial, intellectual and moral education' to prepare them for their domestic mission.[35] In both positive and restrictive ways, gendered notions of domesticity were a powerful influence on women's lives in nineteenth-century England. The shape and character of girls' boarding-schools exemplified the pull and the push of this influence.

A Domestic Model of Schooling

As noted above, schools for boys in England seemed domestic in their arrangements to observers from France. Moreover, whereas on the Continent the Jesuits and other religious orders had established the beginnings of an educational system, the evolution of English education had depended largely on individual initiative. Making a virtue of this lack of system, private schools for boys often made much of their domestic and familial organization.[36] In public schools, pupils were divided up into 'houses' which, following the example set by Thomas Arnold at Rugby, were increasingly headed by married masters whose wives played an important part in the daily life of the house, so that the boys

---

[32] A. Fletcher, *Gender, sex and subordination* (London, 1995), 634–76.

[33] M. Edgeworth, *Letters for literary ladies* (London, 1993), 37.

[34] More, *Strictures*; A. L. Barbauld, *A legacy for young ladies, consisting of miscellaneous pieces in prose and verse by the late Mrs Barbauld*, ed. L. Aikin (Boston, 1826), 25. On Hannah More's views, see A. Stott, 'A singular injustice towards women': Hannah More, Evangelicalism and female education, in S. Morgan, (ed.), *Women, religion and feminism in Britain, 1750–1900* (Basingstoke, 2002), 23–38.

[35] J. O. Squier, *The character and mission of woman* (London, 1937), 21.

lived in a kind of extended family.[37] Arnold saw this domestic atmosphere as a bulwark against the potentially corrupting influence of institutional life. It married well with his conception of the school as a moral entity and with his emphasis on the individualized pastoral care that masters would provide; the school was 'a system of instruction towards moral perfection', not merely a teaching academy.[38] The fluidity of boundaries between the family schoolroom and educational establishments bolstered this domestic conception of the school, a conception further reinforced by the accent placed on the educative function of the family and domestic life. For James Angell James, home was 'the school of character'. John Stuart Mill saw the family as 'the real school of the virtues of freedom'.[39] In emphasizing the home-like character of English schools, Demogeot and Montucci were uncovering the influence of an educational tradition in which home and school were both structurally and rhetorically intertwined.

The first part of the nineteenth century, however, had seen the elaboration of a conception of education that emphasized the distance between school and home. Vicesimus Knox's *Liberal Education*, published in 1781, had helped tip the balance in favour of school, rather than home education for boys: boys must be sent to school, where discipline, exertion, and friendships with other boys would draw out the qualities they would need as men. By the end of the eighteenth century, the public, non-familial environment of the school was increasingly considered essential for the development of masculine virtue.[40] Thomas Arnold's work built on this new emphasis on the value of school education and contributed to the evolution of a particular conception of the school. Although Arnold had encouraged the familial direction of houses at Rugby, he envisioned the school as 'a little world' rather than a family home, insisting upon the importance of emulation and autonomy, and the corporate identity of the school. Reflecting the influence of a Protestant emphasis on self-improvement and self-government, school was perceived as a period of apprenticeship for adult life.[41] Simultaneously, schools themselves were undergoing a process of institutionalization as establishments expanded and were able to maintain relatively continuous high levels of recruitment, and as public and grammar schools became more stable and less dependent on the skills and charisma of individual headmasters. This stability was reflected in the new buildings with which public and grammar schools sought to underline

---

[36] Bryant, *London experience,* 156.   [37] Honey, *Tom Brown's universe,* 11.

[38] Quoted in D. Newsome, *Godliness and good learning: four studies on a Victorian ideal* (London, 1961), 52.

[39] J. A. James, quoted in Davidoff and Hall, *Family fortunes,* 109; J. S. Mill, 'On the subjection of women' (1865), ed. S. Collini, *On liberty and other writings,* 2nd edn. (Cambridge, 1993), 160.

[40] Cohen, 'Gender and the public/private debate'.

[41] T. W. Bamford, *Thomas Arnold on education* (Cambridge, 1970); Newsome, *Godliness and good learning,* 28–91.

their historic antecedents and institutional solidity, and through which they affirmed their adherence to an Arnoldian conception of the school.[42] Despite the domesticity of some of their arrangements, English schools for boys asserted their public and institutional character no less categorically than their more impersonally structured French counterparts.

In a period when women's role was often idealized as private and domestic, the characterization of educational institutions as essentially public and masculine had implications for the development of girls' schooling. Whilst Knox and Arnold argued that boys could only properly be educated in large public institutions, authors like John Chirol, who published an investigation of female education in 1809, contended that 'even the best boarding-schools are good for nothing, because they are not adapted to the constitution or destiny of woman'.[43] Though Hannah More and Anna Laetitia Barbauld emphasized the need to extend female education, they felt that girls, being destined for family life, were best educated at home, and that female virtue could only be cultivated in a domestic setting. In 1787 Barbauld turned down Elizabeth Montagu's suggestion that she start a girls' school, on the grounds that 'the best way for women to acquire knowledge is from conversation'.[44] This resistance to the development of schools for girls was also fuelled by hostility towards female institutions *per se*. Although after the Reformation the idea of a 'Protestant nunnery' was periodically revived and occasionally garnered considerable support, convent schools were regarded with suspicion. Catholic emancipation in 1829 and the re-establishment of the Catholic hierarchy in 1850, at a time when the number of convents in Britain was rapidly increasing, fuelled such sentiments. As a number of historians have demonstrated, as well as expressing a form of Protestant patriotic nationalism, opposition to convents and convent education reflected hostility to a model of feminine institution that was felt to undermine domesticity and patriarchal control of property. Female institutions—which carried an echo of the convent—dangerously foreign and Catholic as they were, were characterized as artificial and contrary to women's domestic, familial nature.[45]

[42] Honey argues that this conception of the school as an educational community was 'probably more powerfully and fully developed [in Britain] than anywhere else in the world' *Tom Brown's universe*, p. xxi, chs. 1 and 3; W. Whyte, 'Building a public school community, 1860–1910', *History of Education*, 32 (2003), 601–26.

[43] J. L. Chirol, *Enquiry into the best system of female education, or boarding school or home education attentively considered* (London, 1809), 19.

[44] A. Barbauld to E. Montagu, 1774, quoted in M. Hilton, ' "Child of Reason": Anna Barbauld and the origins of progressive pedagogy', in M. Hilton and P. Hirsch (eds.), *Practical Visionaries: women, education and social progress, 1790–1830* (London, 2000), 30.

[45] F. Cobbe, 'Female Charity, lay and monastic', *Fraser's Magazine*, 66 (1862), 774–88; 'Two views of the convent question', *Macmillan's Magazine*, 19 (1869), 534–43; N. Auerbach, *Communities of women: an idea in fiction* (Cambridge, Mass., 1978) ch. 1; W. L. Arnstein, *Protestant versus Catholic in Mid-Victorian England: Mr Newdegate and the nuns* (London, 1982); B. Hill, 'A refuge from men: the idea of a protestant nunnery', *Past and Present*, 117

Despite such opposition, schools for girls continued to multiply. However, whereas boys' establishments sought to emphasize their institutional character, amongst female establishments, 'there are many schools, the conductors of which have adopted as much as is practicable in a public establishment a system of domestic education and therefore afford a pleasing substitute for *home*, to the children placed under their care'.[46] The SIC found that girls' schools were 'often spoken of as intended to be more a home than a school'.[47] The same sentiment was expressed by many other schoolmistresses: Elizabeth Sewell, a successful teacher and author who kept a school on the Isle of Wight in the 1850s, was 'indignant if [her establishment] was called a school, it was a family home'.[48] Far from seeking to underline the distance between family and school, English schoolmistresses were building on the domestic tradition in English education to assimilate their establishments as much as possible to the home, to an extent that far exceeded any attempt to preserve a degree of domesticity in boys' schools. Women teachers sought to reconcile their establishments with a notion of femininity that idealized women's domestic nature and maternal role, and with an Evangelical ideal of domesticity that conceived of the home as a feminine preserve, a sanctuary from the world of business, and as the school of character.

The familial character of school life was reinforced by its setting. As noted above, some schools were first started in the family home, and most were established in ordinary town houses. This, as the SIC noted, was also true of many boys' schools. However, rather than making modifications which would give their establishments a more institutional quality, schoolmistresses accentuated the domestic character of the houses they occupied. Girls shared small bedrooms, ate in a dining-room, and might spend evenings in the family drawing-room.[49] Elizabeth and Ellen Sewell's school occupied 'a cheerful and friendly house'. One pupil, Mary Fraser, remembered sharing 'a great airy bedroom, furnished with bright chintz' with her sister. It was decorated with watercolours by one of their schoolmistresses.[50] The schoolroom itself might retain a domestic character. Arriving at her new school in Brighton in 1872, Alice Whichelo noted in her diary, 'First day at school. It is a very nice place. The schoolroom is just like a drawing-room.'[51] At Leam House near Leamington Spa, where Bessie Parkes was a pupil, lessons initially took place in the family

[46] A. Taylor, *Hints on the education of girls* (London, 1814), 67.   [47] 'Report', *SIC* i. 2.

[48] M. C. Fraser, *A diplomatist's wife in many lands* (London, 1910), i. 223.

[49] This was the case at Hannah Pipe's school in London in the 1850s. There pupils spent evenings reading or singing in the schoolmistress's drawing-room. Stoddart, *Life*, 58.

[50] Fraser, *Diplomatist's wife*, i. 220.

[51] Journal entry, 5 Nov. 1872, Alice Whichelo's journal for 1872, Cambridge, King's College, Cambridge, Papers of E. M. Forster, GBR/0272/EMF/21/1.

Illustration 1. Charlotte Brontë's sketch of Miss Wooler's school at Roe Head (*c*.1831–2); reproduced by permission of the Brontë Parsonage Museum, Haworth.

sitting-room. A designated schoolroom was added only in 1844, about ten years after the school was opened.[52] Charlotte Brontë's sketch of Miss Wooler's school at Roe Head, where she was first pupil and then teacher, illustrates how the grander English schools might be indistinguishable from an ordinary country house, the detail lavished on the trees in the foreground emphasizing its bucolic surroundings.

Emphasis on the home-like nature of girls' schools was coupled with a desire to avoid publicity. The SIC report observed ruefully that 'the privacy of girls' schools occasions greater difficulty in obtaining satisfactory information than is found in the case of boys'.[53] In Devon, one schoolmistress returned C. H. Stanton's circular, saying, 'we have worked alone, independently of control from without, and lived too much as in a home with our pupils to like the idea of this kind of public investigation'.[54] Doubtless the reluctance of some to undergo investigation was due to a fear that their inadequacy might be exposed, but it also reflects the middle-class character of these institutions. Emphasizing the private character of schools was a means to safeguard their social status. In a

---

[52] B. Parkes, Autobiographical material, undated, Girton College, GCPP Parkes 1/1–3; Pigot, *Directory for Herefordshire, etc.*, 319.
[53] 'Report', *SIC* i. 2.   [54] C. H. Stanton, 'Devon and Somerset', *SIC* vii. 69.

period when government intervention was exclusively associated with elementary schools for the working classes, schoolmistresses were anxious to assert their independence from any kind of public scrutiny, both to preserve their own middle-class standing and to reassure parents. Reporting for the SIC, Joshua Fitch observed, 'all the sharp lines of demarcation which divide society into classes, and all the jealousies and suspicions which help to keep these classes apart, are seen in their fullest operation in girls' schools'.[55] If the school was a private family, free from government intervention, parents might be sure that their daughters would come into contact only with girls of the same milieu. At the same time, the schoolmistresses' desire to protect their schools from publicity reflected the need to conform to the idea that women's sphere was essentially private and domestic. As Hannah More had stressed, women who stepped outside their 'lesser domestic territory' were usurping 'a wider foreign empire'.

The need to respond to prevailing notions of femininity also had an impact on the size of schools. The SIC found that 'girls are often educated at home or in schools too small to deserve the name'.[56] J. L. Hammond calculated that the average number of pupils in Norfolk girls' schools was twenty-four. In Lancashire, James Bryce found only five schools with more than forty pupils. Most had around twenty-six.[57] This chimes with studies of schools in the early part of the century. Though in the 1790s some schools like Abbey House in Reading or Belvidere House in Bath might cater for as many as sixty scholars, typically schools would have around twenty pupils.[58] Evidence about fifty-six schools established by schoolmistresses born between 1800 and 1860 gives an average of only twenty-four per establishment.[59] Bryce and Hammond, working with a conception of the school that emphasized the importance of numbers, excluded schools with fewer than ten pupils from their study. In doing so, they failed to recognize that many schoolmistresses consciously limited the number of pupils they would take in. In the 1860s Louisa Carbutt never accepted more than twenty-four pupils at her school in Cheshire. Elizabeth Sewell refused to take more than seven.[60] Moreover, successful schoolmistresses tended not to expand but to reduce the number of pupils they would take in. In 1818 Mrs Field, who kept a school on Holywell Street in Oxford, announced that in future she would limit the number of

---

[55] J. G. Fitch, 'West Riding of York', *SIC* ix. 281.

[56] H. Roby, 'Instructions to assistant commissioners appointed to examine education in certain selected areas', *SIC* vii. 480.

[57] J. L. Hammond, 'Northumberland and Norfolk', *SIC* viii. 24; J. Bryce, 'Lancashire', *SIC* ix. 803.

[58] Skedd, 'Education of women', 153; Bryant, *London experience*, 145–8.

[59] The mean number of pupils in these 56 establishments was 24, ± 1.9 (Standard Error of the Mean). See the biographical sample described in Ch. 2 for details of this sample.

[60] Herford, *In Memoriam*, 44; Fraser, *Diplomatist's wife*, 223.

boarders she took to six, in order that they might better 'benefit from her maternal solicitude and care'.[61]

Large establishments were considered ill suited to girls. As Anne Pendered noted, they bore 'too near a resemblance to the world at large'. For Elizabeth Sewell, 'there is no connection between the bustling mill-wheel life of a large school and that for which they are supposed to be preparing . . . to educate girls in crowds is to educate them wrongly'. Keeping schools small reinforced the familial atmosphere, and served to mark the difference between these establishments and the artificial and foreign institution of the 'nunnery'. Thus Dorothea Beale was critical of the 'conventual' large Clergy Daughters' School at Casterton where she taught in the 1850s; pupils there lacked family influences.[62] Conversely, responding to a father's enquiry about her school, Anne Price, a London schoolmistress in the 1870s, wrote that his daughter 'should receive every kindness as our number being limited, I am enabled to make our domestic life that of a family circle'.[63] Restrictions on the size of schools also reflected ideas about feminine weakness. The SIC noted that 'ladies are generally found to shrink from the labour and responsibility of large schools'.[64] Not only were large establishments inimical to the development of domestic virtue, they endangered a conception of femininity predicated on frailty and dependence.

The extension of secondary schooling for girls in the nineteenth century was stimulated by the demands of an increasingly literate society, by parents' social aspirations, and by the needs of middle-class women whose employment opportunities were more and more constricted. It was also influenced by the growing interest in women's education, underpinned by the new importance attributed to women's domestic role in a context where Evangelical ideals of domesticity were gaining increasing currency. The schools established in the first half of the nineteenth century ranged from the fashionable Miss Pinkerton's Academy style 'seminaries' which placed great emphasis on elegant and ladylike accomplishments, to village boarding-schools like Sarah Bennet's establishment in Melton Mowbray, where, in the 1830s, girls received an elementary education supplemented with history, geography, and music, and included schools like the academically solid Laleham School, founded in Clapham in the 1850s by Hannah Pipe, who explicitly rejected the title of 'seminary' for her establishment. Yet, diverse as these institutions were, and despite the

---

[61] Advertisement from *Jackson's Oxford Journal*, 17 Jan. 1818, cited in Skedd, 'Education of women', 183.

[62] A. E. Pendered, *Remarks on the education of girls* (London, 1823), 5; E. Sewell, *Principles of Education, drawn from Nature and Revelation, and applied to female education in the upper classes* (London, 1865), ii. 219; D. Beale, 'Girls' schools past and present', *Nineteenth Century*, 25 (1888), 546.

[63] Anne Price to Gill, 20 Dec. 1878, LLIB, Gill MSS.   [64] 'Report', *SIC* i. 560.

idiosyncrasies inherent in institutions established by private individuals who were under no obligation to conform to any administrative procedure, the influence of gendered notions of domesticity meant that the boarding-schools for girls that proliferated in England in the first half of the nineteenth century shared certain features. Domestic in setting, familial in atmosphere, small and intensely private, the schools for girls developing throughout the first part of the nineteenth century could be said to conform to a domestic model of schooling.

By the 1860s, the boys' schools describing themselves as 'educational homes' were increasingly coming under attack and their proprietors all but accused of charlatanism.[65] The domestic model of girls' school was criticized in similar terms. This disparagement reflected the increasing dominance of Arnoldian conceptions of liberal education. The public-school model of large, hierarchically structured establishments offering an education dominated by Classics which was designed to form the character of an 'English gentleman' was being taken as the standard of schooling.[66] Those reporting for the SIC were heavily influenced by this conception of the school and, as seen above, tended to imply that girls' schools, established on a different footing, did not 'deserve the name' of 'school'.[67] At the same time, motivated in part by their awareness of the growing dominance of the Arnoldian model, schoolmistresses and feminists sought to 'reform' girls' education, developing new types of girls' school: large institutions that were public in character and which would assimilate female education more closely to that of boys.[68] Already the 1840s and 1850s had seen the creation of a growing number of proprietary schools, established by groups of share-holding parents, or by Protestant denominational societies;[69] By the 1860s, the small, privately owned, family-like schools which had multiplied in the first part of the century were being sidelined by establishments like Bedford College School, Cheltenham Ladies' College, and the North London Collegiate. Yet the earlier domestic model of female schooling elaborated by schoolmistresses throughout the country had strengthened the notion that girls should receive a rational intellectual education, contributed significantly to the development of female

---

[65] Arnold, 'A French Eton'.

[66] Bamford, *Thomas Arnold*; Honey, *Tom Brown's universe*, ch. 1.

[67] The same blind spot with regard to schools which did not conform to the dominant model led middle-class observers to disparage working-class private schools. Gardner, *The lost elementary schools of Victorian England* (London, 1984), 3–10.

[68] Pedersen, *Reform*, chs.1–3, 5; Fletcher, *Feminists*; B. Caine, *Victorian Feminists* (Oxford, 1992), 54–102.

[69] E. Clark and W. Sturge, *The Mount School, York, 1785–1814, 1831–1931* (London, 1931); C. Curryer and E. Pike, *The story of Walthamstow Hall* (London, 1938); P. Manisty and H. Osborne, *A history of the Royal School for daughters of officers of the army, 1864–1965* (Bath, 1965).

schooling, and provided a precedent on which schoolmistresses in the 'reformed' schools would continue to draw.

FRANCE—THE CONSOLIDATION OF A CONVENT MODEL OF SCHOOLING

The Development of Schooling for Girls in France

Private boarding-schools for girls were also proliferating in France at the end of the eighteenth century, prompting observers like Antoine Caillot, author of a manual for girls' boarding-schools published in 1816, to comment on 'this crowd of boarding-schools established in France over the past twenty-five years'. Jeanne Campan, an influential schoolmistress and pedagogue, also noted that 'a prodigious number of boarding-schools were established in Paris' at that time.[70] Circumstances in France, however, differed from those in England. Lay boarding-schools for girls on the Continent had sprung up in direct response to the gradual decline and eventual closure in 1792 of the convent schools that had prospered under the *Ancien Régime*.[71]

In the early modern period, the daughters of aristocratic families in France, like their English counterparts, had often been sent away to other households for instruction.[72] From the seventeenth century, however, convent boarding-schools, created as a result of the Counter-Reformation interest in education and the multiplication of female religious orders, were the dominant force in female instruction. By 1641, the Visitandines, who had a special responsibility for girls' education, had established eighty-seven convent schools in France. The Ursulines also specialized in teaching, as did the Congrégation de Nôtre-Dame, which had eighty-four houses in France by 1789.[73] Their educational mission was to provide free education for poor girls as part of a programme of re-christianization. To finance this work, however, many orders established fee-paying boarding-schools, so that the development of charitable schooling went hand in hand with the extension of schooling for bourgeois and aristocratic girls.[74] Between 1610

---

[70] A. Caillot, *Tableau des exercices et des enseignements en usage dans un pensionnat de jeunes demoiselles* (Paris, 1816), i. 242; J. Campan, *De l'éducation, suivi des conseils aux jeunes filles, d'un théâtre pour les jeunes personnes et de quelques essais de morale* (Paris, 1824), i. 335.

[71] M. Sonnet, 'Education', in N. Zemon-Davis and A. Farge (eds.), *Histoire des femmes: XVIe–XVIIIe siècles* (Paris, 1991), 126.

[72] Hufton, *Prospect*, 65.

[73] R. Chartier, D. Julia, and M. M. Compère, *L'éducation en France du XVIe au XVIIIe siècle* (Paris, 1976), 233–44. For excellent detailed studies see E. Rapley, *Les Devotes: women and the church in seventeenth century France* (Montreal, 1990), ch. 6 and M. Sonnet, *L'éducation des filles au temps des Lumières* (Paris, 1987). Sonnet's work, to which the following paragraphs are indebted, is a mine of information.

[74] Sonnet, *L'éducation*, 42–3.

and 1660 a total of forty-one religious orders founded convent boarding-schools in Paris, and by the end of the seventeenth century there were about 500 teaching convents in France.[75]

Convent boarding-schools were highly formalized establishments, often catering for large numbers of pupils and staff. The Maison Royale de Saint-Cyr, established by Mme de Maintenon in 1686 to educate the daughters of impoverished noble families, catered for 250 pupils.[76] The Ursuline convent on the rue Sainte-Avoye in Paris in the 1760s, took seventy pupils. The corollary was the development of ladders of authority. In the schools of the Congrégation de la Mère Dieu, the *maîtresses de classe* (form mistresses) who taught the pupils were supervised by the *mère préfète des pensionnaires* (superior mistress of the boarding-school), herself under the authority of the Mother Superior. Daily management was in the hands of the *econome* (bursar).[77] Such large numbers also called for the division of pupils into classes, and in their arrangements the female teaching orders drew on the system elaborated in the Jesuit *Ratio Studiorum* (1599). The principle was that pupils moved individually through a hierarchy of seven classes, each divided into groups of ten known as *dizaines*, headed by a captain chosen for his scholastic success.[78] Following this example, the Ursulines tended to divide their pupils into four groups. At Port Royal, the girls were classified as 'petites', 'moyennes', and 'grandes'.[79] At Saint-Cyr, the girls were divided into four classes by age, differentiated by the colour of the sash they wore. Each class was split into *dizaines*, headed not by the most successful pupils but by the best behaved.[80]

The size of convent institutions also called for careful organization of time and space, a practical requirement that married well with a Counter-Reformation emphasis on the need for constant industry and order in women's lives.[81] Establishments like the Ursuline convents followed comprehensive (and remarkably enduring) *règlements* (or regulations), which set out detailed instructions as to how the school should be structured and how each day should be filled.[82] Space was also carefully regulated and buildings were modified to suit the needs of

---

[75] Ibid. 39; E. Rapley, 'Fénelon revisited: a review of girls' education in seventeenth century France', *Social History*, 20 (1987), 301.

[76] Chartier *et al.*, *L'éducation*, 243–4; C. Lougee, 'Noblesse, domesticity and social reform: the education of girls by Fénelon and Saint-Cyr', *History of Education Quarterly*, 14 (1974), 87–113.

[77] Sonnet, *L'éducation*, 79, 123–4.

[78] Rapley, 'Fénelon'; Rapley, *Dévotes*, 145–66; P. Janelle, *The Catholic Reformation* (Milwaukee, 1948), ch. 7; A. Farrell, *The Jesuit code of liberal education* (Milwaukee, 1938), chs. 13, 14.

[79] Sonnet, *L'éducation*, 145, 201.

[80] Chartier *et al.*, *L'éducation*, 243–4.

[81] L. Timmermans, *L'accès des femmes à la culture, 1598–1715* (Paris, 1993), 440, 494–7.

[82] After a second edition published in 1734, the Ursuline *Règlement* was constantly in print until 1868, by which time it had grown from 508 to 800 pages. It gave detailed instructions as to how each day should be ordered and set out prayers for almost every action of the day, including one to be said as the pupil tied her belt. Sonnet, *L'éducation*, 165–6.

institutional life. Pupils would sleep in large dormitories; they heard Mass in a chapel to which they would return for the prayers which punctuated the school day, and one room would be set aside as the *parloir* (or locutory) where girls might receive occasional visits from their parents.[83] The use of the *parloir* points to the degree to which pupils were isolated in convent boarding-schools. The principle of enclosure was central. At Saint-Cyr, girls were forbidden to leave the school precincts until they left for good. 'You should congratulate yourselves', Mme de Maintenon told the sisters, 'on having preserved [your pupils] from the corruption of the secular world until the age of twenty.'[84] Though most convent schools did not forbid temporary absences, they were strongly discouraged. Of the pupils at five Parisian convent schools in the eighteenth century, only 5% of the girls ever took temporary leave.[85] It was only through the air-lock of the *parloir* that pupils would have any contact with the world outside the convent.

Interest in educational questions continued to grow in the eighteenth century. The number of books published on education rose from fifty-one between 1715 and 1759 to 161 from 1760 to 1790.[86] In the 1760s, one in four Parisian girls aged between 7 and 14 had access to schooling of some sort. Female literacy was also rising, so that by the end of the eighteenth century 44% of brides in the north of France were signing marriage registers.[87] But the 1760s also marked the beginning of a period of downturn for religious schooling. Under attack from Enlightenment sceptics, and affected by the expulsion of the Jesuits in 1762, the convent boarding-schools began to decline. The trend was exacerbated by the growing influence of Rousseauist ideas favouring maternal education, and by criticism of the worldliness and frivolity of the education offered in the grand convent schools favoured by the aristocracy.[88] Numbers at the Ursuline convent on the rue Sainte-Avoye fell from about seventy in the 1760s to thirty in the 1770s.[89] Some middle-class families were able to benefit, sending their daughters to previously exclusive schools, which dropped their prices to attract new recruits. Between 1790 and 1792, however, the Revolutionary Assemblies ordered the suppression of all male and female religious orders, entailing the closure of all the schools they had established and bringing an abrupt halt to the tradition of convent education for girls.[90]

---

[83] Ibid. 67–74.

[84] Françoise de Maintenon, *Entretiens sur l'éducation des filles*, ed. Th. Lavallée (Paris, 1854), 39.

[85] Sonnet, *L'éducation*, 207. This should not necessarily be interpreted as a constraint. Paule Constant argues that in the eighteenth century many women sought the seclusion of the convent, and that leaving this female sanctuary was often experienced as a painful rupture rather than a liberation. P. Constant, *Un monde à l'usage des demoiselles* (Paris, 1987).

[86] Sonnet, 'Education', 117. [87] Sonnet, *L'éducation*, 82–3.

[88] S. de Genlis, *Discours sur la suppression des couvents de religieuses et sur l'éducation publique des femmes* (Paris, 1790).

[89] Sonnet, *L'éducation*, 79.

[90] A. Dansette, *Religious history of Modern France*, trans. J. Dingle (Edinburgh, 1961), i. 41–50.

Lay Boarding-Schools for Girls in an Administrative Framework

The impact of the Revolution on the development of girls' schooling was complex. The closure of the convents had prompted the elaboration of various proposals for the establishment of new secular systems of education to replace the eighteenth-century network of religious foundations.[91] Ultimately, however, none of the plans for the development of girls' secondary education was followed through, and the only tangible contribution by the state to female education after 1789 was Napoleon's creation of the *Maisons d'Éducation de la Légion d'Honneur*, intended to educate the daughters of officers and soldiers who had received the *Légion d'Honneur* medal.[92] In 1801 the religious concordat with the Pope led to the proliferation of new and dynamic forms of female congregation which eventually came to dominate the provision of schooling for girls.[93] At the same time, influenced by the Rousseauist idealization of the maternal role, the Revolution had seen the elaboration of an ideal of Republican motherhood which emphasized that women's contribution to society should be made through the home. Whereas, through the vote and their participation in public life, men would participate directly in the new world of democracy, women would participate indirectly, through the cultivation of Republican virtues in the home, and the education of future citizens.[94] The idea that women's contribution to society should be made exclusively through the home was reinforced in the early years of the nineteenth century. Napoleon, like the ideologues of the Restoration, Louis de Bonald and Joseph de Maistre, saw feminine domesticity and strengthening the patriarchal family as fundamental to the restoration of order following the Revolutionary upheavals.[95] The Emperor's notion of the education that would prepare women for their role in the new order was far from

[91] Mayeur, *L'éducation*, 27–32; D. Julia, *Les trois couleurs du tableau noir: la Révolution* (Paris, 1981), 310–29.

[92] On the history of the *Maisons d'Éducation de la Légion d'Honneur*, see R. Rogers, *Les demoiselles de la Légion d'Honneur* (Paris, 1992); Rogers, 'Competing visions'. The schools established at St Denis and St Germain-en-Laye are still in operation today. I am indebted to Elvire de Coëtlogon, Intendante of the Maison d'Éducation de la Légion d'Honneur, Les Loges, St Germain-en-Laye, from 1989 to 1999, who welcomed me as an Assistant at the school in 1993 and introduced me to the history of girls' education in France.

[93] Dansette, *Religious history*, i. 117–29; C. Langlois, *Le Catholicisme au féminin: les congrégations françaises a supérieure générale au XIXe siècle* (Paris, 1984); H. Mills, 'Women and Catholicism in provincial France, 1800–1850: Franche-Comté in national context', D.Phil. thesis (Oxford, 1994), ch. 4.

[94] J. Landes, *Women and the public sphere in the age of the French Revolution* (Ithaca, 1988); G. Fraisse, *Muse de la raison: la démocratie exclusive et la différence des sexes* (Aix-en-Provence, 1989); O. Hufton, *Women and the limits of citizenship in the French Revolution* (Toronto, 1990); L. Hunt, *The family romance of the French Revolution* (Berkeley, 1992); J. Scott, *Only paradoxes to offer: French feminists and the Rights of Man* (Cambridge, Mass., 1996); S. Desan, *The family on trial in Revolutionary France* (Berkeley, 2004).

[95] M. Albistur and M. Armogathe, *Histoire du féminisme français du Moyen Age à nos jours* (Paris, 1977), 239–49.

the scientific and classical curriculum envisaged by some of the Revolutionary projects. He saw religion as the essence of girls' education, and envisaged only a limited curriculum, three-quarters of which was devoted to needlework and domestic economy, for his *Légion d'Honneur* schools.[96] De Maistre emphasized women's domestic role and argued that women 'should not seek to aspire to knowledge, nor let any one think they have that pretension'.[97] Women were seen as having particular responsibility for religion and the revival of Catholic piety. Increasingly the separation between male and female spheres was underscored—at least rhetorically—by the division between women brought up within a Catholic tradition that coloured every aspect of their experience of home and school life (whether they attended a lay establishment or a convent school), and men brought up in *lycées* and *collèges* by the heirs of a tradition of Enlightenment scepticism.[98]

Yet the Revolutionary projects had firmly established the radical principle that girls' education was a matter of national concern and mooted the idea that it should be provided for by the state. Before opening the *Légion d'Honneur* schools, Napoleon had considered establishing a network of girls' schools aimed at the daughters of public servants.[99] Though this idea was abandoned, that it was considered reveals the extent to which that principle had taken root. Furthermore, there was room for manoeuvre within the notion that women's sphere was the home. The politicization of family life during the Revolution had given a new significance to the private sphere of the home and family, and while the duties and capacities of men and women were seen as distinct, they were perceived as complementary. In the 1820s authors like Jeanne Campan and Claire de Rémusat published treatises emphasizing that while women's role was domestic, their duties as 'the wives and mothers of citizens' gave them an influence that stretched beyond the home.[100] They should receive a rational education to prepare them for these responsibilities. Campan argued that 'a solid instruction must render a woman able to appreciate her husband's virtues, to manage his wealth through wise economy, to share his position without ridiculous ostentation, to console him if he falls from favour, to educate her

[96] Rogers, *Demoiselles*, 23–4.

[97] Joseph de Maistre to his daughter, quoted in Albistur and Armogathe, *Histoire*, 244.

[98] C. Ford, *Divided houses: religion and gender in modern France* (Ithaca, 2005).

[99] This idea had already been mooted in the 1760s, by Nicolas Beaudeau, in an article entitled 'De l'éducation nationale' (17 mai 1766). Extracts in S. Bell and K. Offen (eds.), *Women, the family and freedom: the debate in documents*, 2 vols. (Stanford, 1983), i. 73–9; Rogers, *From the Salon*, 47–8.

[100] C. de Rémusat, *Essai sur l'éducation des femmes* (Paris, 1824), 87; Campan, *De l'éducation*; P. Guizot, *Éducation domestique ou lettres de famille sur l'éducation*, 2 vols. (Paris, 1826); On the politicization of family and the private sphere, see M. Darrow, 'The new domesticity, 1750–1850', *Feminist Studies*, 5 (1979), 39–65, and Desan, *Family on trial*. For discussion of these pedagogues' ideas see B. Corrado-Pope, 'Maternal education in France, 1815–1848', *Proceedings of the Western Society for French History* (1975), 368–73; Rendall, *Origins*, 112–25; and Rogers, *From the Salon*, ch. 1.

daughters in all the feminine virtues and to guide her sons in their early years'.[101] As directress of the *Légion d'Honneur* schools she developed a course of studies that included literature, history, geography, and geometry as well as needlework, a much more extensive curriculum than that envisaged by Napoleon.[102] The Revolution had made female education a public issue, had strengthened and politicized a potentially valorizing notion of feminine domesticity, and had underlined the need for women to develop the skills which would prepare them to respond to fluctuating circumstances.

At the same time, the closure of the convents had opened up a space in which lay boarding-schools for girls could flourish. By 1804 there were seven lay establishments or *pensions* in Lille and in 1808 there were at least sixty in Paris.[103] Many authors were doubtful about school education for girls, insisting instead on the role of *la mère-éducatrice* (the mother-educator), a powerful theme in French writing on women's education.[104] Only Campan argued in favour of school education for girls, although even she claimed to believe that maternal education was the ideal.[105] Nonetheless, lay boarding-schools for girls continued to multiply. The increase was fostered by the growing interest in girls' education, by parental demand, and by the needs of women who sought to provide for themselves through their work. Most significantly, it was underpinned and legitimated by the long-standing tradition of female schooling.

Throughout the period the capital was a centre of female education. By 1845 there were 253 lay boarding-schools in Paris, catering for 15,087 pupils.[106] Letters addressed by the prefects of provincial departments to the *Ministre de l'Instruction Publique* in the late 1830s reveal the patchy distribution of *pensions* in other regions. There were very few lay establishments in the more rural departments. In the Cantal the only boarding-schools for girls were religious establishments.[107] Lay schools flourished, however, in both established university and commercial cities and in the newer industrial towns. In the university city of Douai, there were three *pensions* and two religious institutions catering for a total of 612 pupils by 1819. In Bordeaux in 1852 the local directory listed

---

[101] Campan, *De l'éducation*, i. 4.   [102] Rogers, 'Competing visions', 159–60.

[103] État indicatif des établissements d'instruction pour l'un et l'autre sexe, existant en l'an XII dans la commune de Lille, Lille, Archives Départementales du Nord (hereafter AD Nord), 1 T 121–2. F. V. Goblet, *Dictionnaire administrative et topographique de Paris* (Paris, 1808), 146–8. The term *pension* was usually used by contemporaries to refer to lay boarding-schools; however, it was also sometimes used without the qualification of '*religieuse*' to describe convent boarding-schools. Here, *Pension* will always indicate a lay establishment.

[104] Corrado-Pope, 'Maternal education'; I. Havelange, 'La littérature à l'usage des demoiselles, 1750–1830', Thèse de 3ᵉ cycle (École des Hautes Études en Sciences Sociales, Paris, 1983–4), p. xix.

[105] Campan, *De l'éducation*, pp. i, xi–xii.

[106] Résultats de l'inspection des pensionnats de demoiselles, 1846 (Extrait du *Recueil des actes administratifs de la préfecture du dépt de la Seine*, 4ᵉ année, No. 2, 29), Paris, Archives Nationales (hereafter AN), F¹⁷ 12431.

[107] Dossier of responses to the Minister's circular of 1837 regarding the Seine ruling, AN, F¹⁷ 12432.

thirty-seven boarding-schools, and by the same year there were at least sixteen *pensions*, catering for 762 girls, in Lille.[108]

The 1840s and 1850s saw the convent schools gaining in strength and number. In Paris, however, lay establishments continued to outnumber convent schools. In 1855, there were at least 195 *pensions* in Paris, catering for around 13,529 girls. In the same year there were just twenty-two religious establishments with 1,721 pupils in the capital.[109] The situation in the provinces was somewhat different. An 1864 survey reveals that although *pensions* were still numerous in large towns and cities, overall, religious establishments outnumbered lay schools. One report suggests that *pensions* accounted for only 46% of girls at school in the Nord in 1854. Similarly, an inspection of boarding-schools in the city of Bordeaux in 1865 reveals that women religious catered for more girls than lay schoolmistresses.[110] Nonetheless, in 1865 there were still sixteen thriving lay boarding-schools in Lille, and in the same year the Bordeaux directory listed a total of seventy-four *pensions* in the city.[111] Although the figures for the period after 1860 do suggest the growing dominance of religious establishments in girls' education, lay boarding-schools were still a significant presence.

It is difficult to estimate what proportion of the population was catered for in these establishments, especially for the period before 1850, when lay boarding-schools served a larger proportion of the whole. For the period after 1850, taking the 1864 survey as a guide, and relating it to calculations of what proportion of the population could be described as bourgeois, suggests that, in 1864, about 25% of girls of middle-class origin were attending lay boarding-schools, and 38% were attending religious establishments.[112] Allowing for the very approximate nature of these figures, this suggests that in the 1860s over half of all middle-class girls were attending either a religious or a lay boarding-school in France.

---

[108] État nominatif des institutrices employees dans les Pensionnats de Demoiselles, *c*.1819, Douai, Archives Municipales de Douai (hereafter AM Douai), 1 R 32; *Annuaire général du commerce de Bordeaux* (Bordeaux, 1852), 147; Rapports sur les écoles primaires libres de filles, 3 juillet 1852, AD Nord, 1 T 123–9.

[109] *Almanach Impérial* (Paris, 1855), 1043–5. Figures for the number of pupils and counting the number of religious establishments from Rogers, *From the Salon*, 168.

[110] Réponses à la circulaire ministérielle du 16 juillet 1864, AN, F[17] 6843–9; Rapport sur l'enseignement primaire des filles en réponse à la circulaire ministérielle du 16 juillet 1864, AD Nord, 1 T 80/62*; Rapport sur l'enseignement primaire des filles, 1865, Archives Départementales de la Gironde (hereafter AD Gironde), 6 T 17.

[111] *Annuaire de l'Arrondissement de Lille, du Commerce, de l'Industrie, de la Magistrature et de l'Administration* (Lille, 1865), 471; *Annuaire Général du Commerce de Bordeaux* (Bordeaux, 1865), 217–18.

[112] The 1864 survey counted 2,338 lay boarding-schools and 3,489 religious establishments. Inspection reports suggest that the average number of pupils in lay and religious schools was around 50, which would mean that lay and religious schools were catering for around 116,900 and 174,000 girls respectively in 1864. There were 3,177,000 girls aged 10–19 in the population as a whole in 1861; B. R. Mitchell, *European Historical Statistics, Europe 1750–1950* (London, 1975), 35. Jardin and Tudesq calculate that 15% of the population were of bourgeois origin in 1847; *Vie de la nation*, 211.

In keeping with the principle established during the Revolution that female education was a public matter, this expansion was accompanied by the development of a system of inspection and administration, clearly influenced by the establishment, in 1808, of the *Université*. Building on the revolutionary proposals which envisaged the creation of a national system of state-controlled education, the *Université* administered and supervised the government-funded *lycées* and municipal *collèges* established in 1802. It was also responsible for authorizing and inspecting private boarding-schools for boys.[113] In 1801, the prefect of Paris declared that private schoolmistresses should be authorized by the mayor of the *arrondissement* in which they lived. In 1810, a ruling was passed in Paris that set up an arrangement parallel to that envisaged for private boys' schools within the *Université*. It would provide a model for the administration of girls' secondary education in the first half of the nineteenth century.[114] The 1810 decree required all schoolmistresses to obtain official authorization before opening their schools, having been 'examined in respect to their aptitude' by a committee nominated by the prefect.[115] Voluntary inspectresses, *dames inspectrices*, would visit girls' schools and report annually on the schools in their *arrondissement*. Every schoolmistress was required to place a sign at the entrance to her school indicating her name and the nature of her establishment. A further ruling in 1816 established a distinction between *institutions*, where the curriculum was relatively advanced (including ancient as well as modern history, literature, and geography), and *pensions*, where the curriculum was more limited. Correspondingly separate diplomas were required for *maîtresses d'institution* and *maîtresses de pension*. This framework of authorization and inspection was extended beyond Paris in 1820 when the *Ministre de l'Instruction Publique* urged prefects in other departments to establish similar rulings.[116]

This pattern was repeated in 1837 when the prefect of the Seine passed a new ruling. Its terms extended the curriculum to be covered by schoolmistresses seeking authorization, and required the *dames inspectrices* to make sure that school buildings were salubrious, large enough for the number of pupils, and carefully enclosed. Copies were sent out to prefects in the provinces, who were again encouraged to emulate the Seine department. The suggestion was taken up

---

[113] P. Savoie,'Introduction', in *Les enseignants du secondaire, XIX–XXe siècles: le corps, le métier, les carrières* (Paris, 2000); P. Gerbod, *La condition universitaire en France au XIXe siècle* (Paris, 1965).

[114] Rogers, *From the Salon,* 47; Règlement pour les écoles de filles, 20 Aug. 1810, AD Seine, VD⁴ 21–5496.

[115] Before being sent before the committee, they had to address a formal petition to the mayor of their *arrondissement*, indicating what they would teach and including their birth and marriage certificates and a document certifying they were of good conduct.

[116] Règlement concernant les maisons d'éducation de filles dans le département de la Seine, Préfet Chabrol, 20 June 1816, AD Seine, VD⁶648–1; Instruction ministérielle, 19 June 1820, quoted in E. Kilian, *De l'instruction des filles à ses divers degrés: Institutions et pensions, écoles primaires, supérieures et élémentaires* (Paris, 1842), 8–9.

with varying degrees of enthusiasm, and truly welcomed only in the departments where large towns housed significant numbers of schools.[117]

In 1850, however, the specialized administration for *pensions* and *institutions* was dismantled under the provisions of a new law on elementary education. The *Loi Falloux* established the first nationally enforced standards in girls' education, but it ignored any distinction between elementary and secondary education in girls' schooling. Instead, it classified all female establishments as *enseignement primaire*, and placed them under the supervision of the primary inspectorate, now under the supervision of a new *Conseil Supérieur de l'Instruction Publique*, which had overall jurisdiction over both elementary schooling and over the secondary schools and higher education establishments of the *Université*. Any woman intending to open a lay school for girls need only obtain an elementary teaching diploma or *brevet*. Significantly, the principle of the *lettre d'obédience*, which dispensed members of religious orders from the requirement to obtain the *brevet*, was preserved.[118] Seen by some as a major setback to the development of girls' education, indicative of the reactionary Catholicism of the new regime, the *Loi Falloux* should be seen in the context of the raft of measures which attempted to reduce the influence of secular schoolmasters, who were seen as partly responsible for the upheavals of 1848.[119] At the same time, its provisions carry an echo of the hostility to feminist demands and the frequent attacks on the figure of the female intellectual which were a common theme of the period.[120] Certainly, the safeguarding of the *lettre d'obédience* had a damaging effect on lay schoolmistresses because it sponsored the proliferation of convent schools which gradually came to outnumber lay schools in many areas. Yet, even if its provisions tended to favour religious establishments, by incorporating lay boarding-schools into the fabric of the national education system, the *Loi Falloux* reinforced the notion that female education was a public matter. At the same time, it sponsored the expansion of primary schooling for girls by stipulating that all towns with a population of more than 800 must establish a girls' school.

Both the provisions of the *Loi Falloux* and the prefectoral and ministerial rulings that preceded it fell far short of Revolutionary visions of a publicly funded system of secondary education for girls. Proposals for the development of female schooling requiring substantial investments of public money were repeatedly

[117] Règlement du 7 mars pour les pensions de demoiselles du département de la Seine, 1837, AN, F[17]12431; Dossier of responses to the Minister's circular of 1837 regarding the Seine ruling, AN, F[17] 12432. Some of the rulings established in response are reproduced in *REF* 1 and 2 (Jan. and Feb. 1845).

[118] 'Loi sur l'enseignement', 15 Dec. 1850, *Recueil des lois et actes de l'Instruction Publique* (Paris, 1848–91), III. 120.

[119] Gréard, *L'enseignement*, 52–4; J.-V. Daubié, *La femme pauvre au XIXe siècle*, 3rd edn., 2 vols. (Paris, 1992), i. 113–17; Gerbod, *Condition*, 226–340.

[120] M. Riot-Sarcey, *La démocratie à l'épreuve des femmes* (Paris, 1994), 83–274 and J. McMillan, *France and Women, 1789–1914: gender, society and politics* (London, 2000), 90–5; J. Bergman-Carton, *The woman of ideas in French art* (London, 1995).

rejected.[121] Moreover, enforcement of the various rulings was erratic. Although the 1837 provisions threatened unauthorized schoolmistresses with closure, in practice this was rarely carried out. There was often a gap between the theory of regulation and what could actually be put into practice.[122]

Nonetheless, the development of an administrative framework to oversee the expansion of lay schooling for girls testifies to the continuing strength of the idea that girls' schooling was of national concern and should come under public jurisdiction. Shaped by the rulings of the administrative authorities, supervised and authorized by publicly appointed officials, *pensions* were, in some degree, public institutions. With the sign required by the authorities at its entrance, a girls' boarding-school was an obvious presence in the urban landscape. Even if some sought to evade the prescriptions of the authorities, French lay boarding-schoolmistresses showed no signs of the indignation expressed by their English counterparts at the first sign of public intervention. In temporarily opening up the female education market to lay schoolmistresses, and in anticipating the development of a system of public administration for girls' schools, the Revolutionary Assemblies had opened the way for the development of lay educational establishments that were public in character. Yet, though these schools had sprung up to replace the *Ancien Régime* convents, or perhaps because of this, the lay institutions of the nineteenth century did not radically depart from the patterns established by their eighteenth-century predecessors. Indeed, the most powerful factor in explaining the proliferation of lay institutions for girls in the nineteenth century was, paradoxically, the deeply rooted traditions of female schooling developed in the convents of the seventeenth and eighteenth centuries.

The Consolidation of a Convent Model of Schooling

In 1849 an inspectress visiting Élisa Liot's school in Paris observed that 'this establishment cannot be regarded as an ordinary *pension*. It is more like a large family, where the older pupils are like sisters, almost like mothers to the younger pupils.'[123] In the eighteenth century some private boys' schools had sought, like their English counterparts, to emphasize the domestic character of their arrangements, and in the nineteenth century some schoolmistresses took a similar line.[124] As the report on Liot's school suggests, however, these were exceptions to the rule.

---

[121] See Ch. 4.

[122] J.-N. Luc, *L'invention du jeune enfant au XIXe siècle* (Paris, 1997), 306–7.

[123] Inspection pension Liot, Aug. 1849, AD Seine, VD⁶ 148–2.

[124] M. Grandière, 'L'éducation en France à la fin du XVIIIe siècle: quelques aspects d'un nouveau cadre éducatif, les "maisons d'éducation", 1760–1790', *Revue d'Histoire Moderne et Contemporaine*, 33 (1986), 440–62; P. Marchand, 'Un modèle d'éducation à la veille de la Révolution: les maisons d'éducation particulière', *Revue d'Histoire Moderne et Contemporaine*, 22 (1975), 549–67; M.-M. Compère, 'Les pensions à Paris (1789–1820)', *Revue du Nord*, 78 (1996), 823–35.

Girls' boarding-schools in France were considerably larger than their English counterparts. According to Mme Campan, most schoolmistresses would have around fifty to sixty pupils, a number which required 'order, extreme cleanliness, precise discipline, careful and numerous divisions of pupils and subjects of study'.[125] In 1841 Mlle Duban's *pension* in the first *arrondissement*, which had thirty-eight boarders and ten day girls, was described as 'a little, well-kept school'.[126] In the 1840s Parisian schools were often somewhat larger. Of thirty-three schools established in the first *arrondissement* between 1845 and 1848, three had over one hundred pupils and the average number of pupils, day girls included, was forty-eight.[127] Although, especially in the provinces, smaller institutions with only twenty to thirty pupils were common, most French schoolmistresses do not seem to have limited the number of pupils they would receive in the same deliberate way as their English counterparts. A survey of the schools of sixteen schoolmistresses born between 1780 and 1860, and teaching in different parts of the country, gives an average of sixty-seven boarding and day pupils.[128] Most girls' boarding-schools in France were too large and too hierarchically structured to be plausibly likened to a family. The contrast between these large French establishments and their smaller English counterparts reveals the powerful pressures shaping the domestic model of school in England, and the influence of the convent tradition of female schooling in France. In very practical terms, the lay boarding-schools that sprang up to replace the convents of the *Ancien Régime* drew heavily on the institutional patterns established by their predecessors.

One of the clearest signs of this legacy was the physical structure of lay *pensions*. Unlike in England, where schoolmistresses might simply receive pupils into their own home, in France many institutions were housed in specially adapted, or even specially constructed buildings. The plan of Mme Achet's school, which had fifty-six pupils in 1846, shows that the school occupied a building surrounding a central courtyard. A chapel, at the back of which was the antechamber and *parloir,* occupied most of one side of the courtyard. Lessons were held in three separate classrooms and the girls slept in two large dormitories, the larger containing twenty-five beds. As in many schools, there was also an infirmary. At Mme Achet's, meals were taken in a large room known as the *salle a manger* (*sic*), but in most establishments this was called the refectory.[129]

---

[125] Campan, *De l'éducation*, i. 313.

[126] Inspection pension Duban, 1841, AD Seine, VD⁶ 158–3.

[127] Inspections, 1845–8, AD Seine, VD⁶158–3. In 1845, the mean number of pupils in the schools of the first *arrondissement* was 47.5, ± 4.4 (Standard error of the mean). In Bordeaux in 1851 the average number of day and boarding pupils in fifteen schools visited by the inspector was 42. Rapport de Benoit, Inspecteur Primaire, Pensions et Institutions de Demoiselles, 16 Dec. 1851, Bordeaux, AD Gironde, 6 T 12. The mean number of pupils in these 15 schools in 1851 was 41.7, ± 4.3.

[128] The mean number of pupils in this sixteen schools was 67.1, ± 9.2. See the biographical study described in Ch. 2 for details of this sample.

[129] Inspection pension Achet, 1846–7, AD Seine, VD⁶ 158–1; Dossier Achet, *c.* 1842, AD Seine, DT Supplément/1.

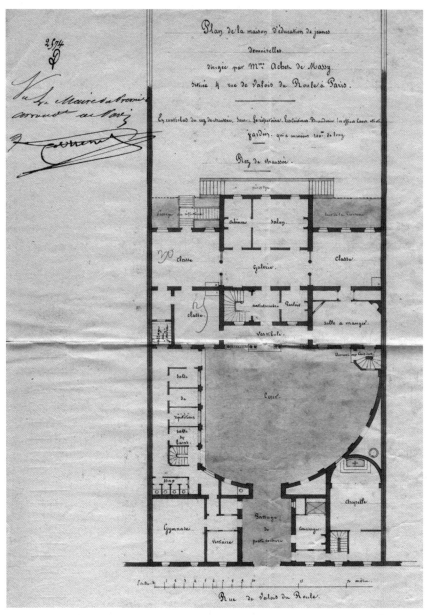

Illustration 2. Plan of Mme Achet's school, Paris (*c.*1842), AD Seine, VD⁶ 158–3; reproduced by permission of the Archives de Paris.

Not all schoolmistresses could provide such elaborate arrangements. In the 1860s Julie-Victoire Daubié drew attention to the difficulties faced by lay schoolmistresses, who, unlike their religious counterparts, could often only afford 'a small, dark, unhealthy room' in which to teach.[130] However, the expectation was clearly that girls' schools should be housed in specially adapted buildings, organized in ways that reflected the formal character and function of the school. The administrative authorities were critical of schoolmistresses who established themselves in buildings that had not been modified to meet the specialized needs of a school, and conversely heaped praise on those who were able to build from scratch. In Tourcoing in 1830, when objecting to the proposed opening of a school by the Demoiselles Mutuel, the mayor referred to the fact that 'the house, which was never intended as a boarding-school, is not suitably arranged'. Admittedly, his judgement was discounted by the prefect, who saw that the mayor's objective was to protect a nearby convent from a potential rival; but it is significant that the question of space could be important enough to call the existence of a school into question.[131] In contrast, in 1829 Mme Martinez's school in Paris, 'to a large extent built as a boarding-school', was considered 'well arranged . . . It could serve as a model of cleanliness and order.'[132] Those who were able to expand and improve the houses their schools occupied sought to do so and to build more classrooms. Thus census reports indicate that Mme Ploux had been gradually taking over neighbouring houses, and by 1866 the prospectus boasted of four 'belles classes', a refectory that could seat a hundred girls, and a chapel.[133] Far from domestic in setting, these schools physically embodied the inherited traditions of a formal institutional model of schooling.

The *règlements* which had governed daily life in the *Ancien Régime* convents were also carried over into lay boarding-schools. Encouraged by authors like Campan, who noted somewhat caustically, however, that 'regulations are not difficult to draw up, the difficulty is in carrying them out and enforcing them', schoolmistresses drew up their own rulings and were required to submit them to the prefect. Those that have survived evoke strictly organized days punctuated with prayers and religious instruction.[134] Complementing the *règlements*, many schools adopted hierarchical structures that mirrored those established in the convent schools. Pupils were divided up into classes in ways that drew on Jesuit

[130] Daubié, *Femme pauvre,* ii. 115.

[131] Dossier Mutuel, Tourcoing, 1830, AD Nord, 1 T 122/6.

[132] Rapport de Mme la Marquise de Macmahon, 15 Nov. 1829, AD Seine, VD[6] 158–3; Inspection pension Villeneuve, 1841, AD Seine, VD[6] 158–3.

[133] Prospectus, Mme Lavergne Mirande, *c.*1866, Archives Municipales de Bordeaux (hereafter AM Bordeaux), Fonds Ploux/8.

[134] Campan, *De l'éducation,* i. 315; Règlement concernant les Maisons d'Éducation de Filles dans le Département de la Seine, 1 Dec. 1821, AN, F[17] 12341; e.g. Règlement, Mme Bazin, *c.*1842, AD Seine, VD[6]650–1 and Règlement, Mlle Viard, 26 Aug. 1841, VD[6]649–1.

precedents and affected the organization of learning, and in many establishments the schoolmistress appointed a second-in-command, known as the *directrice des études*.[135] At Mme Deslignières' institution, one of the most successful Parisian schools from the 1840s to the 1870s, which educated between 100 and 120 pupils at a time, the schoolmistress herself was rarely seen except on her fortnightly visits to the classrooms, when she would hear the girls' marks read out. Mlle Suleau, the *sous-directrice,* undertook the daily management of the school; Mlle Froment, *directrice des études,* headed the teaching staff. The music teachers came under the management of the *directrice de la musique.*[136]

The space allotted to a *parloir* at Mme Achet's school points to the continuing attachment to the idea of enclosure in lay establishments. In her description of a typical Parisian boarding-school of the 1850s, Marie Sincère (the pseudonym of Marie Romieu) noted that in many schools, a *dame du parloir* would sit by the main entrance to the school, watching over all comings and goings and chaperoning any visits to pupils.[137] Earlier in the century the Ecouen branch of the *Légion d'Honneur* school 'had established the enclosure of the convents', as Mme Campan noted with approval, emphasizing that it helped to preserve the purity of the pupils' efforts to better themselves and to emulate their peers.[138] The administrative authorities also underlined the value of enclosure. In the Seine, a prefectoral ruling of 1821 specified that if a school overlooked a street, its outside windows must be papered over.[139] This was as much to prevent the girls looking out as to stop passers-by looking in, and successive rulings emphasized that inspectresses should pay particular attention to how well schools were enclosed.

Evidence from inspection reports and from the rules drawn up for the administration of lay boarding-schools thus reveals the continuing sway of a convent model of female schooling over the administrative authorities, who drew on the *Ancien Régime* traditions of girls' schooling in the same way as those who created the *Université* harked back to eighteenth-century precedents in boys' schooling.[140] Although, in the second half of the eighteenth century, convents had attracted increasing criticism, they nonetheless proved a source of inspiration for many of the projects being elaborated for the development of girls' education. Stéphanie de Genlis was critical of the aristocratic convent schools of the *Ancien Régime,* but still envisaged a network of 'cloistered schools' as the best means of extending female schooling, and drew heavily on Mme de Maintenon's directions for Saint-Cyr in elaborating her plan.[141]

---

[135] See, for example, the Paris schools of Mlle Anglade where in the 1840s the assistant mistresses were divided into 'maîtresse de première classe, maîtresse de deuxième classe' etc. Inspection pension Anglade, 1841, VD⁶ 367–10.

[136] Mme Brada (pseud. of Henrietta Consuela de Puliga), *Souvenirs d'une petite du Second Empire* (Paris, 1921), 35–7; Inspection pension St Aubin Deslignières, 1872, AD Seine, VD⁶ 1731–10.

[137] Marie Sincère (pseud. of Marie Romieu), *Les pensionnats de jeunes filles* (Paris, 1853), 11.

[138] Campan, *De l'éducation,* i. 338.   [139] Règlement de la Seine, 1 Dec. 1821.

[140] Savoie, *Enseignants,* 20–32.   [141] Genlis, *Discours,* 23–6.

Although in the early nineteenth century convent schooling was a frequent point of reference, in the 1830s and 1840s, as Rebecca Rogers' research reveals, there were increasing calls for girls' education to be established on a more domestic footing, not only offering them practical skills, but reflecting their essentially private and familial nature. Inspectors criticized lay boarding-schools for placing too much emphasis on the accomplishments, and prefects expressed a new suspicion of female communal life and wariness about the public status of lay schoolmistresses.[142] Schoolmistresses like Mme Pivand in Paris, who had twenty-two boarders and twenty-three day girls in 1835, were criticized by the inspectress for 'trying to give the impression of being the director of a grand establishment, and not that of the mother of a family'.[143] As would perhaps be expected, Protestant commentators tended to be particularly hostile to convent schooling, expressing their opposition in ways that echoed English criticism of religious orders as contrary to the family and to women's domestic nature.[144] Significantly, evidence concerning the schools established by Protestant women in France suggests that they were more often inclined to emphasize the familial and domestic character of their schools than their Catholic counterparts. Mme Coulon's school in Paris, though successful, never had more than forty pupils and was described as 'une grande famille' by the inspectress.[145]

Yet among the Catholic majority the institutional model of female schooling was never fundamentally called into question. Indeed, the success of convent schools is proof of the model's enduring authority, and of continuing attachment to the idea of a school education as a period when pupils should be preserved from outside influences. Catholic lay schoolmistresses continued to establish large, hierarchical institutions that carefully enclosed their pupils, yet were public in character, benefiting from the precedents set by the founders of the new religious orders, 'strategists operating in the public spaces of the community'.[146] At the same time, the chief response on the part of the authorities to the impulse for reform was not to withdraw from female schooling in favour of domestic education, but to control and supervise schools ever more closely.[147] The power of the model was such that even when seeking to develop an explicitly secular

---

[142] Rogers, 'Boarding schools'.

[143] Inspection pension Pivand, 1836, AD Seine, $D^2T^1$110.

[144] A. Coquerel (fils), *De l'éducation des filles en réponse à Monsieur l'Evêque d'Orléans* (Paris, 1868), 18.

[145] Inspection pension Coulon, 1838, AD Seine, $VD^6$158–3. Rebecca Rogers makes the same observation: *From the Salon*, 175.

[146] Mills, 'Women', 200. Emily Clark sees a similar phenomenon in the confraternities of the *Ancien Régime*: see '"By all the conduct of their lives": a laywomen's confraternity in New Orleans, 1730–1744', *William and Mary Quarterly*, 3rd Ser. 54/4 (1997), 769–94; R. Rogers, 'Retrograde or modern? Unveiling the teaching nun in nineteenth century France', *Social History*, 23 (1998), 146–65.

[147] Règlement de la Seine, 1 Dec. 1821.

system of girls' education in the 1880s, legislators talked of establishing 'a lay noviciate' of teachers to staff it. [148]

The lay *pensions* of the nineteenth century ranged from grand institutions like the Parisian schools of Mme Achet and Mme Deslignières to more humble establishments like Mme Ploux's school in Bordeaux, which grew gradually in size and only late in the day acquired the space to establish the chapel characteristic of the *Ancien Régime* religious houses. Though they might do so with differing degrees of success, these lay boarding-schools aspired to emulate the Catholic institutional model of the convent boarding-school, a model which still represented the dominant conception of female schooling. In their large size, hierarchical structures, careful organization of time and space, and in the value attributed to the principle of enclosure, lay *pensions* built on and consolidated long-standing traditions in French girls' education. Like the Catholic institutions they emulated and competed with, these private lay boarding-schools, and the administrative networks which developed around them, anticipated and provided a model for the state institutions that gradually came to supplant them.[149]

Examining the development of girls' schooling on either side of the Channel reveals the significant part played by private lay boarding-schools in the history of female education in the first half of the nineteenth century. In both countries, these institutions were multiplying, and offering schooling to a growing proportion of middle-class girls. In England, by the 1860s private schools were providing education for just over half of all girls of middle-class origin. In France, the picture is complicated by the growing competition lay schoolmistresses faced from religious establishments; nevertheless, in the same period, lay boarding-schools were catering for over 20% of girls of middle-class origin. However, girls' schooling developed along very different lines on either side of the Channel. The case of Mlle Bray—the English schoolmistress who had failed to display a sign advertising her Parisian school—illustrates some of these contrasts. Whereas the inspection committee perceived Mlle Bray's establishment as a public institution which must conform to rules that the state had established for the regulation of girls' schools, Mlle Bray's response demonstrates an English hostility to government intervention, fuelled by the sense that schooling was considered a matter of private interest.[150] Her response to the committee was analogous to that of the Sussex schoolmistress who answered an SIC circular saying, 'I think sir, you

---

[148] Ferrouillat, Rapport de la Commission de la Chambre sur la création d'une École Normale, 1881, quoted in Mayeur, *L'enseignement*, 108.

[149] D. Julia, 'Le choix des professeurs en France: vocation ou concours? 1700–1850', *Paedagogica Historica*, 30 (1994), 175–205; Savoie, *Enseignants*, 'Introduction', and S. A. Curtis, *Educating the faithful: religion, schooling and society in nineteenth-century France* (Dekalb, Ill., 2000).

[150] Procès verbaux du Comité de Surveillance du 1er arrdt., 13 May 1841, AD Seine, VD[6] 158–3; P. Thane, 'Government and society in England and Wales, 1750–1914', in F. M. L. Thompson (ed.), *The Cambridge social history of Britain, 1750–1950* (Cambridge, 1990), i. 10–32.

have entirely mistaken the character of my establishment, which is not so much a school, as a home for young ladies.'[151] The misunderstanding between Mlle Bray and the Parisian authorities points to a contrast between English and French conceptions of the school; it also reflects dissimilarities between English and French understandings of femininity. Different interpretations of the domestic nature and role of women overlaid and accentuated the separate educational traditions of the two countries. At the same time, it highlights the influence of religion on the experiences of women in France and England.

In France, ideas of feminine domesticity had a political and public flavour. Motherhood and the family were politicized during the Revolution, and through-out the nineteenth century commentators saw the family as a determining element of public life. The corollary was that girls' education was established as a matter of public importance, reinforcing the concept of girls' hools as institutions occupying a public space that dated back to the creation of the Counter-Reformation convents. The exercise of authority by women in Catholic religious orders and the tradition of large-scale female institutions meant that privately established lay schools could build on the convent model of schooling, developing a public, institutional character which was problematic in England. Women teachers, and their establishments, were integrated into a public sphere of administration parallel to that overseeing male teachers and their schools, an institutional form of the mixing and complementarity underlined by Mona Ozouf. In England, conceptions of the family and ideals of womanhood had a different accent, which meant that girls' schools developed along different lines. The powerful influence of a Protestant Evangelical ideal of domesticity that emphasized the separation between the private feminine world of the family and the public masculine world of business meant that English girls' schools tended to be small and to cultivate a familial atmosphere. Their difference from the publicly oriented conception of boys' education was marked and reinforced by their physical location. At the same time the evolution of educational provision in England was marked by the absence of the kinds of networks of religious institutions found on the Continent, an absence which meant that ideas of the home as a pedagogic space continued to be influential, and that schooling was considered to be a matter of private interest. This tradition, and the lack of socially legitimate models of feminine institution-building (most evident in the hostility expressed towards 'nunneries'), coupled with the powerful influence of an ideal of femininity emphasizing separation, rather than complementarity, meant that English girls' schools tended to follow what could be described as a domestic model of schooling.

Yet, while the institutional form of both French and English schools reflected the influence of contemporary conceptions of femininity, in both countries girls' schools were sites of tension and ambiguity, reflecting the intricate play of the influences shaping the two models of schooling. Despite English schoolmistresses'

---

[151] H. A. Giffard, 'Surrey and Sussex', *SIC* xi. 211.

efforts to reconcile their work and their schools with notions of feminine domesticity, they could only do so with a certain degree of ambiguity. There was often a gap between the rhetorical ideal and the reality of women's experience. Indeed, it could be argued that treatises underscoring women's domestic role were a response to the sense that women were increasingly stepping outside the bounds of their feminine sphere. The boundaries between public and private were permeable, and the ideal of domesticity was full of ambiguities; woman's 'natural' role was private and domestic, yet it was a 'profession' for which she must be prepared. The home was a sanctuary from the world, but it was also a woman's 'business' to 'make her home into a seminary'.[152] English schools sought to emulate families and emphasized their private and non-institutional character, but they were nonetheless commercial enterprises, reliant on advertising and financial exchange. Since teaching the children of others was an extension of women's natural role as the teachers of their own children, it could be countenanced by middle-class women who sought to conform to an ideal of feminine domesticity. Yet it was commonly undertaken because that ideal was found wanting. Women established themselves as teachers because they could not rely on their fathers, husbands, or brothers to support them. Domesticity as they enacted it was not private, since it depended on their ability to manage affairs with landlords and parents, bypassing the mediation of the appropriate male representatives. The ideal of domesticity was not a fixed universal principle; it was elastic enough to allow for a positive interpretation of women's role, and the domestic model of girls' school is in some sense an enactment of that interpretation. The women who ran these schools might have felt the tensions implicit in what they were doing, but the structure of their schools represents a conscious attempt to reinforce that ideal. While their work contributed to the expansion of female education, and shored up arguments in favour of rational instruction for girls, these schoolmistresses did not directly challenge prevailing notions of femininity, and gendered notions of domesticity remained a strong self-reproducing current, as the desire to assimilate the school to a home reveals. In its inherent ambiguity, the domestic model of school reflects the powerful influence of an ideal of feminine domesticity while epitomizing the tension between the ideal and the reality of daily life.

The public character of girls' schools was also a source of tension in France, as the question of enclosure demonstrates. Though Mme Campan considered that the *Légion d'Honneur* school at Ecouen had adopted the principle, in 1816 a more rigorous form of enclosure was imposed on the schoolmistresses of the Saint-Denis establishment for somewhat different reasons when a pupil was found to have an anti-monarchical tract in her possession.[153] In the same

---

[152] A. Taylor, *Reciprocal duties of parents and children* (1814), quoted in Davidoff and Hall, *Family fortunes*, 179.

year, the prefect of Paris required all schoolmistresses who had sworn loyalty to Napoleon to swear an oath of support for the new regime.[154] On the one hand, girls' schools were to be enclosed institutions, underlining their distance from the outside world; on the other, schoolmistresses and their establishments were seen to have a public presence which could potentially make them politically threatening. As a result, as the period of the *Loi Falloux* suggests, girls' schools in France were potentially vulnerable to political upheaval. At the same time, while prefects and ministers sought to incorporate girls' schools into the public structures of educational administration, authors like the Catholic Ultramontane intellectual Lammenais were arguing that 'if one thing, by its nature, should be free of public administration, it is without doubt the education of girls, who are destined to a life of retreat and will only be concerned with family affairs'.[155] His contention was inspired more by arguments in favour of freedom of education than by opposition to the development of 'institutional' forms of female education, but even those who supported the development of girls' schooling by the state were dubious about the conception of girls' education as public. Whilst arguing in favour of a proposal to establish an *École Normale* (or teacher training college) for women, Lamartine told the Chamber of Deputies, 'there is no public education for women . . . Public education is only appropriate for those who are destined, like ourselves, for an active and public life. Women are destined for the family, therefore they must draw from the family their principal education.'[156] In the 1840s, lay schoolmistresses were operating in an increasingly hostile climate amid renewed calls for girls to be educated domestically. At the same time, they were facing intense competition from religious establishments. With the weight of tradition behind them, they continued, however, to build on the model of the convent to establish large, hierarchical institutions that were public in character. But the anxieties aroused by the question of enclosure and the public administration of female schooling point to the tensions that shaped the development of girls' education. The following chapters explore how these strains and ambiguities played themselves out in the lives of French and English schoolmistresses and their pupils.

---

[153] Rogers, *Demoiselles*, 171.

[154] Lettre du Préfet de la Seine aux maires d'arrdt., 7 Nov. 1816, AD Seine, VD[6] 159–2.

[155] Félicité de Lammenais in *Le Conservateur*, 5 (1819), 30. Quoted in Mayeur, *L'éducation*, 47.

[156] Speech of Lamartine to the Chamber of Deputies, 20 May 1835. Quoted in Rogers, 'Boarding schools', 165–6.

2

Becoming a Schoolmistress

It was a commonplace in England in the first half of the nineteenth century that governesses were, as Mary Maurice put it, 'the children of affluent parents' forced by 'a sudden loss of fortune, a failure in business or death' to become teachers if they could not marry.[1] Lady Eastlake defined a governess as 'a being who is our equal in birth, manners and education, but our inferior in worldly wealth'.[2] In this period, 'governesses' were distinguished not so much by their place of work—the term was frequently used to refer to those working in schools—but by their social standing.[3] Teaching, as an extension of the maternal role, was the only occupation a middle-class woman could adopt without losing caste. According to this image of the lady teacher, the only qualifications asked of a woman who wished to become a governess were gentility and poverty. Indeed, it was only need that could justify a lady undertaking any work other than the domestic duties of a wife and mother.[4] Paradoxically, her very lack of training was her qualification, since it marked the governess as being of gentle birth, unlike the trained teachers who worked in elementary schools.

Such ideas meant that governesses and schoolmistresses were characterized as tragic figures, victims of unexpected reverses in their family's fortune. In England, they figured prominently in contemporary fiction, even generating a new form—the 'governess novel' of the 1840s and 1850s. Describing the travails of the governess—failed by the bankruptcy or lack of foresight of her father, ignored by aristocratic parents who neglected their children, or insulted by the nouveau riche—was a way to criticize contemporary mores, and to draw attention to the woman teacher's plight.[5] In the same period, images of

[1] Mary Maurice, *Mothers and governesses* (London, 1847), 18.

[2] E. Eastlake 'Vanity Fair, Jane Eyre and the Governesses Benevolent Institution', *Quarterly Review*, 84 (1848), 176.

[3] The term was been used more to distinguish 'lady' teachers from elementary schoolmistresses, rather than defining the location of their work; see, for example, the 1857 publication *Hints to a young governess on beginning a school*. Its continued use in the school context indicates the importance of the social standing that the term implied, and the degree to which women could alternate between private governessing and school teaching.

[4] M. J. Peterson, 'The Victorian governess: status incongruence', in M. Vicinus (ed.), *Suffer and be still: women in the Victorian age*, 2nd edn. (London, 1980), 3–20.

[5] K. West, *Chapter of governesses: a study of the governess in English fiction, 1800–1949* (London, 1949); M. Poovey, *Uneven developments: the ideological work of gender in mid-Victorian England* (Chicago, 1988), 126–57; C. Wadsö Lecaros, *The Victorian governess novel* (Lund, 2001).

'indigent gentlewomen', women teachers prominent amongst them, became a theme of Victorian painting.[6] Richard Redgrave's painting of 'The Poor Teacher' (Illustration 3) provided a vivid illustration of the stereotype of the 'lady teacher'. An elegant young woman, dressed in dark clothes, sits with her head bowed in the foreground, a black-edged letter resting on her lap. She has turned away from the piano, on which rests the music for 'Home sweet home'—a reminder of how she has been forced to leave her proper place in the family home. Two pastel-clothed girls play in the garden outside the window, sunny, in contrast to the sombre interior; a third pupil looks out into the garden. Possibly based on a scene observed at Mrs Matthew's school, Westbourne Place, where Redgrave taught drawing, the image highlights the isolation of the lady teacher from her own kind and hints at the tragic circumstances which led to the decision to become a schoolmistress or governess.[7]

Illustration 3. *The Poor Teacher*, Richard Redgrave, RA (1845), oil on canvas; reproduced by permission of V&A Images, Victoria and Albert Museum.

[6] D. Cherry, *Beyond the frame: feminism and visual culture, Britain, 1850–1900* (London, 2000), 33–40; S. Casteras, *Images of Victorian womanhood in English art* (London, 1987), 114–16.

[7] R. Parkinson, *Victoria and Albert Museum: catalogue of British oil paintings* (London, 1990), 239.

In France, too, teaching was often presented as 'the only honourable occupation' for well-bred young women whose fathers had died or gone bankrupt, or who had been unable to find a husband.[8] Popular novels like Mathilde Bourdon's *Souvenirs d'une institutrice* (1859) evoked the 'always arid career' of the governess, and real schoolmistresses frequently drew on the romantic rhetoric of fiction in describing their own condition.[9] Elise Chambordon appealed to the *Ministre de l'Instruction Publique* for help, saying that 'you are too good not to protect the daughter of a military man whose unhappy situation is so deserving of interest'.[10] Women teachers were also commonly presented as social-climbing tradesmen's daughters, or luxury-loving *grandes dames*, who saw school teaching as an easy way to supplement their income.[11] On both sides of the Channel, it was assumed that women did not become teachers out of choice, and that they would not have had any training for their work.[12]

In the 1840s and 1850s, however, a growing number of contemporaries were questioning the idea that all schoolmistresses were 'reduced gentlewomen'. Harriet Martineau used evidence from the 1851 census to demonstrate the many fields in which women were active. She challenged her readers to recognize the self-deluding nature of a vision of society that perceived women as being universally provided for by men.[13] The census recorded 67,551 women teachers amongst the active female population (without distinguishing between elementary schoolmistresses, private governesses, and boarding-schoolmistresses).[14] In France, Joséphine Bachellery, a well-known Parisian schoolmistress, called for the extension of opportunities for teachers because so many bourgeois girls needed to find their own means of support.[15] As Marie Sincère noted, many women had been preparing to teach 'since childhood'.[16] Commentators like Bachellery and Martineau were pointing to the fact that many middle-class women not only worked, but *expected* to work: the situation of women teachers in the first part of the nineteenth century was often more complex than the 'reduced gentlewoman' stereotype implies.

---

[8] M. Sincère (pseud. of Marie Romieu), *La femme au XIXe siècle* (Paris, 1858), 100.

[9] M. Bourdon, *Souvenirs d'une institutrice* (Paris, 1859); A. Esquiros, *Histoire d'une sous-maîtresse* (Paris, 1861).

[10] Elise Chambordon au Ministre de l'Instruction Publique, 23 Jan. 1838, AN, F17 12432.

[11] J. Marchef-Girard, *Les femmes, leur passé, leur présent, leur avenir* (Paris, 1860), 485–7.

[12] It is an assumption that historians of education have tended to accept. Pedersen, *Reform*, 106, 114; J. S. Pedersen, 'School-mistresses and Headmistresses: elites and education in nineteenth century England', *Journal of British Studies*, 15 (1975), 136–62; Dyhouse, *Girls*, 47, 58–9. Françoise Mayeur and Rebecca Rogers argue that authorization procedures contributed to defining a new kind of professional lay schoolmistress in France, but both emphasize the importance of social criteria in the way schoolmistresses were defined and defined themselves. Mayeur, *L'éducation*, chs. 3 and 4; Rogers, *From the Salon*, ch. 4.

[13] H. Martineau, 'Female industry', *Edinburgh Review*, 222 (1859), 293–337.

[14] Figures from P. Corfield, *Power and the professions in Britain, 1700–1850* (London, 1995), 33.

[15] J. Bachellery, *Lettres sur l'éducation des femmes* (Paris, 1848), 3.

[16] Sincère, *Pensionnats*, 28.

BECOMING A SCHOOLMISTRESS IN ENGLAND

The Social Origin and Itinerary of Schoolmistresses

The stereotypical image of the governess or schoolmistress in England was of a lady of 'reduced circumstances', whose pupils differed from her more in wealth than in rank. Publicity for schools alluded to the schoolmistresses' social credentials and occasionally detailed the difficult circumstances that had induced them to take up school teaching. An 1861 advertisement for Mrs Davies' 'Ladies' College for the Daughters of Gentlemen' explained that she was 'the widow of the late Professor Davies', and one for Miss Leeke's 'Select Finishing School for the Daughters of Gentlemen' in Yorkshire specified that she was the daughter of a clergyman of the established church.[17]

Like Miss Leeke and Mrs Davies, many English schoolmistresses were drawn from the professional and business classes. This emerges clearly from a proso-pographical study of the lives of seventy-four English teachers born between *c.*1780 and 1850.[18] Classifying the schoolmistresses in this biographical sample according to their fathers' occupation reveals that of the sixty-seven women in the sample for whom the information is available, thirty-nine (58.2%) came from the gentry and professional classes (see Figure 2.1). Nineteen (28.4%) were daughters of merchants, businessmen, and manufacturers. The overwhelming majority of schoolmistresses in the sample (86.6%) could thus be described as belonging to the middle and upper middle classes.

Reliance on biographical sources tends to over-represent women from more privileged backgrounds; however, records from the Governesses' Benevolent Institution (GBI), founded in 1846 to assist aged and unwell governesses, give a similar picture. Between 1846 and 1848, of twenty applicants, eleven were the daughters of professional men, six were the daughters of businessmen and merchants, and only three (whose fathers were all lesser government clerks) could be described as being members of the lower middle class.[19] A study of schoolmistresses active in Oxfordshire and Wiltshire in the late 1840s and early 1850s suggests that opening a boarding-school might also be an option for women of more humble backgrounds. Although five of the fourteen boarding-schoolmistresses for whom the information is available were the children of

---

[17] *Crockford's*, pp. xxiii–xxiv.

[18] The information comes from the biographies and autobiographies of women identified as teachers in P. Bell, *Victorian women: an index to biographies and memoirs* (London, 1989), and B. Kanner, *Women in English social history*, 3 vols. (New York, 1987–90), iii: *Autobiographical writings*, from school histories, and from the biographies of famous pupils. All the women included were at one time either proprietors of or teachers in middle-class schools for girls.

[19] Governesses' Benevolent Institution (hereafter GBI), *Report of the Committee of Management* (London, 1843–9).

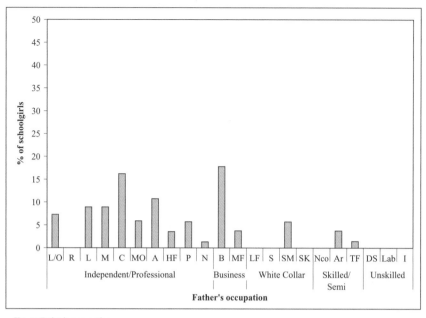

Figure 2.1. The social origin of sixty-seven schoolmistresses in the English biographical sample.

clergymen and businessmen, two were the daughters of domestic servants, and three were the offspring of shopkeepers or tradesmen.[20] Nevertheless, the image of schoolmistresses and governesses being 'the daughters of gentlemen' (insofar as professional men and businessmen were described as such) does seem to reflect the social origin of a high proportion of boarding-school teachers.

[20] Based on those identified in the Post Office directories as keeping 'ladies'' schools, 'boarding-schools', or 'seminaries', and who had boarding pupils in their households at the time of the 1851 census. *Post Office directory of Berkshire, Northamptonshire, Oxfordshire with Bedfordshire, Buckinghamshire and Huntingdonshire* (London, 1847, 1854); *Post Office directory of Hampshire, Wiltshire and Dorsetshire* (London, 1855).

Evidence from the biographical sample also suggests that the image of women being forced into teaching by 'a sudden loss of fortune' does highlight a common phenomenon. Only five of the seventy-four schoolmistresses are explicitly recorded as having become teachers solely from a sense of vocation. But of the fifty-two whose early lives are described in some detail, seventeen (33%) had seen their fathers experience financial difficulties, crises that were causally linked to the decision to begin teaching. In 1793 the losses sustained by Nathaniel Lawrence, a Birmingham merchant, led his daughters Eliza and Sarah to take positions as governesses. After their parents died, they provided for the family of seven daughters through their successful boarding-school at Gateacre, near Liverpool.[21] Rachel Martineau took a position as a governess and later opened a school after a blow to the family finances and the death of her father in 1826.[22] Anne Clough opened a small school for girls in 1841 when her father, a cotton merchant, ran into business difficulties.[23] At the end of the period the Lawrence sisters who founded Roedean, descendants of the family at Gateacre, began to work as teachers when it became clear that the family finances were suffering from their father's decision to abandon his successful practice as a solicitor.[24]

The idea that 'if a woman did not marry by a certain age, she immediately opened a school' also appears to be confirmed by the experiences of the schoolmistresses in the study.[25] Fifty-four (73%) never married, and only ten (14%) continued to teach after they married. Teaching was primarily the work of unmarried women. None of the teachers in the sample took up teaching for the first time after marriage.[26] Of the ten who continued to work after they married, two became assistants to husbands who were themselves teachers and four others continued to teach only because their husbands had fallen ill. These figures reflect the taboo against married women's work and tend to support the view that teaching was an expedient resorted to mainly by unmarried women in a society where it was expected that ladies would be provided for by their husbands. In the 1850s, women who had subscribed to annuities from the GBI were required to wind up their accounts if they married.[27]

Closer examination, however, suggests a more complex picture than this story of unmarried women forced into teaching by spinsterhood and business failure. The Liverpool schoolmistress Sarah Lawrence argued that 'in general, notwithstanding the care with which the situation must ever abound, no set of females (except perhaps the few who are very happily married) have more substantial happiness than those who enter with all their hearts into the

---

[21] D. E. de Zouche, *Roedean School, 1885–1955* (Brighton, 1955), 14–15.

[22] H. Martineau, *Autobiography* (London, 1983).

[23] B. A. Clough, *Memoir of Anne Jemima Clough* (London, 1897), 20.

[24] de Zouche, *Roedean*, 10–11.   [25] Stanton, 'Devon', *SIC* vi. 75.

[26] This excludes two who became teachers when they were widowed.

[27] GBI, Ladies' accounts, London, London Metropolitan Archives, E4.

employment of education and discharge its duties conscientiously'.[28] Although the Lawrence sisters had been unexpectedly thrown into teaching by their father's bankruptcy, Sarah clearly looked upon teaching as potentially offering more fulfilment than any situation other than that rare one of being 'very happily married', and may have chosen to remain a teacher rather than to marry. Several other teachers in the sample refused offers of marriage. Dorothea Beale declined several proposals, and argued that many women would be better suited for active life as nurses or teachers.[29] Mary Smith, a schoolmistress in Glasgow and Carlisle in the 1850s, claimed to have rejected two offers of marriage on the grounds that 'I did not want matrimony, it was congenial labour I wanted . . . I often thought that my plainness and my poverty were my safeguard.'[30] For both Beale and Smith this decision was underpinned by a sense of religious mission, which echoes the notions of vocation and service expressed by many Protestant philanthropists in this period, but this was not the case with all those who chose to teach rather than to marry. Underlining the convention that married life was incompatible with work for women, these examples also indicate that while most women teachers were unmarried, for some this was a matter of deliberate choice.[31]

Similarly, not all schoolmistresses were the victims of unexpected changes in their family's finances. Many had grown up in the knowledge that they would become teachers, often being prepared for this role by their education. Thirty-two (62%) of those in the biographical sample whose early lives are described in detail had lost their father, or seen him experience financial difficulties, before the age of 15. These young women would have known from an early age that in the event they did not marry, they would have to teach. Like many of the candidates for GBI annuities, described as 'educated for a governess', the upbringing of thirty-three of the teachers in the sample is explicitly recorded as having been determined by the expectation that they would become teachers.[32] Anna Carpenter had been brought up to be a governess by her mother, and her own daughters Mary and Anna were similarly prepared, their father remarking in 1819 that 'the plan to which I look forward as a future resource for my elder girls . . . is a school for girls, in which my elder girls might be directed by their mother, who could also superintend

---

[28] Quoted in de Zouche, *Roedean*, 14.

[29] Dorothea Beale to Roden Noël, quoted in Kamm, *How different*, 37.

[30] M. Smith, *Autobiography of Mary Smith, schoolmistress and Non-Conformist* (London, 1892), i. 196, 122.

[31] F. Prochaska, *Women and philanthropy in nineteenth-century England* (Oxford, 1980). Olive Banks argues that some women consciously avoided marriage, 'fearing the effect it would have on their freedom': O. Banks, *Becoming a feminist: the social origins of first wave feminism* (London, 1987), 6. The legal restrictions placed on married women's control of property could have a significant impact on their lives. A similar phenomenon has been observed in America: L. V. Chambers-Schiller, *Liberty a better husband: single women in America: the generations of 1780–1840* (New Haven, 1984).

[32] For example, one candidate in 1843 is described as 'educated for a governess and eventually became a partner in a school', Harriet F., a candidate in 1845, had been 'educated for the profession', GBI, *Report* (London, 1843), 19.

the household affairs until they had experience'.[33] When Charlotte and Emily Brontë arrived at the Clergy Daughters' School in 1824, 'governess' was noted in the register as their future occupation.[34] Elizabeth Day wrote that she 'could not remember a time when I did not look forward to being a teacher' and was educated by her mother, who, like her five sisters, had been a governess herself.[35]

The image of the lady who became a teacher after a sudden change in her personal circumstances was in part a fiction that usefully concealed the actual situation of the daughters of many impecunious professional men, who had always expected to have to teach if they did not marry. The stereotypical image of the 'reduced gentlewoman' had to be maintained in order to support an ideal of femininity centring on marriage and motherhood, and to bolster a notion of masculinity predicated on men's ability to provide for their families. In fact, many professional families fell short of maintaining these ideals in practice, and educating girls 'for a governess' was often the only way in which daughters could be provided for. That this was a problem encountered by many middle-class families is clearly demonstrated by the establishment of institutions like St Mary's Hall, Brighton (1838), for the daughters of impoverished clergy and the Royal Naval Female School, Richmond (1840), for naval officers' daughters. Such institutions were intended to provide the education appropriate for a gentleman's daughter at low cost, on the understanding that 'those whose abilities and circumstances permit will go forth as governesses'.[36] In the same way as considerable effort was put into preparing sons for a professional career, attempts were made to prepare daughters for educational work. Thomas Sewell, an unsuccessful solicitor, sent his sons to Winchester and Oxford in the 1820s in the expectation that they would adopt a profession, and dispatched his daughters Elizabeth and Ellen to boarding-school in Bath 'for the advantage of the masters'. When the Sewell sisters opened their school in 1852, their efforts were supported by their male siblings, three of whom were fellows of Oxford colleges, and one of whom went on to establish a public school for boys. The second generation of Sewell daughters were for the most part educated at their aunts' school and two later became teachers, as did three of the third generation. The men of the family continued to be prominent in the universities and public schools.[37] Educating daughters could be part of a family strategy to prepare children of both sexes for a future where financial security could not be guaranteed.

---

[33] A. W. Matthews, *Life of Sarah Bache*, 7; quoted in J. Manton, *Mary Carpenter and the children of the streets* (London, 1976), 23.

[34] Cited by L. Gordon, *Charlotte Brontë: a passionate life* (London, 1995), 15.

[35] Quoted in N. Glenday and M. Price, *Reluctant revolutionaries: a century of Head Mistresses, 1874–1974* (London, 1974), 10; S. Burstall, *The story of Manchester High School for girls* (Manchester, 1911), 37–8.

[36] *Second Report of St Mary's Hall, Brighton: an institution for educating the daughters of poor clergy, August 1st 1838*, 7.

[37] E. Sewell, *Autobiography of Elizabeth Missing Sewell* (London, 1907), 24; M. Owen, *The Sewells of the Isle of Wight* (Manchester, 1906).

The Education of Schoolmistresses

The girls who attended St Mary's Hall were offered a general education as a preparation for becoming a teacher, and a period at boarding-school was the most common form of educational activity of teachers in the sample. Forty-six (68%) of those whose early lives are well documented had been sent away to school. However, their educational experiences were very diverse and rarely limited to continuous attendance at a single establishment. When Hannah Pipe's father, a Birmingham cutlery merchant, died when she was 8, she was 'educated for a governess'; her experience shows how school attendance might simply be one element of a varied educational itinerary. She attended a day school run by the Society of Friends, had Latin and piano lessons from friends, went to a boarding-school near Birmingham, and then took classes destined for women teachers given by W. B. Hodgson of Chorlton High School, before opening her first school at the age of 17.[38]

Many women in the sample had equally heterogeneous educational experiences, and continued to study throughout their lives. Some went to considerable lengths to further their own education and fit themselves for their work as teachers. While running her girls' establishment in Carlisle in the 1850s, Mary Smith took French lessons with a Miss Patrickson who had spent twelve years in Paris, and studied alone to improve further.[39] Having established a school near Manchester in 1852, Elizabeth Wolstenholme worked by herself to prepare for the secondary examinations administered by the University of Cambridge, which she passed in 1869.[40] Ten of the teachers in the study attended lectures offered by Literary and Philosophical Societies and Mechanics' Institutes as well as studying alone.[41] In Bristol in the 1820s, Mary Carpenter was going to lectures on natural history and chemistry.[42] Public lectures offered, as the mid-century educational reformers realized, an accessible and socially acceptable means for women to extend their education.[43] Even before specially designed courses were introduced, future teachers were using public lectures as a means of further extending their professional knowledge and preparing themselves for their work.

Some schoolmistresses also sought to gain practical skills. Forty-three (58%) of the women in the sample are known to have had some experience of teaching before becoming schoolmistresses, often by taking on the education

---

[38] Stoddart, *Life*, 12–27.   [39] Smith, *Autobiography*, i. 153.

[40] E. Crawford, The *women's suffrage movement: a reference guide* (London, 1999), 188–9.

[41] M. D. Stephens and G. W. Roderick, 'Middle class self-help—the literary and philosophical societies', in M. D. Stephens and G. W. Roderick (eds.), *Samuel Smiles and nineteenth century self-help in education* (Nottingham, 1983), 16–47; M. Tylecote, *The Mechanics' Institutes of Lancashire and Yorkshire before 1851* (Manchester, 1957), 185–7.

[42] J. E. Carpenter, *The life and work of Mary Carpenter* (London, 1879), 31.

[43] A. J. Clough, Paper for the North of England Council for the Promotion of Higher Education for Women, 1868, quoted in Clough, *Memoir*, 138; P. Phillips, *The scientific lady: a social history of women's scientific interests, 1520–1918* (London, 1990), 193–247.

of younger siblings.[44] Elizabeth Sewell managed the education of her younger sisters according to a programme she had worked out with her fellow teacher and sister Ellen.[45] Penelope Lawrence began teaching her younger brothers and sisters after obtaining a Froebel diploma from a Dresden training college and later became a distinguished educator.[46] Sunday school teaching was also a common feature of the early lives of many teachers, whether Anglican or Nonconformist. Sarah Bache, who had a successful school in Edgbaston in the 1820s, first taught at the Birmingham New Meeting Sunday school in the 1790s and later spoke of the influence that one of her fellow teachers at this time had had on her.[47] Louisa Carbutt also taught for the first time in a Sunday school.[48] Others sought to gain experience in France so that they might also improve their French, a phenomenon explored in Chapter 7. Far from being inexperienced amateurs, many schoolmistresses were practised teachers who had sought to qualify themselves for their work.

Notions of 'self-help' and 'self-improvement', prevalent at the beginning of the nineteenth century, had particular relevance to middle-class women, who, like working-class men, were excluded from traditional structures of learning. Numerous publications aimed at facilitating or encouraging home study were published at this time and many were directed specifically at women. Schoolmistresses could also refer to a growing number of advice manuals and guides for teachers published in this period.[49] Manuals like *Hints to a young governess on beginning a school* (1857) offered practical advice on devising curricula and timetables and on methods of teaching and awarding merit, and emphasized the importance of tailoring methods to children's abilities and interests. The burgeoning teachers' periodical press also offered advice.[50] *The Governess, a repertory of female education*, a periodical published for the first time in 1855, seems to have had a significant impact on some schoolmistresses, judging by the letters reproduced at the end of each volume. It espoused the view that although by nature they were better educators than men, women must be trained to teach, and published articles on methods of teaching arithmetic and Tudor history, reported on training establishments, reviewed recently published textbooks, and examined new pedagogical theories.[51]

---

[44] The real figure is probably higher, since it is likely that early teaching work, particularly when it took place in the family, was thought so commonplace as not to be worthy of record.

[45] Sewell, *Autobiography*, 39.   [46] de Zouche, *Roedean*, 9.

[47] Matthews, *Sarah Bache*, 9.

[48] Herford, *In Memoriam*, 15; Malcolm Dick has suggested that middle-class involvement in Sunday schools was more substantial than has often been suggested: 'The myth of the working class Sunday school', *History of Education*, 9 (1980), 27–41.

[49] Other examples include S. F. Ridout's *Letters to a young governess on the principles of education* (London, 1838), *Hints to a young governess on beginning a school* (London, 1857), and *A word to a young governess by an old one* (London, 1860).

[50] L. Fletcher, *The teacher's press in Britain, 1802–1888* (Leeds, 1978).

[51] *The Governess, a repertory of female education* (1855–56).

It is difficult to know how many teachers periodicals like *The Governess* reached, or how many women followed the advice of books like *Hints to a young governess*. Clearly, some schoolmistresses did refer to manuals. Miss Miller, proprietor of an establishment for young ladies in Darlington, praised Henry Dunn's *Normal School Manual* (1837), written for elementary teachers but which had influenced her work in educating middle-class girls.[52] The proliferation of manuals and periodicals for teachers suggests that there was a demand for them. Even when formal structures for the training of teachers were limited, middle-class women were studying to prepare for their work, gaining teaching experience, and seeking to extend their expertise. However, by the 1840s calls for the more systematic education of schoolmistresses and governesses were multiplying and institutions were established which offered formalized training and certification to women.

Training for Schoolmistresses

The opening of Queen's College in London in 1848 has often been seen as a key moment in the development of women's education.[53] Established in conjunction with the GBI and offering lectures to women by professors from King's College, the aim of its founders was to 'exclude unqualified teachers from the profession; and gradually to raise the general tone of female education'.[54] Six of the forty-three women in the sample born after 1820 were students at Queen's; Frances Buss felt that the College had 'opened a new life' to her, 'to come into contact with the minds of such men was indeed delightful, and it was a new experience to me and to most of the women who were fortunate enough to become students'.[55] But although the College had initially been planned specifically to provide instruction for governesses, by 1848 the annual report was stressing that 'the committee disclaim any idea of training governesses as a separate profession'.[56] It had also abandoned a plan for the registration of women teachers. By 1853, regular lectures on 'the theory and practice of education' had been dropped and the formal connection with the GBI severed.[57] Queen's College was to be an institution for the higher education of young ladies, not a training college. Those who were destined to become governesses, like those of their male counterparts who would become public schoolmasters, were best prepared for their work, not by the pedagogical training deemed appropriate for working-class teachers whose primary task would be to instruct

---

[52] Miss Miller to H. Dunn, 1 Dec. 1845, British and Foreign Schools Society Archive (hereafter BFSS), 319, Middle Class schools—women.

[53] M. Bryant, *The unexpected revolution: a study in the history of the education of women and girls* (London, 1979), 21–2; E. Kaye, *A history of Queen's College, London, 1848–1927* (London, 1972).

[54] GBI, *Report* (1845).

[55] France Buss to Dorothea Beale, 13 Jan. 1889, London, North London Collegiate Archives (hereafter NLC), Buss family papers, B1.

[56] GBI, *Report* (1848), 17.   [57] Kaye, *Queen's College*, 53.

their pupils, but by a general liberal education, which was the best preparation for a professional whose principal duty was to educate, and to form the character. However, the move away from teacher training was not solely inspired by the growing influence of this Arnoldian conception of the teacher—it was also influenced by the ambiguities inherent in formalizing training expressly for middle-class women. Teaching was seen to be a legitimate occupation for women because it drew on their maternal qualities and 'natural' abilities. Offering formal training for teaching, which implied that women needed to be taught to teach, endangered this understanding of femininity. Moreover, it called into question the ability of men to provide for their families. When faced with the prospect of contradicting widely held notions about gender roles, the men who established Queen's College drew back. The notion that women teachers constituted 'a definite class' was rejected, as were existing practices of teacher training among schoolmistresses.[58]

Other institutions, however, did try to offer specialized education for schoolmistresses. Founded in 1846, the College of Preceptors was committed to vocational instruction.[59] This commitment was in part self-interested, since most of the College's members were not university graduates, and thus, like all women teachers, suffered from the absence of a means to prove their professional worth. To counteract this, the College established examinations in the theory and practice of education that tested candidates' knowledge of teaching methods, and required an understanding of educational philosophy and theories of learning. Schoolmistresses were encouraged to sit these examinations, which were in effect the first secondary teaching diplomas open to women.[60] By delivering certificates to women teachers and recognizing their expertise and pedagogical knowledge, the College attracted the support of many schoolmistresses. Sarah Ellis, best known as the author of *The women of England* (1839), but also a successful schoolmistress, was one of the first subscribers to the College's Ladies' department. Elizabeth Wolstenholme and Frances Buss both joined the College of Preceptors and in 1869 the latter was appointed to its council.[61] By 1862 there were at least forty-eight women licentiates, associates, and members of the College.

---

[58] F. D. Maurice, *Queen's College: its objects and methods* (London, 1848), 5. On pedagogical training for teachers, see C. de Bellaigue, 'The development of teaching as a profession for women before 1870', *Historical Journal*, 44 (2001), 963–88.

[59] *Fifty years of progress in education: a review of the work of the College of Preceptors, 1846–1896* (London, 1896), 7; J. V. Chapman, *Professional roots: the College of Preceptors in British society* (Theydon Bois, 1985); R. Willis, 'Professional roots: the Royal Incorporated College of Preceptors and Private Teachers from 1846–1850', *History of Education Society Bulletin*, 64 (1999), 91–9.

[60] See the 'selection from the examination papers', *Educational Times* (2 Oct. 1847), 3–5; 'Editorial', *Educational Times* (Sept. 1848), quoted in Chapman, *Professional roots*, 26.

[61] 'Ladies' department', *Educational Times* (2 Oct. 1847), 5; *A list of the Council of the Board of Examiners, Fellows, Licentiates, Associates and other members of the College of Preceptors* (London, 1862); Chapman, *Professional Roots*, 69.

The reports of the SIC uncover further efforts to offer pedagogical training to middle-class teachers. In Devon, a manufacturer's daughter had established a school for training governesses. It offered a general education supplemented with lessons on the art of teaching and practice sessions in a model school. Mary Porter, who headed the school in 1865, estimated that in the six years of her principalship, 115 of her pupils had become successful governesses.[62] The Chantry School, Frome also trained middle-class girls as teachers and was run along similar lines.[63] Private institutions too offered instruction for teachers, as an advertisement dating from the 1840s that announces training lectures for governesses at Mrs Morrell's South Globe Institution in Highgate suggests.[64] Further evidence concerning this and other establishments has not survived; however, there is evidence to suggest that middle-class teachers were looking to the elementary training colleges for training.

Like seven of the schoolmistresses in the sample, a small but nonetheless significant number of middle-class women were attending the elementary training colleges. Of 270 applicants to Borough Road College between 1830 and 1850, thirty-four (13%) were clearly intending to become boarding-schoolmistresses and private governesses.[65] Borough Road College was the training college of the British and Foreign School Society, where future elementary teachers learned the principles of monitorial instruction, yet it was not uncommon for boarding-school proprietors to recruit assistants from the College. Usually specifying that they did not intend to seek places in the schools of the Society, these middle-class students wished, like Sarah Harridge, an applicant in 1834, to 'receive more training . . . and thus better discharge her duties'.[66] Middle-class women also frequented the new elementary training establishments founded in the 1840s and 1850s. By 1864, there were eighteen such training colleges open to women in England.[67] The disappearance of many of the early registers makes it difficult to establish precisely how many middle-class schoolmistresses attended training colleges; however, even in the 1850s and 1860s, when the proportion of middle-class candidates seems to have been declining, there was nevertheless a steady intake of private students who were not destined for elementary teaching.[68]

---

[62] Evidence of Mary Eliza Porter, *SIC* v. 625–9.

[63] Evidence of Susan Kyberd and Revd. Fussell, *SIC* v. 708–11.

[64] Prospectus, Mrs Morrell's South Globe Institution for Young Ladies, London Metropolitan Archives, GBI Governess Papers, I (1846), 467.

[65] The sample was based on letters of application in three randomly selected periods, 1830–4, 1840–2, 1849–50; Applications and testimonials to Borough Road College, 1817–1858, BFSS, Applications to Borough Road College, 4, 437–49.

[66] S. Thoroughgood to the Ladies' Committee of Borough Road College, Feb. 1834, BFSS, Applications and testimonials to Borough Road College, 4, 438.

[67] L. Jones, *The training of teachers in England and Wales* (Oxford, 1924), 16–29; R. W. Rich, *The training of teachers in England and Wales during the nineteenth century* (Cambridge, 1933).

[68] Frances Widdowson suggests that the proportion of students with a professional background at Whitelands College fell from 7.1% in 1847 to 2.3% in 1867: *Going up into the next class: women and elementary teacher training, 1840–1914* (London, 1980), 21–27; S. Williams, 'The recruitment

Significantly, it was in the 1850s that Whitelands College was criticized for educating too many governesses.[69]

Anne Clough, who went on to become the first principal of Newnham College, Cambridge, having first taught in her own school, was one of the middle-class students attending the Borough Road College. Her interest in education led her to pursue her training in a second establishment, the Home and Colonial School Society (HCSS) Institution, founded in 1836. This college was intended to train teachers, particularly infant-school teachers, on principles derived from Pestalozzi. It was a progressive establishment, which in the 1850s contributed to diffusing the ideas of Friedrich Froebel, the founder of the Kindergarten movement who emphasized the importance of child-centred approaches. Anne Clough found the HCSS Institution's methods inspiring and felt that 'from their lessons the children would acquire a greater love for information'.[70] When she needed an assistant for her own school, she recruited Selina Healey from amongst its students.[71] Four of the seventy-four teachers in the biographical sample attended this institution, and in the 1850s Frances Buss encouraged her assistants to follow its courses.[72] The enthusiasm of these schoolmistresses for the HCSS Institution exemplifies the interest in pedagogical innovation expressed by several teachers in the sample. It underlines the ways in which private schoolmistresses seized opportunities to develop their expertise and were committed to undergoing some form of professional instruction. In doing so they were sometimes aware that on the other side of the Channel, their counterparts had long been subject to a formal system of certification offering much-prized diplomas to middle-class schoolmistresses.[73]

BECOMING A SCHOOLMISTRESS IN FRANCE

The Social Origin and Itinerary of Schoolmistresses

The 'reduced gentlewoman' was a common figure in writing about women's education in France as well as in England. In *L'institutrice*, published in 1840,

---

of elementary mistresses and their social class in the nineteenth century: with special reference to Whitelands College London, 1841–1870', *Early Child Development and Care*, 54 (1990), 29–56; a study of recruitment to Hockerill College in the 1850s suggests a similar pattern: M. Heafford, 'Women entrants to a teachers' training college, 1852–1860', *History of Education Society Bulletin*, 23 (1979), 14–20.

[69] Cited in Widdowson, *Going up*, 22.

[70] Diary entry for 1849, quoted in Clough, *Memoir*, 73.

[71] 'Appointments to schools', *Quarterly papers of the Home and Colonial School Society* (Jan. 1861); BFSS, Home and Colonial School Society Reports, 814.

[72] Kamm, *How different*, 45. The Miss Ainsworths, who succeeded Jane and Maria Byerley at their school in Stratford-upon-Avon in 1836, are listed amongst the donors to the Society in the annual report for 1853.

[73] Letter to the Council of the College of Preceptors, Frances Goodacre, *Educational Times* (1 Dec. 1847), 47.

Louise Colet caricatured the figure of the 'teacher with ambitions'—typically the daughters of Napoleonic generals, or ruined businessmen, or the illegitimate children of aristocrats, educated in luxury, but who found on the death or bankruptcy of their parent that they must provide for themselves. She also, however, evoked two other 'types' of schoolmistress: the devoted teacher and the career-teacher, recruited from more humble backgrounds. The former dedicated herself to working for others at great personal cost. The career-teacher, on the other hand, was 'the daughter of one of those little merchants or petty Parisian bourgeois who say to their children . . . "you must work as we ourselves worked". The career-teacher becomes a teacher, but she could equally become a laundress, a dressmaker or a shop assistant.'[74]

Colet's article is satirical. However, evidence of the social origin of teachers from two prosopographical studies of French schoolmistresses shows that she was right to emphasize that private schoolmistresses were recruited from a wide spectrum of society (see Figure 2.2). A prosopographical sample based on 408 *déclarations d'ouverture* (the documents which schoolmistresses were required to produce when applying for authorization to open a school) reveals that of the 169 women whose father's occupation is known, fifty-eight (34%) were the daughters of professional men or men of independent property. However, forty-two (24%) were the children of skilled workers, and twenty-three (13%) were the daughters of men employed in what might be described as white-collar occupations—lesser civil servants, schoolmasters, and shopkeepers; the latter were a significant presence in both samples. These figures can be compared to evidence from a study, drawing on biographical material, correspondence, and journals, of forty French teachers. Although fourteen (52%) of the women in this biographical sample were the daughters of professional men or men of independent property, three (11%) were the daughters of men in clerical occupations. Overall, these surveys suggest that schoolmistresses in France were recruited primarily from the urban middle and lower middle classes.[75]

---

[74] 'L'institutrice par vocation' means literally 'the teacher by vocation'. Although in certain circumstances 'vocation' was used to imply a sense of mission, it could also be used more neutrally to mean career. L. Colet, 'L'institutrice', in J. Janin (ed.) *Les français peints par eux-mêmes* (Paris, 1840), i. 82.

[75] In the first case, samples were taken from the records for the Seine, the Gironde and the Nord. The 233 Seine *déclarations* were for the most part taken from 17 of 237 boxes of *déclarations* of all types and are reasonably well spread through the period because of the early instalment of administrative procedures in Paris: AD Seine, DT Supplément. The 80 Nord *déclarations* come from applications for permission to take the teaching diploma prompted by a prefectoral ruling of 1830 and from *déclarations d'ouverture* for boarding-schools registered between 1830 and 1870: AD Nord, 1 T 118/2 and 1 T 122/1–8. The 95 Gironde *déclarations* come from a register of *déclarations d'ouverture* for 1821–88 and from the *déclarations* for private schools from 1850 to 1893: AD Gironde, 48 T 1 and 47 T 1–17. The information on teachers collected from the archives will henceforth be referred to as the *déclarations* sample to avoid confusion with the biographical samples. The French biographical sample was constituted in the same way as the English study. Particularly useful in locating the biographies and autobiographies

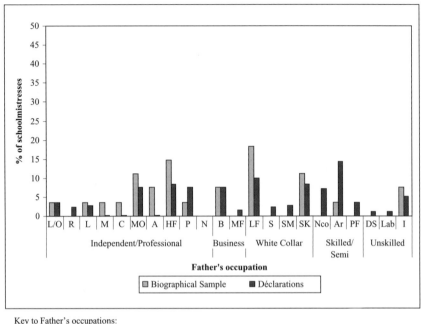

Key to Father's occupations:

L/O	Landowner/independent gentleman	MF	Manufacturer / Industrialist
R	Rentier	LF	Lower Functionary
L	Lawyer (barrister or solicitor)	S	Elementary schoolmaster / *Instituteur*
M	Medical man (surgeon or physician)	SM	Salesman / Commercial Clerk
C	Clergyman	SK	Shop-Keeper, Tradesman, Inn-Keeper
MO	Military or Naval Officer	Nco	Soldier / Sailor / Constable
A	Architect / Engineer / Journalist / Artist	Ar	Artisan
HF	Higher Functionary	TF	Tenant / Small Farmer
P	Public schoolmaster / *Universitaire*	DS	Domestic Servant
N	Notary / senior clerk	Lab	Labourer / Factory Worker
B	Businessman / Merchant	I	Illegitimate

Figure 2.2. The social origin of twenty-seven schoolmistresses in the French biographical sample and 169 schoolmistresses in the *déclarations* sample.

It is often difficult to identify and disentangle the factors influencing the decision to become a schoolmistress. Recalling Colet's 'devoted teacher', some stated that a commitment to education was the reason they had become teachers. Mme Duchambon wrote in 1838 that 'my only ambition, my only reward is to find happiness in the accomplishment of all my duties'.[76] Since she was

of schoolmistresses were D. Bertholet, *Les français par eux-mêmes* (Paris, 1981) and M. Yalom, 'Women's autobiography in French, 1793–1939: a selective bibliography', *French Literature Series*, 12 (1985), 197–205. Rebecca Rogers' data gives similar results with 43.8% of a group of 64 Parisian schoolmistresses being the daughters of men in middle-range occupations: Rogers, *From the Salon*, 130.

[76] Mme Duchambon au Maire du 1er arrdt., 24 Mar. 1838, AD Seine, VD6 158–3.

writing to ask for special treatment from the authorities, she may have been currying favour by presenting herself as devoted to her work. Mme Duchambon also emphasized that 'for me, teaching is a vocation', which, although it could simply mean 'an inclination', also had a religious resonance. The way faith might influence professional commitment will be examined in Chapter 4, but it could also determine the route which a Catholic woman took in becoming a schoolmistress. Teaching sisters were recruited from the same strata of society as secular schoolmistresses, and, given the cloistered conditions of the lives of many *sous-maîtresses* or assistants, there may have been little to choose between working in a lay and a religious establishment. If religious vocation was an important motivation for many teaching sisters, working in a convent school also offered practical advantages: there was no need to obtain a *brevet* and religious establishments offered greater economic security.[77] Unfortunately, detailed information on the reasons why lay schoolmistresses chose the secular path is seldom forthcoming. In his 1838 treatise on girls' education, Charpentier commented that many schoolmistresses were the daughters of 'parents who could not reconcile themselves to seeing their children entering the cloister without a clear vocation' (offering an interesting glimpse of the role played by a teacher's family in making the decision).[78] A more prosaic interpretation is that, unlike teaching sisters, lay schoolmistresses were able to provide not only for their own future but also for that of their families. Several of the teachers writing to the *Ministre de l'Instruction Publique* in the 1840s cited the need to support parents and siblings as the reason they wished to teach.

Marital status does not seem to have played a significant part in the decision to become a teacher. French schoolmistresses, unlike their English counterparts, did not view teaching only as an alternative to marriage, or married life and schoolmistressing as mutually exclusive. On the contrary, twelve (30%) of the teachers in the biographical sample married and continued to teach whilst married. Three more gave up teaching, but sought positions as inspectors after they married. Five (13%) were widowed or separated from their husbands before they became teachers. Only three (8%) gave up teaching on marriage. Moreover, ten of the eighteen schoolmistresses in the biographical sample who married established their schools after marriage: of these, five were married to men who were themselves teachers, but in all these cases the man assisted his wife rather than establishing or maintaining his own school. The *déclarations* study gives a similar picture. Sixty-nine (35%) of the 199 teachers from the Seine, and thirty (33%) of the ninety-five women from the Gironde in the *déclarations* sample for whom the information is available, were married when they opened their schools.

[77] R. Rogers, 'Retrograde or modern'.

[78] L. Charpentier, *Des moyens d'améliorer et de généraliser l'éducation des jeunes filles* (Paris, 1838), 53.

Marriage did not mark the end of a woman's teaching career, and becoming a teacher was not the last resort of women who could not find a husband.

A high proportion of schoolmistresses in the sample were the daughters of professors, schoolmasters, and civil servants. Contemporaries like Colet suggested that there was a particularly strong link between teaching and shopkeeping, and it was commonly believed that 'many women had moved without difficulty from the shop to the school'; the *déclarations* offer several instances of this kind of transition.[79] Marie Rispal, for example, had been an umbrella manufacturer before she established her school in Paris in 1849.[80] But in both the *déclarations* and the biographical samples, the daughters of civil servants and teachers outnumbered shopkeepers' children. Significantly, professors in boys' *lycées* were predominantly recruited from amongst the sons of men working in the civil service.[81] The information provided by both samples suggests that for the daughters, as well as for the sons, of *petits fonctionnaires*, teaching was a favoured occupation. In families where status was important, but there was little capital, preparing children for a career in education could be a means to provide for them in a manner appropriate to their social standing.

Viviane Isambert-Jamati's research into the Dubois-Goblot family provides a case-study of this kind of strategy. Alexandre Dubois, a tax inspector, sent his sons—of whom one later became a mathematics teacher in Paris—to school in their native Pont-Audemer, and then to the *collège* at Rouen. Meanwhile, his daughters attended a local *pension* and then were sent to Paris, where they prepared for the teaching examinations. On returning to Pont-Audemer in 1844 they opened a school, in the running of which they were fully supported by their father and brothers.[82] Like Dubois, other civil servants and teachers fostered their daughters' education and sponsored their work as teachers. In 1848, M. Munnier, the director of the infant school in Orléans, wrote to the Minister to ask for a special dispensation to permit his daughter Adélaïde to take the *sous-maîtresse* diploma.[83] Earlier in the year, the prefect of the Loiret had written to the Minister on behalf of M. Nouel, professor at the *collège* in Orléans, and his daughter.[84]

Connections with the *Université* or loyal service to the state might weigh in schoolmistresses' favour. Thus, the rector of the *Académie* (the regional educational authority) of Orléans supported M. Munnier's request, underlining the latter's hard work.[85] When Mme Millet requested permission to take the

[79] Gréard, *L'enseignement*, 15   [80] Dossier Rispal, 1849, AD Seine, D2T1 110.

[81] A. Prost, *L'enseignement en France, 1800–1867* (Paris, 1968) 68; P. Gerbod, 'La vie universitaire sous la Restauration, 1830–1848', *Revue d'Histoire Moderne et Contemporaine*, 13 (1966), 40.

[82] V. Isambert-Jamati, *Solidarité fraternelle et réussite sociale: la correspondance familiale des Dubois-Goblot, 1841–1882* (Paris, 1995), chs. 6–9.

[83] M. Munnier au Ministre de l'Instruction Publique, 13 May 1848, AN, F17 12431.

[84] Préfet du Loiret au Ministre de l'Instruction Publique, 23 Jan. 1848, AN, F17 12431.

[85] Recteur de l'Academie d'Orléans au Ministre de l'Instruction Publique, 25 July 1848, AN, F17 12431.

examinations for the *Maîtresse d'Institution* diploma it was noted that her mother-in-law was an inspector of infant schools in the Seine, and that this 'honourable alliance' provided a special guarantee of her suitability as a teacher.[86] Similarly, in recommending Zoë Hubert for a paid position as an inspector, the deputy of the Loiret underlined not only that she was an experienced teacher, but also that her father and brother were senior secretaries at the *Préfecture* and that another brother was a *lycée* professor; 'all in all, Mlle Hubert belongs to one of those families with whom everything one could wish for is a rule of conduct and a duty'.[87] If civil servants and teachers were particularly inclined to helping their daughters and sisters to become schoolmistresses, then the state was also keen to encourage them in this. Clearly, the strategies of families like the Dubois or the Huberts closely resemble those adopted by professional families like the Sewells in England. However, in contrast to their English counterparts, these families were dealing with a bureaucracy that not only provided employment for the men of the family, but also influenced the course of their sisters' and daughters' education and the content of the instruction they would offer. It incorporated their schools into a pre-existing hierarchy of institutions and authority. Such structures shaped the lives of schoolmistresses in France, and sponsored the emergence of career patterns of promotion and advance.

Education and Diplomas

The example of the Dubois sisters exemplifies the way in which some families sought to further their daughters' education in order to better prepare them for teaching work. Unfortunately, little is known about the early education of other schoolmistresses. It does seem that a period at school was a common experience for future teachers. Of the twenty-one teachers in the biographical sample whose childhood is described in some detail, thirteen (69%) had been sent to school. Julienne Dantier, who later headed a thriving Parisian school and ultimately became a school inspector, clearly regarded her time at St Denis as the basis for her future success. There, she had 'been rewarded with the highest praise and encouragement of her superiors'.[88] Mme Dantier may have been exaggerating the quality and importance of her education, since she was seeking employment as an infant-school inspector. But others shared this sense that schooling could have an important impact on a teacher's career. In 1842, Augustine Goblot recorded that her teacher Mme Olympe 'told me that she is very pleased with my way of working, and that she can clearly see that I am working to improve my future prospects'.[89]

---

[86] Préfet de la Seine au Ministre de l'Instruction Publique, 3 Oct. 1845, AN, F17 12431.

[87] Député du Loiret au Ministre de l'Instruction Publique, 29 July 1843, AN, F17 12431.

[88] J. Dantier au Ministre de l'Instruction Publique, 25 Apr. 1855, AN, F17 20516.

[89] Augustine Dubois to Eugénie Dubois, 9 Sept. 1842, quoted in Isambert-Jamati, *Solidarité*, 111.

Yet flexibility and informality was also often a feature of female education in France. Schoolmistresses often owed their education to family or friends or to private study. Jeanne Sauvan, who had a school in Paris from 1811 to 1828, then gave lectures at a training school for elementary teachers, and finally was made an inspector of girls' schools, went to considerable lengths to gain an education. Recorded by her biographer as barely able to read at the age of 12, by the time she was 20 Mlle Sauvan was acting as amanuensis to the successful pedagogical author J. N. Bouilly, whose *Contes à ma fille* had gone through five editions by 1815.[90] Ernest Renan's sister Henriette was also largely an autodidact. Taught to read Latin by some former nuns, she studied alone hard enough to obtain the *diplôme de maîtresse d'institution*—the highest qualification a schoolmistress could obtain—while she was working as an assistant in a Parisian *pension* in 1836.[91]

Although little is known about the early education of the forty teachers in the French biographical sample, at least thirty (75%) had obtained some kind of formal qualification. Of the sample of *déclarations* from the Seine, 231 teachers (98%) were certified, as were ninety-one (96%) of those in the Gironde. Given that the schoolmistresses in the *déclarations* were by definition those who had sought to conform with regulations, it is not surprising that so many had undergone the formal examinations prescribed by the authorities. Nonetheless, the number of qualified teachers points to the importance and influence of the systems of certification developed by the authorities since 1810.

One of the first formal attempts to regulate girls' schools was the ruling passed in August 1810 by the prefect of the Seine. It specified that the prospective teacher would be sent before an examination committee to be questioned on the subjects they wished to teach.[92] By 1815 it had been decided that those wanting to open a *pension* would be examined on French grammar, arithmetic, history, and geography. The jury would decide if they had 'sufficient notions' for a teacher and award them a diploma.[93] In 1820, when the *Ministre de l'Instruction Publique* exhorted prefects in other departments to follow the example of the Seine, the prefect of the Gironde followed orders and established his own regulations. Less exacting than his Paris colleague, he required a prospective schoolmistress only to prove that she had some knowledge of religion, reading, writing, grammar, and arithmetic, the same criteria adopted by the prefect of the Nord when he finally established regulations for boarding-schools in 1830.[94] The ruling of 1837 for the department of the Seine increased the demands made of women teachers. Those seeking the diploma for a *pension* would now need to pass examinations

---

[90] E. Gossot, *Mlle Sauvan, première inspectrice des écoles de Paris*, 2nd edn. (Paris, 1880), 13, 31.

[91] E. Renan, *Ma soeur Henriette* (Paris, 1896), 17–24.

[92] Règlement pour les écoles de filles, 20 Aug. 1810, AD Seine, VD4 21–5496.

[93] Arrêté du Préfet de la Seine, 10 Feb. 1815, AD Seine, VD4 20–5188.

[94] 'Écoles de degré supérieur et pensionnats de filles, 30 décembre 1820', Recueil des actes administratifs de la Gironde (Bordeaux, 1822), 165–70. Extrait des registres et actes de la Préfecture du 6 juillet 1830, AM Douai, 1 R 32.

in moral instruction, religion, reading, writing, grammar, arithmetic, French history, and geography. They would also be examined on the elements of physics, natural history, music, needlework, or modern languages if they were proposing to teach one of those subjects.[95] Again, the prefect of the Gironde issued a ruling along similar lines, commenting that the absence of such a ruling till then was 'an omission it would be wise to rectify in the interest of improving education'.[96] The prefect of the Nord appeared to be less interested in raising the level of education. His decree of 1842 dispensed with specialized exams for *pension* teachers, who were simply required to obtain the elementary *brevet*, with the exception of those teaching in towns with a population of more than 3,000, who needed the *brevet supérieur*.[97]

The Nord ruling anticipated the provisions of the *Loi Falloux* of 1850, which, as we have seen, dismantled the prefectoral rulings for *pensions* and meant that boarding-schoolmistresses only needed the *brevet*, obtained after an examination in religious and moral instruction, reading, writing, elements of the French language, arithmetic and weights and measures, and needlework.[98] To establish a school 'of the first order', candidates also needed to pass an examination testing their knowledge of elementary geography and history, elementary physics and natural history, basic agriculture, industry and hygiene, technical drawing, singing, and gymnastics.[99]

The prefectoral rulings and the requirements of the *Loi Falloux* indicate that the authorities hoped to ensure that the women who intended to open schools for girls had at least an elementary level of instruction. However, little effort was made to develop facilities for their education and training, partly because the rulings were motivated as much by the need to control and contain the spread of schooling for girls as to improve the standard of female education. The case of Mme Stevens demonstrates the extent and the limitations of provision for future teachers in Paris. In 1834, she had written to the Minister to request that her establishment be given the title of *École Spéciale des Institutrices* because it specialized in preparing girls for the teaching diplomas. After consultation, the prefect refused.[100] The main grounds for this were that there was a clear conflict of interest since Mme Stevens had been charged with vetting candidates for

---

[95] Règlement du 7 mars pour les pensions de demoiselles du département de la Seine, 1837, AN, F17 12431.

[96] 'Règlement pour les pensions de demoiselles de la Gironde, 11 juin 1842', Actes administratifs de la Gironde (Bordeaux, 1842), 212–13 ; Réponses à l'enquête du Ministre suivant le règlement de la Seine de 1837, AN, F17 12432.

[97] Arrêté du Préfet sur les pensions et institutions de filles, 29 Apr. 1842, AD Nord, 1 T 30/16.

[98] 'Loi sur l'enseignement', 15 Mar. 1850, Lois et actes de l'Instruction Publique, iii. 120.

[99] 'Décret Impérial, precede d'un rapport, relatif aux écoles primares de garçons et de filles, et aux maisons d'éducation de jeunes demoiselles', 31 Dec. 1853, Lois et actes de l'Instruction Publique, vi. 661.

[100] Dossier Stevens, 1834–5, AN, F17 12432. Despite her name, there is no indication that she was a foreigner. Dossier Blum-Léger, 1839, AN, F17 12432.

the teaching examinations since 1828 and was paid 1,200F p.a. by the prefect to do so. She would interview prospective teachers one day a week and instruct them as to how to prepare for the examinations. Those she judged unable to succeed would be sent away. In refusing Mme Stevens permission to change the title of her school, the prefect commented that he was of the opinion that 'there is no reason to establish an *École Normale* for women, because there is no shortage of schoolmistresses, and we should rather be trying to reduce their number', adding that were an *École Normale* established it would have to be supported by public funds.[101] His remarks suggest that among the administrative authorities, interest in raising standards in girls' schools was limited. Women's education was not of sufficient importance to require more substantial intervention and there was little support for spending public money on girls' education.[102] The same year as Mme Stevens saw her request refused, a petition to the *Chambre des Pairs* calling for the creation of a central *École Normale* for female elementary teachers sank without trace.[103] The *Loi Guizot* of 1833 had required all departments to establish male *Écoles Normales*, but when considering female education in 1836, the Minister simply recommended that something be done for future *institutrices*.[104] Though departments, municipalities, and central government did eventually establish bursaries in privately established *cours normaux*—teacher-training courses attached to lay or convent schools, or to day schools, rather than independent training colleges that developed in the absence of publicly funded *Écoles Normales*—it was not until 1879 that the *Loi Paul Bert* stipulated that training colleges for women be established on the same basis as men's.[105]

Although the state did little to sponsor the development of training institutions, evidence from the biographical sample and *déclarations* indicates that women did seek preparation for the examinations and for teaching. Five schoolmistresses in the biographical sample had followed some kind of training course, and institutions that specialized in training teachers were springing up around the country, with or without public assistance. Many Parisian boarding-schools were preparing their pupils for the teaching diplomas.[106] Alongside this instruction, aspiring teachers could benefit from a growing number of manuals aimed at candidates for the diploma.[107] In Paris, as well as *pensions* offering examination preparation, there were specialized *cours* for teachers. The first of these was established in

---

[101] Préfet de la Seine au Ministre de l'Instruction Publique, 25 Feb. 1835, AN, F17 12432.

[102] Daubié, *Femme pauvre*, ii. 101–3; Mayeur, *L'éducation*, 88–93.

[103] Riot-Sarcey, *Démocratie*, 94–9; Rogers, *From the Salon,* 84–90.

[104] Prost, *L'enseignement*, 91–9; A. Quartararo, *Women teachers and popular education in nineteenth century France* (Newark, 1995).

[105] F. Mayeur, 'La formation des institutrices avant la loi Paul Bert: les cours normaux', *Revue d'Histoire de l'Église de France*, 81 (1995), 121–30.

[106] Préfet de la Seine au Ministre de l'Instruction Publique, 25 Feb. 1835, AN, F17 12432.

[107] For example, E. M. Lefranc, *Nouveau manuel complet et méthodique des aspirantes aux diplômes de maîtresse de pension ou d'institution*, 2nd edn. (Paris, 1845); Mme E. Charrier, *Dictées pour l'Hôtel de Ville* (Paris, 1845).

1831 and offered free lectures to teachers on Sunday afternoons.[108] Outside Paris there were other opportunities. In the Gironde, Mme Dupuy, who had herself attended a lecture course on monitorial instruction, opened a boarding-school which trained Protestant teachers at Sainte-Foy in 1818. Consistently producing successful candidates for teaching certificates in Bordeaux, it still existed, under the management of a Mme Delhorbe, in 1868.[109]

Like their counterparts in England, schoolmistresses in France also followed courses intended for elementary teachers. As one inspector wrote ruefully in 1857, 'despite our precautions . . . the departmental scholarships and the pains taken by the *Académie* [of Rennes] have simply contributed to training more assistants, more *maîtresses de pension,* and more governesses and private teachers'.[110] In Bordeaux, a report of 1871 noted that 'the students' only desire is not to leave the city and to obtain positions in one of the innumerable Bordeaux boarding-schools'.[111] Clearly, attendance at an *École Normale* might be a means of social advancement for young women originally intended for elementary teaching who had been able to win a scholarship for the *cours*. However, these elementary training courses were also providing, at a price, instruction for middle-class women who hoped to become boarding-schoolmistresses. Indeed, some of the *cours normaux* which attracted state investment and semi-public status had evolved from the private initiatives of *maîtresses de pension,* an example of the interest in professional training expressed by some schoolmistresses which will be more fully explored in Chapter 4.[112]

Obtaining a diploma did not necessarily guarantee that a prospective schoolmistress was intellectually equipped for teaching. Joséphine Marchef-Girard, a prominent educational reformer, commented in 1869 that it was difficult to believe that the examination committees for the *brevet de capacité* were able to detect merit in the candidates before them. The curriculum and approach were outdated and old-fashioned.[113] Several years before, Henri Léon had also criticized the certification system, more particularly the courses designed to prepare girls for the examinations, which, he claimed, simply taught them to memorize what was required without understanding: 'they successfully pass their examinations without too much effort, but in reality, they have little solid

---

[108] Kilian, *L'instruction,* 25.

[109] Comité cantonal Protestant de Bordeaux au Baron Cuvier, 1 Apr. 1828, AN, F17 12505. Rapports sur l'école normale de Sainte Foy, 1844–54, AN, F17 9765. P. Goy, *L'éducation des filles: discours prononcé dans l'École Normale de Sainte Foy, le 6 juillet 1868* (Paris, 1868).

[110] Inspecteur Général Vincent au Ministre de l'Instruction Publique, 1857, AN, F17 9765.

[111] Rapport sur le Cours Normal de Bordeaux, 12 May 1871, AN, F17 9765.

[112] For example, the *Cours Normal* of the Corrèze had been established in 1843 in the boarding-school Mme Féart had first opened in 1837. Préfet de la Corrèze au Ministre de l'Instruction Publique, 27 Oct. 1843, AN, F17 9763.

[113] Marchef-Girard, *Femmes,* 488; Dossier Marchef-Girard, AD Seine, DT Supplément/154; *Collège Sévigné, le livre du centenaire, 1880–1980* (Paris, 1982), 11–16; entry in G. Caplat (ed.), *Les inspecteurs généraux de l'instruction publique: dictionnaire biographique, 1802–1914* (Paris, 1986).

education'.[114] An examination paper on French history from the 1840s does suggest that the chief skill tested by the committee was an ability to memorize.[115] That the standard was not very high in Bordeaux either is implied by the nonchalant attitude of Zéline Reclus, a successful schoolmistress from Orthez, who, according to her obituary, when 'passing through Bordeaux with her family, took the opportunity to sit the teaching certificate'.[116] Furthermore, even if prefects sought to ensure that no one could open a school without some kind of qualification, as we have seen, enforcement was patchy and many women continued to take positions as assistants and establish *pensions* without authorization. In 1829 a report on institutions in the first *arrondissement* in Paris noted that most assistants had no diploma, and in 1845 only 164 of 508 assistants (32%) in Parisian schools had the correct diploma.[117]

Nonetheless, many schoolmistresses attached considerable importance to seeking a diploma. Ondine Valmore insisted that she wanted to be a teacher and needed to pass her examinations, despite her mother's lack of enthusiasm. She would get up at seven and study till lunchtime. After a walk she resumed her studies until dinner, when she was called upon to make conversation with her parents' guests. She would snatch an hour or two more of study before going to bed at ten. In August 1844, she obtained the diploma with high grades in every subject and took up a post at Sophie Bascans' school at Chaillot in February 1845.[118] Louise Michel also worked hard for the *brevet*. In 1851, she enrolled for the preparatory course at a private boarding-school in Lagny, where she applied herself to grammar and arithmetic and looked forward to the examinations with trepidation. 'And on top of all this,' she wrote to her friend Victor Hugo, 'the idea of the examination in August, which, every second rises before me like a ghost, is enough to break a heart stronger than my own.'[119] Failing at her first attempt, she eventually obtained the *brevet* in 1852.

Women were also seeking certificates in ever-increasing numbers. In 1845, there were 317 candidates for the Seine examinations, of whom 250 obtained a diploma. In 1855, under the new system instituted by the *Loi Falloux*, 356 *brevets* were issued by the Paris *Académie*. In the Gironde by the 1860s, the number of candidates was rising, from 120 in 1860 to 183 in 1864.[120] At the same time

[114] H. Léon, *Les indiscretions de Jehan de Bomoloque à l'endroit des maîtresses de pension* (Paris, 1855), 32.

[115] 'Questionnaire raisonné sur l'histoire de France pour les examens de l'Hôtel de Ville de Paris', *c.*1846, AN, F17 12432.

[116] Quoted in H. Sarrazin, *Elisée Reclus ou la passion du monde* (Paris, 1985), 18.

[117] Rapport de Mme la Marquise de Macmahon, 15 Nov. 1829, AD Seine, VD6 158–3 ; 'Résultats de l'inspection des pensionnats de demoiselles, Paris, 1846', AN, F17 12431.

[118] F. Ambrière, *Le siècle des Valmore: Marceline Desbordes-Valmore et les siens* (Paris, 1987), ii. 77–8, 109–10.

[119] Quoted in L. Michel, *Je vous écris de ma nuit: correspondance générale, 1850–1904*, ed. X. Gauthier (Paris, 1999), 57.

[120] 'Résultats de l'inspection des pensionnats de demoiselles, Paris, 1846', 40; Gréard, *L'enseignement,* 55; Aspirantes au brevet de capacité, 1829–75, AD Gironde, Vt III.

as the numbers of women taking the teaching examinations were rising, the age at which they did so was falling. The average age at first diploma of teachers in the biographical sample born before 1820 was 33.0, but that of teachers born after 1820 was 20.9, a statistically significant difference.[121] This was partly the effect of a growing tendency for middle-class girls to use the diplomas or *brevet* as a school-leaving examination.[122] However, it is also a symptom of the way in which teaching was becoming a profession with a relatively stable career ladder of promotion and advance.

Emerging Career Patterns

In 1869 Julie-Victoire Daubié complained bitterly that, in a family with both sons and daughters working in education, whereas the sons might eventually obtain a professorship, their sisters, 'even if they were more intelligent, more committed to their studies, more interested in education, could only hope for a position as an assistant, the *nec plus ultra* of their present and of their future'.[123] Even before the creation of the *Université* in 1808, legislation had sought to create avenues of advancement for male teachers, and, in theory at least, a young man might begin his career as a penniless *maître d'études* and finish it as professor in one of the Parisian *Facultés*.[124] There was no parallel attempt to legislate in support of similar conditions for women teachers. But the correspondence exchanged between the Minister and prefects, and between schoolmistresses (or their parents) and the authorities, suggests that the idea that teaching might be a career with a ladder of promotion and advance for women was nevertheless gaining currency.

Daubié's contention that most *sous-maîtresses* had little hope of any kind of promotion accords with the state of affairs depicted by Louise Colet, who saw boarding-school proprietors as a breed apart from their assistants and from private governesses. The *maîtresse de pension,* Colet claimed, was 'almost always aged between forty and sixty: she is the administrator, rather than the teacher of the establishment she directs'.[125] Joséphine Marchef-Girard, however, who unlike Daubié and Colet was a teacher herself, claimed that most school proprietors had begun their careers as assistants.[126] This is supported by evidence from the French prosopographical samples. Of sixty-three women seeking permission to establish schools in the eighth *arrondissement* of Paris between 1850 and 1866, forty-nine (78%) had previously been assistants in someone else's school, as

---

[121] For those in the French biographical sample born before 1820, the mean age at diploma was 33.0, ± 2.09 (Standard error of the mean). For those born after 1820, the mean age was 20.9, ± 1.33. Those born after 1820 obtained their diplomas at a significantly younger age than those born before 1820 ($P < 0.05$, Unpaired t-test, $t = 4.17$, df = 17).

[122] See Ch. 6.

[123] Daubié, *Femme pauvre*, ii. 128–9.   [124] Savoie, *Enseignants*, 'Introduction'.

[125] Colet, 'L'institutrice', 81. Mayeur, *L'éducation*, 65, 80.

[126] Marchef-Girard, *Femmes*, 495.

had at least twenty-nine of the eighty teachers from the Nord (33%) in the *déclarations* sample.[127] Moreover, the administrative authorities in Paris seem to have been actively seeking to sponsor this career path. In 1816 the minimum age for taking the *sous-maîtresse* examination was set at 18 and that for *maîtresses de pension* at 21. This was raised to 25 in the ruling of 1821: the authorities had some kind of progressive pattern in mind.[128]

There was still considerable diversity in teachers' itineraries. Like their counterparts in England, French schoolmistresses might have their initial experience of teaching when they took on the education of their siblings. Working as a private governess was also a common experience. Four of those in the sample and fourteen (22%) of seventy women opening schools in the eighth *arrondissement* of Paris between 1850 and 1866 had previously been governesses.[129] Some of those in the sample of *déclarations* moved back and forth between school-teaching and governessing a number of times. Mme Martin had been an assistant in a Belleville school from 1842 to 1845; she had then worked as a private governess until 1848; in 1850 she established a *cours secondaire* before opening her own boarding-school in 1852.[130] Significantly, it was not unheard of for teachers to move between teaching in convent schools (which did not necessarily imply taking orders) to working in lay establishments. The daughter of a private schoolmaster in Lyon, Mlle Elas, who ended her career directing the Catholic *cours normal* of Valence, had taught in lay schools from 1834 to 1843 and in religious establishments from 1843 to 1864.[131] Five of the schoolmistresses in the Seine *déclarations* sample had previously taught in a religious establishment before opening their own secular school. Moreover, many of those who had attended elementary training courses would themselves have been students in a religious establishment, since a large proportion of *cours* were run by women religious.[132] Nonetheless, working as an assistant in a lay establishment was becoming a characteristic—if not quite universal—stage in the careers of many schoolmistresses. As a result, by the end of the period it is possible to identify a 'typical' career pattern.

There is little evidence of how a young woman who wished to become an assistant in a boarding-school went about doing so. In the Seine, the ruling of 1810 had established a central *bureau d'indication*, 'intended to supply schoolmistresses

---

[127] Clearly, these figures cannot tell us what proportion of assistants failed to establish their own schools. According to Marie Sincère, many *sous-maîtresses* could not find work after they reached the age of 35 and were obliged to return to their families with the few savings they had earned: Sincère, *Pensionnats*, 35.

[128] Arrêté du préfet de la Seine, 29 Apr. 1816, AD Seine, VD4 20–5191. Règlement concernant les maisons d'éducation de filles dans le département de la Seine, 1 Dec. 1821, AN, F17 12431.

[129] Calculated from Registre des déclaration d'ouverture d'établissements scolaires libres, 8e arrdt., 1850–66, AD Seine, Vbis 11 R15.

[130] Dossier Martin, 1852, AD Seine, D2T1 110.

[131] Rapport sur le Cours Normal Catholique de Valence (Drôme), 3 July 1864, AN, F17 9764.

[132] Mayeur, 'La formation'; Curtis, *Educating the faithful*, ch. 2.

with the assistants they need, and to indicate vacancies in schools to assistants'.[133] The lady director of the *bureau* would keep a list of Parisian schoolmistresses, and all those taking the *diplôme de sous-maîtresse* were required to register with the *bureau*. The *bureau* is mentioned in successive rulings up to 1850, but its records have not survived so it is difficult to know how effective it was as an employment agency. Informal networks and personal connections seem to have been more important in helping future teachers to find work. Ondine Valmore obtained her position at Mme Bascans' school through a complicated web of family friends linking her to George Sand, who had sent her daughter Solange to the school.[134] In Strasbourg, Amélie Weiler appealed to friends and was put in touch with a Mlle Schneider, who agreed 'to take care of my prospects and to guide me in what I need to read to prepare myself for teaching'.[135] Another common route was simply to begin teaching in the school one had attended.

At 36, Amélie Weiler was older than most teachers seeking their first appointment, a fact which she regretted, because she found studying for the diploma laborious and uninteresting. 'I never imagined', she wrote, 'how hard it would be to be a schoolgirl again at thirty-five.'[136] The average age at first appointment of schoolmistresses in the sample born before 1820 was 25.[137] However, Weiler was not alone in studying for the diploma quite late in life. As seen above, for those in the sample born before 1820, the average age at first diploma was 33, which reflects not only the slow and patchy implementation of the legislation on teaching certificates, but also the fact that many schoolmistresses of this generation prepared for the diploma while already working as assistants. Whether they took the diploma before or after taking up their first position as a teacher, conditions for *sous-maîtresses* could be difficult. They were usually required to sleep in the dormitories with their pupils, and were almost constantly on duty, supervising, teaching, and marking. Salaries, moreover, were low. According to Julie-Victoire Daubié, in 1845 the average yearly wage for an assistant in Paris was between 200F and 400F, less than that for a female domestic servant.[138] Because of the shortage of opportunities many accepted positions where they were simply 'au pair', receiving no payment except board and lodging.[139]

How schoolmistresses who began as assistants made the transition from being underpaid and overworked *sous-maîtresses* to establishing their own schools is difficult to ascertain. Many would have held two or three previous teaching positions, but it is still hard to see how the average teacher would have been able

---

[133] Règlement pour les écoles de filles, 20 Aug. 1810.   [134] Ambrière, *Valmore*, i. 112.

[135] A. Weiler, *Journal d'une jeune fille mal dans son siècle, 1840–1859*, ed. N. Stoskopf (Paris, 1994), 414.

[136] Ibid. 415.

[137] The mean age at first appointment of the schoolmistresses in the French biographical sample born before 1820 was 24.9, ± 1.86 (Standard error of the mean).

[138] The average wage for female servants in Nancy was 252F in 1853. That of female servants in Paris was 400F. T. McBride, *The domestic revolution: the modernisation of household service in England and France, 1820–1920* (London, 1976), 60.

to save enough money to open her own school. One fairly common route was for teachers to take on the school in which they had previously been assistants. Twelve of the schools in the sample of *déclarations* from the Nord had been passed on in this way. After Ondine Valmore had spent about a year working at Mme Bascans', during which time she had made a considerable impression on both pupils and schoolmistress, she was approached by a Mlle Bausset, *maîtresse de pension* in Lyon, where Ondine had spent her childhood. Mlle Bausset offered her '1,000F in salary, only two hours per day of teaching; the rest of the day entirely at my own disposition; after an agreed period of time, an interest in the establishment'. The agreement not only offered Ondine the prospect of eventually owning her own establishment, it also provided for Mlle Bausset's eventual retirement.[140]

Another route taken by would-be *maîtresses de pension* underlines the importance of marriage in schoolmistresses' careers. In France, as noted above, marriage did not preclude women from working as schoolmistresses. In fact it was fairly common for marriage to signal the transition from the position of *sous-maîtresse* or day-school proprietor to *maîtresse de pension*, possibly because the husband contributed some of the social or financial capital required for buying or setting up the school. Ten of the schoolmistresses in the sample established their schools after marriage, and, significantly, for the teachers in the Seine *déclarations* sample for whom the information is available, age at marriage was closely correlated with age at establishment.[141] Sophie Bascans was a highly successful schoolmistress as well as being Ondine Valmore's first employer. Having obtained the diploma and authorization for a day-school for girls in 1832, she married Ferdinand Bascans, a journalist and the professor of history in her school, in 1838, the year in which her establishment was first counted as a boarding-school by the inspectors.[142] Similarly, it was just after her marriage that Julienne Dantier established what was described in 1858 as 'one of the foremost Institutions for girls in Paris'. She had worked as an assistant in a Parisian school before her marriage to Henri Dantier, an author and teacher of literature and history in a number of Parisian boarding-schools. By 1847, Mme Dantier and her husband were installed in a school on the Quai de Billy, probably the same institution in which she had previously been a *sous-maîtresse*.[143]

---

[139] Daubié, *Femme pauvre*, ii. 121.   [140] Ambrière, *Valmore*, ii. 132.

[141] Comparing the ages at which the twenty schoolmistresses from the Seine in the *déclarations* sample for whom the information is available married and established their schools reveals a significant correlation between age at marriage and age at establishment ($P < 0.05$, pearson's r, t = 1.38, df = 22).

[142] Dossier Bascans, 1832, AD Seine, DT Supplément/13; Procès Verbaux du comité de surveillances des pensions et institutions du 1er arrdt., 18–22 Nov. 1838, AD Seine, VD6 158–3. Biographical information also from *Correspondance de George Sand*, ed. G. Lubin (Paris, 1964–91), v. 858, G. d'Heylli (pseud. of Edmond Poinsot), *La fille de George Sand* (Paris, 1900).

[143] Note sur Mme Dantier, 10 Dec. 1858, AN F17 20516. Inspection pension Dantier, 1847–8, AD Seine, VD6 158–3. Additional biographical information from Caplat (ed.), *Inspecteurs généraux*, 277–8.

Contemporary authors often satirized the *sous-maîtresses* who made eyes at male professors, ridiculing or pitying their hopes for marriage as 'a virtually unattainable dream'.[144] Like three other teachers in the sample, both Sophie Bascans and Julienne Dantier had married boarding-school teachers. Their example shows how marriage to a professor might be more than the fulfilment of romantic hopes: it could be the springboard they needed to move from the position of assistant to schoolmistress and the basis of a successful career. Whether marriage to a man who was not also a teacher had a significantly different effect on a schoolmistress's career is not clear. The husbands of the seven schoolmistresses in the biographical sample who continued to teach after marriage included an architect, a doctor, a sculptor, and a journalist. By the 1850s and 1860s, however, being married was becoming more of a hindrance for French schoolmistresses as the celibate ideal of the teaching sister gained influence. In the Nord it was noted that Mme Gorin had been losing pupils since her marriage, and that 'to a certain extent, this is the case for all the married schoolmistresses'.[145] Comparing teachers in the biographical sample who were born before and after 1820 reveals a statistically significant difference in the proportion of married teachers.[146] The path of professional advance that had been emerging since the prefect of the Seine's first ruling in 1810 was not only increasingly fixed, by mid-century it was increasingly closed to married women.

Evidence from the prosopographical samples suggests that although early nineteenth-century stereotypes of schoolmistresses and governesses contained elements of truth, they concealed the multiplicity of routes into teaching taken by women in England and France. They also failed to render the complexity of motives behind the decision to become a schoolmistress and the way in which families and individuals invested in education and training to better prepare the future teacher for her work. On both sides of the Channel, families with meagre financial resources were investing in the social capital that education could provide. Their decision to do so, and the importance that women teachers attached to undergoing some kind of preparation for their work, constituted a radical challenge to the idealized images of domestic womanhood found in the prescriptive literature of the period. It undermined the principle that women should be provided for by their fathers or husbands, opening up a space in which the notion of a feminine career outside the convent could take root. At the same time, by suggesting that being a woman was insufficient preparation for teaching, the interest in training undermined a conception of femininity predicated on the idea that women were naturally maternal. Such tensions remained largely

---

[144] Sincère, *Pensionnats*, 34.   [145] Dossier Gorin, 1865–66, AD Nord, 1 T 122/2.

[146] Comparing the proportions of married and never-married schoolmistresses of women in the sample born before and after 1820 reveals that a significantly larger proportion of those born after 1820 never married (P < 0.05, chi2 = 6.81, df = 1).

unacknowledged, concealed in part by the useful fictions of 'reduced gentle-women'. However, when, in both England and France, schoolmistresses began to campaign for the development of teaching as a profession for women, these ambiguities were brought to the fore.

Although on both sides of the Channel recruitment into teaching was more complex than has usually been recognized, a comparison of the social origins of teachers in England and France reveals significant differences. Fifty-eight (86.6%) schoolmistresses in the English sample were recruited from professional and business backgrounds. This compares with sixteen (59%) in the French biographical study and seventy-four (44%) in the *déclarations* sample. The contrast points to the impact of the early bureaucratization of secondary schooling for girls in France and to the different factors shaping middle-class identity on either side of the Channel.

In France, the system of certification established by the authorities supported the notion that teaching could be a lifelong career and sponsored the emergence of fairly fixed ladders of promotion and advance. This encouraged the recruitment of girls from middle- and lower-middle-class families already integrated within state structures through the civil service and the *Université*. At the same time, the system of certification favoured women's upward social mobility. Although comparing the occupations of fathers and husbands can only be a very rough indicator of social mobility, the biographical sample reveals that schoolmistresses in France were considerably more likely to marry professional men than they were to have originated from professional families.[147] By becoming teachers, women could move up the social scale in a context where status was allied with service to the bureaucratic state for a considerable proportion of the middle class.[148] In England, by contrast, entry into the profession was not formally regulated, nor were career itineraries clearly defined, although many women did seek training to prepare for their work. In the second half of the century, the development of schemes for training and promoting teachers favoured the emergence of a pattern of recruitment and mobility among elementary teachers which resembled the situation in France.[149] Becoming a governess or schoolmistress, however, tended to be a means to protect against downward mobility in a social context where middle-class status was often unstable, and this pattern continued even after the

[147] Comparing the proportions of schoolmistresses with professional fathers with the proportions of schoolmistresses with professional husbands reveals that a significantly larger proportion of women in the French biographical sample had professional husbands than professional fathers ($P < 0.05$, chi2 $= 5.35$, df $= 1$). Comparing the proportion of professional fathers and husbands in the *déclarations* sample points to the same conclusion. Rebecca Rogers identifies the same trend: R. Rogers, 'Professional opportunities for middle class women in Paris', in M. Hietala and L. Nilsson (eds.), *Women in towns: the social position of urban women in historical context* (Stockholm, 1999), 116–17.

[148] Garrioch, *Formation*, 244, 262–8; A. Daumard, *Les bourgeois et la bourgeoisie en France depuis 1815* (Paris, 1991), 74.

[149] Widdowson, *Going up*.

development of higher education for women. [150] Jane Austen's Colonel Campbell, whose 'income by pay and appointments was handsome', but whose 'fortune was moderate', provided his ward Jane Fairfax with an education because he hoped thereby to be 'supplying the means of a respectable subsistence hereafter'.[151] For women like the fictional Jane Fairfax, becoming a teacher was a means to maintain the social status quo, and those teachers who married were not likely to marry professional men if they did not already have professional fathers.[152]

But English schoolmistresses were much less likely to marry, or to continue teaching after marriage, than their French counterparts. Maintaining bourgeois status in England often involved a delicate balancing act between appearance and reality for impoverished professional families. The precariousness of their situation intensified the need to conform to these ideals, and since domesticity was predicated on the assumption that husbands could provide for their wives, in England there was often intense pressure for married women not to work. In these circumstances, the association between education and motherhood meant that teaching was the only acceptable occupation for middle-class women, but it was regarded as an alternative to marriage rather than a possible source of employment and social advance. Even then, as the literary and artistic energy lavished on the figure of the governess suggests, the position of the lady teacher—both a middle-class and a working woman, and a childless woman performing the function of a mother—was a focus of anxiety and tension.[153]

In France, except at moments of political upheaval, service to the state offered greater security, lessening anxieties about married women's work.[154] In fact, marriage could be an important element in the development of a schoolmistress's career, and it is significant that although forlorn schoolmistresses do appear in French fiction, there was no equivalent to the phenomenon of the English 'governess novel'. Even Mathilde Bourdon's *Souvenirs d'une institutrice* may be more indicative of the literary influence of the English phenomenon—the author specifically mentions *Jane Eyre*—than of responses to the situation of schoolmistresses in France. As the following chapter suggests, legal and economic factors reinforced the contrasts between England, where marriage often marked the end of a teacher's professional life, and France, where it might be a means to professional advance.

---

[150] Janet Howarth identifies this phenomenon in her study of early Oxbridge students; education was 'not a means of moving up in the social scale, but an insurance against downward mobility': J. Howarth, 'Public schools, safety-nets and educational ladders: the classification of girls' secondary schools, 1880–1914', *Oxford Review of Education*, 11 (1985), 67.

[151] J. Austen, *Emma* (1816; London, 1996), 137.

[152] The roughly similar proportions of professional men amongst the fathers and spouses of the schoolmistresses who married confirms that becoming a teacher was not likely to be a vector of upward social mobility in England. There was no statistically significant difference between the proportions of professional fathers and spouses of the schoolmistresses in the English sample who married ($P < 0.05$, chi2 = 2.45, df = 1).

[153] Peterson, 'Victorian governess'; Poovey, *Ideological work*, ch. 5.

[154] R. Tombs, *France 1814–1915* (London, 1996), 129.

3

The Business of School-Keeping

Schoolmistresses in England and France were thus not always 'reduced gentle-women' thrown into teaching by sudden misfortune, despite the prevalence of that stereotype. A second, frequently recurring image of the woman teacher in the nine-teenth century—more common in France than in England—was the caricature of the self-interested profiteer, and since it was assumed that women only worked outside the home through necessity, schoolmistresses were always vulnerable to the accusation that their primary aim was monetary gain. Portalis, writing in 1807, claimed that 'boarding-schools for girls are in general, nothing but profit-seeking enterprises, veritable commercial speculations'.[1] Similarly, an article in *Fraser's Magazine* in 1845 commented that 'one might be tempted to believe that the end most schoolmistresses propose to themselves in teaching is to get themselves handsome houses, furnish sumptuous drawing-rooms, keep livery servants'.[2]

The frequency with which these two stereotypes of the boarding-schoolmistress recur—the reduced gentlewoman and the self-interested profiteer—point to tensions and ambiguities surrounding the issue of women and money in nineteenth-century France and England. Such stereotypes also highlight an important aspect of the work of women teachers: the degree to which teaching was a commercial enterprise. As their contemporaries recognized, private schoolmistresses were as much entrepreneurs as teachers. Establishing and administering a boarding-school, even a small-scale enterprise started in the family home, required investment and financial planning, as well as an under-standing of market forces and commercial and legal practice.[3] Critics who claimed boarding-school proprietors were more concerned with profit than with the welfare of their pupils were expressing anxieties about women operating in a commercial sphere from which they were theoretically excluded.

The historiography of female enterprise in England has tended to suggest that the eighteenth century saw a constriction of women's business and commercial

---

[1] Jean Etienne Marie Portalis, Ministre des Cultes sous l'Empire, 'Rapport sur les associations religieuses de femmes à sa Majesté Impériale et Royale', 24 Mar. 1807, quoted in L. Grimaud, *Histoire de la liberté de l'enseignement en France* (Paris, 1944–1954), iv. 195.

[2] 'An inquiry into the state of girls' fashionable schools', *Fraser's Magazine*, 31 (1845), 703.

[3] Much of their work mirrored that of women working in more commercial sectors: S. Nenadic, 'The social shaping of business behaviour in the nineteenth century women's garment trades', *Social History*, 31 (1998), 625–45.

activity. By 1800, it has been argued, new legal practices imposing restrictions over women's control over property meant that women participated in business chiefly by providing a 'hidden investment' of labour and capital (in the form of dowries and loans).[4] Studies of the French bourgeoisie have also emphasized the part women played in business through marriage alliances and their contribution to the household economy, although research on female guild masters has demonstrated the vitality of female business in France in the eighteenth century, and Bonnie Smith has argued that it was not until the 1860s that women like the wives, mothers, and sisters of industrialists in the Nord began to draw back from direct participation in family businesses.[5]

Recently, narratives of women's withdrawal from commercial activity in the nineteenth century have been challenged. Research on the eighteenth century 'middling sort' and studies of nineteenth-century female entrepreneurs have demonstrated that women continued to be active in a wide range of commercial activities.[6] At the same time, Stena Nenadic and others have demonstrated how the preoccupation of business history with large-scale operations directs attention away from women's economic activity—usually conducted on a smaller, more informal basis—despite a growing awareness of the contribution made by small businesses to economic development.[7] Women employed various strategies to build up successful enterprises, yet because the benefits they sought were not the financial profits considered the measure of success in business, they have been overlooked. It is clear that women did continue to operate in business and commerce in the nineteenth century, despite the influence of ideas of domesticity and femininity, and despite legal changes restricting married women's control over their property. What is less clear is what impact such legal changes had on those who were economically active, and how businesswomen themselves negotiated the gap between an ideal which emphasized women's distance from the world of commerce, and the reality of their experience.

---

[4] I. Pinchbeck, *Women workers and industrial revolution* (London, 1930); A. Erickson, *Women and property in early modern England* (London, 1993); Davidoff and Hall, *Family fortunes*, ch. 6.

[5] Daumard, *Bourgeoisie*, 357–65; N. Z. Davis, 'Women in the crafts in sixteenth century Lyon', in Barbara A. Hanawalt, *Women and work in pre-industrial Europe* (Bloomington, Ind., 1986), 167–97; D. M. Hafter, 'Female masters in the ribbon-making guild of eighteenth-century Rouen', *French Historical Studies*, 20 (1997), 1–14; Smith, *Ladies*, ch. 3.

[6] M. Hunt, *The middling sort: commerce, gender and the family in England, 1680–1780* (London, 1996), ch. 5; M. Prior, 'Women and the urban economy: Oxford, 1500–1800', in M. Prior (ed.), *Women in English society, 1500–1800* (London, 1985), 93–117; P. Sharpe, 'Dealing with love: the ambiguous independence of the single woman in early modern England', *Gender and History*, 11/2 (1999), 209–32; C. Wiskin, 'Urban businesswomen in eighteenth-century England' and H. Barker and K. Harvey, 'Women Entrepreneurs and Urban Expansion: Manchester 1760–1820', in R. Sweet and P. Lane (eds.), *Women and urban life in eighteenth-century England: 'on the town'* (Aldershot, 2003), 87–110 and 111–30.

[7] Nenadic, 'Social shaping'; A. Kwolek-Folland, *Incorporating women: a history of women and business in the United States* (New York, 1998), 2–5; M. Yeager, 'Introduction', in M. Yeager (ed.), *Women in business* (Cheltenham, 1999), pp. i, ix–xciii.

Examining the business of school-keeping in England and France uncovers an important aspect of the work of nineteenth-century schoolmistresses. It helps further our understanding of the economic activity of middle-class women, and of the ways in which they negotiated the cultural ramifications of their work. Moreover, highlighting the impact of economic factors on girls' schooling can modify the traditional analysis of the development of female education. The historiography of women's education has tended to emphasize the ephemeral nature and instability of private girls' schools in the early nineteenth century, inferring poor educational standards from lack of financial security. However, as historians of family business have noted, mobility was a characteristic of small enterprise and not necessarily indicative of failure.[8] Despite the rhetorical prejudice against women's participation in commerce in the nineteenth century, schoolmistresses were clearly operating as business entrepreneurs. But the recurrence of stereotypical images of schoolmistresses in nineteenth-century art and literature shows concerns about the relationship between femininity, independence, property, and commerce crystallizing around the figure of the woman teacher: how did schoolmistresses themselves respond to the complex web of cultural norms, legal restrictions, and economic influences which shaped school-keeping as a business for women?

THE BUSINESS OF SCHOOL-KEEPING IN ENGLAND

Starting A School

In 1849, W. H. Bainbridge commented that, whereas in France one encountered women 'in almost every shop, sitting in a little counting house with pen in hand, and ledger before them, daily acting as clerks', in England, 'education is almost the only work in which [women] can engage, and that is legitimate, because it supposes her to fill a mother's place'. 'It is a proud distinction to the women of England', he continued, 'that they are fitted for home.'[9] As we have seen, this veneration of the home was a considerable influence on the development of girls' schooling in England. In a context where, as Bessie Rayner Parkes noted, 'if a lady has to work for her livelihood, it is universally considered to be a misfortune', it was essential for a middle-class schoolmistress to distance herself from the idea that teaching was a business.[10]

But English schoolmistresses were operating in a commercial sphere. Although they emphasized the domesticity of their arrangements, establishing a school

[8] S. Nenadic, 'The small family firm in Victorian Britain', in Geoffrey Jones and Mary B. Rose (eds.), *Family capitalism* (London, 1993), 91; G. Crossick and H. G. Haupt, *The petite bourgeoisie in Europe, 1780–1914* (London, 1995), 65.
[9] W. H. Bainbridge, *A lecture for the purpose of promoting the establishment of a governesses' institution in Liverpool* (London, 1849), 26–7.
[10] B. Rayner-Parkes, *Essays on women's work* (London, 1865), 74.

often consisted of more than opening up the family home. Of forty-one schoolmistresses in the biographical sample of English teachers for whom the information is available, twenty-eight (68%) either began by renting a separate property, or went on to establish an independent household after a few years of school-keeping. Eleven (27%) actually acquired the building in which their school was housed. There is little detailed information on the ways in which they went about renting and purchasing property, but these figures clearly indicate that the women who set up their own schools must have had some financial expertise and understanding of the legal mechanisms surrounding the ownership of property.

There were considerable constraints on married women's ownership of property in England: the principle of coverture meant that a wife's legal identity was subsumed within her husband's and the control of her property passed to him. As a result, she could not sue or be sued. Marriage settlements that protected women's property and limited the impact of coverture were widely used in the early modern period. However, by the end of the eighteenth century, changes in legal practice had reduced the scope for women to act as independent economic agents.[11] In addition, by the nineteenth century, borough custom—which had often made provision for women to engage in trade as separate individuals, and thus to contract independently as a *feme sole*—was only preserved in London. The records of the GBI highlight the ambiguity of the situation of married women who had business interests. In 1847, referring to the plan to let premises to a Mrs Mercatti, the Institution's accountant noted that she is 'a married woman and therefore not legally bound by any such agreement'. But he added that 'at the same time, it appears that she is a lady of respectability and property and in the habit of acting independently of her husband'.[12] His comment suggests both that people were very aware of married women's legal incapacity, and that there was a degree of flexibility in practice.

Nevertheless, the law was making it increasingly difficult for married women to operate as independent entrepreneurs, and this, coupled with the dominant cultural assumption that marriage was a profession in itself, may help to explain the small number of married schoolmistresses in England. The case of Mrs de Wahl, a schoolmistress from St John's Wood, who had sold her establishment to the Reverend and Mrs Braune in the 1860s, highlights the vulnerability of married schoolmistresses before the law. When Reverend Braune failed to fulfil his agreement, Mrs de Wahl challenged him in court. She was defeated on the grounds that since her husband (from whom she was separated) was still living, the action should have been brought in his name.[13] Given the odds stacked against

[11] Erickson, *Women.*
[12] Paley Chapple to Revd James Laing, 26 Nov. 1847, London Metropolitan Archives, GBI, Governess Papers, I, 559.
[13] R. Mair, *The educator's guide for teachers, parents and guardians* (London, 1866), 40.

married women, it is not surprising that it was customary for schoolmistresses working with their siblings to give up their involvement in the family school if they married. Four of the six Byerley sisters who ran a successful school in Warwick from 1810 to 1841 ultimately withdrew from the school, and when Frances Byerley received a proposal of marriage shortly after the school first opened, 'fearful it might be a disadvantage to her sisters in the school line, [she] I believe, refused'.[14] Fanny may have been concerned that her withdrawal would create more work—however, she would also have feared that the school might suffer financially if her husband chose to withdraw her share of the investment in it.

Even unmarried women, formally free from the legal restrictions on ownership of property, were considered credit risks. Bessie Parkes was to remark that it was not surprising that women rarely established their own businesses because 'girls never have any capital, they hardly know what it means', and as a result, 'it is equally impossible to borrow, as they can give no security'.[15] Clearly, prejudice against women in business could have a real influence over their ability to raise loans.

In the early nineteenth century, however, formal credit agreements did not play a significant part in the establishment of small enterprises. Limited capital was required to establish oneself as a small-scale entrepreneur, and even those with larger ambitions relied on personal savings, family loans, marriage dowries, and wholesaler credit.[16] Thirteen of the twenty-one women in the biographical sample for whom the information is available had made use of some form of family fund or inheritance and thirteen had benefited from a loan from a friend or family member. The career of Sarah Bache gives an insight into the way that savings, legacies, and family loans could be combined with the profits of school-keeping to fund the establishment and expansion of a successful school.

In 1801 Sarah moved with her sister Susan to a large house in Great Charles Street, Birmingham, where they opened a school. They had both spent fifteen years as mantua-makers and their mother and one married sister had recently died. It seems likely that it was by combining what they had saved with small amounts inherited that they were able to take this step. The school initially charged 12s. 6d. a quarter, and was highly successful. When Susan married in 1805 she was replaced as Sarah's partner by another sister, Phoebe. By 1809 they were making 300 guineas a year, and in 1816, the school moved to new premises in Islington House, Edgbaston, where there was room for boarders who were charged £26 p.a.[17]

In about 1822 the sisters decided to buy Islington House, an indication of their continued success. To do so, they borrowed money from their brother-in-law

---

[14] Frances Byerley (snr.) to Josiah Wedgwood II, 21 Mar. 1810, Keele University Library (hereafter KUL), Wedgwood papers, 12395–13.

[15] Parkes, *Essays*, 143.

[16] Nenadic, 'Small family', 86–114; J. Benson, *The penny capitalists* (Dublin, 1983), 73; Crossick and Haupt, *Petite bourgeoisie*, 69.

[17] Phoebe Penn to Anna Carpenter, Dec. 1809, Matthews, *Sarah Bache*, 57.

Lant Carpenter. By November 1833, Sarah was writing to complete her repayments and thanking him for 'the kind manner in which you supplied our wants . . . and also for the convenient opportunity you have afforded me in reducing our interest and so lessening our expenditure'. Obtaining a loan from a family member, as Sarah realized, could mean credit on favourable terms. They had borrowed £300 and £350 respectively from Carpenter and by 1825 negotiations for the house were proceeding slowly.[18] 'Our landlord has at last consented to our offer,' Sarah told her sister, 'but drew up an agreement in such a manner we could not with safety sign, without further information, so it is not signed yet, and is in our attorney's hands; but I suppose it will be settled in about a week. It has been a troublesome business and made me many ugly walks to town.'[19] It would seem that Sarah Bache was herself undertaking the negotiations for sale, although she turned to a lawyer for expert advice. Her tone implies that there was nothing extraordinary in these proceedings. She was active in the management of her own affairs and dealt with lawyers and contracts with few feminine qualms as to the propriety of stepping outside the domestic sphere.

Other schoolmistresses showed equal awareness of financial mechanisms. Rachel Martineau, who opened her school in Liverpool in about 1838, was able to draw on the £35 she had put in a savings bank to accumulate interest in 1830. Having obtained excellent terms on her first appointment as a governess in 1829 (100 guineas p.a., when in 1866 Robert Mair estimated that the best governess would be paid £100 p.a.), she was clearly, as her sister recognized, 'made for power, prosperity and responsibility'.[20] By 1859, having enjoyed wide renown and success for her Liverpool establishment, she had retired to Weybridge and lived independently. When Elizabeth and Ellen Sewell established their school on the Isle of Wight in 1852, they purchased the leasehold of a house called Ashcliff by taking out an insurance on Elizabeth's life worth £1,200.[21] As these examples demonstrate, opening a school was not always simply a matter of opening up the family home to pupils. Though some schoolmistresses did begin in this way, many undertook more ambitious schemes, revealing themselves fully capable of operating within the world of business as they negotiated loans and contracted leases.

Family Strategies

In establishing their school at Gateacre near Liverpool in 1807, the Lawrence sisters were fulfilling 'mother's favourite plan'. She had hoped that 'after residence in different families should have given to each of us a due share of experience,

---

[18] It is not clear why the loans were made separately, rather than as a lump sum to one sister.

[19] Sarah Bache to Anna Carpenter, n.d., Matthews, *Sarah Bache*, 78.

[20] Harriet Martineau to James Martineau, 18 Aug. 1829 and Harriet Martineau to James Martineau, 28 Dec. 1830, HMCO, MS J. Martineau 1; Harriet Martineau to Fanny Wedgwood, Mar. 1844, in *Harriet Martineau's letters to Fanny Wedgwood*, ed. E. Arbuckle (Stanford, 1983) 75.

[21] Sewell, *Autobiography*, 141.

we should all unite together for the purpose of conducting the education of young people on a more extensive scale'.[22] On her marriage to Robert Holmes in 1810, Eliza Lawrence left the school to her sisters' care. The four remaining sisters lived from its proceeds until, in 1839, the school was transferred to the Miss Hollands and the sisters moved to Leamington Spa. The school's longevity is a mark of its success, but it was also successful in terms of family strategy. As the description of 'mother's favourite plan' implies, school-keeping avoided family break-up.

In 1841 Charlotte, Emily, and Anne Brontë were considering opening their own school as an alternative to governessing in others' schools and private homes. Charlotte wrote to her friend Ellen Nussey that 'I have often, you know, said how much I wished such a thing; but I never could conceive where the capital was to come from for meeting such a speculation'.[23] Now it appeared that the project would be realized as Aunt Branwell could loan them £100. Charlotte wondered whether it would be possible to open a respectable school, 'not by any means showy', with that amount and, with the need to avoid competition with similar establishments in mind, weighed up the merits of various locations. She had already witnessed the 'consumptive state of health' of Miss Wooler's school after a rival institution was opened in Bradford.[24] Emily was hopeful that the sisters should be able to earn their livings together. 'This day in four years', an autobiographical fragment begins, 'I wonder whether we shall [be] . . . established to our heart's content . . . in our own sitting-room in some pleasant and flourishing seminary.'[25] In the event, the Brontës decided that it would be more profitable in the long term to spend £50 of their aunt's money on going to Brussels to learn French, but their letters reveal the ways in which a school might be started, both to make the most of limited family resources and to provide collective emotional security.

The letters exchanged between the Byerley sisters and their third cousin Josiah Wedgwood reveal how important kinship relationships could be in ensuring the success or failure of an establishment. The Byerleys had drawn on money left to them by their great-uncle to open their Warwick school in 1810. However, rather than drawing it all at once, they had entrusted the legacies to Josiah Wedgwood's care. He sent money as they needed it and kept a close eye on their business. In 1814, he loaned them £230, because at the end of the year Anne Byerley had found that the combined expenses of furnishing new premises and their mother's medical bills exceeded the sisters' income, despite an increase in the number of pupils.[26] Like Lant Carpenter's arrangement with Sarah Bache, it

    [22] Sarah Lawrence, de Zouche, *Roedean*, 14.
    [23] Charlotte Brontë to Ellen Nussey, 19 July 1841, quoted in C. Shorter (ed.), *The Brontës: life and letters* (New York, 1969) i. 213.
    [24] Charlotte Brontë to Ellen Nussey, 12 Nov. 1840, ibid. 194.
    [25] Autobiographical fragments, ibid. 216.
    [26] Anne Byerley to Josiah Wedgwood II, 12 Feb. 1814, KUL, Wedgwood papers, 12326–13.

was not an interest-free loan, and the correspondence clearly indicates that the sisters were expected to make regular interest payments until they could pay back the sum borrowed.

The Byerleys also looked to Josiah and to other relatives for advice. In 1810, he contributed to the debate as to whether they should buy or rent a house.[27] Frances Byerley answered, saying that 'Mr Parkes [her future father-in-law], with the rest of our friends here, is of the opinion that it will be much more to our advantage to rent a house'.[28] The sisters could rely on the support and experience of a network of friends and relations in financial decision-making. Fanny's response suggests that all advice was carefully evaluated. It was not simply a question of doing as their wealthy uncle suggested.

Family, however, could also be a considerable drain on resources, and the finances of the Byerleys' school improved and declined with the health of family members, including not only that of the sisters themselves, but that of their mother and brothers.[29] The Byerley sons were a particular burden. In 1815 the sisters discovered that their brother Frank had abandoned his medical studies in troubling circumstances, and were keen to find him a new situation 'in which he can begin to regain his character'.[30] The response from Josiah Wedgwood is revealing. He urges them to encourage Frank to emigrate and advises them not to lend their elder brother Josiah more money.[31] Far from being dependent, the Byerleys were providing for the men of the family.

Feminine Enterprise

As the Byerleys' situation indicates, the financial independence of schoolmistresses undermined conventional notions of femininity. Maria soon became confident of her ability to manage money and to stand her ground. When Josiah Wedgwood wrote to request the interest on his loan, she replied that 'I have stated exactly what we owe you, and all the other sums that are set down in your paper, we know nothing about'.[32] Later that year, Josiah asked the sisters to sign an account stating that they had a standing debt with him of £284 9s. 6d. Maria's reply is illuminating. 'We must request you to excuse us from signing the note which you have sent" she writes, 'it may be ignorance on our part but we cannot promise to pay on demand what would entirely ruin us if the demand were made.'[33] By 1823 the debt was repaid and Maria wrote jubilantly that 'it gives us satisfaction to

[27] Draft letter from Josiah Wedgwood II to Frances Byerley, 27 Nov. 1810, KUL, Wedgwood papers, 12238–13.

[28] Frances Byerley to Josiah Wedgwood II, 1 Dec. 1810, KUL, Wedgwood papers, 12340–13.

[29] Frances Byerley to Josiah Wedgwood II, 4 May 1811, KUL, Wedgwood papers, 12347–13.

[30] Maria Byerley to Josiah Wedgwood II, 6 Nov. 1815, KUL, Wedgwood papers, 12240–13.

[31] Josiah Wedgwood II to Maria Byerley, Jan. 1816, KUL, Wedgwood papers, 12240a–13.

[32] Maria Byerley to Josiah Wedgwood II, 18 Jan. 1817, KUL, Wedgwood papers, 12242–13.

[33] Maria Byerley to Josiah Wedgwood II, 28 Oct. 1817, KUL, Wedgwood papers, 12247–13.

find ourselves now quite clear, and with a tolerable school to go on with'.[34] The confidence and authority of Maria's letters belies her protestation of ignorance. Similarly, Fanny's claim that her sisters had a 'dread of involving themselves with pecuniary matters' is surprising, given their successful management of the schools' finances.[35] Perhaps Maria and Fanny were being disingenuous and seeking to appeal to Josiah Wedgwood's sympathy by portraying themselves as women who knew nothing of money. Or perhaps emphasizing their financial inexperience was a way of reconciling their work with conventional notions of femininity. Either way, their letters are evidence of the degree to which the relationship between schoolmistresses and business was complex and ambiguous.

Sarah Bache's correspondence gives a further insight into the tensions that could arise from a middle-class woman's involvement in business. In 1805, she wrote to her sister Anna, then also engaged in running a school, that Phoebe had recently become governess to a family who had had five different teachers in two years. She did not expect her to stay more than a half-year, 'as I believe they rather choose to take new ones upon trial, and then pay them no wages—that's management Anna—we must learn how the world manages these affairs, if we are to be rich; but if that be not our object, we may go on in the old-fashioned way'.[36] Initially almost admiring of this unscrupulousness, she then appears to renounce it in favour of the 'old-fashioned way'. The cultural prejudice against women's engagement in commercial activity meant that those who were successful could not be seen to be so; it meant that schoolmistresses like Sarah Bache found it hard to reconcile a sense of achievement on realizing profits with a notion of femininity emphasizing dependence and renunciation. A second incident provides further illustration. In 1809, and again in 1810, the sisters raised the fees for their school. On both occasions, Phoebe wrote to inform her sister, explaining that they felt forced to do so to reduce the number of applicants to the school. Accepting as many pupils as applied would endanger their health. An announcement in *Avis's Birmingham Gazette* underlined the point and added that 'they hope to be exonerated from the charge of caprice or ingratitude.'[37] Although the sisters may have used their fragile physical health to conceal a healthy concern for profit, their evident unease at being associated with financial self-interest testifies to the influence of conservative notions of femininity.

Transitions

In her history of Manchester High School for girls, which was established in 1873, Sara Burstall noted that 'to mark the character of the school as a public institution not conducted for private profit', fees were paid on a fixed termly basis, and not

---

[34] Maria Byerley to Josiah Wedgwood II, 12 Feb. 1823, KUL, Wedgwood papers, 12263–13.
[35] Frances Parkes to Josiah Wedgwood II, 27 June 1812, KUL, Wedgwood papers, 14086–15.
[36] Matthews, *Sarah Bache*, 46.   [37] Ibid. 59.

divided into interminable extras as they had been in the girls' boarding-schools of the first part of the nineteenth century.[38] The middle years of the century had seen a movement from small privately owned institutions to larger establishments, public in character. As Sara Burstall's comment shows, this change was a self-conscious one. Influential schoolmistresses like Frances Buss and Dorothea Beale hoped to make a useful education available to all middle-class girls. However, they recognized that this could not be achieved without funding which drew on more than fees. The move would also benefit women teachers. The position of teachers in private day-schools, Anne Clough noted, was 'often very painful. They are poor themselves, struggling for subsistence; the parents are economical, if not poor, and there is a constant haggling between the two.'[39] Rather than struggling to make ends meet, schoolmistresses in the system of 'Victoria schools' that she envisaged would have access to external funds. The network of schools established by Maria Grey and Emily Shirreff offered women teachers similar protection from miserly parents and a guaranteed income. They established the Girls' Public Day School Company (GPDSC), selling shares to prospective parents and supporters at a cost of £5 each. As Emily Shirreff emphasized, this was raising funds 'by the ordinary commercial means, as in the case of any other scheme of recognized public utility'.[40] Manchester High School was established following a similar plan. Frances Buss adopted a different strategy, transferring the North London Collegiate School to the control of a charitable trust.[41]

Although Anne Clough and others emphasized the benefits of the new arrangements, the transition from private ownership might involve sacrifices for schoolmistresses who had built up successful private schools on their own terms. Frances Buss was significantly reducing her personal income and financial autonomy. Her somewhat hagiographic biography emphasizes the selflessness of this measure but letters reveal that at the time she experienced a sharp sense of loss.[42] Emily Davies understood: 'to a person of your eager and ambitious temperament to be under a slow, bothering board must be particularly trying'.[43] Other schoolmistresses experienced similar frustrations and new challenges when dealing with occasionally obstructive trustees or shareholders. Dorinda Neligan, headmistress of the GPDSC school in Croydon in 1874, was even charged with untruthfulness by the local committee of shareholders.[44] Schoolmistresses in the first part of the century had operated with confidence in the world of

---

[38] Burstall, *Manchester*, 41.

[39] A. J. Clough, 'Hints on the organization of girls' schools', *Macmillan's Magazine*, 14 (Oct. 1866), 434.

[40] E. Shirreff, *The work of the National Union* (London, 1873), 13.

[41] A. Ridley, *Frances Mary Buss and her work for education* (London, 1895), 93; K. Anderson, 'Frances Mary Buss, the founder as headmistress, 1850–1894', in *The North London Collegiate School, 1850–1950* (Oxford, 1950), 37–9.

[42] Ridley, *Frances Buss*, 93.

[43] Emily Davies to Frances Buss, ?1873, NLC, Frances Mary Buss and family, B1.

[44] L. Magnus, *The jubilee book of the Girls' Public Day School Trust* (Cambridge, 1923), 61.

business, despite legal limitations and cultural obstacles. Though they might seek to play down the relationship between school-keeping and commerce in public, some clearly enjoyed the degree of financial autonomy and independence that it could confer. In the second half of the nineteenth century, the new endowed schools and those established by the GPDSC offered greater financial security to schoolmistresses and provided the conditions necessary for girls' schools to become enduring institutions. But the move away from teaching as a commercial enterprise may have limited teachers' autonomy and the opportunities for entrepreneurship enjoyed by schoolmistresses in the first part of the century.

THE BUSINESS OF SCHOOL-KEEPING IN FRANCE

Starting A School

According to Octave Gréard, in the first part of the nineteenth century in France, 'teaching was chosen as an easy option . . . many women had moved without difficulty from the shop to the school'.[45] Gréard was right in some respects—a high proportion of French schoolmistresses were recruited from the ranks of the commercial and shop-keeping middle class and some moved directly from shop- to school-keeping. His claim that this was an 'easy option', however, underestimates the degree to which establishing a school involved complicated legal and financial transactions and often a substantial initial investment.

This complexity is clear from the declarations of bankruptcy registered by schoolmistresses. In assessing the case of Mlle Delagrange, in February 1814, the *Tribunal de Commerce* argued that there were grounds for leniency, given that her debts 'were largely the result of the enormous sums that the Demoiselle Delagrange had spent for the foundation of her establishment'. She could not be blamed for the fact that many of her pupils were withdrawn because of the war. Mlle Delagrange's case provides detailed information about the cost of establishing a school. It reveals that she owed a total of 38,014F to her creditors, of which 12,500F was rent due to the owners of the house her school occupied. The sum included 4,104F owed to a builder who had made the alterations required to convert the house to a school, 300F owed to an upholsterer, and large amounts due for textiles, china, and the hire of musical instruments. There were also significant sums owed to the twenty-five teachers and domestic servants she had employed.[46] In 1817, the highest rents in Paris ranged between 2,500F and 22,600F, and of the wills registered in 1820, only those leaving more than

---

[45] 'un métier facile à exercer.' Gréard, *L'enseignement*, 15.
[46] Bilan des affaires de Antoinette Charlotte Boule Dauphin Delagrange, tenant pension de demoiselles, 106 rue de Sèvres, 3 Feb. 1814, AD Seine, D11 U³ 48/1049.

500,000F included furnishings worth more than 15,000F.[47] Mlle Delagrange was aiming high.

Opening a school, even on a less ambitious footing, required capital and a degree of financial acumen. Jeanne Campan's correspondence shows the calculations involved. Having lost her fortune during the Revolution, and with a sick husband and son to support, she wrote, 'I knew that I must go on... I decided that I could establish a boarding-school for girls.' On one level, her story conforms to the stereotype of the reduced gentlewoman. But she then adds that in order to cover her costs she would need 100 pupils, each paying 1,200F p.a. Mme Campan claimed she was making 20,000F a year by 1804, but by 1807 she had 30,000F worth of debts and saw being appointed head of the *Légion d'Honneur* school as the only means to extricate herself.[48] There is little evidence as to what went wrong; nevertheless, it is clear that both she and Mlle Delagrange were making complicated financial calculations in establishing their schools, however unsuccessful they ultimately were.

The sources give no indication of how Mlle Delagrange or Mme Campan obtained the initial capital required to set up their establishments, but opening an establishment was likely to involve some kind of credit arrangement. Given the size and number of her debts, perhaps Mlle Delagrange relied on the credit accorded to her by different tradesmen, banking on the fact that her school would soon be successful enough to allow her to repay the sums owed. Studies of small-scale enterprise suggest reliance on wholesaler credit when starting up was common practice amongst small-scale entrepreneurs.[49]

It was difficult for women to obtain funding in more formal ways. Between 1690 and 1840 women made up only 3% of all borrowers in Paris using a notary to arrange a loan.[50] This may reflect women's lesser involvement in economic activity, but also the impact of legal constraints on both married and single women. From 1804, the *Code Civil* specified that a woman could not contract any engagement without the written consent of her husband. Unmarried women were not deemed accountable and could not sign credit notes or witness civil acts.[51] The evidence suggests that many schoolmistresses relied on family loans to obtain the capital needed for establishing a school, and restrictions on women's legal capacities may have meant that women had to rely more heavily than men on familial support and informal personal agreements. Mme Vigogne, another Parisian schoolmistress forced to close her school in 1814, had managed to raise

[47] Daumard, *Bourgeoisie*, 22–3, 128.
[48] Campan, *De l'éducation*, ii. 15; Rogers, *Demoiselles*, 28.
[49] Crossick and Haupt, *Petite bourgeoisie*, 69.
[50] T. Hoffman, G. Postel-Vinay, and J.-L. Rosenthal, 'Private credit markets in Paris, 1690–1840', *Journal of Economic History*, 52 (1992), 299.
[51] *Les Huits Codes* (Paris, 1830), Code Civil, Art. 217; M. Bordeaux, 'Droits et femmes seules: les pièges de la discrimination', in C. Klapisch and A. Farge (eds.), *Madame ou Mademoiselle: itinéraires de la solitude féminine* (Paris, 1984), 19–58.

35,780F through personal loans. In 1838 Mlle Bodart, who wanted to ensure that she had enough to 'buy a day school with a good reputation, obtained 10,000F from M. Quarre, given to her as payment of the sum he owed to Mlle Bodart's stepfather, a liqueur-seller.[52]

Most often, women teachers drew on funds from within their family. In some cases, it was more a family investment than a loan. When, in 1811, M. Sauvan, who had lost his fortune during the Revolution, spent the remaining 40,000F on buying a school for his daughter in the fashionable Parisian district of Chaillot, Jeanne was expected to provide for the whole family, not to repay the sum.[53] When Eugénie, Augustine, and Aurélie Dubois opened their *pension* in Normandy in 1847, their father lent them money. It was not enough for them even to cover their costs in the first year the school was open, so Augustine sought work as a seamstress to make ends meet. However, in 1853, Eugénie refused her brother-in-law's offer of assistance, saying, as he reported, that 'she had had a very good year' and that 'her affairs were already in good order'. By 1855, the sisters were contemplating buying a house.[54] Personal loans and agreements between family members, like that between the Dubois sisters and their father, would not necessarily appear in notarial or banking records. Nonetheless, they were often binding contracts requiring some understanding of the 'masculine' subject of interest rates and credit mechanisms.

Schools on The Market

The clearest indication that school-keeping was a business in nineteenth-century France is that schools were commonly bought and sold. The Paris ruling of 1810 required schoolmistresses conceding their establishments to a new proprietor to obtain the authorization of the prefect.[55] It was the goodwill of the school, not the school buildings, that was sold on in this way, as is clear from an 1845 advertisement announcing the sale of a boarding-school; it specifies that 'the establishment is prosperous, contains 80 pupils, of which 55 are boarders'.[56] Such sales indicate that, although schoolmistresses might come and go, schools might endure for several decades. The establishment taken over in about 1847 by Mme Dantier had been in existence since 1817, though it had been bought and sold several times.[57]

---

[52] Créances de Mme Vigogne, 16 Feb. 1814, AD Seine, D11 U^3 49/1073; Dossier Bodart, 1838–9, AD Seine, VD^6 142–2.

[53] Gossot, *Sauvan*, 45.

[54] Isambert-Jamati, *Solidarité*, 118, 128.

[55] Règlement pour les écoles de filles, 20 Aug. 1810, AD Seine, VD^4 21–5496.

[56] *REF*, 4 (Apr. 1845), 72.

[57] Rapport d'inspection des Dames Inspectrices du 1er arrdt., 1817; Préfet de la Seine au Maire du 1er arrdt., 12 June 1823, AD Seine, VD^6 158–3; Inspections pension Auger, 1838–1841, AD Seine, VD^6 158–3.

The reputation of an establishment and its schoolmistress had a definite monetary value. In 1865, Mlle Bronville, who had had to transfer her school to a new *quartier* because of Paris's programme of Hausmannization, claimed compensation, calculating precisely what the loss of reputation and clientele would cost her. Mlle Bronville argued that since a schoolmistress's success was dependent on the esteem of the neighbourhood, the move would be costly. She estimated that it would take her four years to 'win the confidence of parents'. On the basis of three and a half years' worth of net profits (which she estimated at 18,366F p.a.) she claimed compensation of 42,000F, a sum roughly equivalent to the assets of middle-range Parisian businessmen in 1847.[58]

Like Mlle Bronville, other teachers looked on schools as financial institutions with a measurable market value. In about 1845, the school *inspectrice* noted that a Mlle Keraval had 'brought pupils from Mme Guillois' establishment, of which she had purchased the goodwill,' to the former Mlle de Rosace's school in the first *arrondissement*.[59] Mlle Keraval was operating as an entrepreneur, buying up two schools and combining them for maximum profits. In 1842 the prefect of the Seine was obliged to publish a special ruling, reiterating the regulations concerning the buying and selling of girls' schools, originally set down in 1810.[60] This not only suggests that some schoolmistresses were ignoring those regulations—plainly having a good reputation in the eyes of parents was not always synonymous with fulfilment of the administrative authority's requirements—but also points to increasing anxiety about the idea of education as a commercial enterprise, an anxiety perhaps exacerbated by the fact that it was women who were engaging in this kind of speculation.

Ironically, the administrative regulations applying in Paris unintentionally encouraged the commercialization of school-keeping. From 1810, prefectoral rulings stipulated that no woman under the age of 21 (raised to 25 in 1821) could run a boarding-school, or could do so without obtaining a diploma and authorization. Some schoolmistresses simply ignored this regulation and established schools without official authorization. Others formed partnerships. In 1877 'Mme Couturier who does not have the teaching diploma', 'contracted a new engagement with Mlle Allainmat, who will continue to manage Mme Couturier's institution in her name, and will receive, as previously, a monthly salary for doing so'.[61] If they drew up a formal contract, it has not survived, but the form their partnership took was that of the *commandité simple*, the most common form of business association at the time.[62] This kind of arrangement was not limited

[58] L. Bronville, *Mémoire en défense et expertise pour Mlle Laure Bronville (Pensionnat, demi-pension et externat de demoiselles) contre la ville de Paris* (Paris, 1865), 3–8 ; Daumard, *Bourgeoisie*, 77.

[59] 'Maisons visitées par Mlle Hubert', n.d. ?1845, AD Seine, VD[6] 158–3.

[60] Règlement pour les écoles de filles, 20 Aug. 1810.

[61] Préfet de Police au Procureur du Roi, 12 Dec. 1877, AD Seine, DT Supplément/3.

[62] J.-L. Dansette, *Histoire de l'entreprise et des chefs d'entreprise en France, 1780–1880: genèse du patronat* (Paris, 1991) 241.

to Paris; in 1867 a Mlle Bonvoisin, acting as the figurehead for Mrs Baron, an Englishwoman who did not have the necessary diploma, declared her intention to open a school at Bourbourg, in the Nord.[63] The regulations concerning boarding-schools for girls, which in one sense contributed to the professionalization of teaching by requiring schoolmistresses to undergo some form of certification, also promoted a more businesslike approach to schoolmistressing. Women might regard their schools not only as educational institutions, but also as investments.

Family Strategies

The career of Eléonore Ploux, née Chapuis, who bought the Bordeaux school of a Mme Berdalle in 1824, offers an example of this double vision of the school. The school regulations she drew up in 1840 reveal the seriousness of her educational purpose.[64] Mme Ploux was lauded by her successors as one of the foremost schoolmistresses of Bordeaux and was highly recommended as an educator by the departmental school inspector.[65] But she was also a businesswoman and her school was a commercial enterprise. The daughter of a commercial clerk, she had been teaching at the school of Mme Berdalle de Lapommeray before her marriage in January 1824 to François Ploux, a professor of commerce, who probably also taught in Mme Berdalle's school. The Chapuis family were not wealthy—she was given no dowry—however, because of her teaching work she was not completely penniless, bringing 700F to the marriage. Despite the small sums involved, the couple drew up a marriage contract, establishing a *société aux acquets*, meaning that any subsequent earnings would be shared between them.[66] The importance of this is clear because two months after their marriage the Ploux couple bought out Mme Berdalle and took over her school.[67]

Under Mme Ploux, the school quickly became successful and began to expand, taking over a whole house in the rue Arnaud Miqueu. Mme Ploux shared the teaching with one assistant and her husband. Three children born between 1826 and 1828 were in all probability sent out to nurse, thus permitting Mme Ploux to continue teaching; the household also included François Ploux's mother, aunt, and sister.[68] In 1834 François Ploux died, leaving his wife and children about

[63] Inspecteur primaire à M. Jarry, Inspecteur d'Académie, 21 Oct. 1867, AD Nord, 1 T 124/3.

[64] Règlement, 1840–1850, AM Bordeaux, Fonds Ploux/8.

[65] M. Benoit, Inspecteur Primaire, État de situation des écoles de filles dans l'Académie de la Gironde, 1851–2, AD Gironde, 6 T 12.

[66] Contrat de mariage: François Ploux et Eléonore Chapuis, Maître Rauzan, 29 Jan. 1824, AD Gironde, 3^E 41400.

[67] The school was valued at 2,000F, but instead of buying it outright, the Ploux simply agree to take over the debts Mme Berdalle had accrued in establishing it. Contrat de cession: pension de Mme Berdalle de Lapommeray à M. François Ploux et Eléonore Chapuis, son épouse, 23 Mar. 1824, AM Bordeaux, Fonds Ploux/8.

[68] État Civil, and Recensement 1831, 21 rue Arnaud Miqueu, AM Bordeaux, 1 F 17. On the use of wet-nurses in France, see E. Shorter, *The making of the modern family* (New York, 1975) 189.

7,000F.[69] Three years later, she presumably drew on this inheritance because she bought the house on the rue Arnaud Miqueu.[70] In 1855 she negotiated an association with a M. Bonnet, acting in the name of his 18-year-old daughter, Thérésia. By this agreement, Mme Ploux sold the goodwill of her school, and its furniture, for 8,500F. She would receive 400F a year to act as 'first associate' in the eyes of the administrative authorities (thus concealing the fact that Theresia did not have the teaching certificate) and agreed to let the schoolhouse at 9,000F p.a. She would continue to live in the upper apartment above the school.[71] A similar agreement was negotiated with Mme Mirande in 1866.[72] When Eléonore Ploux died in 1876, she still owned the former school building. Having bought the school for 2,000F in 1824, Mme Ploux had been able substantially to increase the value of her investment, becoming a property-owner whilst supporting her children and providing for her old age. School-keeping, for her, was as much about business as about education. In terms of the traditional evaluation of business success, focusing on profits and expansion, her achievement would not be valued highly. But Mme Ploux was highly successful in terms of family-income strategy, as well as being a successful and respected educationist.

Marriage had marked the beginning of a new stage in Eléonore Ploux's career as a schoolmistress, and, as suggested in Chapter 2, marriage seems frequently to have coincided with the moment of transition from being a *sous-maîtresse* to opening an establishment. There is no direct evidence to confirm that the husbands of other schoolmistresses contributed financially to the establishment of their wives' schools. However, working partnerships between schoolmistresses and their husbands were common. The Ploux establishment was a joint enterprise: the contract between the couple and Mme Berdalle, and subsequent leases for the house on rue Arnaud Miqueu, involve both Eléonore and her husband in all engagements. Other teaching couples worked in tandem, rather than in the same institution. When Emma Willard visited Paris in 1830–1, she was taken to the school of Mme Morin, whose husband owned a well-known institution at Fontenay-aux-Roses.[73] That a foreign visitor should be taken to Mme Morin's establishment suggests that the couple's arrangement was not considered unusual. Similarly, in the 1860s and 1870s, Claude Despernex and his wife Marie Clarisse Bayrel each headed their own establishments in the first *arrondissement*, a fact noted entirely without comment by the school inspector.[74] If the financial contribution of husbands to their wives' schools is obscure, it is clear that marriage to a professor could be the foundation of a fruitful partnership.

[69] Inventaire après déces: François Ploux, 29 Apr. 1834, AD Gironde, 3[E] 41412.

[70] Note de ?Ernest Ploux, 17 Dec. 1884, AM Bordeaux, Fonds Ploux/5.

[71] Contrat certifié: Mmes Ploux and Quere, et M. Bonnet de Larbogne, 28 July 1855, AM Bordeaux, Fonds Ploux/8.

[72] Bail de la maison au 21 rue Arnaud Miqueu, 15 Feb. 1866: AM Bordeaux, Fonds Ploux/8.

[73] E. Willard, *Journal and letters from France and Great Britain* (New York, 1833), 142.

[74] Dossier Fischer, 1881, AD Seine, DT Supplément/89.

As mentioned above, some schoolmistresses were expected to support their families, but such arrangements were often reciprocal and frequently a teacher's husband, her siblings, parents, and children participated in the establishment and management of the *pension*. Daughters frequently worked as assistants until they married or took over the school themselves. Mme d'Astuq-Bruley, who had a school in the first *arrondissement* of Paris from 1812 to 1815, was helped by her daughter.[75] Propriety meant that the male professors employed in girls' schools were for the most part aged over 35 and married, so that sons and brothers were rarely directly involved with instruction or the daily running of girls' schools. They might, however, intervene at moments of crisis or advise over difficult decisions. When Parisian schoolmistresses Mmes Collard and Lemaître were censured by the prefect in 1819, it was their brother, a notary, who took the first step of writing to the mayor to defend them.[76] The Dubois sisters in Normandy worked together, but also turned to their brother-in-law, a salesman of broad acquaintance, when they needed a new assistant and asked an architect nephew for advice on converting the house they bought in 1872.[77] The school could be a family enterprise in more than one sense. First, it could be part of a strategy intended to provide for the various members of a nuclear family at different stages in life (as in the case of Mme Ploux's establishment). Second, it might be a family business inasmuch as the schoolmistress would draw on the labour and expertise of her family to ensure the prosperity of her school, and families would collaborate in order to provide for female members. Third, the school could become an element of family patrimony, transferred from generation to generation.

Feminine Enterprise

Keeping a girls' school nevertheless remained a distinctively feminine business. Many schools were expected to provide for younger generations of women in the family, and numerous institutions were transmitted from mother to daughter, or aunt to niece. On Marie Litais' death in 1808, the school she had founded in Paris in 1796 was taken over by her widowed sister, Veuve Lelarge, who also took charge of her five children. In 1830 two daughters of the family wrote to the mayor of the first *arrondissement*, asking permission to present themselves as candidates for the *diplôme de maîtresse de pension*, so that they could assume the running of the school.[78] Although she was married to a lawyer, Marie Litais needed to supplement his income and to provide for daughters who, if they did not marry, would be reliant on their own resources.

[75] Rapports des Dames Inspectrices sur les pensions du 1er arrdt., 1812, 1813, 1814, 1815, AD Seine, VD[6] 158–3.

[76] Mlle Collard et Veuve Lemaitre au Maire du 1er arrdt., 12 June 1819, AD Seine, VD[6] 158–3.

[77] Isambert-Jamati, *Solidarité*, 118, 128, 145.

[78] Marie Madeleine et Luce Zémélina Litais au Maire du 1er arrdt., 26 Nov. 1830, VD[6] 158–3.

Other schoolmistresses reserved their profits for the use of daughters and female relatives. Eléonore Ploux used the yield from her school to allocate 15,000F to her daughter when she married in 1845. The marriage contract specified that in the event of a separation, the groom's father's estate would be collateral against repayment in full of this sum.[79] Mme Ploux's business acumen extended beyond the school and the contract demonstrates a sense of the odds stacked against women. Eugénie Dubois shared this awareness. She had groomed her nieces as potential successors, and when they decided not to take on the school she wrote: 'My intention is to leave to my nieces the savings we have acquired . . . May my nephews forgive me, but young men always manage, it is young women who need support.'[80]

That women like Eugénie Dubois were so aware of the financial difficulties that women might face demonstrates the distance between an ideal of domesticity and actual circumstances. This is further illustrated by the Reclus family. Zéline Reclus ran a school for Protestant girls in Orthez from 1831 to 1882. Her daughter Noémi knew that it was Zéline's work which fed the family of six daughters and four sons: 'it's on her that everything depends . . . father's work, which he exhausts himself doing, is purely done out of devotion, of sublime devotion, but devotion does not feed a family'.[81] Reversing the conventional gender order, it was the wife who provided for the family's needs and the husband who lacked commercial sense. Even when a schoolmistress was married to a professor, the *maîtresse* was usually the figure of authority. In 1845, when Mme Bachellery was being pursued by the prefectoral authorities for infringing their ruling, at no point did her husband—also a schoolmaster—intervene. The letter she wrote to justify her conduct makes it clear that the engagements she had entered into were in her own name.[82]

In contemporary satires, the henpecked husband of the *maîtresse de pension* often featured alongside the profit-seeking schoolmistress. Henri Léon caricatured the man who, 'entering the household, must shed a large portion of his manly character, in order to conform to the requirements of his condition . . . he is generally referred to as Mme's husband'.[83] Such images paralleled Daumier's caricatures of husbands unmanned by their 'bas-bleu' wives.[84] They reveal more about contemporary hostility towards female authority and intellectual endeavour than about actual power relationships within the *pension*. Yet, as

---

[79] Contrat de marriage: Henri Medaile et Jeanne Ploux, 29 Nov. 1845, AM Bordeaux, Fonds Ploux/3.

[80] Eugénie Dubois à Augustine Goblot, 24 Jan. 1875, quoted in Isambert-Jamati, *Solidarité*, 160.

[81] Noémi Reclus à Zoë Tuyes, Autumn 1857, in L. Carrive (ed.) 'Lettres écrites par les filles du pasteur Reclus à Zoë Tuyes, 1856–1863', *Bulletin de la Société pour l'Histoire du Protestantisme Français*, 143 (1997), 189.

[82] Mme Bachellery au Maire du 1er arrdt. (copie), 24 Nov. 1845, AD Seine, VD[6] 158–2.

[83] Léon, *Indiscretions*, 12.

[84] Bergman-Carton, *Woman*, ch. 3.

the examples above reveal, the division of labour within girls' boarding-schools did not always correspond to the accepted understanding of male and female roles, raising the question of how women facing legal constraints that offered a narrow definition of the feminine sphere were able to operate outside that domain.

It is difficult to know what the legal status of married teachers was. Technically, Joséphine Bachellery was not able to sign a lease or contract a loan without her husband's express and written permission, although the *Code Civil* had provided for married women who exercised a trade independent of their husband's. If a woman had the status of *marchande publique* she could contract engagements without requiring her husband's permission (she still required her husband's permission to be considered *marchande publique* in the first place).[85] However, there is little indication that married schoolmistresses were usually *marchandes publiques*. Nowhere in the rulings are married *maîtresses de pension* required to have this special legal status. Moreover, in 1837 the prefect of the Manche asked that, under the terms of the *Code du Commerce*, schoolmistresses be made to produce their husband's authorization to act as *marchande publique*.[86] This implies that though the law provided for married women to act as independent economic actors, schoolmistresses tended not to adopt this official status, perhaps indicating that in practice the husband's consent was taken for granted when a married woman engaged in business.

The degree to which the Napoleonic codes set new limits on women's freedom is a matter of debate.[87] Although it placed strict limits on women's legal capacities, the *Code Civil* maintained the Revolutionary principle that unmarried women could inherit on broadly the same grounds as their male siblings.[88] Adeline Daumard argues that marriage settlements highlighted the importance of a wife's contribution to the family economy and contends that women might in reality have more influence than the law suggests. The history of business demonstrates that middle-class women were active in commerce until late in the nineteenth century. In the families of professionals and public servants, wives played a semi-official role.[89] Nonetheless, the fact that a special legal status had to be created to enable wives to act as independent businesswomen demonstrates that women entrepreneurs operated against the grain of society.

---

[85] Hafter, 'Female masters', 3–4; R. Marion, 'What's that "E" at the end of "Marchande"?', *Proceedings of the Western Society for French History*, 22 (1995), 109–17; *Huits Codes*, Code Civil, Art. 220, Code du Commerce, Art. 4.

[86] Préfet de la Manche au Ministre de l'Instruction Publique, Mar. 1837 AN, F¹⁷ 12432.

[87] N. Arnaud-Duc 'Les contradictions du droit', in G. Fraisse and M. Perrot (eds.), *Histoire des femmes en occident*, iv. *Le XIXe siècle* (Paris, 1991), 87–120; Desan, *Family on trial*, 283–311.

[88] H. D. Lewis, 'The legal status of women in nineteenth century France', *Journal of European Studies*, 10/3 (1980), 178–9.

[89] Daumard, *Bourgeoisie*, 359–63; Dansette, *L'entreprise*, 228–9. The wife of a sub-prefect was commonly known as 'Madame le sous-préfet'. Sincère, *Femme*, ch. 5.

Moreover, if practice meant that businesswomen were able to act more freely than theory permitted, this freedom was always vulnerable. When, in 1843, Mme de Montmirel expressed her interest in buying a school in the first *arrondissement* in Paris, the mayor noted that 'M. de Montmirel seems little disposed to authorize this'. Although his wife had run a successful day-school before their marriage and was clearly an efficient and capable teacher, she was dependent on her husband's goodwill—M. de Montmirel always had the power to overrule her decision, which ultimately he did.[90] Schoolmistresses who became successful businesswomen were the exception proving the rule of feminine domesticity and subordination.

The scarcity of autobiographical material makes it difficult to know how women teachers in France reconciled their business activities with conventional notions of femininity, or how they reacted to constraints and difficulties. Julienne Dantier was proud of the way in which she supported herself by teaching. Applying for a position as a school inspector in 1857, she emphasized that, as a young woman, 'my work provided for me, and it is to work that I have always turned to furnish the means of living honourably and in a manner worthy of the dignity of my family'.[91] The Dubois sisters also took pride in their financial success. In 1848, Augustine noted: 'we have had a superb Easter . . . I think that in the end we will triumph. In the town, our school is now reputed to be the most prosperous: we have the girls from all the best families.' If Mme Campan—who emphasized the importance of being inspired by a genuine love for children rather than simple need—sometimes suffered from the tensions between the ideal of feminine domesticity and her commercial activity, she never sought to conceal the commercial aspect of her work; the sentiments expressed by Julienne Dantier, Eugénie Dubois, and others suggest that for some schoolmistresses economic self-sufficiency was a considerable source of satisfaction.[92]

Difficulties and Changing Circumstances

Though some schoolmistresses were able to live comfortably from their earnings, others found it difficult to keep their heads above water. At least eight Parisian schoolmistresses were declared bankrupt between 1814 and 1842, most likely only a tiny fraction of the proportion who failed in business or were forced to withdraw. Some, like Mlle Delagrange, were victims of political upheaval. Others were simply unable to attract enough pupils or were poor managers. Visiting Mme Martin's establishment in Chaillot in 1815, the inspectress noted that

90 Maire du 1er arrdt. au Préfet de la Seine, 6 Feb. 1843, AD Seine, VD⁶ 158–3.
91 Julienne Dantier à L'Impératrice Eugénie, 28 May 1857, AN, F¹⁷ 20516.
92 Augustine Dubois à Edouard Dubois, 24 Apr. 1848, Isambert-Jamati, *Solidarité*, 155; Campan, *De l'éducation*, ii. 16, 23–5.

she 'only had five pupils left; she did not know whether she could continue'.[93] Inspection reports throughout the period 1810–67 make frequent mention of schools closed through financial difficulty. In 1835 a Mme Duhamel, a schoolmistress from the first *arrondissement* in Paris, was found to have left the country, because of 'the poor state of her finances'.[94] It is not clear whether Mme Duhamel was simply guilty of poor management, or was more unscrupulous. Mme Lescaze's fraudulent intentions are clear. In 1843, having obtained payment for the next term, she sent her pupils home and then disappeared, leaving her creditors to fight over the furniture.[95] As well as demonstrating that school-keeping was financially risky, these examples emphasize the perception of the *pension* as a commercial enterprise and undermine the notion that middle-class women were divorced from business and ignorant about legal and commercial practice.

Even those who never faced bankruptcy or the prospect of being forced to sell their school might encounter financial difficulties or be left with little to show for their labour. The wife of an architect, Mme Nicolas had had successful schools in Vervins and Avesnes in the 1820s and 1830s. By 1844, however, she was in Paris, living 'in a state of deplorable poverty, and . . . asking for assistance' from the *Ministre de l'Instruction Publique*.[96] Mme Nicolas' situation was extreme, but even a relatively successful schoolmistress might die in straitened circumstances. Sophie Delécourt had taken over the Lille school her mother had established in 1807, and in 1859 it was a prosperous establishment, providing a living for three Delécourt sisters. Yet when Sophie died in 1881, she left her sisters only 311F.[97] In the 1840s, Joséphine Bachellery had also faced destitution. In 1845 she had bought the goodwill of a school in the first *arrondissement* at the cost of 30,000F, having contracted some sort of credit agreement attached to the lease of the house she was renting at 12,500F p.a. But when the prefect of the Seine issued a ruling that forbade schoolmistresses from taking adult boarders the delicate balance of her finances was upset. As Mme Bachellery argued, they were a valuable source of income. She pleaded with the prefect to allow her until the end of her lease, claiming that 'the salvation or ruin of my family' depended on his decision.[98] The correspondence surrounding the issue of adult boarders shows that one of the reasons why the prefect sought to forbid them was precisely their profitability;

[93] Rapport sur les pensions du 1er arrdt., 1814–15, AD Seine, VD[6] 158–3.

[94] Mme Duchambon au Maire du 1er arrdt., 18 Dec. 1835, AD Seine, VD[6] 158–3.

[95] Maire du 1er arrdt. au Préfet de la Seine, 22 July 1843, AD Seine, VD[6] 158–3.

[96] M. Nicolas au Préfet du Nord, 22 Feb. 1832, AD Nord, 1 T 118/2. Mme Nicolas au Préfet du Nord, 15 May 1832, AD Nord, 1 T 122/1; M. Dumouchel, Inspecteur primaire au Préfet du Nord, 23 Oct. 1844, AD Nord, 1 T 118/2.

[97] M. Dumouchel, Inspecteur primaire au Préfet du Nord, 23 Oct. 1844, AD Nord, 1 T 118/2; Sophie Charlotte Delécourt à M. Grimond, Inspecteur primaire, 8 Nov. 1859, AD Nord, 1 T 120/2; Déclaration de la succession de Sophie Charlotte Delécourt, 9 Feb. 1882, AD Nord, 3 Q 318/161.

[98] Mme Bachellery au Maire du 1er arrdt. (copie), 24 Nov. 1845, AD Seine, VD[6] 158–2.

it highlighted the commercial dimension of school-keeping.[99] He presumably decided in favour of leniency in Mme Bachellery's case, however, because by 1847 she was at the head of a large school in the rue du Rocher, with ninety pupils in her care, and when she died in 1872 she left her heirs a total of 10,784F.[100] This was not much in comparison to the assets of 100,000–200,000F held by 31% of Parisian businessmen in the late 1840s, but compares relatively favourably with the estates of professional men, of whom 49% were worth less than 10,000F in 1847.[101]

Establishing a boarding-school had always been a risky undertaking, but in the mid-nineteenth century private schoolmistresses faced new ideological, economic, and political challenges. The *Loi Falloux* had sponsored the proliferation of convent schools by exempting those in religious orders from the teaching diploma. For many lay schoolmistresses, this had direct and immediate consequences. Competition with other schoolmistresses had always been a feature of school-keeping—school inspectors had described it as 'that open wound which gnaws at girls' boarding-schools'.[102] The worst competition was with the convents. Joséphine Bachellery wrote of a concerted campaign against lay schoolmistresses in the countryside, pitying those 'women of true merit, whose hard work and courage can little resist their daily attacks'.[103] Bachellery's anti-clericalism may have led her to exaggerate, yet lay schoolmistresses in the Nord were indeed being squeezed out by the convents. Henriette Seigner was forced to give up her boarding-school in Merville having lost the battle for survival against a new convent school. In 1866, the Religieuses Augustines de Sainte Marie took over the boarding-school established by Mlle Thèry in Bergues twenty-five years earlier. Three years later, in 1869, the Congrégation de la Mère-Dieu took over the school opened in Lambersart in 1851 by her sister Pauline.[104] This phenomenon had a clear economic dimension. How, Julie-Victoire Daubié asked in the 1860s, could a private schoolmistress hope to survive in the face of the wealth of convents? Religious establishments had the resources to attract the best male professors, and to offer parents the prospect of 'a palace, with spacious salons, courtyards, magnificent vestibules and airy gardens'. Joséphine Marchef-Girard noted that, faced with convent schools which

---

[99] Arrêté du Préfet de la Seine portant interdiction d'admettre des Dames en Chambre dans les pensions et institutions de demoiselles, 26 Aug. 1845, AD Seine, VD⁶ 648–1; Arrêté relatif aux dames en chambre, 6 Sept. 1845, AD Seine, VD⁶ 158–3.

[100] Déclaration de la succession de Joséphine Bordaz, femme Bachellery, 24 Dec. 1873, AD Seine, Q 12609.

[101] Daumard, *Bourgeoisie,* 77–9.

[102] Legros, Delegué du Ministre de l'Instruction Publique pour l'inspection des pensions de jeunes filles à Paris au Ministre de l'Instruction Publique, 2 June 1845, AN, F¹⁷ 12432.

[103] Bachellery, *Lettres,* 135.

[104] Recteur de l'Académie de Douai, 13 July 1853, AD Nord, 1 T 122/5; Déclaration d'ouverture, Religieuses Augustines de Ste Marie (de Paris), 5 rue des Cavaliers à Bergues, 24 Oct. 1866, AD Nord, 1 T 124/2; Déclaration d'ouverture, Congrégation de la Mère Dieu, 29 Nov. 1869, AD Nord, 1 T 124/6.

constituted 'an immense co-operative network', 'lay boarding-schools perish in isolation'.[105]

At the same time, schools and many other small businesses succumbed to the political upheavals of the middle of the century. Between 1848 and 1852, 27% of the companies liable to pay the *patente* (a tax on business) disappeared.[106] In 1849, the inspectress of the first *arrondissement* in Paris noted that the school established by Mme Mondielli had closed and referred to 'the crisis currently facing boarding-schools for girls'.[107] Parisian schools were particularly vulnerable, since many had a high proportion of foreign pupils, almost all removed as the situation worsened. Private schoolmistresses in Paris also faced a new problem when the process of Hausmannization forced up rents and in some cases physically displaced long-established schools, like that of Mlle Bronville, who had claimed compensation from the city.[108] No damages were ever paid and her new school closed a few years later. The 1848 revolution and the changes brought about by the new regime had direct consequences for boarding-schools for girls.

Long-term changes in economic structure and a general shift towards larger-scale corporations and finance also had an impact. One way to understand the increasing success of convent education is to place it in economic context. As Joséphine Marchef-Girard had recognized, convents—belonging to a larger network with the security of church funding behind them—were simply more suited to the new business climate than individually owned lay schools for girls. Significantly, having worked alone during the 1850s, Mlle Marchef-Girard went on to participate in the creation of establishments like the vocational schools set up under the aegis of the *Société pour l'Enseignement Professionnel des Femmes*, and the Collège Sévigné, backed by the *Société pour la Propagation de l'Instruction parmi les Femmes*.[109] Both were semi-public institutions supported by subscription, rather than privately owned enterprises.

In the 1860s lay women continued to establish boarding-schools for girls and their establishments continued to provide schooling for a significant proportion of middle-class girls. However, lacking both the social prestige and the financial and institutional backing that convent schools could draw upon, private institutions were operating in an increasingly difficult climate. In the 1880s they faced new competition from the publicly funded *lycées*. Recognizing this, Augustine Goblot decided that her daughters would not take over the school established in Pont-Audemer by their aunts. 'There is no future in girls' boarding-schools', she argued. They were too vulnerable financially and could not compete with either

---

[105] Daubié, *Femme pauvre*, ii. 116–17; Marchef-Girard, *Femmes*, 499.

[106] Crossick and Haupt, *Petite bourgeoisie*, 53.

[107] Inspection pension Mondielli, 1849, AD Seine, VD^6 158–3.

[108] Gréard, *L'enseignement*, 55.

[109] Dossier de Mlle Marchef-Girard, AD Seine, DT Supplément/154; *Collège Sévigné, le livre du centenaire, 1880–1890* (Paris, 1982).

the convents or the *lycées*. Her daughters would attend the state *École Normale* and would make their careers in the *lycée* system.[110] The gap between education and private enterprise was widening.

Despite the prejudice against women's participation in commerce in the nineteenth century, schoolmistresses in both France and England were entrepreneurs, able to negotiate credit agreements and use legal mechanisms, and often took pride in commercial success. Like other enterprises, schools could fail, succumbing to the pressures of competition, poor management, or the effects of economic and political disruption. James Bryce commented that 'their existence in any given spot does not seem to be determined by the number of children to be instructed so much as by the number of ladies without any occupation who desire to support themselves in this way,' and historians of girls' education have echoed this sense that girls' boarding-schools were unstable and not established with any understanding of the laws of supply and demand.[111] The appearance of mobility, however, sometimes belied considerable stability. Establishments like those of Mme Dantier or the Miss Byerleys were successful schools for over forty years. Changing ownership and location has sometimes obscured longevity. Furthermore, the economic objectives of schoolmistresses were not necessarily expansion or maximizing profits. As Robert Mair noted in 1866, 'lay capitalists do not buy schools'.[112] The examples of Mme Ploux, Sarah Bache, and the Byerley sisters demonstrate that instead school-keeping was often a successful element of family income strategies.

Although women in France and England might share similar objectives in establishing themselves as schoolmistresses, examining the careers of teachers reveals important and interrelated contrasts between schoolmistresses in the two countries. First, there is an openness about the business work of French schoolmistresses that is absent from the English sources. And second, the proportion of married schoolmistresses was much higher in France than in England. Seeking to make sense of these contrasts uncovers the interaction of various factors—an asymmetry in attitudes towards women's work and marriage, differences in the legal status of women, and disparities in the economic development of the two countries.

W. H. Bainbridge was not alone in remarking on the greater involvement of women in business on the Continent.[113] According to the census of 1856, 5% of the active female population in France worked in commerce and finance, as compared to only 0.06% recorded for the same occupations in England in

---

[110] Isambert-Jamati, *Solidarité*, 153, 165.

[111] J. Bryce, 'Lancashire', *SIC* ix. 794; Kamm, *Hope deferred*, 141; Mayeur, *L'éducation*, 58–9.

[112] Mair, *Educator's guide*, 26.

[113] Emma Willard and Jessie Boucherett had made similar observations, as did many English visitors to France throughout the period. Willard, *Journal*, 34; S. Marandon, *L'image de la France dans l'Angleterre victorienne 1848–1900* (Paris, 1967), 255.

1861.[114] The categories used by census enumerators to record female occupations were never simply descriptive, so that the work of many English businesswomen may have been concealed because of the way women's work was counted.[115] However, even if the figures are unreliable, the fact that female occupations may have been recorded more fully in France is itself indicative of a greater acceptance of women's economic activity. The businesswomen of the Nord were so openly involved in business that 'they acquired a collective reputation for shrewd business sense, industriousness, and even cunning'. In France, even those who were not directly responsible for any kind of commercial activity were praised for their commercial acumen, they were 'bonnes ménagères' who knew how to manage the household economy.[116] Significantly, 'la tenue des livres' was a common feature of the curriculum in French girls' schools, but bookkeeping was only very seldom taught in English establishments.

The study of schoolmistresses' lives demonstrates that women in England did operate in the commercial sphere. However, in public, they emphasized the domesticity of their arrangements, playing down the degree to which school-keeping was a business. The most frequently recurring stereotype of the woman teacher was that of the impoverished governess. The powerful influence of an ideal of domestic femininity meant that the relationship between women and money was complex, and any involvement with commerce had to be concealed. When Jane Harrison was paid for her writing for the first time, she did not tell her father: 'he held old-fashioned views as to women earning money. To do so was to bring disgrace on the men of the family.'[117] The power of the 'reduced governess' stereotype hints at the anxieties surrounding the anomalous situation of middle-class women who earned money.[118]

In France, by contrast, an eminent schoolmistress such as Mme Campan might openly discuss the calculations involved in establishing a school, and the buying and selling of schools was officially sanctioned and regulated. Images of the schoolmistress, luxuriously dressed in lace and embroidery, who 'nurtures profits more than intellect', were common.[119] The prevalence of the profit-seeking image points to the openness with which the business of school-keeping was conducted in France, where the idea of women engaging in commerce was less problematic (although criticism of the profit-seeking schoolmistress was partly an expression of discomfort at the idea of women operating in a commercial sphere). Nonetheless, the financial importance and cultural significance of small family enterprises in France meant that middle-class women continued to play a

[114] Figures calculated from Mitchell, *Statistics,* 149, 160.

[115] E. Higgs, 'Women, occupations and work in nineteenth-century censuses', *History Workshop Journal,* 23 (1987), 70.

[116] Smith, *Ladies,* 48; Marcus, *Apartment stories,* 41.

[117] J. E. Harrison, *Reminiscences* (London, 1925), 38.

[118] Peterson, 'Victorian governess', 3–20.

[119] 'Elle en soigne les revenus mieux que les études'; Colet, 'L'Institutrice', 11.

prominent and important part in economic life in the first half of the nineteenth century.[120]

French attitudes to women's business activity go some way to explaining the higher proportion of married schoolmistresses in France. It is also possible that differences in child-rearing practices had an influence: whereas breast-feeding was increasingly the norm for middle-class mothers in England, the common recourse to wet-nurses in France, particularly among the urban middle class, may have made it more feasible for married women like Mme Ploux to combine work with family life.[121] As her example and that of other teaching couples suggest, for schoolmistresses, marriage might provide an opportunity for pooling resources and skills to the best advantage of both partners. To a certain extent, in French society more generally, marriage was viewed as a business arrangement; it cemented partnerships and often provided capital for starting a business. In turn, the association of women with property and investment contributed to the acceptance of their business activities. However, differences in the legal status of women also had an impact. It is difficult to know exactly what impact legal restrictions on married women's ownership of property had in practice. If women in France could not sue or be sued without their husband's permission and were sometimes faced with the reassertion of a husband's authority, marriage settlements could give them a degree of control over their property.[122] At the same time, the status of *marchande publique* continued to have real weight. In England, married women did run their own schools, seeming to operate relatively freely despite the theoretical limitations on their capacity to do so. However, the law of coverture could be a real hindrance to their freedom to act. Moreover, the status of *feme sole* trader was increasingly restricted. Such legal restrictions surely contribute to explaining the small number of married schoolmistresses in England.

By the 1850s, however, the pattern of school-keeping in both England and France was changing. Although recent studies have rightly argued that women continued to be economically active in the nineteenth century, the experiences of middle-class schoolmistresses suggests that discomfort about the involvement of women in business was on the increase, and that women's enterprise was badly affected by changes in the law and in business practice. In France, even the bourgeoises of the Nord began to withdraw from active participation in business.[123] Already in the 1840s, the rulings of the prefect of the Seine against adult boarders and regulating the sale of schools suggest unease at the ways

[120] Smith, *Ladies*, ch. 3; M. Perrot, 'Fonctions de famille', in M. Perrot (ed.), *Histoire de la vie privée*, iv. *De la Révolution à la Grande Guerre* (Paris, 1986), 109.

[121] Shorter, *Modern family*, 189; R. Woods, *The demography of Victorian England and Wales* (Cambridge, 2000) 285.

[122] Crossick and Haupt, *Petite bourgeoisie*, 69; Daumard, *Bourgeoisie*, 363–4; Lewis, 'Legal status', 181–2.

[123] Smith, *Ladies*, 48.

in which schoolmistresses made education a business. Simultaneously, those in business were dismissive of the idea that a school was a commercial enterprise. Hence, in 1842, the declaration of bankruptcy of a Parisian schoolmistress was dismissed because the *Tribunal de Commerce* argued that 'given that Mlle Revol describes herself as a schoolmistress, that as such she is not a *commerçante*, and that only *commerçants* have the right to the status of bankruptcy'.[124] Moreover, changes in the economy and company law in both countries were accelerating the transition from small- to large-scale enterprise, making the position of individual private schoolmistresses increasingly difficult. At the same time, in both England and France, teachers were calling for the development of teaching as a profession and seeking to introduce new publicly-sponsored institutional forms. Education, they argued, should cease to be a commercial enterprise. As we shall see, whereas growing prejudice against women's involvement in business and changing economic circumstances endangered school-keeping as a business, the language of professionalism had connotations that made it particularly attractive and useful to women teachers. On both sides of the Channel, the transition from education as a business to education as a profession involved the elaboration of an image of the woman teacher that reinforced the disassociation between women and business.

[124] Faillite de Mlle Revol, Henriette Camille, maîtresse de pension de demoiselles à Vaugirard, 7 Apr. 1842, AD Seine, D10 U^3 Registre 21/3047bis.

4

Teaching as a Profession

In both England and France in the first part of the nineteenth century, many women became teachers to provide for themselves or as part of a family strategy. As a result, schoolmistresses were vulnerable to the charge that they were inexperienced amateurs, or more concerned about profits and status than pupils, and images of the 'reduced gentlewoman' amateur governess and the profit-seeking school proprietor abounded. Historians of women's education have tended to recycle these images, emphasizing the lack of qualification of schoolmistresses in the first part of the nineteenth century against the professionalism of their successors in the high schools and *lycées* established in the second half of the century.[1] As we have seen, however, many private schoolmistresses in the first half of the century had sought out some kind of training for their work and had always expected they would become teachers. Some decided to begin teaching because they were interested in education. Even if they had become teachers by necessity, many sought to develop their pedagogical knowledge.

Schoolmistresses' interest in training and commitment to their work has been overlooked, partly as a result of the way in which the history of women's activities has been interpreted through the lens of male work. Viewing the professions as fixed and closed institutions, most historians of women's work in England see women as obliged to storm, or steal, into the professional citadel, and link this process closely to feminist campaigns to develop employment for women. Others have argued that professionalization was a mechanism intended to exclude women from a particular occupation.[2] Certainly the use of the term 'semi-profession' to describe occupations which have been female-dominated suggests the degree to which women's claims to professional status are contested, and it is clear that professionalism has often been constructed as male. However,

---

[1] Pedersen, *Reform,* 63–171; Pedersen, 'Schoolmistresses'; Vicinus, *Independent women,* 163–210; Dyhouse, *Girls,* 58–78; Mayeur, *L'enseignement,* 241–364; Margadant, *Madame.*

[2] L. Holcombe, *Victorian ladies at work: middle class working women in England and Wales 1850–1914* (Hamden, 1973); D. Copelman, *London's women teachers: gender, class and feminism, 1870–1930* (London, 1996); Corfield, *Power,* 188. On professionalization as a mechanism for exclusion, see M. Rossiter, *Women scientists in America: struggles and strategies to 1940* (Baltimore, 1982), and B. Smith, *The gender of history: men, women and historical practice* (Cambridge, Mass., 1998).

this is only part of the story; it ignores the continual process of self-definition and construction in which professional groups are engaged and the ways in which women have contributed to shaping the institutions and ideals that bolster professional identity.[3] As this chapter demonstrates, in the nineteenth century, schoolmistresses on both sides of the Channel were developing a form of occupational expertise which they themselves claimed as 'professional'—a term of particular value for them not only because of the social status it laid claim to, but also because of the degree to which it resonated with the notions of vocation, mission, and service associated with femininity. Uncovering the part women played in developing teaching as a profession poses a challenge to the masculine/feminine, professional/amateur dichotomies implicit in much writing about the history of women's education: it reveals that women did not simply adopt an existing model of educational professionalism. On the contrary, they were deeply implicated in the development of teaching as a career for women, and helped shape the way it evolved as an occupation for men.

The historiography of the professions in France has taken a somewhat different turn, reflecting the centrality of the state in the development of occupations such as medicine and engineering.[4] Studies of women's work have focused on the role played by governments in opening up the professions.[5] In studying women's education historians have also tended to concentrate on state initiatives, and have contended that the development of female schooling owed relatively little to the women's movement. Instead, it has been argued that the creation of a corps of female professors in the 1880s was an example of 'state feminism'.[6] However, recent work on women religious has challenged this exclusive focus on the state by demonstrating that the congregations were key agents in the professionalization of occupations such as social work and nursing, as well as teaching.[7] These studies have called historians' attention to the work of teachers outside the *Université*, yet the work of lay schoolmistresses—neither subject to a

---

[3] R. Torstendahl, 'Essential properties, strategic aims and historical development: three approaches to theories of professionalization', in M. Burrage and R. Torstendahl (eds.), *Professions in theory and history* (London, 1990), 544–8; M. Larson, *The rise of the professions: a sociological analysis* (Berkeley, 1977). For a more detailed analysis of the relevance to re-evaluations of the history of the professions to the development of teaching, see de Bellaigue, 'The development of teaching'.

[4] J.-M. Chapoulie, 'Sur l'analyse sociologique des groupes professionnels', *Revue Française de Sociologie*, 14 (1973), 86–114; G. L. Geison (ed.), *Professions and the French State, 1700–1900* (Philadelphia, 1984); S. Rothblatt, 'How "professional" are the professions? A review article', *Comparative Studies in Society and History*, 37 (1995), 194–204.

[5] C. Bodard-Silver, 'Salon, foyer, bureau: women and the professions in France', in M. Hartman and L. Banner (eds.), *Clio's consciousness raised: new perspectives on the history of women* (London, 1974), 72–83; L. Clark, *The rise of professional women in France* (Cambridge, 2000).

[6] Mayeur, *L'éducation*, chs. 4 and 5; Mayeur, *L'enseignement*, 61–9; Margadant, *Madame*; Quartararo, *Women teachers*; S. Gemie, *Women and schooling in France, 1800–1914* (Keele, 1995); S. Gémie, 'Institutional history, social history, women's history: a comment on Patrick Harrigan's "Women teachers and the schooling of girls in France"', *French Historical Studies*, 22 (1999), 619.

[7] C. Langlois, 'Le Catholicisme au féminin', *Archives des Sciences Sociales des Religions*, 57 (1984), 43–7; Mills, 'Women', ch. 4; Rogers, 'Retrograde'; Curtis, *Educating the faithful*.

systematic state-directed process of professionalization, nor incorporated within a professionalizing religious corps—has received little attention. Examining the efforts of lay schoolmistresses who sought to contribute to the development of the teaching profession calls into question the strict distinctions made between lay and religious women and also between secular and religious moves towards professionalization.[8] At the same time it highlights that, as for England, it is misleading to think of women 'entering' a profession whose parameters were already firmly established. Long before the establishment of publicly funded schools for girls and training institutions for secondary teachers, schoolmistresses on both sides of the Channel were expressing commitment to their work and developing their expertise. By the mid-nineteenth century women teachers were claiming professional status and prestige for their work.

TEACHING AS A PROFESSION IN ENGLAND

The role of the schoolmistress

Historians have tended to argue that the increasing influence of Evangelical ideals of domesticity in the early nineteenth century contributed to restricting the scope of the lives of middle-class women. Sharp distinctions drawn between the male sphere of commerce and the professions and the female sphere of the home contained women's activities within strict limits. But the idealization of domestic womanhood was not necessarily an obstacle to the expansion of schooling for girls. The notion that women's domestic role was 'a profession' emphasized its importance, and, by placing it on a par with male occupations, reinforced claims that the best preparation for domesticity was a rational intellectual education.[9]

Many schoolmistresses reiterated such claims, stressing the value of female education and elaborating a conception of their role that underlined the importance of their work. At her London school in the 1850s, Hannah Pipe concentrated on 'training those powers of the mind and heart that fit a woman for the thoughtful and intelligent performance of her duties in life', emphasizing that those duties would be performed in the home.[10] For Sarah Ellis, 'education . . . must be a preparation of the character for what will be its duties and avocations in afterlife', a future which she saw as entirely domestic, but which required 'the development of the faculties, moral as well as intellectual'. In her eyes 'a woman of cultivated understanding and correct religious principle, when engaged in educating the rising generation, in reality fills one of the most responsible stations to which a

---

[8] This approach is indebted to the work of Hazel Mills, who challenges the distinction usually made between lay and religious women: 'Catholic women', 8.

[9] More, *Strictures,* i. 109–10. [10] Stoddart, *Life,* 58.

human being can aspire'.[11] Notions of feminine domesticity both inspired these schoolmistresses in their work and reinforced their sense that it was important and necessary.

Just as women teachers emphasized the private nature of their establishments as a way of reconciling their work with these ideals, many schoolmistresses characterized their role as maternal and established warm personal relationships with their pupils. Charlotte Brontë's teacher, Miss Wooler, liked to stroll arm in arm with her pupils around the dining-room. She exchanged letters with her former pupils, and on Charlotte's marriage in 1853 it was Miss Wooler who gave her away.[12] Other schoolmistresses referred to their charges as 'my children'. Alice Ottley described her first pupils at Worcester High School for girls as 'my children' and 'my first brood'. Frances Buss kissed each child goodbye at the end of the school day, stayed in close contact with many of her former pupils, and referred to their husbands as 'my sons-in-law'.[13] Pupils frequently shared this sense that the relationship between themselves and their teachers was maternal. Remembering Jane Gardiner in 1842, one student wrote that 'she was inestimable, for to me she was mother, instructress and the kindest and truest of all my friends'. Hannah Pipe was described by her pupils as 'the schoolmother', and actively cultivated this image, encouraging them to come to her for informal chats.[14]

In practice, not all relationships between teachers and their pupils were as harmonious as the language of maternal affection might suggest. When herself a teacher in Miss Wooler's school, Charlotte Brontë craved privacy and freedom from the clinging affection of her pupils. She remarked furiously to her diary that 'if these girls knew how I loathed their company, they would not seek mine so much as they do'.[15] Nor were all schoolmistresses gentle in the exercise of authority. At Margaret Bell's school in the 1860s 'absolute submission to their principal was expected and given'.[16] Nevertheless, the image most frequently evoked by schoolmistresses and their pupils was that of 'the adoptive motherhood of the school'.[17] When authors like W. R. Greg could label unmarried and childless women as 'redundant' and 'incomplete and unnatural beings', the maternal metaphor was a way in which schoolmistresses could reconcile their situation with ideals of domestic womanhood.[18]

---

[11] Ellis, *Women*, 60, 126.   [12] W. Gerin, *Emily Brontë* (Oxford, 1967), 497.

[13] M. James, *Alice Ottley: first Head-Mistress of the Worcester High School for Girls* (London, 1914), 71; Ridley, *Frances Buss*, 63, 76.

[14] E. A. Gardiner, *Recollections of a beloved mother* (London, 1842), 27; Stoddart, *Life*, 47.

[15] C. Brontë, Roe Head Journal, *c*.1836, Gordon, *Charlotte Brontë*, 57.

[16] Georgiana Burne-Jones, *The Winnington letters of John Ruskin*, ed. J. Van Aikin Burd (London, 1969), 33.

[17] J. Ludlow, review, *North British Review*, 19 (1853), 151–74, cited in J. Uglow, *Elizabeth Gaskell: a life* (London, 1985), 317.

[18] W. R. Greg, 'Why are women redundant?', *National Review*, 14 (Apr. 1862), 433–5.

At the same time, the language of motherhood was the only socially legitimate means of expressing and exercising female authority. Frances Buss found stepping outside this language a traumatic experience: having handed over the control of her school to trustees in 1871, she found it difficult to ensure that her views were taken into account, writing that 'it tears me to pieces to have always to be asserting myself. . . I sobbed myself to sleep like a child.'[19] The schoolmistress in the biographical sample who was most at ease with authority was Dorothea Beale. Instead of emphasizing motherliness, she saw education as a God-given mission, drawing inspiration from the example of Abbess Hilda of Whitby and the notion of sisterhood, thus associating herself with a religious tradition of female professionalism which, as will be seen below, had a considerable impact on schoolmistresses in France.[20]

Like Dorothea Beale, many schoolmistresses were inspired by notions of Protestant mission and drew on the language of piety to express their seriousness of purpose and commitment to education. The Evangelical Anglican Jane Gardiner rose daily at 5 a.m. in order to study as preparation for her task of sending forth 'solidly educated Christian women', writing on her first appointment as a governess that 'I feel deeply the importance of the task I have to fulfil'.[21] Another Anglican, Sarah Bennet, who kept a school in Melton Mowbray in the 1840s, claimed that 'next to the Christian ministry, the office of the instruction of youth is the most important'.[22] In the same vein, many schoolmistresses emphasized the sense of moral responsibility they had for their pupils. When one of Helen Higginson's pupils left the Unitarian school she kept in Derby with her sisters in the 1820s, she noted that 'it is a comfort for us to feel that she is much improved and so well prepared in many essential points for the situations she will be called on to fill at home'.[23] Jane Byerley, also a Unitarian, similarly expressed her pride in a former pupil, Sophy: 'she is a noble minded intelligent ingenuous creature, in fact she is everything that I wish her to be and that I fondly hoped she would be when I used to study her youthful mind, and narrowly watch her opening dispositions'. She added that though Sophy had been taken to Bath (presumably by her family) she had left the city 'sick of its miscalled pleasures'.[24] Both Higginson and Byerley felt that they had done rather better than their pupils'

[19] Frances Buss to Annie Ridley, 1871, Kamm, *How different*, 134.

[20] Kamm, *How different*, 79, 121; C. Dyhouse, 'Miss Buss and Miss Beale: gender and authority in the history of education', in F. Hunt (ed.), *Lessons for life: the schooling of girls and women, 1850–1950* (Oxford, 1987), 22–38. The Catholic tradition also had attractions for other Protestant women: see E. Yeo, 'Protestant feminists and Catholic saints in Victorian Britain', in E. Yeo (ed.), Radical femininity: women's self-representation in the public sphere (Manchester, 1998), 127–44.

[21] Gardiner, *Recollections*, 4, 28.

[22] G. Bennet (ed.), *The Christian governess: a memoir and selection from the correspondence of Miss Sarah Bennet* (London, 1862), 60.

[23] Helen Higginson to Edward Higginson, 21 Dec. 1825, HMCO, MS J. Martineau 8, fo. 46.

[24] Jane Byerley to Elizabeth Gaskell, 14 June 1826, J. Chapple, *Elizabeth Gaskell: a portrait in Letters* (Manchester, 1980), 8.

mothers would have done, but their letters also indicate the degree to which they hoped not only to instruct their pupils but also to form their characters. Like the notion of religious mission, the idea that a teacher had a moral responsibility to educate gave schoolmistresses' work added meaning. As Helen Higginson remarked, 'the reflection that their intercourse with us and with each other must have a lasting influence on their characters in their work, and that it may extend its effects beyond the grave gives a dignity to even our homely endeavours and an importance to our occupations'.[25] The language of religious and moral mission gave the work of these teachers a dynamic, outward-looking thrust and gave schoolmistresses the scope to imagine their influence extending beyond the home.

This approach often fuelled a more robust vision of womanhood than that advanced in the prescriptive literature. Mrs Lalor, who kept a school in Hampstead in the 1850s, was recommended for 'her power of forming conscientious, thoughtful, earnest independent characters'.[26] Anne Clough's aim, according to one of her students, was 'to put us in the way of becoming useful, helpful women, able and willing when the time came to take up our share of work in the world and to serve each other for the good of all'.[27] This sense that girls had an existence independent of their domestic role inspired some schoolmistresses to expand the traditional curriculum beyond that 'solid instruction' recommended by authors like Sarah Ellis, and it should not be inferred from the informality and domesticity of arrangements in girls' schools that the intellectual education offered was necessarily poor, or methods haphazard. Hannah Pipe's pupils were amongst the first students to benefit from new opportunities for higher education. Many schoolmistresses went to considerable lengths to extend their own instruction in preparation for teaching. Some made a virtue of the informality inspired by ideals of domesticity to develop innovative pedagogical approaches. Having studied Pestalozzi and Froebel, Louisa Carbutt emphasized the importance of giving attention to each girl and refused to admit more pupils than she could educate in this way.[28] Although Elizabeth Sewell mistrusted elaborate theories, she shared this belief in child-centred methods, arguing that 'the mode of dealing must in every case be a subject of separate study'.[29] Women teachers were elaborating a 'domestic model' of girls' education, inspired both by contemporary ideals of femininity and by notions of child-centred learning.

These schoolmistresses sought to develop their pupils' intellectual horizons and offered girls a stimulating example to follow. Helen Higginson expressed

[25] Helen Higginson to Edward Higginson, 21 Dec. 1825, HMCO, MS J. Martineau 8, fo. 46.

[26] Elizabeth Gaskell to Lady Kay Shuttleworth, 12 Dec. 1850, *Letters of Elizabeth Gaskell*, ed. J. A.V. Chapple and A. Pollard (Manchester, 1997), 137–40.

[27] Clough, *Memoir*, 97.

[28] Herford, *In Memoriam*, 45; Stoddart, *Life*, 175–80; For the contribution of women to progressive education, see the essays in Hilton and Hirsch (eds.), *Practical visionaries*.

[29] Sewell, *Principles*, ii. 30. Private schoolmasters also profited from the flexibility of their arrangements to experiment: D. Leinster-Mackay, 'Pioneers in progressive education: some little known proprietary and private school exemplars', *History of Education*, 9 (1980), 213–17.

her admiration for a fellow schoolmistress who offered her pupils an intellectual education she expected would produce 'reasonable, or rather, *reasoning* women' and corresponded with her brother at theological college in preparation for keeping her own school.[30] She asked him 'to write to us on subjects of such importance and interest as those in which you are now engaged', and attended lectures on chemistry and astronomy at the Derby Mechanics Institute. Pupils at her school studied both subjects, as well as geography, history, geometry, and arithmetic.[31] Dorothea Beale recalled that her teachers 'were women who had read and thought; they had taken pains to arrange various schemes of knowledge, and so we left with the consciousness that there were large tracts to be explored by us'.[32] Describing their efforts to stimulate their pupils' intellectual growth, teachers like Hannah Pipe and Dorothea Beale went beyond platitudes, insisting that women needed solid instruction in order to be better mothers. In the 1850s Hannah Pipe wrote in her diary of her awe when faced with the task of instruction in secular, very undomestic, very *male* terms: 'education appears to me to continually more complex, a more vast, difficult, arduous undertaking . . . A boundless, unnavigable sea leading to an unexplored continent lies before me.'[33] Emphasizing the importance of instruction, Beale argued that 'a right education is the development of all the powers, physical, intellectual, and moral, and . . . this is *a good in itself*'.[34] Reflecting a Protestant emphasis on self-improvement, many of the English schoolmistresses in the biographical sample thus expressed their belief in the importance of intellectual instruction, reinforced the notion of intellectual equality between men and women, and challenged the view that women were simply 'relative creatures'.[35]

The importance these schoolmistresses attached to providing a serious education for their pupils derived in part from concerns about what girls might face once they had left school. Women teachers stressed the importance of the work they did to prepare girls for a future in which a life of secure domesticity might not be guaranteed. In the 1820s, Frances Broadhurst argued that girls must be taught as much as possible, 'for you know not what may be their lot in life'.[36] Sarah Ellis emphasized that the uncertainty of their financial situation meant

[30] Helen Higginson to Edward Higginson, Oct. 1823, HMCO, MS J. Martineau 8, fo. 34.

[31] Helen Higginson to Edward Higginson, 23 Oct. 1825, and 1 Feb. 1826, HMCO, MS J. Martineau 8, fos. 40, 53.

[32] Beale, 'Girls' schools', 542.   [33] Stoddart, *Life*, 52

[34] D. Beale, 'On the education of girls, by a Utopian', *Fraser's Magazine*, 74 (1866), 512.

[35] Ruth Watts has explored the relationship between Unitarians and women's education. Clyde Binfield's research demonstrates that other dissenting schoolmistresses also attached considerable importance to intellectual instruction, and the Quaker attention to women's intellectual development is well documented. See Watts, 'Female education', Binfield, *Belmont's Portias; K. Allen and A. Mackinnon, ' "Allowed and expected to be educated and intelligent": the education of Quaker girls in nineteenth century England', *History of Education*, 27 (Dec. 1998), 391–402; C. Leach, 'Religion and rationality: Quaker women and science education, 1790–1850', *History of Education*, 35/1 (2006), 69–90.

[36] F. Broadhurst, *A word in favour of female schools* (London, 1826), 53.

that middle-class women must be educated in order to be prepared for 'entering a lower sphere'.[37]

By the 1840s calls for the more systematic education of schoolmistresses and governesses were multiplying.[38] It was in this period that the 'governess novel' emerged as a distinct genre, responding to and fuelling anxieties about the situation of middle-class women who could not depend on familial resources. As we have seen, the process of becoming a schoolmistress was more complex than stereotypical image of the Victorian governess suggests. None of the schoolmistresses in the sample reacted in the same way to the proliferation of images of distressed gentlewomen as the fictional Ann Salter, in 'Dr Deane's Governess', who was inspired by Redgrave's image of 'The Poor Teacher' to adopt a demeanour of romantic melancholy.[39] Nor did the sense of commitment and engagement with their work articulated by many schoolmistresses bear much relation to the quiet resignation of fictional governesses. Where schoolmistresses did allude to the sad life of the governess, it was in campaigning for reform and for the extension of girls' education.

Like Frances Broadhurst, Dorothea Beale and Frances Buss saw a key part of their work as preparing young women for any eventuality. They argued that 'a good education is a sort of insurance . . . a wealth which cannot so easily take to itself wings and fly away'.[40] Drawing rhetorical force from images of the 'reduced gentlewoman', Frances Buss declared that she wanted to lighten the sufferings of 'women of my own class', 'brought up to be married and taken care of and left alone in the world, destitute'. Although neither explicitly challenged an ideal of middle-class domesticity predicated on the notion that fathers and husbands would provide, their own situations, and the idea that girls needed 'a sort of insurance', undermined that ideal. Furthermore, in arguing that women needed a better education in order to provide for themselves in the future, they had large aims. Both Buss and Beale envisaged the extension of professional opportunities for women and their first aim was 'that teaching should . . . take its true place as foremost among the learned professions'.[41]

The development of the profession

The role and status of the teacher were undergoing profound changes during the nineteenth century. The elaboration of a new ideal of liberal education, drawing on new psychological theories that stressed the importance of a methodical approach to teaching, meant that 'the teacher was important for scientific reasons. Only he disciplined minds; only he could determine which faculties

---

[37] Ellis, *Women*, 20.   [38] Peterson, 'Victorian governess'; Pedersen, *Reform*, ch. 5.

[39] J. Ingelow, 'Dr Deane's governess', in *Studies for stories* (London, 1864).

[40] D. Beale, *Reports issued by the Schools Inquiry Commission on the education of girls* (London, 1869), Preface, p. xxxiii.

[41] Ridley, *Frances Buss*, 93, 91.

needed strengthening, and consequently, which programme of study best suited the student.'[42] Simultaneously developments in medicine and law were setting precedents of institutionalization and control that many other occupations sought to emulate, laying claim to professional status. Reinforcing these initiatives, increasing importance was attributed to competitive examinations. In 1854, the Northcote-Trevelyan report recommended that entry to the civil service should depend on examination success, and from 1858 the University Local Examinations offered independent testing to secondary schools.[43] The proficiency aspired to by the middle-class professionals was coming to be prized above social status and 'amateurish' was becoming a term of disparagement. Anxieties about the situation of middle-class women had generated support for the notion that girls' education should be extended and teaching developed as a profession for women. That support was also related to the gradual formalization of professional qualifications and must be situated within the context of shifting notions about the status of teaching.[44]

Women teachers took a share in the wider discourse, claiming a new authority and expertise in educational matters. In the 1820s Anne Pendered and Frances Broadhurst published treatises defending school instruction. They claimed that women teachers, who could devote their lives to teaching, were best placed to take charge of the education of girls.[45] Other schoolmistresses showed a clear interest in discussing educational matters. In the 1810s, the Birmingham schoolmistress Sarah Bache and her stepsister Anna Penn exchanged letters discussing their reading of Locke.[46] Helen Higginson used conversations and correspondence with a fellow teacher to discuss teaching methods and pedagogical treatises.[47] Schoolmistresses published textbooks and treatises offering practical advice and developing their views on education. Many reveal an understanding of the importance of tailoring methods to children's abilities and interests that seems progressive when compared to the mechanical style of much of the teaching then available in boys' schools.[48] Sarah Jolly's *Thoughts on the vocation and profession of the teacher* (1854) called on teachers to study their pupils in order to understand the process of learning.[49] As seen above, some schoolmistresses developed inventive teaching methods that drew on recent pedagogical theories. Journals like *The Governess* discussed Pestalozzi's ideas of child-centred learning and Jacotot's theories of learning by association, one article on infant education

[42] S. Rothblatt, *Tradition and change in English liberal education* (London, 1976), 130.
[43] J. Roach, *Public examinations in England, 1850–1900* (Cambridge, 1971).
[44] For a fuller discussion see Bellaigue, 'The development of teaching'.
[45] Pendered, *Remarks*, 10; Broadhurst, *A word*, 10–15.
[46] Sarah Bache to Anna Penn, Nov. 1801, Matthews, *Sarah Bache*, 28.
[47] Helen Higginson to Edward Higginson, Oct. 1823—Feb. 1826, HMCO, Martineau Papers, J. Martineau 8, fos. 3–116.
[48] Roach, *Secondary education*, 70–1; Bamford, *Public schools*, 62–5.
[49] Sarah Jolly, *Thoughts on the vocation and profession of the teacher* (London, 1854), 47.

emphasizing that women had been instrumental in this area.[50] Clearly, women teachers were not only drawing on ideals of feminine domesticity to express the importance of their work and their commitment to it, they were also participating in the construction of education as a discipline.

A corollary was the growing importance schoolmistresses attached to specialized training. Many women teachers sought some kind of preparation for their work, but some were also instrumental in developing teacher training. Frances Buss was especially active, sending her assistants to the HCSS Institution and stressing, in her evidence to the SIC, that every teacher should be trained in the art of teaching.[51] As a member of the College of Preceptors, which had attracted the support of many women teachers, she helped establish the first chair of education in the country in 1873.[52] Dorothea Beale had also underlined the value of training when she addressed the SIC, and in 1885 she opened St Hilda's College in Cheltenham for that purpose. The importance of women educators in the history of teacher training has rightly been acknowledged. But their efforts have usually been perceived as motivated by the need to compensate for the inadequacies of girls' secondary education.[53] This interpretation ignores the long-standing interest of many schoolmistresses in 'the science and art of education' as well as their commitment to making teaching a professional career for women. In addition, it conceals the radicalism inherent in the idea of training women teachers. The founders of Queen's College had drawn back from a project that weakened the assumption that women were teachers by nature, but women like Emily Shirreff explicitly rejected the idea that women could become competent teachers through 'the ordinary contact with children'.[54] The support of schoolmistresses for teacher training challenged conservative notions of femininity and offered women the possibility of a valued professional existence outside the home.

Professional networks, like the College of Preceptors, strengthened the professional identity and authority of teachers and provided a forum for the exchange of ideas. Schoolmistresses' organizations further reinforced teachers' sense of the importance of their work, and stimulated feelings of shared identity and professional authority. Anne Clough described how, at the sessions of the London Association of Schoolmistresses (LSM), which met from 1866 to 1887, 'the mistresses . . . learned to combine; they were no longer alone, each in her own small sphere which had been dull and monotonous; they were now becoming part of a system and gathering strength'.[55] The London group was not the only such association. The Manchester Board of Schoolmistresses, of which Elizabeth Wolstenholme was a prominent member, pre-dated the London association

---

[50] *The Governess*, 1 (July 1855), 31. On Jacotot, see 'Expertise and profesional development outside the *Université*' below.

[51] Evidence of Frances Buss, *SIC* iv. 52–67.   [52] Chapman, *Professional roots*, 73.

[53] Jones, *Training*, 30.   [54] Shirreff, *National Union*, 23.   [55] Clough, *A memoir*, 110.

and there were sister organizations in Bristol, Leeds, and Newcastle.[56] Women teachers sought to build on this sense of solidarity and shared expertise to raise the status of teaching as an occupation for women. In 1866 the LSM refused to join the College of Preceptors' Scholastic Registration Association until it agreed to campaign for the registration of women teachers on the same grounds as that of men, and a key aim of the National Union for the Education of Women, founded in 1872, was 'to raise the social status of female teachers by encouraging women to make teaching a profession'. [57]

New opportunities for exchange also helped foster the interest in pedagogical experimentation that already influenced the work of a number of schoolmistresses. The LSM discussed the language-teaching methods being developed by Professor Max Müller and the advantages of interspersing intellectual work with physical exercise.[58] Child-centred pedagogical strategies continued to have particular appeal. In 1879, Mary Porter presented a paper calling for greater sensitivity to each pupil's interests and abilities. She argued that pupils would learn their lessons better if more active methods were used, interspersing question and answer sessions with independent study and group work.[59] Although, as will be suggested below, schoolmistresses like Anne Clough and Frances Buss were beginning to stress the necessity of integration into the dominant male education system, they were sceptical about wholesale adoption of the methods and principles that shaped boys' schooling. Elizabeth Sewell argued that forcing the same curriculum on all pupils was 'a kind of intellectual despotism'.[60] Dorothea Beale spoke for many in saying, 'I do not want girls' education to be what that of boys is now, but that both should move on together to a higher ideal, not as yet realized by either.'[61]

Some historians have argued that the mid-century schoolmistresses were constrained by a 'double conformity'—to domestic notions of femininity and to masculine educational standards—which hampered their efforts to develop teaching as a profession for women.[62] In fact, women teachers had an ambivalent attitude to those standards, and the relationship between ideals of domestic femininity and teachers' sense of professional identity and authority was more

---

[56] London Association of Schoolmistresses, *List of members* (May 1869), Girton College, GCPP Davies 9; R. Pope, 'Ladies' educational organizations in England, 1865–1875', *Paedagogica Historica*, 16 (1976), 336–60.

[57] Minutes, 14 June 1867, Minute book of the London Association of Schoolmistresses, 1866–74, Girton College, GCPP Davies 9; 'The objects of the National Union for the Education of Women', in Shirreff, *National Union*, 48.

[58] Minute Book, 1866–74, Girton College, GCPP Davies 9.

[59] M. Porter, 'The lecture system as applied to school teaching', 1879, Papers given and presented for the London Association of Schoolmistresses, NLC, Place of the school in history, RS7iv.

[60] E. Sewell, 'The reign of pedantry in girls' schools', *Nineteenth Century*, 23 (1888), 220.

[61] Beale, 'Girls' schools', 553.

[62] This hypothesis was first developed in S. Delamont, 'The contradictions in ladies' education', in S. Delmont and L. Duffin (eds.), *The nineteenth century woman, her cultural and physical world* (London, 1978), 134–63.

complex. None of the schoolmistresses in the study publicly questioned the belief that women shared an essentially feminine nature, which differentiated them from men. However, this belief could be a source of strength. Both Elizabeth Sewell and Dorothea Beale argued that 'women alone can understand, and therefore truly educate women'.[63] Though this implied an adherence to conventional notions of femininity, it also strengthened their conviction that teaching must be developed as a profession for women. It pushed Elizabeth Sewell to imagine a corps of female lecturers and led Dorothea Beale to act in distinctly 'unfeminine' ways. In 1856 she resigned from her position as mathematical tutor at Queen's, citing 'the want of womanly influence' as one reason for her action.[64] She had been disappointed by the move away from teacher training at the college, and the institution was troubled by disagreements between female members of staff and the male principal.[65] She also resigned from her next post on discovering that she was required to follow the directions of a male board of governors. On her arrival at Cheltenham, she sought to ensure that women teachers predominated on the staff and could work without male interference. In 1871, when the school's shareholders refused to implement her plans for the institution, she and the other teachers resigned in protest.[66] Estelle Freedman has argued that at certain points in history, a separatist approach was the only viable strategy open to women.[67] Elizabeth Sewell and Dorothea Beale used such a strategy, their understanding of women's separate nature underpinning and reinforcing their claims for professional authority.

Like schoolmistresses earlier in the century, Dorothea Beale also drew on ideas about women's role as the guardians of religion in expressing the importance of her work. Her Protestant faith also reinforced her belief in teaching as a profession and led her to question that all women were destined for marriage and domesticity, arguing that for some 'their whole being is amply satisfied by a life like mine . . . in which they can live for others and minister to others' needs'. For her, women teachers constituted a 'sisterhood of service'.[68] The notion that women's role was to serve others presented teaching as a lifelong career and strengthened her sense of teachers as a unified corps of workers. Her focus on the idea of service also resonated with the increasingly powerful idea that the professional middle classes represented a moral force, motivated by an ethic of service, rather than one of self-interest. That women teachers were seeking to locate themselves within this ideology is clear from Frances Buss's exhortation

---

[63] Sewell, 'Reign', 231; Dorothea Beale; Kamm, *How different*, 28.

[64] Sewell, 'Reign', 232; Beale, 'Girls' schools', 545.

[65] S. Gordon, 'Studies at Queen's College, Harley Street, 1848–1868', *British Journal of Educational Studies*, 3 (May 1955), 148.

[66] Dorothea Beale to Frances Buss, 2 Oct. 1871, NLC, History of the School, B1.

[67] E. Freedman, 'Separatism as strategy: female institution-building and American feminism, 1870–1930', *Feminist Studies*, 5 (1979), 516.

[68] E. Raikes, *Dorothea Beale of Cheltenham* (London, 1908), 37, 53.

that 'teaching should cease to be a mere trade—so many hours grudgingly given for so much pay—and that it should take its place as foremost among the learned professions, in which the excellence of work, and not work's reward, is the object of ambition'.[69] Ideals of domestic femininity and notions of vocation could thus intersect with 'the powerful ideological matrix' of professionalism and enhance the status of teaching as an occupation for women.[70]

Although networks like the LSM were crucial in developing schoolmistresses' sense of teaching as a profession, as Anne Clough emphasized, in order to achieve the extension and improvement of women's education, schoolmistresses needed 'some recognition from those who rule, whether in the country or at the universities'.[71] The LSM had been instrumental in obtaining that recognition. It had originated from Emily Davies's efforts to obtain the admission of girls to the Cambridge University Local Examinations, and many of its members had met when presenting their pupils as candidates in 1863. Anne Clough felt that this had created 'a bond of union' between the schoolmistresses, a bond later reinforced by their successful campaign, again led by Emily Davies, to ensure that girls' schools were included within the remit of the SIC.[72] The inclusion of girls' schools in the investigation indicates the degree to which the notion of reforming women's education had gained support in government circles, if not in wider public opinion. Anne Clough, Frances Buss, Dorothea Beale, Mary Porter, and other schoolmistresses were called to give evidence. The commissioners also discussed a 'memorial respecting the education of girls', submitted by a group of women teachers from schools scattered all over the country.[73] These women now considered themselves, and were regarded as, educational experts, a measure of the new authority and assurance that organizations like the schoolmistresses' associations had helped to foster.

But official recognition also entailed change. The growing dominance of a public-school model of education at mid-century saw the gradual eclipse of the small intimate establishments opened by women teachers. Appreciating the influence of current developments in boys' education, Frances Buss recognized that a new type of 'public' girls' school was required and transferred her school to the control of a body of trustees. The new schools must be embedded in existing social practice, and founded on a more substantial and enduring financial basis than private enterprise.[74] At the same time, the need for recognition identified by Anne Clough influenced the development of the profession. The SIC had concluded that in order to correct the low standards in girl's education, 'the first remedy is to provide all English women of the middle class with the opportunity

---

[69] Ridley, *Frances Buss*, 91.

[70] G. Sutherland, 'Examinations and the construction of professional identity: a case study of England, 1800–1950', *Assessment in Education*, 8 (2001), 8.

[71] Clough, 'Hints', 439.   [72] Clough, *Memoir*, 110.

[73] Minutes of evidence, *SIC* iv, v. 'Memorial respecting the education of girls', *SIC* ii. 192.

[74] Ridley, *Frances Buss*, 93; Anderson, 'Frances Mary Buss, the founders as headmistress', 37–9.

of higher liberal education'.[75] In terms reminiscent of those used by the founders of Queen's College, training schools were condemned as producing 'teachers and nothing else'.[76] They did recommend a system of certification and registration for both male and female teachers, but this was dropped when the Endowed Schools bill passed through parliament.

Women teachers continued to invest in the notion of teacher training, and the period after 1870 saw the creation of a number of training colleges. However, the conclusions of the SIC had strengthened what Michael Burrage identifies as a peculiarly English tradition of practice-based professional training. In England, public schools and universities played a culturally significant role in offering a general liberal education, deemed an essential prerequisite for work in the professions, but provided no specific vocational training. Professional education was provided through practice.[77] Providing formal training for teachers would have required that the existing socially approved model of public-school and university education be dismantled. Mid-century educational reformers were enmeshed within the public-school and university tradition, and unable to challenge existing structures.[78] Moreover, vocational training for middle-class teachers would have had the radical effect of making the occupation accessible to those who had not received the liberal education of a gentleman, thus weakening the relationship between the middle classes and the professions. The social legitimacy of the idea that the best professional education was a general liberal education led to the expansion of higher education for women, but devalued pedagogical training for female teachers. As Sophie Bryant noted, 'the women educated at the universities persisted in neglecting professional training. Either they despised it, or could not afford it, or could get entrance to the schools without it.'[79]

By the 1870s the dominance of the liberal idea of education meant that pedagogical training for teachers, an important element of the ideal of the professional teacher upheld by many schoolmistresses, had declined in importance. Although organizations like the GPDSC and the Association of Head Mistresses continued to promote teacher training, and although secondary training institutions were established in many universities later in the century, the headmistresses of the later part of the nineteenth century tended to follow a different professional tradition, which corresponded to that of public-school masters. In 1878, when his opinion on the provision of teacher training in Cambridge was solicited, the Headmaster of Eton declared that the best qualification for a teacher was

---

[75] 'Report', *SIC* i. 62.   [76] Ibid. 613.

[77] M. Burrage, 'From practice to school-based professional education: patterns of conflict and accommodation in England, France and the United States', in S. Rothblatt and B. Wittrock (eds.), *The European and American university since 1800* (Cambridge, 1993), 180–3.

[78] C. Harvie, *The lights of liberalism: university liberals and the challenge of democracy, 1860–1886* (London, 1976), 211.

[79] Glenday and Price, *Reluctant revolutionaries*, 31.

'some of that spirit, which in a word is best described as manliness'.[80] Women teachers were moving towards a professional model predicated on masculinity. It is a process vividly illustrated by a photograph of Sara Burstall, possibly taken in 1905 on the occasion of her accepting an honorary Master of Arts degree from Trinity College, Dublin (Illustration 4). In full academic dress, with degree in hand, she faces the camera in a portrait which asserts the confidence of the High School Headmistress, a fully qualified educator, who forged her own image, and bore very little resemblance to the passive 'Poor Teacher' of 1845. But it is also a portrait of assimilation into a pre-existing tradition, the female body concealed and disguised by gowns and mortarboard. Significantly, in 1892, when asked whether one of her colleagues was a lady, Edith Wilson's reply was that she did not know, but that 'at any rate, she is a gentleman'.[81]

TEACHING AS A PROFESSION IN FRANCE

The role of the schoolmistress

In France, as well as in England, the schoolmistresses' role was frequently likened to that of a mother. Ernest Legouvé suggested that for a schoolmistress, 'maternal love has become a career'.[82] The *dames inspectrices* were keen to encourage this understanding of the teacher's role. Thus, while Mme Pivand was criticized for her unmaternal lack of attention to her pupils, Mme Barizon was praised for being 'a teacher who cares for her pupils with maternal concern and who does her duty conscientiously'.[83] Schoolmistresses themselves drew on the language of motherhood. Mme Garnier, who held a school in Paris in the 1820s, claimed that she supervised her pupils 'with the care of a tender mother', and 'sollicitude maternelle' was a phrase which frequently recurred in school prospectuses. In the 1850s Marie Sincère noted that many Parisian teachers were addressed by their pupils as 'Petite Mère'.[84] The strength of feeling in favour of maternal and domestic education meant it was important for lay schoolmistresses to emphasize a motherly approach. It was also a way for teachers to reconcile their work to

---

[80] Quoted in P. Searby, *The training of teachers in Cambridge University: the first sixty years, 1879–1939* (Cambridge, 1982), 8. For further details on the interest of women teachers in training in the second half of the century, see Kamm, *Indicative past*; Glenday and Price, *Reluctant revolutionaries*; P. Hirsch and M. McBeth, *Teacher training at Cambridge: the initiatives of Oscar Browning and Elizabeth Hughes* (London, 2004).

[81] E. C. Wilson, *Catherine Isabella Dodd, 1860–1932* (London, 1936), 7.

[82] E. Legouvé, 'Femmes', in F. Buisson (ed.), *Dictionnaire de pedagogie*, 2nd edn. (Paris, 1914), i. 997.

[83] Inspection pension Pivand, AD Seine, D² T¹ 110; Inspection pension Barizon, 1843, AD Seine, Vbis R¹ 6–7.

[84] Rapport sur l'institution de Mme Garnier, May 1823, AD Seine, VD⁶ 158–3; Sincère, *Pensionnats*, 20.

Illustration 4. Portrait of Sara Burstall, (*c*.1905); reproduced by permission of the Archives at Manchester High School for Girls.

dominant ideals of femininity. Such claims were not entirely rhetorical, and French schoolmistresses sometimes established warm relationships with their charges. As a pupil in Le Mans in the 1850s, Adèle Riobé emphasized the 'maternal affection' of her former teacher there, and threw herself into the arms of 'Mme C' on returning to the school to visit.[85]

[85] C. Riobé, *Notice sur ma fille* (Le Mans, 1863), 179.

Yet the images evoked by both teachers and their pupils were often less conventionally feminine. Jeanne Campan wrote of herself as being 'at the head of a little scholastic government'.[86] Her contemporary, Mme de Renneville, compared the schoolmistress to 'a monarch at the heart of her court', an image also used by Marie Sincère—they were the 'queens' of their 'subjects'.[87] Similarly, French pupils were likely to describe their schoolmistresses as distant figures of great authority. Thérèse Martin recalled that Mme Campan 'imposed a great deal of respect. When she entered a classroom, everyone rose. She never went so far as to speak to all the pupils.'[88] Mme Brada (the pseudonym of Henrietta Puliga), a pupil at Mme Deslignières' Paris school in the 1850s, described her schoolmistress as 'a perfect despot, everyone in the house, without exception, feared her'.[89] The orphaned Henriette Picanon, a pupil at Mme Dupuy's school in Sainte-Foy in the 1830s, remembered that 'although [Mme Dupuy] often emphasized to me when I was a child that she would take my mother's place, her dignified and majestic appearance commanded respect, there would be absolute silence in the classroom when she appeared'.[90] The authority of these schoolmistress even extended over parents. George Sand saw her wishes overridden by Sophie Bascans, her daughter's schoolmistress, who refused to excuse Solange from religious instruction.[91]

Pupils' descriptions of their teachers resonate with the imposing, distant schoolmistresses of other contemporary accounts. Mme d'Olbreuil, the paragon depicted in Antoine Caillot's evocation of an ideal *pension* for girls, was 'severe and gracious' and embodied reserved authority.[92] In the 1850s, Marie Sincère suggested that most schoolmistresses were either 'worldly and distinguished' or 'cold and monastic'.[93] This distance and authority were often reinforced by the physical arrangements of institutions. Mme Deslignières lived somewhat apart from her pupils, occupying a house separated from the school by the garden; the pupils encountered her only infrequently. In this, she resembled the fictional, and rather sinister-seeming, Mme Arcin, the schoolmistresses in Fanny Villars' *Deux ans de la vie d'une jeune fille* (1868): 'once or twice a day, she leaves her room, and appears silently in the classrooms . . . She moves slowly, and without apparent movement, crosses the three rooms, simply turning her head left and right . . . the pupils are extremely afraid of her, precisely because of her habitual invisibility.'[94]

---

[86] Campan, *De l'éducation*, ii. 25.

[87] S. de Renneville, *Lettres d'Octavie, jeune pensionnaire de la Maison St Clair, ou essai sur l'éducation de demoiselles* (Paris, 1806), 213; Sincère, *Pensionnats*, 20.

[88] T. M. Martin, *Souvenirs d'une ancienne élève de la Maison d'Education de la Légion d'Honneur d'Ecouen* (Saint Dizier, 1924), 35.

[89] Mme Brada (pseud. of Henrietta Consuela de Puliga), *Souvenirs*, 29.

[90] Mme Picanon (Henriette Picanon), *Mon frère et moi, souvenirs de jeunesse, accompagnés de poèsies d'Eugène Picanon* (Paris, 1876), 13.

[91] d'Heylli, *Fille de George Sand*, 27.   [92] Caillot, *Tableau*, i. 2.

[93] Sincère, *Pensionnats*, 121.

[94] F. Villars, *Deux ans dans la vie d'une jeune fille* (Paris, 1868), 18.

Keeping emotional as well as physical distance was sometimes a policy. Jeanne Campan observed that prudent schoolmistresses, finding themselves at the head of 'little scholastic governments', should 'avoid letting subordinates become too familiar with those in authority'.[95] At Mme Bazin's school in Paris in the 1840s, assistants were instructed that excessive familiarity with pupils would dent the proper respect the girls owed them. Teachers 'must always preserve their dignity and whilst being accessible to all pupils, must not forget to observe a certain reserve which would ensure and preserve their authority'.[96]

This concern with order and hierarchy points to the influence of Catholic ideals and practice on girls' schooling and on women's experiences in France. In the nineteenth century, conceptions of the Catholic 'femme forte' emphasized women's moral superiority and authority within the home, where their role was described as 'the government of the interior'.[97] At the same time, just as convent schools provided a precedent for the development of large female institutions that were not domestic in character, the commanding positions occupied by women in religious orders provided a model of feminine authority and legitimized the expression of that authority in terms that stretched beyond the boundaries of conventional notions of femininity. Using language that prefigured the monarchical images evoked above, Mme de Genlis wrote that 'an abbess is a kind of queen'.[98] Joséphine Bachellery traced the ability of schoolmistresses to govern large schools back to the precedents set by the convent heads of the *Ancien Régime*, and the power of this model of female professionalism is evident in Bachellery's proposals for developing teaching as a profession, as it is in the projects of other reformers. Although she criticized teaching sisters for their lack of qualifications, she nevertheless envisaged the *École Normale* for laywomen she hoped would be founded as a kind of 'professed house' and referred to future teachers as 'novices'.[99] Mme Caubet-Darius, writing in 1869, would also allude to the model of the teaching sister to describe the *École Normale* she proposed and, as noted above, the legislators of the 1880s conceived of the *École Normale* they intended to establish as a 'lay noviciate'.[100] Such allusions are perhaps not surprising in a period which saw an unprecedented expansion in the number of women religious, as well as the emergence of new and dynamic *congrégations*, organizations which permitted women to be far more

---

[95] Campan, *De l'éducation*, ii. 25.

[96] Règlement de Mme Bazin, *c*.1842, AD Seine, VD⁶ 650–1.

[97] Mills, 'Women and Catholicism', 138–65.

[98] Genlis, *Discours*, 2. She drew this comparison in order to attack the atmosphere of courtly flattery that surrounded abbesses, but the image is nonetheless a powerful counterpoint to more conventional images of maternal authority.

[99] Bachellery, *Lettres*, 61, 214, 219.

[100] Mémoire Caubet-Darius, *c*. Oct 1869, AN, F¹⁷ 2680; Ferrouillat, Rapport de la Commission sur la creation d'une école normale, 1881, quoted in F. Mayeur, *L'enseignement*, 108.

active than their enclosed predecessors.[101] In both their authoritative approach to teaching and in developing projects for professionalization, lay schoolmistresses were drawing on Catholic representations of womanhood and on the socially legitimate, and increasingly powerful, model of the teaching sister.

Lay women teachers also cultivated a public persona, in stark contrast to English schoolmistresses who emphasized the private nature of their work. Schoolmistresses' names appeared on street signs; they invited local dignitaries to attend their prize-giving ceremonies and published the speeches made on those occasions. When celebrated teachers died, prefects and Ministers attended their funerals, and their life and work was recalled in obituaries.[102] They were public figures, as the appearance of *'l'institutrice'* and *'la maîtresse de pension'* as 'types' in the 'tableaux de Paris' and 'physiognomies' then popular attests.[103] This public presence and authority was reinforced by interaction with the state, an exchange that increased in intensity throughout the period as schoolmistresses were subject to a growing body of rules. After 1850, by the terms of the *Loi Falloux*, those who wished to open a school had to announce their intention, not only to the authorities, but also to all the inhabitants of the town. Administrative procedures encouraged the notion that they were public servants and, as a result, private schoolmistresses sometimes appealed for financial aid from the state.[104]

Prefects and other officials also contributed to upholding a notion of motherhood that indirectly reinforced the authority of schoolmistresses. As noted above, teachers who mothered their pupils were often praised and encouraged; Rebecca Rogers has demonstrated that the prefectoral rulings of the Restoration and July Monarchy reveal a desire to propagate a domestic understanding of femininity.[105] However, the conception of motherhood they articulated differs from the intrinsically private notion prevalent in England. In France the Revolution had prompted the elaboration of a theory of social relations that rested on a reinforced understanding of sexual difference, emphasizing the complementarity of women's domestic duties and men's public obligations.[106] The conception of

---

[101] Langlois, *Le Catholicisme;* Mills, 'Women and Catholicism', ch. 4; Curtis, *Educating the faithful;* Rogers, 'Retrograde'.

[102] See, for example, *Trois allocutions adressées aux familles par Mlle Allix* (Paris, 1845); *Discours prononcé par Mme Bachellery, le jour de la distribution des prix, donnés le 25 août 1842 en son Institution, passage Sandrié 2, à Paris* (Paris, 1842); *Institution des jeunes demoiselles dirigée par Mlle Lequien; Discours prononcé à la distribution des prix, le 28 août 1838, Poissy* (Paris, 1838); Gossot, *Sauvan,* 227–30; Cadier-Rey,'Les Protestants', 746.

[103] S. Marcus, *Apartment stories: city and home in nineteenth-century Paris and London* (Berkeley, 1999), 32–42.

[104] Mme Babron au préfet de la Seine, 19 July 1842, AD Seine, VD[6] 650–1; M. Dumouchel, Inspecteur primaire au Préfet du Nord, 23 Oct. 1844, AD Nord, 1 T 118/2.

[105] Rogers, 'Boarding schools'.

[106] Landes, *Women,* ch. 6; K. Offen, 'Ernest Legouvé and the doctrine of "equality in difference" for women', *Journal of Modern History,* 2 (1986), 83–104; J. Burr Margadant, 'Introduction', *The new biography: performing femininity in nineteenth-century France* (Berkeley, 2000), 16–18.

the family, rather than the individual, as the basic unit of society contributed to the politicization of the family and motherhood, as the views of authors from both ends of the political spectrum suggest. For the conservative de Maistre, the ordered family was a metaphor for the ordered monarchy, and for the liberal Claire de Rémusat, every woman was potentially 'the wife and mother of a citizen'.[107] This publicly oriented conception of motherhood was most fully (and hyperbolically) elaborated by Louis Aimé-Martin in a best-selling book which argued that 'the spirit of a people, their morals, their prejudices, their virtues, in other words the civilization of the human race all are learned at the mother's breast'.[108]

Such ideas shaped the public persona developed by French schoolmistresses. Victoire Paveyranne, a schoolmistress in Paris in the 1840s, claimed that her aim was 'to form the young girl, the wife, the mother for society'.[109] Joséphine Bachellery argued that 'the public education of girls, legally confided to maternal schoolmistresses, is a guarantee of the salvation and prosperity of the nation'.[110] A valorization of motherhood also underpinned the recruitment of inspectresses, chosen, according to the ruling of 1820, 'from amongst the mothers of families most recommended by their rank, their character, and especially by the purity of their morals and religious principles'.[111] The same double understanding of motherhood as a qualification and as a public duty underpinned the establishment of the *Société de Charité Maternelle*, and later that of the infant school, or *école maternelle,* system.[112] As surrogate mothers, as lay 'abbesses', and as state-authorized and regulated educators, French schoolmistresses occupied a place in French civic life as well as directing 'little scholastic governments' within the school walls.

The example of the women religious of the *Ancien Régime* also provided a language for the expression of commitment to education, and many Catholic schoolmistresses were inspired by their religious beliefs, describing teaching as a religious mission. The Parisian schoolmistress Mme Duchambon, who had emphasized her interest in education in writing to the Minister in 1838, described this commitment as 'like a vocation'. Mme Mirande in Bordeaux averred her devotion to 'the serious mission of education'.[113] Some schoolmistresses interpreted their mission as an active religious imperative, like the women religious of the seventeenth century, seeing education as 'a tool of christianization'.[114]

---

[107] Albistur and Armogathe, *Histoire,* 239–49; Rémusat, *Essai,* 87.

[108] L. Aimé-Martin, *Des mères de famille, ou la civilisation du genre humain* (Paris, 1838), 27.

[109] Prospectus, externat de Mlle Paveyranne, 18 rue des francs-bourgeois, Paris, *c.*1848, AD Seine, D² T¹ 110.

[110] Bachellery, *Lettres,* p. vii.   [111] Quoted in Kilian, *L'instruction,* 12.

[112] C. Adams, 'Constructing mothers and families: the Society for Maternal Charity of Bordeaux, 1805–1860', *French Historical Studies,* 22 (1999), 65–86; J.-P. Chaline, 'Sociabilité féminine et maternalisme; les sociétés de Charité Maternelle au XIXe siècle', in A. Corbin, J. Lalouette, and M. Riot-Sarcey (eds.), *Femmes dans la cité, 1815–1871* (Grâne, 1997), 69–77; Luc, *L'invention,* 39–51.

[113] Mme Duchambon au Maire du 1er arrdondissement, 24 Mar. 1838, AD Seine, VD⁶ 158–3. Prospectus, Mme Lavergne Mirande, *c.*1855, AM Bordeaux, Fonds Ploux/8.

[114] Sonnet, *L'éducation,* 43.

Mme Bastard de Saulieu, a former teacher and the author of a textbook published in 1826, wrote that her objective was 'to imprint in young hearts the principles of an education based on religion, to illuminate faith in order to reinforce it'. In the same vein, Jeanne Sauvan wrote that 'we educate for this world and for the next'.[115] Drawing inspiration from their faith, by using the language of vocation, these schoolmistresses were also inserting themselves into a long-standing tradition of female education and feminine professionalism.

This emphasis on vocation was often associated with the notion of education as a difficult task that would only be rewarded in heaven. Sauvan reassured future teachers that 'Even when your efforts to do good are unfruitful and unappreciated in this world, is there not a better world where it will all be seen and rewarded?'[116] Joséphine Bachellery wrote that 'I do not know of any occupation which would be better served by expecting reward only in heaven'.[117] Education was 'une carrière amère' offering all those who chose it 'a succession of arduous and sometimes disheartening tasks'.[118] Eléonore Ploux emphasized that 'instruction is not the most of a schoolmistress's tasks, anyone who has acquired a certain amount of knowledge can teach what she has learned, but it requires a special vocation, complete dedication, an almost total abnegation of oneself to carry out all the rigorous duties that being a teacher imposes'.[119] The administrative authorities shared her view. An 1846 report on Parisian *pensions* emphasized that 'of all professions, there is none that imposes more serious duties, which requires more solicitude, more vigilance, than the direction of a *boarding-school*; moreover, the schoolmistress must be called by a kind of vocation to such a delicate mission'.[120]

The association of women with religion and the example of dedicated teaching sisters enabled the expression of professional commitment and seriousness of purpose, without challenging an understanding of gender roles that saw work and ambition as masculine attributes and self-sacrifice as a feminine virtue. At the same time, by underlining the difficulties of the teacher's task, and emphasizing their self-sacrifice and resignation in the face of such difficulties, lay schoolmistresses were associating themselves with a Catholic ideal of feminine submission and abnegation.[121] The language of abnegation, however, had a con-servative tenor. Even if the model of the teaching sister conveyed public authority and commitment, the value placed on resignation might limit the appetite for

---

[115] Bastard de Saulieu (Mme), *Dernière année du pensionnat* (Paris, 1826), p.x; J. Sauvan, *Cours normal des institutrices primaires* (Paris, 1840), 18.

[116] Ibid. 180.   [117] Bachellery, *Lettres*, 67.

[118] A. Le Groing la Maisonneuve, *Essai sur le genre d'instruction qui paraît le plus analogue à la destination des femmes* (Paris, an VII), 68.

[119] Règlement, Mme Ploux, 1840–50, AM Bordeaux, Fonds Ploux/8.

[120] 'Résultats de l'inspection des pensions de demoiselles, Paris, 1846', AN, F^{17} 12431.

[121] M. di Giorgio, 'La bonne Catholique', in Perrot and Fraisse (eds.), *Histoire des femmes*, 175; R. Radford Ruether, 'Christianity', in A. Sharma (ed.), *Women in world religions*, (Albany, NY, 1987) 209; Bertholet, *Les Français*, 176.

change. Abnegation could also be a deterrent to intellectual adventurousness. As we have seen, Eléonore Ploux valued self-sacrifice above instruction. Inspection reports reserved their praise for those, like Mlle Gourleau, commended in 1848 for being 'entirely devoted to her establishment'.[122] Mlle Paveyranne, on the other hand, was recognized as offering solid and extensive instruction, but criticized for her 'insufficient abnegation'.[123] Intellectual competence was being unfavourably compared with self-sacrifice.

These reservations with regard to schoolmistresses' intellectual aspirations, and the greater importance attached to abnegation, were particularly prevalent in Catholic circles. Protestant pedagogues in France more explicitly presented themselves as extending girls' intellectual instruction and were encouraging of their pupils' efforts in the classroom. At Sainte-Foy in the 1820s and 1830s, Mme Dupuy declared that the aim of education in her school was the 'intellectual and moral advancement' of the pupils and directed all her pupils' efforts towards the teaching diplomas. Her faith, like that of Protestant schoolmistresses in England, tended to promote an outward-looking vision of the schoolmistress's role, setting pupils on the correct path for their future development. It contrasts with Eugénie Dubois' exhortation to her pupils to 'instruct yourselves in order to do good, to do good in order to please God, to whom we owe everything'. While Dubois encouraged her pupils to study and fostered an atmosphere of moral seriousness, her conception of the purpose of education emphasized not change, but stillness.[124] The Protestant/Catholic contrast should not be exaggerated; Protestant authors could also argue that women's education must observe 'the supreme laws of her sex, modesty, devotion, piety and charity' and Catholic educators that 'we must extend the circle of female instruction'.[125] Yet many of the Catholic schoolmistresses in the biographical sample expressed a wariness of female intellectual ambition and a potentially restricting ideal of self-sacrifice that their Protestant colleagues did not seem to share.

Expertise and professional development outside the *Université*

Throughout the first half of the nineteenth century, French schoolmistresses expressed a commitment to their work that fostered the notion that women teachers had a particular vision or understanding of educational matters. Although Mme Campan professed to believe that schooling for girls was only preferable to domestic education in the case of orphans, or daughters of mothers who had

---

[122] Inspection pension Gourleau, 1848, AD Seine, VD⁶ 367–10.

[123] Note, *c*.1837, Dossier Paveyranne, AD Seine, D² T¹ 110.

[124] Mme Dupuy, 'Pension normale de jeunes filles Protestantes', *Archives du Christianisme*, 11 (1828), 378; Picanon, *Mon frère*, 33; Prize day speech by Eugénie Dubois, Aug. 1869, quoted in Isambert-Jamati, *Solidarité*, 156.

[125] Discours du president Gauthey, *Séance d'ouverture des cours gradués pour les jeunes demoiselles Protestantes* (Paris, 1859), 8; Mgr. Dupanloup, *La femme studieuse* 3rd edn. (Paris, 1875), 20.

no time to devote to their children, her letters and the programme she outlined for girls' education reveal that she regarded teaching as a career requiring expert knowledge. She saw schoolmistresses as authorities on education whose special skills outweighed the supposed advantages of maternal instruction and must be cultivated.[126] Mme Desplechin, a Parisian schoolmistress who published a study of girls' education in 1825, argued that girls would only be freed from the 'yoke of ignorance' if their education was undertaken by enlightened women who had studied the schools of Sparta and Rome. She concluded her study by saying: 'I think I need add nothing more to prove how important it is for mothers to entrust the education of their daughters to those of mature experience.'[127] Even if motivated in part by the need to defend school instruction for girls against attacks from the proponents of maternal education, Desplechin and Campan were not just challenging accepted notions about the superiority of maternal instruction. They were articulating a vision of their role beyond the conventional image of the teacher as a surrogate second-best mother, and calling into question ideas about women's natural capacities.

The idea that teachers were better equipped than many mothers to instruct their children gained ground throughout the period. The Demoiselles Allix, who held a school in the Vendée in the 1840s, claimed that children's early education was crucial, and must follow a carefully planned system.[128] Mothers, who were naturally indulgent, were usually unable to keep to a methodical plan. Since the Demoiselles Allix had recently added a preparatory course to their *pension*, this statement was partly self-interested—however, like their predecessors, they were asserting their expert knowledge, and calling into question received wisdom about the benefits of maternal education.[129] Joséphine Bachellery was even more sceptical about home education. She saw it as vulnerable to 'the weaknesses of the narrow and often selfish affections of the maternal heart' and stressed the importance of training.[130] By the 1840s some were suggesting that the instruction provided by women teachers was preferable to that of *all* mothers.

One of the Demoiselles Allix's claims to authority was that they had studied various pedagogical strategies and were thus able to choose the most successful and avoid 'vicious methods'.[131] French schoolmistresses seem to have experimented less with new methods than their English counterparts. Nonetheless, Octave Gréard was probably right to suggest that girls' schools were more likely to innovate in teaching methods than boys' at this time, though he wrongly perceived all such experiments as initiated by the male professors.[132] Teachers

---

[126] Campan, *De l'éducation*, i. 295–404, ii. 23–54.
[127] Mme Desplechin, *Essai sur l'éducation par Mme D——, Institutrice* (Paris, 1825), 20.
[128] Luc, *L'invention*, 95–101.
[129] *Trois allocutions adressées aux familles par Mlles Allix*, 14–20.
[130] Bachellery, *Lettres*, 213, 233–5.
[131] *Trois allocutions adressées aux familles par Mlles Allix*, 8, 12.
[132] Gréard, *L'enseignement*, 40–1.

like Mme Desplechin emphasized the need to observe their pupils and to develop new techniques that would stimulate them to learn more, and though the male professors at Mme Deslignières' school were traditional in their methods, the directress herself was said 'to observe carefully which way the wind was blowing and never to forejudge any kind of innovation'.[133]

Several other schoolmistresses in the biographical sample played an active part in disseminating ideas about new educational methods. Jeanne Sauvan was secretary of the ladies' committee of the *Société pour l' Instruction Elémentaire*, founded in 1816 to introduce the monitorial method into French schools.[134] Joséphine Bachellery and Anne Frèrejean were enthusiastic promoters of the method developed by Joseph Jacotot in 1815. This system was often ridiculed for its central tenet: 'Know one thing and relate everything to it.' However, it was influential in popularizing the notion of 'equality of intelligence'—the idea that not only men and women, but people of all classes were of equal capacity and could learn.[135] Jacotot's ideas were a source of inspiration for women who sought to extend the content of female education, as Bachellery noted at his funeral.[136] Other schoolmistresses built on their knowledge of pedagogical techniques to develop their own methods. In Lyon in the 1850s Mlle Dissard was lecturing on German pedagogy.[137] 'She had a very personal teaching method,' one biographer noted, 'she forced children to think and to organize their thoughts logically, she obliged them to speak out, to express their opinions and appreciations.'[138] Developing their own approaches to instruction, building up their knowledge of pedagogical techniques, contributing to their dissemination, lay schoolmistresses were participating in the constitution of a science of education and promoting the notion of themselves as expert practitioners of it.

Interest in pedagogical developments combined with concerns about the uncertainty of their pupils' future prospects led some schoolmistresses to support projects for the development of the profession and, by implication, to undercut notions of feminine dependence. Jeanne Sauvan echoed the concerns of schoolmistresses who reserved their resources to provide for daughters and nieces when she insisted that the instability of the world meant that girls 'must be able to depend on their own efforts, to earn a living'.[139] Without explicitly challenging an ideal of womanhood predicated on motherhood and domesticity, the idea that girls must be educated to provide for themselves undermined the

---

[133] Desplechin, *Essai*, 11; Brada, *Souvenirs*, 93.   [134] Gossot, *Sauvan*, 227–8.

[135] J. Rancière, *Le maitre ignorant* (Paris, 1989); *Cours complet d'éducation d'après la méthode Jacotot, par plusieurs de ses disciples, à l'usage de toutes les familles* (Paris, 1829–30).

[136] 'Hommage publique aux obsèques de Jacotot, 30 July 1840', 'Joséphine Bachellery', in J. Maitron (ed.), *Dictionnaire du mouvement ouvrier français, 1879–1940* (CD Rom, Paris, 1997).

[137] *Education des femmes, D. Lévi Alvarès (1794–1870)*, ed. T. Lévi-Alvarès (Paris, 1909), 24–5.

[138] Abbé Vachet, *Les Lyonnais de hier (1831–1910)* (Lyon, 1910), 129, quoted in C. Pellissier, *La vie privée des notables lyonnais (XIXe siècle)* (Lyon, 1996), 82.

[139] Sauvan, *Cours*, 7, 44.

notion that women would always be protected and provided for by fathers and husbands. In the 1840s Joséphine Bachellery called for the creation of a state *École Normale* for women and argued that young women must be taught 'to create their own future, and like men, to seek in their courageous intelligence the genuine instruction which leads to talent and generates wealth'.[140] Bachellery's idea that women could 'create their own future . . . like men' was more radical than the suggestions made by Jeanne Sauvan and finds little echo in the writing of other schoolmistresses. However, her practical proposals did resonate with other projects for the development of female education elaborated in the 1830s and 1840s, including the proposal for an *École Normale* drafted by the schoolmistress Sophie Mazure and presented to the *Chambre des Députés* in 1833.[141]

Mazure's proposal was influenced by the ideas of Saint-Simonian feminists like Marie-Reine Guindorff and Eugénie Niboyet.[142] Niboyet called for the extension of girls' secondary education, arguing that 'the government must establish at its own cost, a house in every Academic town, where candidates for the secondary teaching diplomas will be tested for a period of three years, by teaching under the supervision and direction of capable and devoted women'.[143] As we have seen, Mazure's proposal came to nothing. Despite this setback, schoolmistresses and pedagogues continued to demand the creation of a fully funded training college for secondary teachers. In 1838, the annual prize of the *Société pour l' Instruction Élémentaire* had gone to a treatise proposing an *Écoles Normale* to train secondary mistresses after the age of 16, and in 1846 Boulay de la Meurthe, the society's president and a member of the Paris examination committee, followed Mazure's example in petitioning the *Chambre des Députés*. He called for government subsidies of 500,000F to establish a network of institutions for female education including the *Écoles Normales* for women.[144] In 1848, seeing political upheaval as an opportunity to innovate, Bachellery wrote to Hippolyte Carnot, the new *Ministre de l'Instruction Publique*, proposing the creation of girls' colleges and again arguing for the establishment of a female *École Normale*.[145] Perhaps influenced by this, Carnot established a commission to investigate the reform of female education. However, in 1848, when Carnot was replaced as Minister, his plans for the reform of girls' education were dropped. As we have seen, de la Meurthe's proposal had already been rejected on the grounds

[140] Bachellery, *Lettres*, 3.
[141] Riot-Sarcey, *Démocratie*, 94–9; Rogers, *From the Salon*, 84–90.
[142] Riot-Sarcey, *Démocratie*, 49–99; C. G. Moses, *French feminism in the nineteenth century* (Albany, 1984), 41–60.
[143] E. Niboyet, *Conseiller des femmes*, cited in L. Abensour, *Le féminisme sous le règne de Louis Philippe et en 1848* (Paris, 1913), 104.
[144] Charpentier, *Des moyens*, 90–4; See also the treatise by Etienne Kilian, a *chef de bureau* in the ministry of education, *l'instruction*. On Boulay de la Meurthe and his proposal, see Mayeur, *L'éducation*, 93.
[145] Bachellery, *Lettres*, 233–5.

of expense, revealing that girls' education was still not considered of sufficient importance to justify public spending.[146]

The question of excluding male professors from teaching in *pensions* also received considerable attention.[147] Already in 1839, Bachellery had suggested that the first step to improve women's education was to remove male teachers, and in 1845 the former Saint-Simonienne Louise Dauriat launched a campaign to obtain their exclusion, claiming that it was essential on the grounds of morality. Her real objective was the professionalization of female education. She argued that not only were women most suited for the work, being 'the first teachers of humankind' they were also better qualified than many male *pension* professors, and already formed a coherent corps: 'the programme of studies that schoolmistresses are required to master forms in them a teaching corps with no need of male assistance'.[148] Her argument clearly demonstrates that teaching diplomas were seen as demarcating the professional woman teacher, and she, like Joséphine Bachellery, criticized teaching sisters who used the privilege of the *lettre d'obédience*. Dauriat's petition was widely debated in the press, and provoked indignant counter-attacks from various professors, who argued that only they could offer girls a full secondary education. In the event, although the inspector who investigated Dauriat's claims had some sympathy with her position, nothing was done to safeguard or advance the position of women teachers.[149] Her campaign highlights the growing interest in developing teaching as a profession for women, but also the influence of those who sought to resist the process.

Dauriat had argued that lay schoolmistresses formed a coherent corps, pointing to this coherence as evidence of the professionalism of women teachers. The need to defend their position against the encroachments of both male professors and teaching sisters could encourage solidarity amongst lay schoolmistresses. There is fragmentary evidence of attempts to build up bonds in the 1840s. One set of contacts revolved around the school headed by Sophie Bascans. Mme Bascans was connected to romantic literary circles through George Sand, whose daughter was one of her pupils, and through Ondine Valmore, the daughter of the poet Marceline Desbordes-Valmore, who, as seen above, was a valued teacher at the school. Through the same network, the Bascans were linked to the feminist

---

[146] The *REF* commented bitterly that the 1846 budget had allocated 2 million francs for the improvement of horse-breeding, 4 million for whale-hunting, but nothing for girls' education: 'Rapport sur le budget', *REF* (Jan. 1846), 5; Mayeur, *L'éducation*, 101.

[147] See Ch. 6.

[148] L. Dauriat, *Mémoire adressé à Messieurs les membres du Conseil Général du Département de la Seine* (Paris, 1846), 5, 12.

[149] Inspecteur Adjoint de la Seine, Dumouchel, a l'Inspecteur General Rousselle, 30 Sept. 1845, AN, F[17] 12432; Lettre à M. les membres du Conseil Royal de l'Instruction Publique de la part des professeurs, 11 Sept. 1845, AN, F[17] 12432; Paul Buessard au Comité Local du 4e arrondissement, 12 Apr. 1847, AD Seine, VD[6] 706–1. The implication was that women were not capable of high-level instruction. For a suggestive discussion of the Dauriat controversy see R. Rogers, 'Le Professeur a-t-il un sexe? Les débats autour de la présence d'hommes dans l'enseignement féminin, 1840–1880', *Clio—histoire, femmes et société*, 4 (1996), 221–39.

circles of Flora Tristan and Pauline Roland. Aline Tristan (Flora's daughter) was employed in the school in 1845. Mme Bascans also had connections with Republican political circles through her husband, a former journalist. It was through these contacts that Ondine Valmore came to be appointed to Carnot's commission on female education in 1848. She was then appointed as one of the first salaried women school inspectors.[150] On the commission, Ondine became acquainted with Marie Pape-Carpantier, one of the leading pedagogical reformers of the mid-nineteenth century. Their association prompted her to think about ways to reform girls' schooling: 'the idea of uniting with you to do solid and useful work has occurred to me . . . There is one thing that needs taking care of, the education of women. For that cause, we who are so few, can nonetheless try to do something.'[151]

Joséphine Bachellery's links to other teachers hint at the existence of a network of Protestant schoolmistresses. Her son married Celine Chatenet, herself a teacher and the daughter of a husband-and-wife team who each had their own *pension* in Chaillot.[152] The Chatenets were Protestant, and though there is no clear indication that Mme Bachellery was of the same confession, she was connected to another prominent Protestant schoolmistress, Anne Frèrejean. Frèrejean was to be the first employer of Julie Velten, herself a Protestant and the first headmistress of the pioneering *École Normale Supérieure* for women established at Sèvres in 1881.[153] It seems plausible to suggest that these women were linked not only by belonging to the Protestant minority, but also by the more robust approach to women's intellectual development which, as seen above, was shared by some Protestant schoolmistresses in France.

Schoolmistresses also participated in more formal associations. As noted above, teachers joined pedagogical societies like the *Société pour l'Instruction Élémentaire*. The *Société des Instituteurs et Institutrices de la Seine*, a mutual aid society established in Paris in 1845, had seventy women members (36% of the whole), including Mme Frèrejean in 1855.[154] The upheavals of 1848 also saw the creation of a profusion of societies and associations, including female organizations. One of these, the *Association des Instituteurs, Institutrices et des Professeurs Socialistes*, founded by Pauline Roland who had herself been a schoolmistress, explicitly concerned itself with female education.[155] Less well known was the group of

---

[150] *Correspondance de George Sand*, pp. v, vi; d'Heylli, *Fille de George Sand*; Ambrière, *Valmore*, ii. 112–99.

[151] Ondine Valmore à Marie Pape-Carpantier, c.1848, Ambrière, *Valmore*, ii. 257.

[152] Dossier Chatenet, 1871, AD Seine, DT Supplément/9; *Annuaire Protestant et statistique complète des églises, sociétés et établissements religieux Protestants de France* (Paris, 1859).

[153] Déclaration d'ouverture Frèrejean, 14 July 1851, AD Seine, D²T¹ 110; P. Perrod, *Jules Favre, avocat de la liberté* (Lyon, 1988), 419–26; Mayeur, *L'enseignement*, 118–20.

[154] *Annuaire de l'instruction primaire et de la société des instituteurs et des institutrices de la Seine* (1855), 131–3.

[155] Albistur and Armogathe, *Histoire*, 308; B. Groûlt, *Pauline Roland, ou comment la liberté vient aux femmes* (Paris, 1991), 185–9.

Parisian teaching assistants who combined to write to the Minister in May 1848, calling for improved conditions and the incorporation of schoolmistresses into the *Université*.[156]

Yet, despite these initiatives and networks, there is little to suggest that numbers of lay schoolmistresses mobilized to support calls for the extension of women's educational and professional opportunities, and despite the potential for influence represented by the Bascans connection, Ondine seems to have abandoned her plans to work with Marie Pape-Carpantier in 1848. Nothing notable, no concerted campaign for the reform of girls' education was to come of her links to feminist and Republican circles, nor did Mme Bachellery's connections develop into an association. The only female organization to emerge from the 1848 upheavals was the *Société pour l'Enseignement Professionnel des Femmes*, formally established in 1862 to promote vocational training for working-class girls, and to which a number of prominent schoolmistresses belonged.[157]

It is difficult to explain why schoolmistresses' associations in France never really got off the ground. One factor was the backlash following the fall of the Second Republic. Coupled with increasing hostility to feminist demands and frequent attacks on the figure of the female intellectual, the laws against association and the real damage suffered by those who had participated in the actions of 1848 discouraged attempts to mobilize support for the development of teaching as a profession.[158] Already in 1846, Louise Dauriat's petitions had been ridiculed because she was considered to 'belong to the detestable school of George Sand' and to 'have more imagination than sense'; after 1848 and the exile or imprisonment of feminists like Pauline Roland and Jeanne Deroin, pamphlets and caricatures ridiculing the *bas-bleu* proliferated.[159] Joséphine Bachellery may also have suffered from her involvement in the 1848 campaigns. In the 1850s she had abandoned her school in Paris and was established in a small town in the Isère. There, her prize-day speeches were much more conservative in tone and content than those she had made in Paris, perhaps indicating that in a climate of opinion increasingly hostile both to feminist ideas and to lay schoolmistresses, she was reluctant to make the kind of far-reaching demands she had articulated in the 1840s.[160] The increasingly difficult financial situation

[156] Eudoxie de Montbarbon, Adèle de Montelar, Clothilde Nanson, A. Albert, Rosine Chabranc, Anne Jadin, Agathe Ricole, Sophie Bon, 2 Ave Marbeuf, au Ministre de l'Instruction Publique, May 1848, AN, F[17] 12432.

[157] C. Lemonnier, *Élisa Lemonnier, fondatrice de la Société pour l'Enseignement Professionnel des Femmes* (St Germain, 1866); *Assemblée Générale de la société pour l'Enseignement Professionnel des Femmes* (Paris, 1869). Albistur and Armogathe, *Histoire,* 321–2.

[158] Riot-Sarcey, *Démocratie,* 183–278; Moses, *French feminism,* 148–51; McMillan, *France and women,* 90–5; Bergman-Carton, *Woman of ideas,* ch. 3; P. Kay-Bidelman, *Pariahs Rise Up! The founding of the liberal feminist movement in France, 1858–1889* (Greenwood, 1982), 3–33.

[159] Inspecteur Adjoint Dumouchel à l'Inspecteur Général Rousselle, 30 Sept. 1845, AN, F[17] 12432.

[160] J. Bachellery, *Discours prononcé le jour de distribution de prix* (Lyon, 1857, 1858).

in which many schoolmistresses now found themselves compounded these problems. As Joséphine Marchef-Girard claimed, competition isolated teachers from one another.[161]

These different factors, however, do not fully explain the non-appearance of schoolmistresses' associations in France or the quietening of calls to develop teaching as a profession for women. As significant as the impact of the post-1848 backlash were two other more deep-rooted explanations. First, there was the influence of Catholic ideals of feminine abnegation and sacrifice, which gave a conservative tenor to the professional ambitions of many schoolmistresses. At the same time, by the 1840s and 1850s, the image of the teaching sister was gaining increasing currency as the number of women religious multiplied and a growing number of congregations concerned themselves with female education, presumably drawing off some of those who might have been active in the kinds of professional organization established in England. In 1846 there were at least 25,000 women religious in France, but by 1866 they had risen to 86,300.[162] Giving formal sanction to the *lettre d'obédience* and to the principle of religious schooling, the *Loi Falloux* only strengthened the legitimacy of the teaching sister. Religious establishments were a danger to lay schoolmistresses in economic terms. But they also represented a cultural threat, undermining the position of lay schoolmistresses, whose relation to the model of the teaching sister was ambiguous and whose 'vocation' was always vulnerable to accusations of financial self-interest. There was increasing pressure on lay teachers to conform to the ideal of the teaching sister. In Cambrai in 1866 married schoolmistresses were falling out of favour, and in Paris prefects and inspectors were increasingly suspicious of schoolmistresses' husbands.[163] In Gravelines in 1856 Mlle Loisel was obliged to close her school because it was felt in the town that 'she does not have the religious character that her profession requires'.[164] Three years previously the 'flighty' Léocadie Lebeau had been forced by the *Recteur* of Douai to give up teaching because 'she did not appear to have any vocation for it'.[165] These pressures were even felt in Protestant circles. In 1855 an inspection report noted that at the Protestant *cours normal* in Strasbourg there was growing support for the idea of insisting that teachers remain celibate.[166] Yet the declining legitimacy of lay schoolmistresses was not the only long-term factor militating against the organization of a schoolmistresses' movement. Added to this was the role played by the state in the

---

[161] Marchef-Girard, *Femmes*, 499.

[162] C. Langlois, 'Les effectifs des congregations féminines au XIXe siècle: de l'enquête statistique à l'histoire quantitative', *Revue de l'Histoire de l'Église de France*, 60 (1974), 44.

[163] Inspecteur primaire à l'Inspecteur d'Académie, 31 July 1866, AD Nord, 1 T 122/1.

[164] Inspecteur de l'arrondissement de Dunkerque à l'inspecteur primaire, 6 Aug. 1856, AD Nord, 1T 124/6.

[165] Préfet du Nord au Ministre de l'Instruction Publique, 8 Feb. 1853, AN, F[17] 9768.

[166] Rapport d'inspection sur le Cours Normal Protestant de Strasbourg, 1855, AN, F[17] 9769.

development of female education, both in the way it dominated thinking about educational reform and in the practical effect of state involvement in female education.

The state and the development of teaching as a profession for women

Since the expulsion of the Jesuits in 1762, successive governments had consciously sought to build up a unified and hierarchically organized teaching corps, a project significantly advanced with the creation of the *Université* in 1808 which included not only professors of *lycées* and *collèges* but also affected private schoolmasters. All were subject to inspection and required to obtain the *baccalauréat* or *licence*.[167] Although the *Université* came under attack at various points and had an embattled air throughout the first decade of the Second Empire, it offered a powerful model of professional development, stimulating corporate loyalties and precluding the need for any independent professional association.[168] Even when teachers' organizations like the *Société des Instituteurs et Institutrices de la Seine* were established, it was felt that a society 'cannot be founded, develop and flourish without the help and support of the authorities'.[169]

Women teachers had no place in the *Université*. Nevertheless, influenced by the notion of the *Université* as 'a corps through which one could progress from the most humble to the highest position', prefectoral regulations and teaching examinations contributed to shaping the notion of teaching as a career through which women teachers progressed, following a relatively fixed pattern of advance.[170] Those elaborating proposals for the development of girls' education were also inspired by the idea of the *Université*, weakening the impulse to form autonomous associations. Already in 1809, Jeanne Campan had mooted the idea that schoolmistresses should be united in a single body. Her vision of the *Maisons d'Education de la Legion d'Honneur* was of 'a kind of *Université* of women, where young people of our sex will be educated'.[171] This notion of a female *Université* recurred forcefully in Joséphine Bachellery's writing. She called for hierarchies of promotion and the rights of women teachers to be formally defined: they should be incorporated into the civil service, and receive pensions on their retirement.[172] Calling for the creation of a training college for women in 1848, the schoolmistress Mme Burat-Johanneau evoked the pre-history of the

---

[167] Julia, 'Le choix des professeurs'; D. Julia, 'Les professeurs, l'église et l'état après l'expulsion des jésuites, 1762–1789', in D. Baker and P. Harrigan (eds.), *Current directions in the making of Frenchmen* (Waterloo, 1980), 459–82; Gerbod, *Condition;* Savoie, *Enseignants,* 20–34.

[168] S. Gemie, ' "A danger to society?" Teachers and authority in France, 1833–1850', *French History,* 2 (1988), 265.

[169] 'Compte rendu de l'assemblée générale de la Société des Instituteurs et Institutrices de la Seine, 5 Juillet 1846', in *Annuaire de l'Instruction Primaire* (1855), 92.

[170] Savoie, *Enseignants,* 22.

[171] Memoire de Mme Campan, 20 Oct. 1809, quoted in Rogers, *Demoiselles,* 62.

[172] Bachellery, *Lettres,* 75.

Université, arguing that 'the Republic of 1792 gave France an *École Normale* for men. I dare to hope that the Republic of 1848 will do no less for women.'[173] For those who sought to extend women's education, the engine of reform was state involvement, not independent initiative, and the professional model to which they aspired was the *Université*. As a result, the efforts of those who sought to improve the situation of women teachers concentrated on seeking integration into state structures of administration, rather than establishing independent networks of support and exchange; the response of the administrative authorities, however, was ambivalent.

Prefectoral and ministerial rulings since 1810 had promoted the idea of teaching as a career. The diplomas authenticated the notion of schoolmistresses as experts who had mastered a body of knowledge, and the authorities were sometimes strict in seeking to ensure that all those teaching had done so. When, in 1832, Mlle Théry wrote to ask that she be excused from taking examinations in geography, the prefect of the Nord insisted that in order to be authorized, she must satisfy the examination committee.[174] Age requirements for authorization bolstered the idea that teachers required experience in order to undertake their work, hence the refusal to authorize Mlle Loyeux, aged only 17, on the grounds that though she had been successful in the examinations, this was not enough.[175] The administrative authorities gave further sanction to the idea that women were experts in education by awarding the medals and prizes of the education department to schoolmistresses in private *pensions*. In 1852, the *Recteur's* medal was awarded to the schoolmistress Zéline Reclus, whose Protestant establishment in Orthez had an excellent reputation.[176] Similar awards were also distributed to other schoolmistresses, and in 1886 Reclus was made an *Officier de l'Instruction Publique*, an honour also conferred on Eugénie Dubois in 1894.[177] If the *Loi Falloux* had set back the progress of female education by designating all girls' schools as primary, these medals show one of the benefits of that measure. Instead of hovering on the margins of the public education system, girls' schools were incorporated into the official administrative structures of the education department and teachers were eligible for its rewards, as well as obliged to conform to its regulations.

There was sympathy too, within the education department, for the idea that teaching should be developed as a female profession. Camille Jubé de la Pérelle, who headed the office responsible for girls' schools and infant schools, felt it was important to develop female education to furnish employment for women.

[173] Mme Burat-Johanneau au Ministre, Mar. 1848, AN, F[17] 12432.
[174] Préfet du Nord à Mlle Théry, 2 July 1832, AD Nord, 1 T 122/1.
[175] Procès verbaux du comité de surveillance du 11e arrondissement, 5 July 1838, AD Seine, VD[6] 648–4.
[176] Cadier-Rey, 'Les Protestants', 746; Inspection Pension St Aubin Deslignières, 27 Apr. 1872, AD Seine, VD[6] 1731–10.
[177] Isambert-Jamati, *Solidarité*, 164.

Teaching was 'at once an honourable and a productive task'.[178] Antoine Legros, the Minister's delegate for female education in the Seine in the 1840s, also stressed the need to provide increased career opportunities for women, although he argued that the creation of a female inspectorate would best provide for 'these young women who, through hard work, hope to earn an honest and respectable living'.[179] However, the various proposals made in the 1830s and 1840s for the creation of women's training colleges and girls' schools had come to nothing, and in 1850 the government gave sanction instead to the expansion of religious schooling, a much cheaper, and anti-revolutionary, option. Before 1867, the most concrete contribution of the state to the development of professional careers in education for women was the creation, along the lines envisaged by Legros, of a corps of female school inspectors. Their appointment illustrates both the extent to which governments and the administrative authorities did seek to develop teaching and educational administration as professions for women, and the limits to 'state feminism'.[180]

In 1844 a ruling issued by the prefect of the Seine noted that 'given that the number of young women intending to become teachers and aiming to obtain the different diplomas has considerably increased, and that there has been an equally considerable increase in the number of girls' schools', it was necessary to step up the inspection of girls' *pensions*.[181] His statement was a coda to an earlier ruling by the *Ministre de l'Instruction Publique* which had approved the nomination of three salaried *dames déléguées* to inspect Parisian *pensions*. The delegates would be paid 2,000F p.a. to assess 'the teaching, the way the school is kept and everything that relates to education' in Parisian *pensions*.[182] The *dames déléguées* were not the first women to be employed by the state in a position of such responsibility. In 1837, the first salaried female inspector had been nominated to oversee the inspection of the infant schools known as *salles d'asile*. By 1848, there were five women paid by the state or municipal authorities to inspect educational institutions—four inspecting *pensions* in the Seine, and one *déléguée générale des salles d'asile*. In 1855, the *salles d'asile* system was revised, increasing the number of female inspectors to eighteen, and in 1862 Marie Caillard was appointed to inspect girls' schools throughout the country. As a result, the corps of female inspectors outnumbered the sixteen male *inspecteurs généraux*. In addition, some *Académies*, including those of Bordeaux and Douai, appointed

---

[178] C. Jubé de la Pérelle, *Des établissements d'éducation de la première enfance et des établissements d'éducation des filles* (Paris, 1849), 29.

[179] A. Legros au Ministre de l'Instruction Publique, 22 July 1845, AN, F[17] 12432.

[180] Gémie, 'Institutional history', 619.

[181] Arrêté relatif au Règlement additionnel du 27 février 1844, 30 Aug. 1844, AD Seine, VD[6] 158–3.

[182] Règlement additionnel concernant les maisons d'éducation de filles du département de la Seine, 27 Feb. 1844, AD Seine, VD[6] 158–3.

their own salaried school inspectors.[183] These appointments signalled the state's engagement with the idea of schoolmistresses as educational experts and the tentative inclusion of female schooling within the structures of the *Université* and education department.

The state's efforts related to a more general trend towards professionalization. In the 1830s the inspectors appointed to visit boys' schools had been criticized for 'lacking in qualifications and in *Université* antecedents'. Measures had been taken to ensure that in future, inspectors would be recruited from the qualified pool of teachers within the *Université*.[184] In appointing Mme Dettman and Zoë Hubert as *dames déléguées* for the Seine, efforts had been made to choose women with qualifications and experience equivalent to those of their male colleagues (although the appointment of Mlle Foucher d'Aubigny, a minor poet, and the niece of a cardinal, shows the continued influence of patronage). Zoë Hubert had obtained all three teaching diplomas and had taught in and directed schools since the age of 16.[185] Marie Dettmann, a widow, had the *diplôme de maîtresse de pension* and had owned a highly regarded school in the first *arrondissement* for fifteen years.[186] Sixteen of sixty-two female inspectors appointed before 1879 had previously been schoolmistresses or assistants, and two more had been private governesses. Appointment as an inspector could be the pinnacle of the schoolmistress's career.[187] After 1855 those responsible for the *salles d'asile* were required to pass a qualifying certificate to be appointed, but even before this, many had obtained some form of teaching qualification.[188] Once appointed, former teachers like Marie Caillard campaigned for standards of female education to be raised and for the conditions in which schoolmistresses worked to be improved.[189] Recruited on the basis of their qualifications and experience, female inspectors like Zoë Hubert represented a new kind of female professional, embodying not only personal authority on the basis of their own merits, but also public authority as the representatives of the state. As Pauline Kergomard would comment in 1889, 'it [still] seems subversive'.[190]

However, neither the educational authorities nor the *dames déléguées* themselves would have characterized their position as subversive. These first steps into public administration by women were an early example of the 'maternalist' notions that later shaped the development of welfare states in Europe and the USA.[191] It is

---

[183] Luc, *L'invention*, ch. 10; Clark, *Professional women*, chs. 1 and 2; Caplat (ed.), *Les inspecteurs généraux*, 77–89.

[184] Quoted in Caplat (ed.), *Les inspecteurs généraux*, 28.

[185] Préfet de la Seine au Ministre de l'Instruction Publique, 2 Apr. 1844; Zoë Hubert au Ministre de l'Instruction Publique, 4 Apr. 1844, AN, F^{17} 12433.

[186] Inspections pension Dettmann, 1838, 1840, 1841, AD Seine, VD^6 158–3.

[187] Calculated from Caplat (ed.), *Les inspecteurs généraux*, 83–9.

[188] Luc, *L'invention*, 331.   [189] Clark, *Professional women*, 35–6.

[190] Quoted in Luc, *L'invention*, 337.   [191] Clark, *Professional women*, 18, 48.

clear that the appointment of inspectresses was underpinned by the idea that, as women, they embodied a maternal understanding which constituted a particular form of expertise. Thus, in 1830 the prefect of the Seine instructed the mayor of the eleventh *arrondissement* to choose new voluntary inspectors from amongst 'the mothers who had given their daughters the same good education that they had received themselves'.[192] Emilie Mallet used the image of maternal femininity to argue for female inspectors: 'there are, in the work of the *salles d'asile*, tiny and utterly maternal affairs, that only women can comprehend and communicate to other women'.[193] The prescriptions for the inspection of girls' schools in the 1850s emphasized that 'respectability and prudent reserve' required that only female inspectors be permitted to visit female *pensions*.[194] If the creation of a female inspectorate sent out important messages about women's professional abilities, it also reinforced a highly conventional view of women's nature and role.

The salaried female inspectors were exceptions that proved the rule, as their titles indicate. Unlike their male colleagues—known as '*inspecteur*'—they were known as '*déléguée*'. This underlined their limited responsibility and marginal status and emphasized their femininity as exceptional; they were simply delegates from the ministry, not part of the general inspectorate. Fortoul, *Ministre de l'Instruction Publique* in 1855 when the *salles d'asile* inspectorate was reformed, made these limitations explicit: 'they take no decisions themselves, but communicate to the Minister all the information which could stimulate useful reforms and inform the deliberations of the central committee'.[195] By this time, there were no longer any women on the central commission of the *salles d'asile* (which had ultimate jurisdiction) despite the fact that the infant school system owed its existence to the work of women like Emilie Mallet.[196] Similarly, the women who sat on the Seine examination committees had seen their authority reduced. In 1849, Victorine Collin, a former *pension* assistant and the author of a number of pedagogical texts, wrote to the Minister to complain about being removed from the committee without reason. The Minister did not reinstate her.[197] Instead he planned to appoint two 'lady examiners', in the expectation that that 'the *inspectrices* will certainly deny themselves the full honour that is being offered them, and will probably show themselves to be as full of sense as they are modest, by limiting themselves, in practice, to the role of attendants'.[198] Although the French state was exceptional in appointing women to salaried

---

192 Préfet de la Seine au Maire du 11e arrondissement, 24 Sept. 1830, AD Seine, VD⁴ 21–5628.
193 Quoted in Luc, *L'invention,* 157.
194 Ministre de l'Instruction Publique aux Recteurs d'Académie, 26 Jan. 1854, AD Gironde, T Fonds du Rectorat/247.
195 Quoted in Caplat (ed.), *Les inspecteurs généraux,* 80.
196 Luc, *L'invention,* 155.
197 Victorine Collin au Ministre de l'Instruction Publique, 29 June 1849, AN, F¹⁷ 12433.
198 'Nouvelles dispositions pour les dames examinatrices', n.d., AN, F¹⁷ 12433. 'Nouvelles dispositions pour les dames examinatrices', n.d., AN, F¹⁷ 12433.

positions as early as 1836, the constraints and limitations imposed on them confirm the suggestion made by Bishop Dupanloup that it hoped to create 'a female *Université*, run by men'.[199] Lay schoolmistresses had focused their attention and efforts on seeking integration into state structures of education rather than on independent initiatives. They had to wait until the 1880s, when a group of anti-clerical Republicans began to question the dominance of religious establishments in female education and to develop alternative forms of girls' schooling, for moves towards full assimilation to begin.

In both England and France in the first part of the nineteenth century the language of motherhood and vocation provided a means for schoolmistresses to express their commitment to education and their seriousness of purpose. At the same time, for teachers in both countries, emphasizing maternal affection was a way of reconciling their work with the powerful forces identifying femininity with motherhood. Far from indicating an amateurish approach, adopting a maternal metaphor or referring to a sense of mission was a way for teachers to express their professionalism, without directly challenging prevailing ideas about women's nature and role. On both sides of the Channel, schoolmistresses were participating in the construction of education as a discipline and seeking to advance the professional standing and authority of teachers.

Comparing teachers in France and England, however, brings out national differences in the understanding of motherhood and domesticity, and in the pull of Catholic and Protestant models of vocation. In England, 'school mothers' sought to emphasize the privacy and domesticity of their establishments, cultivating warm relationships with their pupils. The 'adoptive motherhood of the school' was understood as intensely private and domestic. But ideas of feminine domesticity and religious mission also underlined schoolmistresses' sense of the importance of their work, strengthening teachers' conviction that they contributed significantly to shaping their pupils' moral and intellectual development and often giving their approach a dynamic and outward-looking force. In France, a politicized notion of motherhood and religious models of feminine influence led schoolmistresses to build up a more public persona, which often went hand in hand with the adoption of a more distant and authoritative role inside the school. At the same time, the idealization of feminine self-sacrifice and abnegation might contain the impulse for change, and restrict intellectual ambitions, particularly in a context where the figure of the woman of ideas provoked considerable hostility. Contrasts between schoolmistresses in England and France reflect the influence of confessional difference. The socially legitimate precedent of Catholic women religious provided a language of feminine professional commitment and a model for the development, by lay schoolmistresses in France, of an authoritative

---

[199] F.-A. Dupanloup, *M. Duruy et l'éducation des filles. Lettre de Mgr. L'Evêque d'Orléans à un des ses collègues* (Paris, 1867), 28.

public presence, but at the same time tended to downplay the importance of individual intellectual development. In England, Protestant schoolmistresses also drew inspiration from the language of religious commitment, but were inspired by notions of individual perfectibility to emphasize the importance of their role in guiding their pupils' moral and intellectual growth, an emphasis shared by many Protestant schoolmistresses in France.

Religious difference also goes some way towards explaining the different patterns of professionalization on either side of the Channel. In England, the efforts of individual teachers and schoolmistresses' associations—which, like early feminist organizations, could refer to the traditions of independent association and organization established by Protestant philanthropists—were crucial in raising the standing of women teachers and in gaining recognition of the importance of women's education.[200] In France, Catholic women were also active in philanthropic associations and in developing dynamic female networks.[201] Jean Noël Luc's work on the founders of the *salles d'asile* has revealed the considerable influence such women's associations could have.[202] Yet, significantly, Protestant women were at the heart of the group which developed the *salles d'asile*, and of the few networks of lay schoolmistresses that can be identified in France, Protestant women were disproportionately numerous and influential. As a number of historians have stressed, networks of Protestant teachers and pedagogues contributed in important ways to the educational reforms of the Third Republic.[203] Their prominence, when Protestants constituted less than 2% of the French population, reflects the fact that some of those French women whose English counterparts were organizing professional associations were being absorbed into the Catholic *congrégations* and their energies channelled through religious organizations. The influence of such organizations and the power of the model of professionalism developed by women religious weakened the legitimacy of teachers working outside church structures. It undermined secular notions of female professional commitment, at a time when hostility to female intellectual activity made lay teachers vulnerable. Yet while the *congrégations* and associations for Catholic lay women offered women opportunities for meaningful work, they did so within a male-dominated church hierarchy, emphasizing piety and continuity rather than change; they did not tend to foster the kinds of autonomous organization that developed in England.[204]

---

[200] Rendall, *Origins*, ch. 3; Prochaska, *Women and Philanthropy*.

[201] Mills, 'Women', ch. 6; Duprat, 'Le silence des femmes', Chaline, 'Sociabilité féminine', in Corbin *et al.*, *Femmes dans la cité;* Adams, 'Constructing mothers'.

[202] Luc, *L'invention,* chs. 1 and 6.

[203] F. Mayeur, 'Les Protestants dans l'Instruction Publique au début de la Troisième République', in A. Encrevé and M. Richaud (eds.), *Les Protestants dans les débuts de la IIIe République* (Paris, 1979), 37–57; C. Hirtz, 'L' ENS de Fontenay: les Protestants aux sources de la laïcité française', *Bulletin de la Société pour l'Histoire du Protestantisme Français*, 135 (1989), 281–90.

[204] Curtis, *Educating the faithful*, 175.

However, while differences in Catholic and Protestant traditions of feminine activity do provide some insight into the contrasting development of the teaching profession in England and France, religious differences were only one element of this contrast. A second key factor was the role of the state, which established the conditions of access to the profession in France and integrated women into the administrative structure from very early on. In England, female education was left entirely to private initiative until, in 1864 under pressure from teachers' associations, the first steps towards the official recognition of women teachers as professional educators were made. The difference between the two countries seems analogous to that identified by Seth Koven and Sonya Michel in their study of emergent welfare states. They observe that 'the power of women's social action movements was inversely related to the range and generosity of state welfare benefits for women and children'.[205]

Nevertheless, despite contrasts in the level of government involvement in female education, and despite differences in the intensity of schoolmistresses' associational life, on both sides of the Channel women teachers were contributing to the development of teaching as a profession. In doing so, they posed a challenge to contemporary assumptions about the place of women in society. They articulated notions of motherhood and domesticity that broadened the range of occupations and activities open to women, and challenged the notion of work and professionalism as a male preserve. In both countries, once women teachers were incorporated into public structures of education, training, and administration, long-standing models of female professionalism were partly eclipsed. But the contribution early nineteenth-century schoolmistresses made to developing the science and practice of education, and to expanding the opportunities available to women, was a lasting one.

---

[205] S. Koven and S. Michel, 'Womanly duties: maternalist politics and the origins of welfare states in France, Germany, Great Britain and the United States, 1880–1920', *American Historical Review*, 95 (1990) 1077–1108.

5

Becoming a Schoolgirl

On both sides of the Channel the idea that boarding-schools for girls were populated with the daughters of social-climbing families who sought to emulate aristocratic habits recurred frequently in contemporary writing about female education. Writing in 1797, Clara Reeve deplored the way that 'the children of farmers, artificers and mechanics, all come into the world as gentry. They send them to the same schools with the first gentry in the country, and they fancy themselves their equals.'[1] A decade later in France, Isidore Lebrun was condemning 'those parents enriched by the Revolution' who sought an aristocratic education for their children.[2] The figure of Mme Bovary—sent by her peasant father to a convent school where she absorbed the aspirations and romantic ideas that lead to her downfall—would vividly dramatize the dangers of 'conspicuous education' for girls.[3] Historians have also highlighted the ways in which a growing middle class in England sought to gain respectability and upward mobility through their daughters' education.[4] The mid-century reforms have been interpreted as an attempt by upper-middle-class families to obtain for their daughters an intellectual education that would distinguish them from 'genteelly' educated lower-middle-class girls.[5] The French historiography similarly emphasizes the social aspect of girls' schooling in France, further complicated by a context where the choice of lay school or convent school might have political implications.[6] At the same time, recent studies have questioned the importance attached to school instruction in the first place, maintaining that the family was the central agent of socialization for girls in the nineteenth century, and that schooling was of more limited significance.[7]

Studying the experiences of individual pupils, however, reveals that even spending only a single year at school might have a considerable impact. Moreover,

---

[1] Reeve, *Plans of education*, 60.

[2] I. Lebrun, *Vues sur l'organisation de l'instruction publique et sur l'éducation des filles* (Paris, 1816), 56.

[3] G. Flaubert, *Mme Bovary* (1856).

[4] Miller, 'Women's education'; Burstyn, *Victorian education*, 22; F. Musgrove, 'Middle class families and schools 1780–1880', in W. Musgrave (ed.), *Sociology, history and education* (London, 1970), 122–4.

[5] Pedersen, *Reform*, ch. 1.

[6] Mayeur, *L'éducation*, 38, 63; Rogers, 'Competing visions', 165.

[7] M.-F. Lévy, *De mères en filles: l'éducation des françaises, 1850–1880* (Paris, 1984), 10–12; Dyhouse, *Girls*, 1–2.

in both countries girls in fact spent longer at school than is usually recognized. In a biographical sample collecting information about fifty-six English schoolgirls, twenty-five of the forty-four pupils for whom the information is available (57%) spent more than four years at school. A similar sample of forty-two French pupils reveals that twenty-three of the thirty-one pupils whose early lives are well documented (74%) also spent over four years at school.[8] Coupled with the evidence suggesting that by the 1860s just over half of all middle-class girls in France and England were being sent to private schools, this seems to indicate that a period at school was becoming an ordinary feature of female education in middle-class families. Reflecting this, new words were coined to describe girls at school. By mid-century 'schoolgirl' was being used as an adjective in English and in French 'une pensionnaire' was as likely to refer to a girl at school as to a woman living from an allowance.[9] Time spent at school was increasingly associated with particular forms of behaviour and experience; it was being constructed as a specific phase in a young woman's life, and thereby contributing to the elaboration of notions of female adolescence.

BECOMING A SCHOOLGIRL IN ENGLAND

Social Origin and Motivations

In 1865, examining schools in Yorkshire, Joshua Fitch observed that, 'all the sharp lines of demarcation which divide society into classes, and all the jealousies and suspicions which help to keep these classes apart, are seen in their fullest operation in girls' schools'.[10] Emphasizing the private and select nature of their establishments was one way in which English schoolmistresses sought to reconcile their position with a domestic ideal of femininity. However, it was also a response to parental concern. As another SIC commissioner saw it:

In giving up for so long an interval much of the controlling influence of home associations, [a father] looks for some guarantee that their place shall be supplied by an effective substitute . . . His first object, then, is to find a well-conducted establishment frequented by girls of his daughter's rank, and (if possible) by them exclusively, where the joint influence of teachers and school companions may help to strengthen the good

---

[8] The English sample is based on biographies and autobiographies of women who had been educated at school, listed in Bell, *Victorian women,* Kanner, *Women,* and L. Pollock, *Forgotten children: parent–child relations from 1500–1900,* 6th edn. (Cambridge, 1996). The French sample was constituted in the same way. Particularly useful were Bertholet, *Les Français* and Yalom, 'Women's autobiography'.

[9] *Oxford English Dictionary online,* 'Schoolgirl'. *http://dictionary.oed.com/cgi/entry_main/* last accessed 8 Nov. 2002. *Dictionnaire de l'Académie Française* (1835), 'Pensionnaire', *http://duras.uchicago.edu/cgi-bin/quick_look.new,* last accessed 8 Nov. 2002.

[10] Fitch 'West Riding', *SIC* ix. 281.

principles instilled at home, and to superadd the finished ease and propriety of manner characteristic of an English Lady.[11]

Judging from the frequency with which schools were described as 'exclusive' and 'select', it would seem that this was indeed the key determinant in a parent's choice of school. Writing to a prospective parent in 1878, the proprietor of the Ladies' Collegiate School, Ealing, gave the assurance: 'no tradesmen's daughters in Ealing received'. Cheltenham Ladies' College claimed to be similarly exclusive.[12] Emmeline Pankhurst (née Goulden) clearly felt social considerations were paramount in the choice of her own school, and later identified as the first sign of a feminist consciousness her sense of injustice at the disparity between the long discussions which took place over choosing her brother's place of education, and the manner in which her own school was chosen: 'Beyond the facts that the head mistress was a gentlewoman and that all the pupils of my own class, nobody seemed concerned.'[13]

Evidence from the biographical sample supports the view that the clientele of most boarding-schools was solidly middle class, and that, as the SIC report observed, 'the wealthiest class, as a rule, do not send their daughters to school'.[14] Thirty-four of the fifty-five girls in the sample for whom the information is available (62%) were daughters of professional men, and twelve (22%) were the daughters of businessmen and manufacturers. Only four had fathers with an independent income.

The price of a boarding-school education meant that only the comfortably off could afford it. In Oxfordshire between 1800 and 1810 prices ranged from £16 to about £21 p.a., and in 1810 the Byerley sisters in Warwick were charging £ 31 5s. p.a., plus 'extras'—lessons in dancing and drawing.[15] In the 1850s, a successful London school could charge £ 84 p.a. and in 1865 the average cost of a boarding education in Lancashire was £ 70 p.a.[16] When, according to a *Times* survey from the 1850s, a gentleman could not expect to marry and maintain a gentlemanly style of life with an income of less than £300 p.a., these prices would appear to exclude all but the prosperous middle class.[17] The sample also suggests that fears about social-climbing tradesmen's daughters were not justified. Only five girls (9%) had fathers in lower-middle- or working-class occupations, although sharp 'lines of demarcation' may often have been drawn to distinguish the daughters of professionals from those of

---

[11] Hammond, 'Northumberland', *SIC* viii. 477–8.

[12] M. Wristbridge to Gill, 20 Dec. 1878, LLIB, Gill Collection; Dyhouse, 'Miss Buss and Miss Beale', 32.

[13] E. Pankhurst, [née Goulden] *My own story* (London, 1914), 5. For ease of reference, schoolgirls in the sample will be referred to by the name under which they published, which in most cases was their married name. Their maiden names will be noted in the first reference to them.

[14] 'Report', *SIC* i. 558.   [15] Skedd, 'Education of women', 165–6; Hicks, *Quest*, 13.

[16] Stoddart, *Life*, 66; 'Report', *SIC* i. 558.

[17] J. Burnett, *A history of the cost of living* (London, 1969), 234.

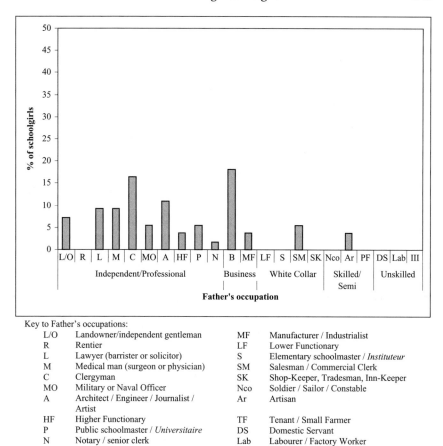

Key to Father's occupations:

L/O	Landowner/independent gentleman	MF	Manufacturer / Industrialist
R	Rentier	LF	Lower Functionary
L	Lawyer (barrister or solicitor)	S	Elementary schoolmaster / *Instituteur*
M	Medical man (surgeon or physician)	SM	Salesman / Commercial Clerk
C	Clergyman	SK	Shop-Keeper, Tradesman, Inn-Keeper
MO	Military or Naval Officer	Nco	Soldier / Sailor / Constable
A	Architect / Engineer / Journalist / Artist	Ar	Artisan
HF	Higher Functionary	TF	Tenant / Small Farmer
P	Public schoolmaster / *Universitaire*	DS	Domestic Servant
N	Notary / senior clerk	Lab	Labourer / Factory Worker
B	Businessman / Merchant	III	Illegitimate

Figure 5.1. The social origin of fifty-five schoolgirls in the English biographical sample of pupils

businessmen, defined as 'trade'. This was clearly how Elizabeth Sewell viewed the distinction. In the 1850s, she wrote to consult parents before agreeing to admit a businessman's daughter, and when the school was rocked by controversy over the girls' illicit reading of passages in Mrs Gaskell's *Cranford*, she promptly expelled the unfortunate girl, blaming herself for having admitted 'trade' to the school.[18]

However, although schoolmistresses like Elizabeth Sewell were clearly catering only for a middle- and upper-middle-class clientele, private schools ranged widely in price and accommodated a broader range of families than figures from the

[18] Fraser, *Diplomatist's wife*, i. 227.

biographical sample might suggest. In 1810, Sarah Bache and her sister offered instruction in basic subjects with history, geography, and literature for £ 1 4s. p.a. for day scholars.[19] In London in the 1860s private girls' schools ranged from expensive establishments charging £ 240 p.a. to day schools charging £ 3 p.a. James Bryce found a similar span in Lancashire.[20] In addition, evidence from the registers of proprietary schools in London reveals that girls were recruited from move diverse backgrounds than the biographical sample suggests, though admittedly these schools were explicitly intended to cater for a broader range of social classes than their private predecessors.[21]

The emphasis placed by parents like the Gouldens on social considerations has been taken as indicative of the lack of serious interest in girls' education. But often the decision to send girls to school, and the choice of establishment, was much more carefully thought over. Mrs Thomas Beddoes visited several schools including the Byerleys' establishment before deciding to send her daughter there in 1812.[22] Elizabeth Gaskell's letters document an intensive search by correspondence to find the right school for each of her daughters. In the 1850s, she sent Marianne to Mrs Lalor's school in London, following an interview with the schoolmistress, because former pupils said that she fostered girls' independence of character and was kind to her pupils, but sent Meta to Rachel Martineau in Liverpool, having 'always felt that hers was the only school that would do for Meta'. Other letters show her discussing the merits of both schools with fellow parents and providing character references for various schoolmistresses of her acquaintance.[23] Before sending her daughters to the Miss Sewells' school in 1862, Mary Fraser's mother also interviewed their future schoolmistress, who visited their home in Italy for that purpose.[24] Such examples point to the considerable care and attention many parents took with their daughters' education, a care not always dictated by the desire to rise up the social scale.

It is difficult to account in more detail for the enthusiasm for female schooling, and it is not clear that attending school would significantly improve a girl's chances of upward marital mobility. Of twenty-five pupils in the English biographical sample who married, only Fanny Kemble, the daughter of an actor, who married an American cotton plantation owner, could be described as having moved up the social scale, and it is not at all clear that it was her education that enabled her to do so. The marriages of other pupils in the sample tend to underline the remarkably endogamous character of the Victorian professional classes. Doctors' daughters married clergymen; clergymen's daughters married doctors or lawyers. Of course

[19] Matthews, *Sarah Bache*, 25.

[20] D. R. Fearon, 'London', *SIC* vii, appendix ix; 'Report', *SIC* i. 58.

[21] Registers for 1865, 1871, NLC.   [22] Hicks, *Quest*, 30.

[23] E. Gaskell to Lady Kay Shuttleworth, 12 Dec. 1850, and E. Gaskell to Marianne Gaskell, 27 Nov. 1852, ed. Chapple and Pollard, *Letters*, 137–40, 214.

[24] Fraser [née Crawford], *Diplomatist's wife*, i. 218.

occupational classification can conceal a considerable variety in income and social status; however, the experiences of the pupils in the biographical sample do not suggest that parents sending their daughters to school could expect them to make socially advantageous marriages as a result.

Pupils' memoirs tend not to elaborate on the reasons they were sent to school. Seven (23%) of those in the sample went away to school after the death of a parent. Caroline Norton was sent to school shortly after her father's early death, but this was in part to improve her character: 'it was perhaps, not so much for education, as for a certain need of discipline that Caroline was sent away from the little circle of home'.[25] However, this is the only mention in the English sample of the 'reform school' justification for school education that appears a number of times in the French biographical sample. The need to educate daughters 'for a governess' was often cited, and, as we have seen, a high proportion of schoolmistresses had spent some time at a boarding-school. Considerations of well-being also seem to have prompted parents to send their children away. Many school prospectuses emphasized the healthy surroundings and fine air of their establishments, and some girls, like Beatrice Webb, who attended Miss Tapp's school in Bournemouth in 1875, were sent to school mainly to improve their health.[26] Fears that foreign climates might have had a bad effect on their children's health also influenced colonial parents. With the expansion of the Empire, a growing number of girls were sent 'home' for their education. Jane Brodbelt was sent to Mrs Fenwick's school in Greenwich from Jamaica in the 1780s and urged by her father to 'stick close to school and apply most diligently to make up your lost time, and don't coax for any holidays from this time to your going home at midsummer'. She learned reading, writing, French, arithmetic, botany, and singing.[27] Clearly, as well as being anxious about his daughter's work ethic, he felt that such instruction was not available in the colonies, a view probably shared by the parents of a girl sent from India to the Miss Franklins' school in Coventry in the 1830s.[28]

Explaining the growth of girls' schooling is further complicated when the importance of home instruction in female education is taken into account. Women's experience of education was very diverse and rarely limited to years of continuous attendance at a single establishment. Of the forty-four pupils in the sample for whom the information is available, thirty-eight (68%) had received some of their education at home. 'Education' was not synonymous with 'schooling'. The five years Bessie Parkes spent at the Miss Fields' school in the 1840s were her only experience of formal instruction, but her education began before her time there. She was also studying Latin and writing abstracts of her

---

[25] J. Perkins, *The life of Mrs Norton* [née Sheridan] (London, 1909), 7.

[26] B. Webb [née Potter], *My apprenticeship* (1926; Cambridge, 1979), 48.

[27] Dr Brodbelt to Jane, Nov. 1789, in G. Mozeley (ed.), *Letters to Jane from Jamaica* (London, 1938), 22.

[28] Dr Brodbelt to Jane, Jan. 1790, ibid. 22. Haight, *George Eliot*, 11.

reading in political economy several years after leaving school.[29] On average the pupils in the sample spent 4.7 years at school.[30] Nonetheless, six (14%) were only at school for a year or less. Similarly, although it was increasingly taken for granted that a period at school was an essential part of the education of middle-class boys, the registers of male establishments suggest that they too might only receive one or two years of formal schooling. Thus the average stay of twenty-eight boarders entering a school in Colchester between 1845 and 1850 was 2.6 years.[31] The brevity of pupils' stays in school has often been taken as a sign of the superficiality of their education; however, attendance at one particular institution could simply be one stage of a much more extended period of instruction, which might involve spells at several different schools. Twenty-two of the girls in the sample (39%) had attended more than one establishment, and this was not considered unusual. In fact, the specialization of establishments into 'preparatory' and 'finishing' schools which was customary in the 1820s indicates the degree to which the practice was an accepted one and suggests that the notion of an 'educational ladder' was current earlier than has often been thought.[32] By the mid-nineteenth century the influence of an Arnoldian conception of the school meant that education was increasingly being assimilated with schooling; however, particularly for women, it was still not necessarily identified with formal instruction at school. Despite this, a schoolgirl like Emily Jones, who attended the Miss Robinsons' school Alston Court for just over a year, could write that, 'it was one of the most telling years of my life'.[33]

Life At School

The studied domesticity of English schools and the absence of formal institutional patterns of schooling mean it is difficult to generalize about school life in England. Descriptions of the daily regime do not feature prominently in the memories of schoolgirls in the sample, suggesting that arrangements were flexible. But even an establishment as small as Elizabeth Sewell's school—which never had more than eight pupils—could not function exactly as a middle-class family. Mary Fraser's memoirs give an idea of the structure of life there in the 1860s. The pupils rose around 7.30 to take their baths before morning prayers. This was followed by breakfast and study until about 8.30. Then came 'hours and hours of lessons of which one hour was always taken for playing in the garden . . . to "freshen" us up'. After dinner, the girls were sent for a two-hour walk, accompanied by

---

[29] Parkes, Autobiographical material, undated; Correspondence with Kate Jeavons, 1846–54, Girton College, GCPP Parkes 1/1–3 and GCPP Parkes 6/49–62.

[30] Standard error of the mean ± 0.4.   [31] Roach, *Secondary education*, 62.

[32] Whittaker, *Boarding schools*, distinguishes between 'finishing', 'preparatory', and 'preparatory and finishing' establishments. Kathryn Hughes notes that governesses might be 'nursery', 'preparatory', or 'finishing governesses': *The Victorian governess* (London, 1993), 60.

[33] E. Jones, *As I remember, an autobiographical ramble* (London, 1922), 35.

a friend, but otherwise alone, returning for tea followed by study until five o'clock. An hour was set aside for 'Evening Toilet' before high tea, which was followed by sketching and reading in the drawing rooms until bed at 9.30.[34] Some of this was unusual. At the Miss Brownings' school in Blackheath in the late 1840s, the Garrett sisters were known as the 'bathing Garretts', because their father insisted they have a bath every week.[35] Nor was dressing for dinner a common practice. Nevertheless, the overall pattern of life at the Miss Sewells' seems to have mirrored that of other schools. At Belvedere House in Bath in the 1790s, the regime differed only in relation to the timing of meals.[36] Supervision, though important, seems often to have been relatively relaxed, and girls were able to leave the establishment and receive visits. Elizabeth Gaskell refers to her daughter's visits to friends and even to her attendance at a ball while at school.[37]

Even if the daily routine was relatively flexible, discipline was often strict and some girls found it hard to adjust to the restrictions of school life. In fact, it was unusual for girls to go for walks alone. Frances Cobbe remembered only a 'dreary hour of walking with our teachers (when we recited our verbs)', and while Bessie Parkes cherished the memory of walks on the moorlands with her governesses, she mentioned that they never made their pupils walk in order of height—implying that such was the more usual practice.[38] The prison metaphor that was common in descriptions of school life in France, as will be seen below, appears in England in connection to this practice. Mildred Ellis, commenting on 'the education of young ladies' for the Central Society of Education, noted that 'the refinements of modern education do not permit . . . spontaneous efforts and generally limit the exercise of young females to a short formal walk in fine weather, coupled two and two like felons, checking every spontaneous effort by the unceasing dullness of school restrictions'.[39]

As well as adjusting to such limits on their physical exertions, pupils also had to accept other kinds of constraints. Mary Fraser recalled that when she first arrived at the Miss Sewells', 'I felt myself in the grasp of discipline so strict that there was no escaping it even in thought, so exacting morally that I was always racing breathlessly to catch up with it, and yet so convincing and admirable that I could not be happy till I had fulfilled its demands'.[40] Frequent reference to the home-like or familial character of girls' schools should not blind us to the strict discipline which might prevail in schools, or, indeed, in

---

[34] Fraser, *Diplomatist's wife*, i. 225.

[35] J. Manton, *Elizabeth Garrett Anderson* (London, 1965), 35.

[36] *Memoirs of Susan Sibbald, 1783–1812* [née Mein], ed. Francis Paget-Hett (London, 1926), 38–45.

[37] *Letters of Elizabeth Gaskell*, ed. Chapple and Pollard, 179–82.

[38] F. Cobbe, *Life of Frances Power Cobbe, by herself*, 2nd edn. (London, 1894), 65; Parkes, Autobiographical material, GCPP Parkes 1/1–3.

[39] M. Ellis, 'Education of young ladies', *Central Society for Education, First Publication* (1838),196.

[40] Fraser, *Diplomatist's wife*, i. 221.

Victorian families.[41] Moreover, discipline was not always so indirectly enforced or as successfully internalized as at the Miss Sewells'. At Richmal Mangnall's school in 1812 Elizabeth Firth recorded seemingly endless incidents that resulted in the 'ladies' being given verses to copy out, being sent to bed, or even being whipped. Punishments were also handed out if the girls failed in their studies; in April 1812 'several of the ladies were sent to bed for losing at spelling'. At Miss Runciman and Miss Roberts' establishment in Brighton, pupils were called together for a weekly 'judgement day' when their misdemeanours (which might include impertinence or a failure to tie one's shoelaces) would be recorded.[42] Many teachers also supervised their pupils' letter-writing and read all incoming correspondence. Jane Brodbelt managed to get round this by making sure her friends only wrote in the holidays.[43]

For some girls the difficulty of adjusting to their new life was such that they became ill. After only a term at school, Theresa Potter collapsed and was brought home.[44] Margaret Nevinson, arriving at school in Oxford in about 1873, felt 'dizzy with bewilderment, that life should have become so unbearable . . . I found myself thrust suddenly amongst strangers in a new environment of girls whom I did not understand, with no liberty nor privacy.'[45] At Christmas she looked so unwell that her father agreed she did not have to return to school. Arriving at school in Clapham in 1872, Alice Whichelo had noted sadly in her diary: 'Came to that dreadful place school very miserable hate it.' A month later she had been removed from the Clapham school and was attending another in Brighton, which she loved.[46] The speed with which Alice was withdrawn suggests that her unhappiness might have been caused by more than schoolgirl bullying; for some unlucky children the difficulty of adjusting to school life were made worse by deliberate cruelty or Spartan conditions. In the 1850s, Alice Ottley and her sisters were removed from one London school because of the teacher's ill treatment of them.[47] Charlotte Brontë's description of the harsh conditions at Lowood School drew on her experiences at the Clergy Daughters' School in Casterton, whose regime Dorothea Beale, when a teacher there, also found objectionable.[48]

Yet the overall picture emerging from the biographical sample suggests that, for many, a period at boarding-school was one of relative freedom, and not

[41] Pollock, *Forgotten children*, ch. 5; J. Tosh, *A man's place: masculinity and the middle-class home in Victorian England* (London, 1999), 89–93.

[42] E. B. Firth, Entry for 12 Apr., Diaries and Travel Journals, 1812–25, Sheffield University Library, MS 58/A–B; Cobbe, *Life*, 62.

[43] Mozeley, *Letters*, 42, 65.

[44] B. Caine, *Destined to be wives: the sisters of Beatrice Webb* (Oxford, 1986), 48.

[45] M. W. Nevinson [née Jones], *Life's fitful fever: a volume of memories* (London, 1926), 21.

[46] Journal entry, 27 Sept., 29 Sept., Alice Whichelo's journal for 1872, King's College, Cambridge, Papers of E. M. Forster, GBR/0272/EMF/21.

[47] James, *Alice Ottley*, 11–12.

[48] Gordon, *Charlotte Brontë*, 15–19; Raikes, *Dorothea Beale*, 36–59.

characterized by constraint and surveillance. In keeping with the domestic atmosphere schoolmistresses sought to accentuate, warm relationships between pupils were often encouraged and pupils had considerable liberty outside lesson times. In many schools, the older pupils would 'mother' younger girls. Jane Brodbelt was 'mother' to her fellow Jamaican, Patty Jones, at Mrs Fenwick's school.[49] At Belvidere House, Susan Sibbald felt great pride in the responsibility, as did Annie Keary at school in the north-east in the 1840s.[50] As a young pupil at Miss Teed's in 1850, Frances Havergal was in awe of the older girls. One in particular was 'the goddess amongst my school friendships . . . and I loved her with a perfectly idolatrous affection,—such as, until that time, I had never given to anyone'.[51] Bessie Parkes established close relationships with many of her schoolfellows, as did Elizabeth Garrett Anderson, who became good friends with the Crow sisters at the Miss Brownings' school. Bessie's correspondence evokes the comfortable intimacy, camaraderie, shared pleasures, and moments of self-discovery of life at school. She refers to birthday celebrations, evenings playing charades, and to times when they 'talked, laughed, acted and screamed'.[52]

Boarding-schools exposed girls to the same group socialization that boys experienced at public schools and colleges. This was perceived as the most important element of their education, whereby young men would 'gain for themselves new ideas and views, fresh matter of thought and distinct principles for judging and acting day by day'—an ideal that seems radical and subversive when applied to girls' education in this period.[53] Miriam Lerenbaum has argued that the conservative bent of authors like Hannah More springs in part from the fact that they had been educated by their fathers at home and missed 'the lively influence of a classroom full of peers, or a young tutor or governess'. As a result, 'they inherit and do not advance beyond the norms and values of the previous generation'.[54] In boarding-schools, however much an ideal of domestic femininity was upheld, there was always more potential for the status quo to be challenged, and schools might provide a kind of collective 'room of one's own' where girls could develop their interests and gain a sense of autonomy. School friendships might even provide an arena for calling accepted notions of women's role into question. Bessie Parkes wrote to Kate Jeavons of her conviction that girls' education must be improved because, she argued, if 'most girls do lead a

[49] *Memoirs of Susan Sibbald*, 84; Mozeley, *Letters,* 48.

[50] *Memoirs of Susan Sibbald*, 84; E. Keary, *Memoir of Annie Keary by her sister* (London, 1882), 50, 56.

[51] M. Havergal, *Memorials of Frances Ridley Havergal* (London, 1880), 33.

[52] Manton, *Elizabeth Garrett Anderson*, 40; Parkes, Autobiographical material, GCPP Parkes 1/1–3; Bessie Parkes to Kate Jeavons, Mar. 1849, GCPP Parkes 6/49–62.

[53] J. H. Newman, *The idea of a university* (1852), Discourse VI, 'Knowledge viewed in relation to learning', s. 9.

[54] M. Lerenbaum, 'Education in the lives and world of late eighteenth century women', *Proceedings of the American Philosophical Society*, 121/4 (1977), 300.

useless life', 'I cannot admit it is a necessary consequence of our state'.[55] Elizabeth Garrett Anderson's friendship with the Crow sisters was one of the pivots of the feminist Langham Place circle. In a less political vein, Annie Keary's friendship with a fellow pupil introduced her to the subject of boys and lovers.[56]

The subversive effects of education in an English boarding-school should not be exaggerated. The recurrent use of images of motherhood by schoolmistresses and the cultivation of a domestic notion of the school served to reinforce a conventional understanding of women's role. There must have been many like Sarah Dendy, who prized the full education they received because 'it made me a better mother to my children than any other training could have done'.[57] Nevertheless, many pupils found that going to school was a distinctive, often liberating experience, and marked a transitional period in their lives. Mary Fraser wrote that 'my childhood came to an end in 1862. The next three years of my life were spent at school.'[58] Frances Havergal was delighted to be going to school in London in 1850, and was told by her sister before she went that, 'I was going to begin a new chapter in my life . . . "One of the great events of your life".'[59] Constance Maynard remembered that 'as I got away to Belstead, a sort of pressure was lifted off me, and I could be myself'.[60] By the 1860s, schoolmistresses and pedagogues were also emphasizing the benefits for girls of spending time at school and associating it with changes in girls' lives. Earlier, different authors had pointed to the physical changes girls went through around the age of 14; the author of *Woman's worth* (1844) described it as 'the seed time', but for Elizabeth Sewell it was also a time of social and psychological development, when pupils must be guided and given responsibilities and freedom in order to train their character.[61] Dorothea Beale spoke of the benefits for girls of spending time at school. There, she argued, they 'do not find their companions ready to bear rudeness and ill-temper; and thus schools exercise a civilizing influence; the character . . . gains in strength and power of discernment, and the sense of responsibility is developed, before the girl is called on to decide the questions of life'.[62]

But the intimacy of life at school was also a source of anxiety. Dorothea Beale worried, like H. M. Bompas, who investigated schools in Wales for the SIC, that one 'flighty girl' could 'infect others and ruin a schoolmistress into the bargain'. The answer, they argued, was either to keep schools small because

---

[55] Bessie Parkes to Kate Jeavons, 24 Jan. 1847, GCPP Parkes 6/49–62.

[56] Keary, *Memoir*, 54.

[57] 'Recollections by Sarah Dendy, née Beard,' in H. MacLachlan, *Records of a family, 1800–1933* (Manchester, 1935), 111.

[58] Fraser, *Diplomatist's wife*, i. 204.   [59] Havergal, *Memorials*, 30.

[60] MS autobiography 47, quoted in D. Gorham, *The Victorian girl and the feminine ideal* (London, 1982), 180.

[61] *Woman's worth or hints to raise the female character* (London, 1844), 162; Sewell, *Principles*, i. 35.

[62] Beale, 'Education of girls', 520.

'they approach more nearly to a home', or to establish day schools where 'indiscriminate association' could principally be avoided by 'strict regulations respecting admission'.[63] The idea that girls at school were in a period of transition between childhood and adult life was gaining ground, as was the view that they would and should draw a new sense of responsibility from the experience of collective life. Unease about the intimacy of life at school, however, was inspired more by concerns about social distinction than by anxieties kindled by developing notions of female adolescence.

BECOMING A SCHOOLGIRL IN FRANCE

Social Origin and Motivations

French boarding-schools for girls catered for a similar clientele to their English counterparts. Detailed information about the social origin of pupils is not often available but it does seem that lay boarding-schools were more likely to cater for middle-class children than for the daughters of noble families. In Paris, for the most part, the daughters of the nobility were sent to convents, of which the Abbaye aux Bois and the Sacré Coeur were the most exclusive; lay schools were generally attended by those lower down the social scale, and shunned by the aristocracy and upper middle classes.[64] Thus, in 1864, the *Recteur* of the Pas de Calais noted that the convent institutions attracted the richer families of the region, whereas smaller lay schools recruited from amongst the children of small merchants and lower functionaries.[65] Similarly, at the end of the century, aristocratic families in Lyon and the Nord eschewed the newly established girls' *lycées*, preferring to send their children to religious institutions. In such families sons too were often sent to religious schools rather than to the *lycées*.[66]

The same conclusion is suggested by the biographical sample of French pupils (see Figure 5.2). Of the thirty-four for whom the information is available, twenty-four (71%) had fathers in professional or business occupations, and only three (9%) had fathers with an independent income. Five (15%) were from lower-middle-class and artisan backgrounds, suggesting that a small but significant number of families from more humble backgrounds were sending their daughters to boarding-school, as contemporaries feared. Nonetheless, twenty-eight (82%) of the pupils in the biographical sample were recruited from middle- and upper-middle-class families. That *pensions* were aimed at this section of

[63] Bompas, 'Glamorgan', *SIC* viii. 40; Beale, 'Education of girls', 520; ibid. 520–1.

[64] Mayeur, *L'éducation*, 38, 78.

[65] Rapport du Recteur du Pas de Calais, 1864, AN, F[17] 6845.

[66] Pellissier, *Vie privée*, 83; Smith, *Ladies*, 184; R. Gildea, 'Education and the *classes moyennes* in the nineteenth century', in D. Baker and P. Harrigan (eds.), *Current directions in the history of education in France, 1679–1979* (Waterloo, 1980), 275–301.

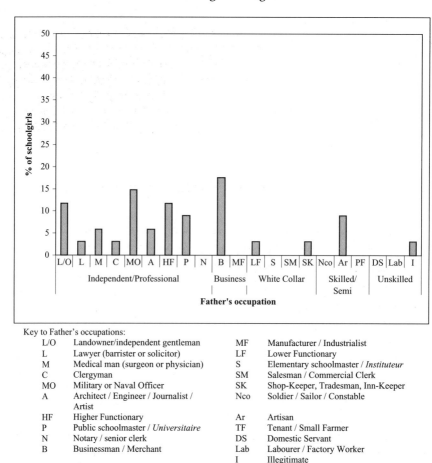

Key to Father's occupations:

L/O	Landowner/independent gentleman	MF	Manufacturer / Industrialist
L	Lawyer (barrister or solicitor)	LF	Lower Functionary
M	Medical man (surgeon or physician)	S	Elementary schoolmaster / *Instituteur*
C	Clergyman	SM	Salesman / Commercial Clerk
MO	Military or Naval Officer	SK	Shop-Keeper, Tradesman, Inn-Keeper
A	Architect / Engineer / Journalist / Artist	Nco	Soldier / Sailor / Constable
HF	Higher Functionary	Ar	Artisan
P	Public schoolmaster / *Universitaire*	TF	Tenant / Small Farmer
N	Notary / senior clerk	DS	Domestic Servant
B	Businessman / Merchant	Lab	Labourer / Factory Worker
		I	Illegitimate

Figure 5.2. The social origin of thirty-four schoolgirls in the French biographical sample of pupils

society is clear from their prices. In 1829, 400F p.a. was considered a 'modest' fee and in the 1860s provincial boarding-schools often cost around 650F p.a.[67] Since the average wage of a male servant in Paris was 720F p.a. in the 1850s, and historians have estimated that an income of at least 2,000F p.a. was necessary to maintain a bourgeois lifestyle in the 1840s, *pension* prices were clearly prohibitive for all but the middle and upper middle classes.[68]

[67] Rapport de Mme la Marquise de Larouzière, Premier arrdt., Paris 1829, AD Seine, VD⁶158–3; Rogers, *From the Salon*, 170.

[68] McBride, *Domestic revolution*, 60; Jardin and Tudescq, *Vie de la nation*, 211.

Yet this picture of solidly bourgeois recruitment requires qualification. As inspection reports reveal, boarding-schools for girls in Paris could be found across the city. This suggests the broad social range in recruitment of such institutions.[69] At the same time, the cost of different institutions varied widely. In the 1840s Mlle Solliers was charging about 700F p.a. at her Parisian school. But in the same period the *Revue de l'Enseignement des Femmes* reported that some establishments in Paris charged as little as 200F p.a. In the 1860s, at Mme Graterolle's *pension* in Bordeaux, where instructions for the boarders' trousseaux indicate clearly that a bourgeois clientele was expected, day girls could attend for 120F p.a.[70]

Although different schools might cater for a broad range of families, within individual institutions there was greater fastidiousness. George Sand reported that as the number of industrialists' children at the Couvent des Anglaises increased, aristocratic families began to send their daughters elsewhere.[71] In her picture of the typical Parisian *pensionnat*, Marie Sincère commented that a schoolmistress would spend much of her time trying to avoid 'Mme X withdrawing her daughter because Mme Y's daughter was at the same school'.[72] The administrative authorities tended to encourage such stratification. Schools like Mlle Chardon's were praised for offering 'solid and simple Christian instruction, exactly appropriate to the social position of the pupils educated there'. By contrast, Mme Fontaine was criticized for providing poor quality and frivolous instruction, all the more damaging because her girls were recruited from the commercial classes.[73] *Pensions* were also segregated in other ways. In Paris in the 1840s, Mme Coulon and Mme d'Ocagne both ran schools for Protestant girls, as did Mme Gerard in Bordeaux and Mlle de Félice in Dunkirk in the 1850s. In the 1860s and 1870s, the Kahn sisters, first Mathilde, then Clara, ran a school for Jewish girls.[74]

Despite this differentiation, there are hints that even within a single establishment pupils might be drawn from a wider range of backgrounds than parents might expect. It is clear from the repeated protests of the inspectresses that in the first decades of the century many girls' schools in Paris accepted both Catholic and Protestant pupils.[75] The social mix might also be more varied. School uniforms—which the administrative authorities in Paris encouraged 'so that in that way at least, there are no differences between those who are rich, and those who are less so'—might have facilitated greater diversity in recruitment, by concealing the

---

[69] See also Rogers, 'Boarding schools', 161.

[70] Prospectus, Mlle Solliers, *c.*1842, AD Seine, VD[6] 158–2; *REF* (Jan. 1846), 7; Prospectus, Mme Léon Graterolle, 1866, AD Gironde, 47 T.

[71] G. Sand (pseud. of Aurore Dudevant, née Dupin), *Histoire de ma vie* (Paris, 1996), 70–80.

[72] Sincère, *Pensionnats*, 50.

[73] Inspection pension Chardon, 1849, AD Seine, VD[6] 184–2; Inspection pension Fontaine, 1852, AD Seine, VD[6] 184–2.

[74] Inspections pensions d'Ocagne, Coulon, 1838, AD Seine, VD[6] 158–3; AD Gironde, 6 T 12. Dossier de Félice, Dunkerque, 1857–8, AD Nord, 1 T 134/1; Déclarations d'ouverture, Kahn, 1869, 1879, AD Seine, DT Supplément/126.

[75] Rapports d'inspection, 1er arrdt., 1812, 1813, 1814, AD Seine, VD[6] 158–3.

obvious material differences between families.[76] Similarly, many schoolmistresses obliged their pupils to refer to each other by a number rather than by name, partly to conceal their family origin—in theory making it possible to draw on pupils from a wide range of backgrounds. Marie Sincère described a typical school visiting day when, despite the sensibilities of Mme X and Mme Y, 'the rich banker's wife rubs shoulders with the little *rentière*, who can save just enough to pay for her daughter's education . . . in another corner, the condescending English woman who is leaving her daughter on the continent for a few years to improve her French pronunciation, parades around'.[77] A rare example of a school register, when matched against local commercial directories, suggests that Sincère's portrayal does have some truth to it. In 1851 Mme Ploux's pupils in Bordeaux included the daughters of the director of the botanical garden and those of a senior government official, but also the daughters of a pin merchant and those of a junior clerk.[78]

It is difficult to uncover the reasoning that prompted parents to choose one school over another. Cost must have been an important factor for some families, but, perhaps not surprisingly, this does not often appear in the memoirs of schoolgirls in the biographical sample. Only Daniel Stern (Marie d'Agoult) refers directly to the social criteria that influenced her Protestant mother's choice—the Sacré Coeur in Paris, deemed to be 'the most "comme il faut" '.[79] Family connections and recommendations were important factors. Louise Ackermann mentions that the school she attended in Paris in the 1830s was headed by the mother of the Abbé Saint-Léon Daubrée, implying that this was a significant consideration in her own mother's choice. Ondine Valmore went to Mme d'Erville's school in Lyon on the recommendation of the family friend Dr Dessaix. Juliette Adam was sent to the school in Chauny where her mother had been a pupil. Similarly, Adèle Riobé's father noted that he and his wife entrusted their daughter 'to the intelligent care of the same lady who had been entrusted with her mother's education'.[80]

In *La femme* Michelet suggested that mothers in thrall to their confessors would insist that their daughters be sent to convent school, and that the choice of religious over lay school was loaded with meaning, as Republican politicians would later also assume.[81] The example of Daniel Stern suggests that this may

---

[76] Règlement concernant les maisons d'éducation de filles dans le département de la Seine, 20 June 1816, AD Seine, VD⁶ 648–1. The injunction was repeated in the ruling of 1821.

[77] Sincère, *Pensionnats*, 50.

[78] Concours 1850–51, AM Bordeaux, Fonds Ploux/6; E. Féret, *Statistique de la Gironde*, 3 vols. (Bordeaux, 1889); *Almanach Général du commerce de Bordeaux et du département de la Gironde* (Bordeaux, 1820).

[79] Daniel Stern (pseud. of Marie d'Agoult, née de Flavigny), *Mes souvenirs, 1806–1833* (Paris, 1877), 152.

[80] L. Ackermann [née Choquet], *Oeuvres de Louise Ackermann: ma vie, premières poésies* (Paris, 1885), iv; Ambrière, *Valmore*, i. 470; J. Adam [née Lamber], *Le roman de mon enfance et de ma jeunesse* (Paris, 1902), 68; Riobé, *Notice*, 17.

[81] J. Michelet, *La femme* (Paris, 1860), 283.

not have been the case. In some regions, like the Haute Savoie, the Corrèze, or the Cantal, where demand for female secondary education was limited and only a religious establishment able to depend on external support could survive, there may have been no choice to make.[82] In areas where there was more diversity, it is clear that boarding-school pupils, like their teachers, moved in and out of religious establishments. Of the thirteen pupils in the sample who had attended more than one school, eight had been sent to a lay and then to a convent school, or vice versa. In the 1810s Amicie Delacoste spent several years at Mlle Midon's school in Le Quesnoy before being sent to the Sacré Coeur establishment in Amiens. Elizabeth de Bonnefonds, who attended the Couvent de St Maur at Montluçon in the 1840s, had first gone to a local lay establishment.[83] In a context where lay schools emulated the model of the convent, and where the education offered to girls, whether in secular establishments or in those run by *congrégations*, was characterized by the importance it attached to religious observance, piety, and religious instruction, the difference between lay and religious schools may not have seemed significant.

In some families, the decision to send a daughter to a convent rather than to a lay school does seem to have been more deliberate, but this was often as much to do with internal family conflicts as with religious or political preference. In the 1850s, Mathilde Shaw was placed by her mother in a succession of convent schools partly in retaliation against her father, from whom Mme Schoebel was estranged.[84] Others may have been attracted by the fact that some convents were able to charge lower fees than their lay counterparts. Overall the biographical sample provides little direct evidence of the increasing dominance of convent schooling highlighted in previous chapters, although it could be argued that the pattern of Amicie Delacoste and Elizabeth de Bonnefonds' education—a short period at a lay school, followed by several years in a convent school—reveals the primacy of religious establishments. Valentine Camecasse recalled that many lay schools in Douai closed in the 1850s because of 'the great vogue for the Dames de Flines' (a local teaching order of nuns).[85] Nonetheless, at least in the first part of the century, there seems to have been less segregation between lay and convent schools than is often assumed; lay boarding-schools and religious establishments were part of the same educational environment.

From the discussion above, it would appear that none of the parents of pupils in the sample selected the school their daughters would attend on the basis of its

---

[82] See the reports on these departments in the Réponses à la circulaire ministérielle du 16 juillet 1864, AN, F^{17} 6843–9.

[83] A. Delacoste [née de Nédonchel], *Souvenirs de la Marquise Delacoste* (Paris, 1886), 60; E. de Bonnefonds, *Mes souvenirs* (Paris, 1869), 51–6.

[84] M. Shaw [née Schoebel], *Illustres et inconnus, souvenirs de ma vie* (Paris, 1906), 29–36 and *passim*.

[85] V. Camecasse [née Luce], *Souvenirs de Mme Camecasse, Douai au XIXe siècle, salons parlementaires sous la IIIe République* (Paris, 1924), 164.

intellectual merit, begging the questions of why girls were sent to school at all and what part it played in their education. Arguments in favour of domestic and maternal education had particular force in France. Authors like Pauline Guizot argued that in order to fulfil their domestic role, girls must be educated at home, and that school instruction was too far removed from their future existence to be of any real benefit.[86] Home instruction was clearly an important feature of girls' educational experience. Nineteen of the forty-two pupils in the study (45%) are recorded as having been taught partly at home, and this is likely to be an underestimate, such experiences being taken for granted and not worthy of note. Élisa Lemonnier, who had first been a day pupil in a Sorèze *pension*, owed most of her education to a cousin, with whom she lived for five years after leaving the school and who 'worked her young cousin harder than she had ever worked previously'.[87]

Despite this, not only were girls' boarding-schools multiplying, but pupils were also spending considerable lengths of time in educational institutions. As noted above, many contemporaries attributed the expansion in female schooling to the pretensions of lower-middle-class parents and the desire for upward social mobility. It seems plausible to suggest that such considerations influenced the decision of Clémence Badère's parents—who ran a hat shop—to send their daughter to boarding-school at Vendôme. When she left school at the age of 18, her education may have been an important factor in her marriage to the son of a *rentier*, who himself was a teacher in the local *lycée*, a match which, she noted, was flattering to her parents.[88] Two other pupils of the twenty-five in the biographical sample who married might also be described as having moved up the social scale through marriage, but for the most part there was considerable continuity between the occupations of fathers and husbands. Social aspirations, however, are not mentioned in the accounts of these, or of other schoolgirls in the sample; instead it would seem that formal instruction was becoming the norm, and that families were sending their daughters to school as a matter of course. In part, they seem to have been building on the eighteenth-century tradition of sending girls to school for one or two years in preparation for First Communion, which in bourgeois families took place between the ages of 10 and 12.[89] Two girls in the sample—Olympe Audouard and Louise Ackermann—mention this as contributing to their parents' decision to send them to school (at the ages of 12 and 10 respectively), and Valentine Camecasse noted that it was after the ceremony that girls at school in Douai usually became half-boarders.[90] None of the other schoolgirls in the sample mentioned First Communion as playing a part in the decision to send them to school. However, most of those in the sample

---

[86] Guizot, *Education domestique*.   [87] Lemonnier [née Grimailh], *Élisa Lemonnier*, 7.

[88] C. Badère [née Delaunay], *Mes mémoires* (Paris, 1886–7), 3–4.

[89] Sonnet, *L'éducation*, 197–9; Levy, *Mères en filles*, 103.

[90] O. Audouard [née Jouval], *Voyage à travers mes souvenirs, ceux que j'ai connus, ce que j'ai vu* (Paris, 1884), 43; Ackermann, *Œuvres*, ii; Camecasse, *Souvenirs*, 162.

started attending school at around the age of 8, and several prepared for the ceremony while at school: it seems likely that the tradition associating a period of schooling with First Communion was a factor in influencing parental decisions.[91]

At the same time school stays were lengthening and pupils were staying on after their Communion. The thirty-two pupils in the sample for whom the information is available spent an average of 5.9 years at school.[92] This was partly an effect of the increasing systematization of school life, accentuated by the incorporation of external examinations into the school curriculum. Describing the education she had received in the 1820s, Julienne Dantier referred to herself as having 'followed the whole course of instruction' at St Denis as if this were exceptional. In 1872, however, in response to a question about 'the time to be spent at school' (itself indicative of a changed attitude to schooling), Mme Deslignières answered that pupils would spend seven years there for a complete education.[93]

Given this apparent trend towards school education as the norm, it seems paradoxical that many pupils' accounts of the start of their school life focus on the exceptional circumstances that led to their being sent away to a *pension*. Nine of the forty-two girls in the study explain the decision to send them to school with reference to family conflicts, six went following the loss of a parent, and nine were sent in order to be educated as a governess.[94] As suggested above, the decision to send Mathilde Shaw to a convent school was related to her parents' disputes. Conflicts of another sort determined Amicie Delacoste's mother to send her to Mlle Midon's school in 1814. Amicie was being bullied by her siblings. George Sand determined to send her daughter Solange to school, exasperated with her indocility and laziness, and fearing that she herself lacked patience as a teacher.[95] Four other girls in the study were apparently sent in order to correct defects in their character. Edmée Capelle was given the somewhat sinister advice that she should dispatch her 11-year-old daughter to St Denis in 1828, 'to curb [her] growing independence under the yoke of boarding-school'. Adeline Lombrail's parents decided to send her to an Ursuline establishment, when she stole some grains of coffee, prompting them to conclude that 'she needed to be constantly watched over, needed pious and intelligent direction'.[96]

It is difficult to resolve the apparent contradiction between the increasing currency of school instruction for girls and these pupils' emphasis on the

---

[91] Of 31 girls, the mean age at the start of school life was 8.6 ± 0.5 (Standard error of the mean); Riobé, *Notice*, 48; Ambrière, *Valmore*, i. 472.

[92] Of 32 girls, the mean number of years spent at school was 5.9 years ± 0.6 (Standard error of the mean).

[93] Julienne Dantier au Ministre de l'Instruction Publique, 25 Apr. 1855, AN, F[17] 20516; Inspection pension St Aubin Deslignières, 8e arrdt., 1872, AD Seine, VD[6]1731–10.

[94] This figure is probably disproportionately high because of the inclusion of future teachers in the sample.

[95] Delacoste, *Souvenirs*, 48; d'Heylli, *Fille de George Sand*, 30.

[96] M. Capelle, *Mémoires de Marie Capelle, Veuve Lafarge, écrits par elle-même* (Paris, 1841–2), i. 34; *Une belle âme: notice et souvenirs de Mlle Adéline Lombrail* (Lille, 1913), 19.

unusual circumstances surrounding the decision to send them to school. Perhaps one way for schoolgirls to reconcile their own experiences with the discourses favouring maternal education was to emphasize the exceptional conditions that led their parents to adopt a different strategy. This dislocation between ideal and practice may also have contributed to another common feature of schoolgirl memoirs—the degree to which the decision to send them to school and their arrival there was described as traumatic. For some unlucky children it was especially devastating because they were not aware of what was to happen. Marie Capelle described how one morning she was taken in her mother's carriage to Saint Denis, 'the great door of the convent closed behind us, and we were received by Mme de Bourgoing, the directress, who kissed me on the forehead and informed me that she had a new daughter and that I would remain with her'. Whilst Mme Capelle talked with Mme de Bourgoing, Marie leant against a window: 'immobile, devastated, I could hear everything and resolved to hide the tears which suffocated me'. Judith Gautier, sent to the convent of Nôtre Dame de la Miséricorde in the 1850s, felt that 'I was betrayed. There was nothing to make me realize what was about to happen to me.'[97]

Even when girls knew that they were going to school, it might be experienced as a punishment. Mme Brada, at school in Paris in the 1850s, wrote that her years at school were 'an exile to which I never became completely accustomed', and on learning that she was to be sent to Amiens, Amicie Delacoste records that she was 'shattered; I loved my family, being separated from them, only to see them very rarely, seemed to me to be barbarous'.[98] On arriving at the school, she fell dangerously ill—a sickness she later attributed to the pain of separation. Valentine Camecasse also became ill on being sent, 'despite my despair at leaving', to convent school in Paris and remained sickly until her return home.[99] While allowing for the hyperbole of hindsight, it seems likely that the trauma evoked in these accounts was genuine and was heightened by the disparity between the rhetoric of maternal education and their experience. Even when becoming a schoolgirl was not so painful, it nonetheless involved a considerable adjustment, as Amicie Delacoste's memoirs testify: 'my independent habits sat ill with the strict discipline of the school . . . I learned to obey and to keep quiet as I must, but I never could do so . . . with good grace.'[100]

Life At School

For many girls adjustment to school life involved a physical transformation. On her arrival at Saint Denis, Marie Capelle was told to change into the uniform black dress, a bonnet, and coarse stockings; 'I closed my eyes so as not to see this

[97] Capelle, *Mémoires*, i. 34; J. Gautier, *Le collier des jours: souvenirs de ma vie* (Paris, 1904), 132.
[98] Brada, *Souvenirs*, 14; Delacoste, *Souvenirs*, 61.   [99] Camecasse, *Souvenirs*, 163.
[100] Delacoste, *Souvenirs*, 62.

lugubrious costume, so different to my little airy dresses of the previous day.'[101] For Juliette Adam, the first sign that she was going to school was when 'my white pinafore was covered over with an ugly black one. It was for school.'[102] Not all *pensions* had uniforms, though even privately-owned provincial establishments exerted some control over what their pupils wore and brought with them to school, stipulating the contents of the 'trousseau' to be prepared.[103] Arriving at school also usually involved being examined in some way and classified. Judith Gautier was questioned by a teacher shortly after her arrival at Nôtre Dame de la Miséricorde in 1854, told she would be in the little girls' class, and given a green belt to wear as a sign of her status, the coloured belts introduced by Mme de Maintenon at Saint-Cyr having been adopted in many nineteenth-century girls' schools.[104] For a new girl, putting on the *ceinture* signalled absorption into the school hierarchy, and the first contact with other pupils.

Having arrived, girls had also to adapt to the daily routine ordained by the *règlements*. Marie Capelle found it hard to adjust to sleeping in a dormitory with two hundred other girls and then being woken up by a signal, and many memoirs of school life give detailed descriptions of early morning procedure.[105] Rising at six or seven in the morning, they would dress in silence, sometimes in a few minutes (the case in many convent schools where vanity was the great bugbear), sometimes with a whole hour for the 'toilette' (as at Ecouen, according to Thérèse Martin).[106] This was usually followed by prayers and an hour of private study, and then the bell would ring for breakfast. As Paule Constant observes, the moment of waking was perhaps the time when the rigour and rules of school life impinged most intensely on the individual, which may explain the clarity with which it is remembered, but it also reflects the regulated and repetitive character the *règlements* conferred on school life in nineteenth-century France.[107] The memoirs of Mme Brada document the rigid school routine at Mme Deslignières', with every moment accounted for. After breakfast, the girls would study until the bell rang for lunch at 12.30. They would eat in silence and then play for an hour in the garden. After four and a half hours of lessons with visiting masters, dinner was served. The girls then had until bedtime (quarter to nine for the eldest) to study or play in the garden. Her description is echoed in many other memoirs of school life.[108]

While following this strict regime, pupils were closely supervised. Prospectuses emphasized that 'supervision of pupils is continual; they are never alone for an instant'. At Mme Villeneuve's school in Paris, school inspectors approvingly

[101] Capelle, *Mémoires*, i. 35.   [102] Adam, *Roman*, 66.
[103] Rapports sur les écoles primaires de filles, 1865, AD Gironde, 6 T 17.
[104] Gautier, *Collier*, 150. See also Brada, *Souvenirs*, 64.   [105] Capelle, *Mémoires*, i. 36.
[106] O. Arnold, *Le corps et l'âme: la vie des religieuses au XIXe siècle* (Paris, 1984).
[107] Constant, *Monde*, 91.
[108] Brada, *Souvenirs*, 32–44; Martin, *Souvenirs d'Ecouen*, 38–40. Riobé, *Notice sur ma fille*, 119–20; Rogers, *Demoiselles*, 50.

noted that a gallery had been specially built in order to facilitate surveillance of the entire school. Other establishments were severely criticized for lax supervision.[109] In many institutions, watchfulness continued even at night and assistants would sleep in the dormitories with their pupils. This was taken as a matter of course by inspectors. This continual supervision points to the widespread suspicion of schoolgirl intimacies, against which other measures were also taken. Pupils were routinely forbidden to walk in groups of less than three. At Mme Ploux's school in Bordeaux the rules stipulated not only that girls should not 'tutoie' each other because 'it engenders a kind of trivial familiarity' but also that special authorization was required for any activity involving fewer than three girls. Girls at Mme Deslignières' establishment were supposed only to refer to one another by number.[110] As we have seen, this was in part a means of avoiding parental upset over the social diversity of schools, but it was also intended to avoid excessive closeness between the girls.[111]

As one guide for schoolgirls' confessions suggested, such closeness might distract pupils from their duties, and must be offered up in the confessional as a sin to be forgiven, an approach that highlights the importance of the moral and religious curriculum in girls' schools.[112] *Le petit manuel de la pieuse pensionnaire* (1836) suggested that its readers adopt a personal *règlement* for the year: 'I will not forget that I have come to school only to acquire, alongside the habit of politeness and manners, a solid virtue and knowledge appropriate to my station. My first objective will be to study my faults in order to conquer them. As well as the study of religion, which is the most necessary, I will give equal attention to my studies and to needlework.'[113] Injunctions intended to discourage pupils from spending too much time on their friendships reflected efforts to encourage pupils to police their own affections and conscience, perceived as the primary lesson to be learned at school.

Continual supervision and self-surveillance were reinforced by the physical restrictions of the schoolgirl's environment. Lay boarding-schools sought to emulate the enclosure of convent schools, and the powerful image of 'les murs de la pension' and references to imprisonment, which appear repeatedly in autobiographical accounts, suggest the very real sense of seclusion many schoolgirls experienced. Mme Brada's abiding memory of school was of the

---

[109] Prospectus in *REF* 1 (Jan. 1846), 7; Inspection pension Villeneuve, 1838, AD Seine, VD[6] 158–3; Rapport sur l'enseignement primaire des filles dans l'arrdt. de Bordeaux, 1849–50, AD Gironde, 6 T 12.

[110] Règlements, 1840–50, AM Bordeaux, Fonds Ploux/8; Brada, *Souvenirs*, 55.

[111] Despite this, in some schools, girls were encouraged to 'mother' younger pupils; however, the fact that this is not mentioned by the schoolgirls in the sample suggests that in practice such ties did not develop into close relationships, perhaps hindered by the more general constraints on friendship between pupils. Sincère, *Pensionnats*, 63; Rogers, *Demoiselles*, 49.

[112] *Examen de conscience d'une pensionnaire, à l'usage des maisons d'éducation* (Paris, 1825), 1838.

[113] *Le petit manuel de la pieuse pensionnaire, ou recueil de réflexions, prières et pratiques de piété à l'usage de la jeunesse Chrétienne* (Paris, 1836), 38. It was in its third edition by 1842.

'unbreachable solidity' of the wall surrounding it. Judith Gautier spent much of her first few days at Nôtre Dame de la Miséricorde planning her escape over the wall of the dark internal courtyard where the girls played. Juliette Adam compared her arrival at school in Chauny to that of an inmate being admitted to prison and recalled the clang of the door behind her. Pauline Kergomard referred to her time at school in Orthez as 'three years of penal servitude'.[114] The result of the inescapable regime and this seclusion was that school life was often profoundly monotonous. Even Adèle Riobé, a happy and willing pupil at Mme B's school in La Flèche in the 1850s, complained to her diary of 'the uniformity of school life', and at her pension in Saint Sorruin, Elizabeth de Bonnefonds remembered that 'many days, and even years passed without anything disturbing the monotony of my schoolgirl life'. Many pupils found this hard to accept. Olympe Audouard noted that 'young girls often suffer from their isolation, and sometimes, they don't hide their unhappiness and protest at their captivity'.[115]

Yet life in French boarding-schools was not always experienced as monotonous and constrained. While she drew attention to the unhappiness of some girls at school, Olympe Audouard also emphasized the 'calm and sepulchral peace' of her convent school, 'a peace which had a definite attraction'.[116] Some literally took refuge at school. In 1839, a Mlle Cabrespine escaped from her mother and an unwelcome marriage proposal by hiding in Mme Colon's establishment in Saint-Denis.[117] For others, being sent away to school provided a welcome opportunity to study. At her *pension* in Paris, where the professor of literature encouraged her to read and write poetry, Louise Ackermann discovered a new freedom, away from her mother's concerns about her reading.[118] In addition, even in the face of continual supervision, rules were transgressed and friendships forged.

Evidence from *règlements*, inspection reports, and memoirs suggests that rules were not always sufficient deterrent against rebellious behaviour. The regulations governing Mme Ploux's school hint at the lack of restraint schoolgirls might demonstrate in practice: 'The recreation period must not be too noisy . . . games which involve chasing one another and races are absolutely forbidden'.[119] At Mme Achet's in about 1845, one pupil climbed out of the window and went for a walk on the roof, as did Fanny Kemble whilst at Mme Faudier's school in Boulogne.[120] Adèle Riobé and her friends even challenged the authority of their

---

[114] Brada, *Souvenirs*, 15; Gautier, *Collier*, 230; Adam, *Roman*, 68; 'Trois ans de bagne', Pauline Kergomard [née Reclus], quoted in F. Rosenzweig, 'Pauline Kergomard, née Reclus (1838–1925) ou comment devient-on républicaine?', in Corbin *et al.* (eds.), *Femmes dans la cité*, 185.

[115] Riobé, *Notice*, 81; Bonnefonds, *Souvenirs*, 54; Audouard, *Voyage*, 168.

[116] Audouard, *Voyage*, 43.   [117] Dossier Colon, 1839, AN, F[17] 12433.

[118] Ackermann, *Œuvres*, p. v.   [119] Règlements, 1840–50, AM Bordeaux, Fonds Ploux/8.

[120] Inspection pension Achet, 1845–7, AD Seine, VD[6] 158–3. Fanny had climbed out of the garret where she was locked as punishment for another offence. F. Kemble, *Records of a girlhood* (London, 1878), i. 43. Interestingly, Colette Cosnier identifies 'the girl on the roof' as a literary trope associated with women who sought to transcend gender boundaries. C. Cosnier, *Le silence des femmes* (Paris, 2001), 13.

schoolmistress, putting together a petition to ask for an extra day's holiday—an interesting demonstration of girls' political awareness in the 1850s.[121] In 1848, Juliette Adam also brought a political element to life at school. Influenced by her Republican father, she organized an *atelier national*, a scheme to create jobs for unemployed workers at Mme André's pension. She was expelled as a result, having already been warned not to talk of politics in the school—a warning which reveals the extent to which girls' schools sought to separate themselves from the world beyond the school walls.[122] Henriette Picanon remembered a similar spirit of insubordination; at her school in the 1840s each generation of pupils passed on satirical comments about their teachers, shared transgressions promoting a subversive sense of community.[123] Similarly, the diaries of Eugénie Servant reveal that friendships were strengthened as girls devised means to get around the rules that governed school life, fostering a subculture that paralleled and sometimes reinforced the official school community.[124] Despite the theoretical restrictions on pupils' freedoms, despite the impressive authority of French schoolmistresses, friendships did flourish and schoolgirls sought to expand the boundaries within which they were expected to live.

At the same time, pupils like Adèle Riobé and Hermance Mésiasse cherished their school friendships and returned to revisit the institutions they had attended, seeing them as the site of former happiness. After leaving school, Adèle Riobé invited former schoolfellows to visit: 'we recalled together the thousand little incidents which are big events in the lives of schoolgirls, the times when we tortured our teachers by getting the giggles, our little disobediences which we thought of then as courageous actions, challenging our dependence'.[125] Like her, many schoolgirls shared the view that friendships established at school had a special character, and school friendships loomed large in the gradually evolving stereotype of *la pensionnaire*. To Pauline Guizot, life at school was characterized by the 'little interests, little intrigues, little mysteries' of schoolgirl intimacies.[126] Marie Sincère took a more positive view, suggesting that at school girls developed disinterested friendships and free exchanges where 'differences in rank and fortune are not taken into account, it is qualities of character which are sought out'.[127] Such impressions contributed to the idea that school was a distinctive experience in a young woman's life.

Looking back, some schoolgirls also associated the time they spent at school with a particular phase in their development. Valentine Camecasse noted that being sent to school corresponded with 'the ungrateful age' when a young girl was not supposed to be seen in public.[128] Her account, written in 1924, unconsciously quotes the phrase first used by Bishop Dupanloup to refer to the

121 Riobé, *Notice*, 179.   122 Adam, *Roman*, 282, 302.
123 Picanon (née Berthoud), *Mon frère*, 12.   124 Rogers, 'Schools, discipline'.
125 Riobé, *Notice*, 179; *Nôtre ange gardien: souvenirs intimes* (Paris, 1891), 23.
126 Guizot, *Education domestique*, 20.   127 Sincère, *Femme*, 90.
128 Camecasse, *Souvenirs*, 164.

period between childhood and adulthood. Dupanloup was amongst the first to identify this interval as a phase of psychological as well as physical development for girls.[129] But the notion that the period between the ages of 12 and 16 was a distinct phase in a girl's life was already well established. In the 1820s and 1830s girls of school age were described as being 'in a chrysalid state' by one doctor, and pedagogues like Mme Carroy sought to design courses responding to the particular needs of adolescent girls.[130] This sense of the period of school life as a liminal stage was probably heightened by the association between schooling and First Communion, often seen, in the words of the Comtesse d'Armaillé, as 'the transition between childhood and youth' and a dramatic experience for many young French women.[131] With girls spending longer at school, this transitional stage was increasingly associated with school life, reflecting and reinforcing a notion of female adolescence that would be more fully elaborated in the second half of the century.[132]

Clearly there was often a considerable discontinuity between the notion of education for innocence and piety articulated by Catholic educators and transmitted to pupils through guides like the *Petit manuel de la pieuse pensionnaire*, and what girls actually learnt and did at school.[133] Yet evidence from the biographical sample does uncover a dominant atmosphere of restraint and containment. The nineteenth century saw the elaboration of a new and positive ideal of Catholic femininity, the 'femme forte'. But older, more negative images also persisted, emphasizing female sexuality, linking women to Eve and the Fall, and generating fears that women were especially susceptible to corruption.[134] The restrictions on girls' intimacy, the rules that governed their every move, and the walls that contained them, reflect the endurance of the institutional model inherited from the *Ancien Régime*. They also reveal the enduring influence of fears of female disorder and unruly sexuality. As the period spent at school came increasingly to be identified with a transitional and unstable phase in girls' development, such fears were heightened. The force of this complex interaction

---

[129] Thiercé, *Adolescence*, 13.

[130] A. M. Bureaud-Riofrey, *Education physique des jeunes filles, ou l'hygiène de la femme avant le mariage* (Paris, 1835), 20–1; Mme Carroy, *Étude et récréation, ou l'intérieur d'un pensionnat: ouvrage divisé en 30 journées, contenant plusieurs histoires morale et instructives, dédié aux jeunes demoiselles* (Paris, 1825).

[131] Comtesse d'Armaillé, *Quand on savait vivre heureux (1830–60): souvenirs de jeunesse* (Paris, 1931), 57; Lévy, *De mère*, 103; Caspard, 'Les trois âges de la première communion en Suisse', in J.-P. Bardet, J.-N. Luc, I. Robin-Romero, and C. Rollet (eds.), *Lorsque l'enfant grandit* (Paris, 2003), 173–83. See the accounts of First Communion in P. Lejeune, *Le moi des demoiselles: enquête sur le journal de jeune fille* (Paris, 1993).

[132] Thiercé, *Adolescence*, 117–24; K. Alaimo, 'Adolescence, gender, and class in education reform in France: the development of Enseignement Primaire Supérieur, 1880–1910', *French Historical Studies*, 18 (1994), 1025–55.

[133] Smith, *Ladies*, 174; G. Houbre, *La discipline de l'amour: l'éducation sentimentale des filles et des garçons à l'âge du romantisme* (Paris, 1997), ch. 4.

[134] Mills, 'Women', ch. 2.

of influences and anxieties even beyond the Catholic community is apparent in the memoirs of Henriette Picanon, who attended Mme Dupuy's Protestant institution in Sainte-Foy in the 1840s. She longed for the holidays, 'when each and every hour was not mercilessly planned ahead of time' and felt that, 'shut up behind the school walls', she knew little of the world.[135]

The clientele of female boarding-schools was broadly similar on either side of the Channel. They catered mainly for the middle and upper middle classes, but might also offer a 'secondary' education to the children of shopkeepers and artisans whose experiences are less often recorded in biographies and memoirs. The proportion of an average middle-class income that would be spent on school fees was roughly the same in England and France.[136] In both countries, the decision to send girls to school was more complex than the focus on social emulation and distinction suggests. It is difficult to discover the reasons why parents chose to send their daughters to school. However, evidence from the biographical samples points to the way in which it might be used as a strategy to deal with the loss of a parent, or with conflicts at home, or, in the case of those 'educated for a governess', as a means of seeking to provide for an uncertain future. For some, especially in France, school was seen as a way of curbing a rebellious disposition. In both countries, however, there are signs that formal instruction at school was increasingly a normal feature of girls' education. In turn, this both reflected and reinforced the notion that the period girls spent at school corresponded to a particular phase in their development.[137]

There were, however, significant differences between the experiences of girls at school in the two countries. French pupils seem more often to have found the moment of being sent away to school a traumatic one, and to have had greater difficulty in adjusting to the constraints of institutional life. The metaphor of the school as prison or the *lycée-caserne* was a powerful literary trope in the nineteenth century, and may have coloured retrospective accounts of school life, exaggerating the sense of imprisonment and monotony.[138] In the absence of counter-narratives, however, it seems plausible to suggest that schoolgirls' emphasis on 'the school walls' does reflect the restrictive and monotonous character of school life in

---

[135] Picanon, *Mon frère*, 60.

[136] Precise figures are difficult to come by, but the fees—including board, lodging, and extra tuition—for schools at the higher end of the scale would have represented 28—34% of the annual revenues of families living on £ 300 or 2,000F p.a., the minimum amount on which it is calculated a middle-class life could be maintained in the 1840s and 1850s. On middle-class incomes, see J. Burnett, *A history of the cost of living* (Harmondsworth, 1969), 234; Tudescq and Jardin, *Vie de la nation*, 111.

[137] In the English sample, girls spent on average 4.7 years at school, $\pm$ 0.4 (Standard error of the mean). In France the average was 6 years $\pm$ 0.6. However this difference is not statistically significant ($P > 0.05$, $t = 1.4$, $df = 47$).

[138] J. C. Caron, *A l'école de la violence* (Paris, 1999), 11–19; R. Lloyd, *The land of lost content: children and childhood in late nineteenth century French literature* (Oxford, 1992), 208–22.

France. Their days were more strictly regulated and their activities more closely supervised than those of their English counterparts.[139] This is not to say that French schoolgirls were all models of innocence and piety. On the contrary, they found ways to rebel against, and remake, the rules under which they lived. In England, girls seem more often to have found school life to be rewarding and sometimes liberating. Though discipline could be strict, the informality that characterized the domestic model of school seems to have tempered the seclusion and constraints of school life. At the same time, schoolmistresses like Dorothea Beale and Elizabeth Sewell were emphasizing the benefits of group socialization and stressing that girls needed to develop a sense of independent responsibility.

These differences reveal a contrasting response to anxieties about social mobility. In France, the close supervision and limits on friendship were partly motivated by the desire to contain the potential for social mixing inherent in a large school. In England, the response was to keep schools small, exclusive, and familial, or to establish day schools where opportunities for inappropriate friendships would be more limited. Such contrasts also reflect distinctions between the formal institutional model adopted in France and the domestic pattern followed in England. More significantly, however, they point to the fundamental difference between a conception of the school associated with Catholic pedagogues and practice which stressed the need to, in the words of Mme de Maintenon, 'preserve pupils from the corruption of the secular world', and one associated with Protestant educators which insisted, as Dorothea Beale put it, that 'seclusion from evil is impossible, but we can strengthen the patient to resist it'.[140] This difference is echoed in recent studies of the sentimental and social education of Protestant girls in England and that of Catholic girls in France. Research by Gabrielle Houbre and Céline Grasser suggests that whereas the socialization of Protestant girls was shaped by the idea of 'self-government', that of Catholic girls was much more focused on the notion of preserving innocence and developing a kind of sensual personal piety.[141]

Differences in the conception of education and schooling had an impact on the shape of girls' lives. Although there was no significant disparity between the time girls spent at school in France and England, French girls were more likely to spend long stretches in a single institution, reflecting the importance attached

---

[139] As will be seen in Chapter 7, visitors from England often commented on the way French girls were continually supervised, even within the family.

[140] Maintenon, *Entretiens*, 39; D. Beale, 'Introduction', in D. Beale and Lucy Soulsby, *Work and play in girls' schools* (London, 1898), 4.

[141] G. Houbre, 'Les influences religieuses sur l'éducation sentimentale des jeunes filles dans la première moitié du XIXe siècle', in *Foi, fidelité, amitié en Europe à la période moderne* (Tours, 1995), ii. 341–54; G. Houbre, 'Demoiselles Catholiques et misses Protestantes: deux modèles éducatifs antagonistes au XIXe siècle', *Bulletin de la société pour l'histoire du Protestantisme français*, 146 (2000), 49–68; Céline Grasser, 'Jeune fille en fleur contre good girls: la construction d'identités féminines bourgeoises au jardin, France et Angleterre, 1820–70', in J.-P. Bardet *et al.*, *L'enfant grandit*, 257–69.

to enclosure and seclusion. Among the thirty-two girls in the English sample who spent more than three years in school education, the average number of institutions they attended was 2.0; among the twenty-eight French girls spending more than three years at school, the average number of institutions attended was 1.4. The difference seems small, but is statistically significant.[142] It seems plausible to suggest that educational practices which meant that French girls were likely to spend the whole of their teenage years in a single institution—often arriving just before the defining moment of First Communion—may help to explain why female adolescence was more clearly defined in France than in England.

Thus, in France, the idea that girls between the ages of 12 and 16 were in a particular transitional phase, and one intimately connected with their sexual and reproductive role, seems to have been a theme in writing about girls' education from the beginning of the century. In the 1830s, Dr Bureaud-Riofrey would describe this phase as the moment when 'the young girl carefully envelops herself within her modesty . . . she can now become a mother'.[143] In England, the notion of girls going through a distinct phase does not emerge so clearly from educational treatises before the 1860s, and when the idea of female adolescence was being more clearly defined in the second part of the century, emphasis seems often to have been placed on girls' new duties and responsibilities, and their sexual development underplayed.[144]

Contrasts between English and French perceptions of adolescence, and differences between the experience of school life in the two countries, were heightened by disparities between French and English understandings of femininity, which also point to the impact of confessional difference on women's experiences. The suspicion of female intimacy and autonomy that characterized many French girls' schools points to an anxiety about female susceptibility and sexuality that was fuelled by the endurance in Catholic thought of a conception of womanhood emphasizing weakness and corruptibility. The survival of these ideas in France contrasted with the situation in England. There, Protestant emphasis on the home as a sanctuary meant that the idea that women were endowed with a superior morality had more fully supplanted earlier negative views of women, and had fostered a desexualized conception of femininity.[145] Significantly, the English edition of Bureaud-Riofrey's treatise on female adolescence omits the

---

[142] English girls spending more than three years at school attended an average of 2.0 establishments, $\pm$ 0.2 (Standard error of the mean). French girls spending more than three years at school attended an average of 1.4 establishments, $\pm$ 0.1 (Standard error of the mean). The average number of schools attended by English girls who spent more than three years in school education was significantly larger than the average number attended by their French counterparts ($P < 0.05$, Unpaired t-test, $t = 2.7$, $df = 47$).

[143] Bureaud-Riofrey, *Education*, 313.

[144] Gorham, *Victorian girl*, 86–108; Dyhouse, *Girls*, ch. 4.

[145] Mills, 'Women and Catholicism', notes the endurance of ideas of female corruptibility in nineteenth-century Catholic thought, alongside a new subtext of female moral superiority; see also Corrado-Pope, 'Angels in the devil's workshop', 312.

chapters on puberty and menstruation that frame the discussion of physical training in the French edition.[146]

The greater degree of surveillance of girls at school in France was thus partly a response a sexualized conception of female adolescence, reflecting the enduring influence of images of dangerous female sexuality. In England, notions of womanhood that played down sexuality and the more diffuse conception of the unstable period of adolescence underpinned the freedom some girls discovered at school. But on both sides of the Channel, schoolgirls were negotiating the gaps between the models that were prescribed for them, and the reality of their experiences. In the process, they were contributing to the construction of new understandings of girlhood. At the same time, through the friendships they formed, and the rebellions they participated in, they were claiming and carving out opportunities for female autonomy and self-determination.

[146] Bureaud-Riofrey, *Physical education; specially adapted to young ladies* (London, 1838).

6

Lessons and Learning

The instruction offered in girls' schools in early nineteenth-century England and France has rarely had a good press. The SIC criticized the teaching in girls' schools for its 'want of thoroughness and foundation, want of system; slovenliness and showy superficiality; inattention to rudiments; undue time given to accomplishments, and those not taught intelligently or in any scientific manner; want of organization'. Similar complaints could be made about many boys' schools, but the Commissioners felt nonetheless that 'on the whole, the evidence is clear that, not as they might be but as they are, the girls' schools are inferior'.[1] In France, Jules Simon made similar criticisms: 'Girls, even in the best boarding schools, receive a futile, incomplete education, entirely taken up with accomplishments, including nothing serious or edifying.'[2] This picture has been reinforced by the memoirs of prominent figures like Frances Power Cobbe and George Sand, both very critical of the instruction they had received.[3]

Closer attention, however, reveals a more complex picture of girls' instruction before 1867. The SIC, working with an Arnoldian conception of liberal education, were likely to disapprove of a pattern of instruction that was not centred on Classics, and worked with gendered notions of intelligence, 'superficiality' and 'thoroughness'.[4] Nor should Jules Simon's remarks be taken at face value. In condemning girls' schooling in the 1860s, he and fellow-critics were seeking to discredit the dominant patterns of Catholic education, thus justifying the creation of a new Republican system of female education.

In France, the period 1800–67 saw a broadening of the curriculum of most girls' schools. Reflecting and reinforcing this evolution, external examinations—in the shape of the teaching diplomas, which were used as a kind of school-leaving certificate—were incorporated into school life, helping to standardize curricula between schools. In England, there was greater diversity

---

[1] 'Report', *SIC* i. 548–9; Kamm, *Hope deferred*, 141–66; Gorham, *Victorian girl*, 22–4; Mayeur, *L'éducation*, 61–5.

[2] Jules Simon, speech to the Corps Législatif, 2 Mar. 1867, Buisson (ed.), *Dictionnaire*, 1022–3.

[3] Cobbe, *Life*, 63; Sand, *Histoire de ma vie*, 191.

[4] M. Cohen, 'Language and meaning in a documentary source: girls' curriculum from the late eighteenth century to the Schools Inquiry Commission, 1868', *History of Education*, 34 (2005), 77–93; '"A habit of healthy idleness": boys' underachievement in historical perspective', in D. Epstein and J. Elwood (eds.), *Failing boys? Issues in gender and achievement* (Milton Keynes, 1998), 19–32.

between schools, but the period also saw a gradual extension of the female curriculum. By the 1860s some schools were presenting candidates for external examinations, further stimulating processes of classification and standardization already well under way in France. The more extensive curricula adopted in boys' public schools and *lycées* in the second half of the nineteenth century were closer to the course of instruction developed earlier in female establishments than to the narrowly classical curricula of earlier boys' schools, a fact which undermines the common equation of 'masculinization' of the curriculum with progress.[5]

LESSONS AND LEARNING IN ENGLAND

The Location and Organization of Learning

The domestic character and familial atmosphere cultivated in their schools by English schoolmistresses extended to the schoolroom. Many girls would have found, like Alice Whichelo, that 'the schoolroom is just like a drawing room'.[6] This influenced and reflected teaching arrangements, as is clear from surviving images of schoolrooms. At Campden House School in Kensington in the 1840s, lessons took place in 'the carved schoolroom'. A lithograph depicting the schoolroom suggests that there was no formal division into classes or uniform teaching (Illustration. 5).[7] The pupils are dotted around the room, some in small groups apparently focused on a teacher. To the far left, a small girl reads to an elderly schoolmistress. In the centre, the teacher's attention is focused on one pupil who is showing a bird in a cage to the other pupils. They, like their teacher, have put aside their books to watch. To the far right, two girls are presenting their drawings to another teacher. Other pupils sit reading or drawing on their own.

This image echoes schoolgirl descriptions of lesson time. Elizabeth Lachlan, a pupil at Miss Shepherd's school in about 1805, remembered how, 'after breakfast, we who learned drawing and music, were summoned to one of the principal apartments. Our masters and attendants waited to receive us. Nearly twenty girls . . . sat round a large table drawing, and one, by turns, moved to receive her lesson on the pianoforte.'[8] At the Misses Runciman and Roberts' school in Brighton in the late 1830s, there were two schoolrooms, but a similar system applied. 'Four pianos might be heard going at once in rooms above and around us, while at numerous tables scattered about the rooms there were

[5] Marjorie Theobald makes a similar point about Australia: 'The sin of Laura: the meaning of culture in the education of nineteenth century women', *Journal of the Canadian Historical Association*, 1 (1990), 257–73.

[6] Journal entry, 5 Nov. 1872, Alice Whichelo's journal for 1872, King's College, Cambridge, Papers of E. M. Forster, GBR/0272/EMF/21/1.

[7] The lithograph is not dated. However, the pupils' dress suggests the late 1830s or 1840s.

[8] E. Lachlan (née Appleton), *Jehovh-jireh: or the provisions of a faithful god* (London, 1850), 28.

Illustration 5. *Interior of the carved schoolroom of Great Campden House, Kensington*, C. J. Richardson (*c*.1840); reproduced by permission of the Royal Borough of Kensington & Chelsea Libraries and Arts Service.

girls reading aloud to the governesses and reciting lessons in English, French, German and Italian . . . In the midst of the uproar we were obliged to write our exercises, to compose our themes, and to commit to memory whole pages of prose.'[9] Rather than addressing a group, teachers would 'hear' pupils 'say' their lessons individually, the girls having studied alone with their textbooks. In some establishments, the schoolroom was more formally arranged, but the same system applied. At the Miss Lees' school in Bath, where Susan Sibbald was a pupil from 1797 to 1800, the pupils sat on rows of forms, but were called up individually by the teacher.[10] Perhaps it is to be expected that schoolmistresses, who had often previously worked as private governesses, would adopt such an approach, but this method—known as the 'individual method'—was also the norm in both elementary and boys' public schools in the first part of the nineteenth century.[11]

By the 1840s, however, 'simultaneous instruction' (meaning the instruction of groups of children at once) was being introduced in elementary schools, and in the 1860s the term was increasingly used to mean 'class instruction' (meaning that the group was restricted to a class of pupils defined by the standard they had reached).[12] In public schools, group teaching was also taking over and the individual approach condemned as an inefficient waste of resources.[13] The SIC agreed with James Bryce that 'though sometimes successful, this "individual" teaching was more often a failure' and portrayed it as a sign of backwardness and incompetence, particularly in the case of girls' schools, where the individual approach was most commonly found.[14] Yet informal classroom organization was often cultivated in the domestic model of school. Moreover, many private schools maintained that they had adopted individual methods for pedagogical purposes, a claim that fits well with the interest in child-centred methods of teaching expressed by influential schoolmistresses.[15] The SIC report suggests that there were many schools where the use of individual methods was as chaotic as at the Misses Runciman and Roberts' in Brighton. But this should not obscure the ways in which some teachers were building on them to develop innovative pedagogical strategies.

The issue of individual versus collective instruction in girls' schools is further complicated by the fact that though schoolmistresses tended to use individual methods, this does not seem to have been the approach adopted by the male visiting masters who taught in many girls' schools.[16] At Brook House in the 1860s the masters who taught Latin, English, history, zoology, and modern languages gave only 'lecture lessons'. The schoolmistress and her assistants would

---

[9] Cobbe, *Life*, 61.   [10] *Memoirs of Susan Sibbald*, 36.   [11] Bamford, *Rise*, 60–1.

[12] B. Simon, 'Classification and streaming: a study of grouping in English schools, 1860–1960' (1967), reproduced in *Intelligence, psychology and education* (London, 1971) 203; G. Sutherland, *Ability, merit and measurement: mental testing and English education, 1800–1940* (Oxford, 1984), ch. 1.

[13] M. Seaborne, *The English school: its architecture and organisation, 1370–1870* (London, 1971), ch. 11.

[14] 'Report', *SIC* i. 290.   [15] See ch. 1; 'Report', *SIC* i. 289.

[16] Twenty-seven of the schools whose curricula are analysed below employed visiting masters.

prepare each pupil for these joint classes.[17] D. R. Fearon found this 'combined' system in use at thirty-nine of sixty London establishments he investigated for the SIC.[18] Fearon felt that the 'combined system' was the best system for teaching girls, sharing F. D. Maurice's view that 'formal, methodical male instruction' was essential for girls. Whereas women teachers provided attention to detail, without male professors, girls would never learn 'the habit of referring all particular cases to some principle'.[19] While Maurice believed that male and female intelligence was complementary, the upshot of his recommendations was to rationalize a kind of sexual division of labour. It was a system under which the German mistress at Brook House chafed, complaining that she spent her time 'grinding' the pupils at grammar before the masters' weekly visits.[20]

Notwithstanding such complaints, evidence from schoolgirl memoirs suggests that in practice the distinction between male and female teachers was not always neatly hierarchical. In many schools visiting masters were only responsible for teaching 'extras', subjects outside the central course of instruction, usually including music, dance, drawing, and occasionally writing and modern languages. Some schoolmistresses sought not to employ masters at all, extending their own studies in order to extend the curriculum.[21] By the 1820s, women were teaching many subjects which, in the eighteenth century, might have been thought of as a male preserve.[22] In the 1860s, at the Miss Robinsons' school in Cheltenham, Miss Catherine was responsible for instruction in Latin, Greek, and Euclid.[23] Even where male masters taught 'solid' subjects, their role was limited. Simply in terms of time, schoolmistresses had the advantage over visiting professors, who only appeared for one or two hours a week. Schoolgirl memories also hint at a somewhat different balance of power. Lawrencina Potter, at school in London in the 1860s, was bored by history lessons with Mr Graham, who dictated notes for an hour a week which his pupils were expected to learn, but drew inspiration from reading Macaulay with one of the schoolmistresses.[24] Though the difference between the lecture system, apparently used by many male visiting professors, and the individual methods used by resident women teachers seems to underline a difference in status between male and female teachers, and between male and female knowledge, evidence from inside schools suggests that in practice the contrast was less marked than might be assumed.

Loose forms of classification had been developing in boys' schools. By the end of the eighteenth century, boys at public schools usually moved through

---

[17] Herford, *In Memoriam*, 112, 117.   [18] Fearon, 'London', *SIC* vii. 407–8, 554–66.

[19] F. D. Maurice, 'What better provision ought to be made for the education of girls of the upper and middle classes?', *Transactions of the National Association for the Promotion of Social Science* (1865), 268–74.

[20] Herford, *In Memoriam*, 112, 58.

[21] Gordon, *Charlotte Brontë*, 36–67; Maria Byerley to Josiah Wedgwood II, 18º Jan. 1817, KUL, Wedgwood papers, 12242–13.

[22] Skedd, 'Women', 125.   [23] Jones, *As I remember*, 37–40.   [24] Caine, *Destined*, 47.

hierarchies of classes, defined by the stage of instruction they had attained, rather than by age or ability.[25] In the 1830s, promotion on the basis of yearly examinations was common, but based on individual achievement rather than on any age-related theory of development.[26] It is not clear whether similar patterns of promotion were used in girls' schools. The informal schoolrooms of the domestic model did not lend themselves to rigid classification of pupils, which was not essential in any case with an individual mode of instruction. However, there are signs that some schools were adopting forms of stratification. In the 1810s pupils might be ranked according to their achievements in different subject areas. Elizabeth Firth moved from the third to the second class of geography during her stay at Miss Mangnall's school near Wakefield.[27] At Roe Head, in the 1830s, Margaret Wooler had introduced a system of instruction which 'required that a good deal of her pupils' work should be done in classes' so that 'new pupils generally had a season of solitary study' to catch up.[28]

Schoolgirl memories provide little information about classification, perhaps because arrangements were made on an ad hoc basis. Asking London teachers about what form they had adopted, D. R. Fearon found that in fourteen schools (23% of a sample of sixty) the response was 'vague'. The same number gave their answer as 'Uniform', and thirty (50%) claimed to classify their pupils separately for leading subjects. His results suggest that if in a considerable number of schools some form of classification was used, arrangements in many continued to be informal. However, in one of the schools investigated by Fearon—the North London Collegiate under Frances Buss—a hierarchical system had been devised. There, pupils were examined on their arrival and the school was classified 'chiefly by the knowledge of English'. The 204 pupils were divided into three classes, which in turn were divided up into groups of about twenty-five for each subject. Each of these groups was the responsibility of a daily governess. Pupils were promoted from class to class according to their marks and to their results in the half-yearly examinations. A similar system was in place at Cheltenham under Dorothea Beale.[29]

Both Dorothea Beale and Frances Buss consciously presented their establishments as developing innovative forms of female instruction. In the 1870s at Buss's new school in Camden, provision was made for separate classrooms, placing it in advance of many public and grammar schools. The Clarendon

---

[25] C. Stray, *Classics transformed: schools, universities, and society in England, 1830–1960* (Oxford, 1998), 22.

[26] Bamford, *Rise*, 64.

[27] Elizabeth Firth's diary, 1812–25, Sheffield University Library, Special Collections and Archives, Elizabeth Firth Manuscripts, MS 58/A–B.

[28] Quoted in Shorter, *Brontës*, i. 85.

[29] Fearon, 'London', *SIC* vii. 554–566; 'Particulars of the Inquiry relating to the North London Collegiate School, 12–14 Camden St, Middlesex', 1865, NLC, History of the School B1; D. Beale, 'The Ladies' College at Cheltenham', *Transactions of the National Association for the Promotion of Social Science* (1865), 279.

Commission which investigated the leading boys' public schools in 1864 had been ambivalent about classrooms, arguing that at Winchester all the teaching had been satisfactorily conducted in a single schoolroom for centuries.[30] For Frances Buss, separate rooms were the means of preserving the intimacy of the domestic model of school: 'the objections still felt to so new an idea as large schools for girls have practically no weight; since separate class-rooms so limit the number of girls together at one time that it is nothing more than a grouping under one roof. . . of half-a-dozen ordinary schools'.[31] Each in its separate room, every class was under the sole jurisdiction of one teacher, who could thus, as Dorothea Beale urged, 'learn to adapt the lessons to the pupils'.[32] The influence of gender is clear. While the single schoolroom was considered by the Clarendon Commission to be of positive value to a young man, since men at the bar or in parliament were expected to work 'amidst many outward causes of distraction', Dorothea Beale and Frances Buss took account of arguments claiming that girls' domestic duties and nature meant they should be educated in a small and familial setting.[33] At the same time, they were influenced by pedagogical concerns. Whilst modernizing girls' education, these schoolmistresses were seeking to preserve the educational advantages of individual instruction.

The Curriculum

One of the chief criticisms made of girls' schools was that they devoted too much time to frivolous 'accomplishments'. Such criticisms were partly fuelled by anxieties about social-climbing tradesmen's daughters, but they also reflect the growing influence of those calling for the development of rational and solid instruction for girls. Hannah More's argument that a programme of intellectual instruction would best qualify girls for their domestic 'profession' echoes throughout the nineteenth century and appears again in the SIC report, which asserted that one important reason to improve female education was that an educated wife could be 'of material service' to her husband.[34] Such arguments contributed to broadening the range of 'solid and substantial' subjects offered in schools in the first half of the nineteenth century.[35] Many observers, however, continued to characterize female instruction as frivolous, criticizing the way in which 'young ladies are made to devote themselves to what are at most the graces of life'. Disparagement of the instruction offered in girls' schools was partly a function of the dominance of a narrow conception of what constituted 'solid' education. Closer scrutiny reveals the gendered nature of attitudes to knowledge and learning.

[30] Seaborne, *English school*, 243.
[31] 'Appeal to raise funds for Camden School for Girls', *c*.1871, NLC, History of the School B1.
[32] Beale, 'Education of girls', 521.   [33] Quoted in Seabourne, *English school*, 243.
[34] More, *Strictures*; 'Report', *SIC* i. 548.   [35] 'Report', *SIC* i. 208.

For all the criticism of 'accomplishments', precisely what they consisted in varied, although prospectuses and educational treatises usually suggest that they included music, drawing, dance, and needlework. The status accorded to French and other modern languages fluctuated. A study of the curriculum in twenty-nine private boarding-schools for girls does suggest that these subjects did account for a considerable proportion of what was taught in girls' schools (Figure 6.1).[36]

French was the subject most often offered, available in twenty-five schools (86%). Music and drawing were similarly popular, taught in twenty-one (72%) and twenty (69%) schools respectively. Dance appeared less frequently, but was offered in twelve establishments. James Bryce estimated that at a typical Lancashire boarding-school in the 1860s, girls would spend 40% of a thirty-hour week on French, music, and drawing.[37] Unfortunately, the sources provide little information on lesson times in private boarding-schools, but the list of subjects most usually offered does imply that, as their critics maintained, 'the accomplishments' formed a substantial part of the curriculum. When Arthur Clough expressed his doubts about the value of his sister's studies in literature, German, and Classics as a preparation for school-keeping, instead emphasizing the value of music, because 'you know how necessary Music etc etc are even to those of a humble kind', he had realistically assessed the importance of such subjects in girls' schooling.[38]

The definition of what constituted an 'accomplishment' was heavily influenced by the close identification of the classical male curriculum with 'solid' education and by gendered notions of 'thoroughness'.[39] While never clearly spelling out which subjects the commissioners considered to be 'accomplishments', the SIC report seems to equate them with those 'branches of instruction more peculiar to female schools', implying that what was not studied in boys' schools was by definition an 'accomplishment'.[40] The categorization of modern languages as 'accomplishments' owed much to the association of French with frivolity and to

---

[36] Figure 6.1 shows the subjects taught in 29 private girls' schools in existence between 1800 and 1880, documenting the frequency with which each subject appeared on prospectuses, in inspection reports, and school memoirs. Wherever possible, the proportion of schools offering subjects as 'extras', rather than including them in the core curriculum, has been noted. The vagaries of the sources and the shifting nomenclature and fluid definition of the subjects of school instruction means that this can give only a broad indication of what was taught. For example, 'Maps' and 'Spheres' (which meant learning to read from geographical and astronomical globes, and was often listed in prospectuses as 'use of the globes') might be given as separate subjects or included within 'Geography' or 'Astronomy'. Similarly, 'Grammar' and 'Composition' might be referred to separately or included within 'English'. Nonetheless, the chart provides a useful indication of the range of subjects that these 29 schools taught, or professed to teach.

[37] Bryce, 'Lancashire', *SIC* ix. 806.

[38] Arthur Clough to Anne Clough, 16 Nov. 1840, *Correspondence of Arthur Hugh Clough*, ed. F. Mulhauser (Oxford, 1957), i. 73; quoted in G. Sutherland, *Faith, duty and the power of mind: the Cloughs and their circle, 1820–1960* (Cambridge, 2006), 25. I am grateful to Gillian Sutherland for drawing this to my attention.

[39] Michèle Cohen makes the same point: Cohen, 'Language'.   [40] 'Report', *SIC* i. 551.

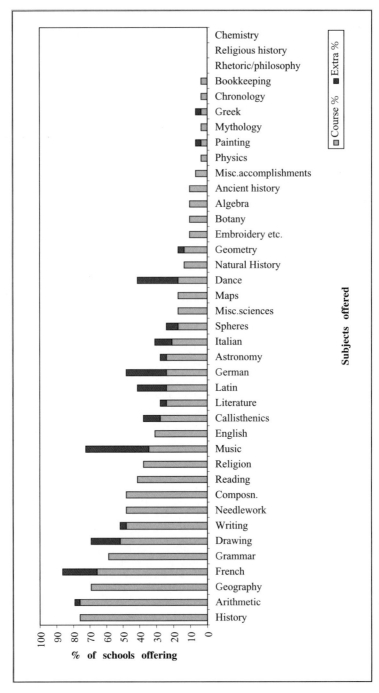

Figure 6.1. The subjects offered in twenty-nine private girls' schools in England (1800–1880).

the conception of Classics as the basis of all serious education.[41] It also derived from the way they were taught through conversation rather than grammar and translation, the favoured methods of teaching Classics.[42] This explains why Dorothea Beale, when seeking to affirm the intellectual rigour of the female curriculum, favoured German. Having regular declensions, it could be taught along the same lines as Latin.[43] In the mid-nineteenth century, French was gradually being absorbed into the 'solid' curriculum in boys' schools. But by this time it was already so firmly entrenched as a subject of serious study in many girls' schools that Sarah Jolly considered it 'a necessary part of education', a view apparently shared by the nineteen schools in the sample which taught French not as an 'extra' but as part of the ordinary curriculum.[44] This was no guarantee of good-quality teaching, and, as Dorothea Beale and Frances Cobbe both remarked, the practice of making French the chief language of conversation in schools often resulted in more 'franglais' than French being learned.[45] Still, in some establishments at least, French language teaching aspired to a high standard.[46] Even Frances Cobbe recognized that many women were proficient in modern languages as a result of their education.[47] Those who dismissed the study of French as an 'accomplishment' were failing to recognize the care with which it was often taught.

Other 'accomplishments' might also be taken more seriously than their label suggests. John Ruskin's letters to girls at Winnington Hall in the 1860s reveal how he introduced pupils to the theory and philosophy of painting.[48] At Mrs Lalor's in the 1850s, Marianne Gaskell was taught harmony 'as a serious science'.[49] A series of articles in *The Governess* emphasized that drawing and music should be taught 'not merely as pleasurable pursuits, but with a view to a strengthening of the mental powers in the first instance'.[50] Although the social value of accomplishments was prized, in some establishments at least the intellectual content of subjects like music and drawing was also brought to the

[41] Cohen, 'Manliness'; Sutherland, 'Secondary education'; Stray, *Classics*, chs. 1–4.

[42] S. Bayley and D. Yavorsky Ronish, 'Gender, modern languages and the curriculum in Victorian England', *History of Education*, 21 (1992), 363–82. For a more subtle investigation of the implications of such gendered distinctions, see M. Cohen, 'Manliness'.

[43] Evidence of Dorothea Beale, *SIC* iv. 726; Cohen makes the same point, 'Language'.

[44] Bryant, *London experience*, 159; P. Gerbod, 'L'enseignement de la langue française en Grande Bretagne au XIXe siècle', *Documents pour l'Histoire du Français Langue Étrangère ou Seconde*, 2 (1988), 11; Jolly, *Thoughts*, 44.

[45] Beale, 'Education of girls', 520; Cobbe, *Life*, 66.

[46] At the Miss Franklins' in Coventry, Marian Evans translated Maria Edgeworth into French and was given Pascal's *Pensées* as a prize: Haight, *George Eliot*, 12.

[47] F. Cobbe, *Female education and how it would be affected by University Examinations* (London, 1862), 14.

[48] *Winnington letters*, ed. Van Aikin Burd.

[49] Elizabeth Gaskell to Lady Kay Shuttleworth, 12 Dec. 1850, Chapple and Pollard (eds.), *Letters*, 137–40.

[50] W.M. 'The accomplishments taught at boarding schools, and their real value', *The Governess, a Repertory of Female Education* (1855–6).

fore. Furthermore, if subjects such as music and needlework formed an important part of the female curriculum, they were by no means as dominant as many suggested. In the sample schools, history, arithmetic, geography, and grammar were more often offered as part of the course of instruction than drawing or music.[51] Evidence from these establishments suggests that girls' schools were developing broad curricula that included subjects not generally included in the male curriculum until later in the century.

History, not widely taught in boys' schools until the second half of the nineteenth century, was one of the subjects most commonly offered in girls' schools, and was often regarded as a particularly feminine topic.[52] For John Relly Beard, it was especially appropriate for women because of the role they would play in their daughters' education. Understanding history, they would be able to draw moral lessons from it for their children.[53] Similarly, whereas in 1875 science was taught in only sixty-three of 128 endowed schools for boys, scientific subjects had long been offered in girls' schools.[54] Twelve of the twenty-nine schools in the sample (58%) taught at least one scientific subject. Botany in particular was often deemed especially suitable for girls because, as the authors of an 1817 textbook maintained, 'it can be pursued in retirement; there is no danger of its inflaming the imagination, because the mind is intent upon realities'.[55] The author of an 1844 treatise on 'Woman's worth' was convinced that women's love of flowers would stimulate their interest in botany, an interest which should be encouraged because knowledge of scientific subjects would enable them to challenge the detractors of the Bible.[56] As Jane Rendall argues, the rhetoric of Protestant domesticity offered a context within which female instruction could gradually be extended without threatening the existing social and gender order.[57] Just as women's study of history could be justified with reference to their maternal role, girls' instruction in sciences was related to conceptions of feminine weakness and to notions of women's particular responsibility for safeguarding religion.

[51] Accomplishments—including modern languages—accounted for more than a third of the subjects offered in only 5 of the 29 schools.

[52] J. Roach, 'History teaching and examining in secondary schools, 1850–1900', *History of Education*, 5 (1976), 127–40; E. Davies, *The higher education of women* (1866; London, 1988), 126.

[53] J. R. Beard, 'What should a woman learn?', *Monthly Repository*, 56 (Aug. 1831), 529.

[54] A. J. Meadows, W. H. Brock, 'Topics fit for gentlemen: the problem of science in the public school curriculum', in Brian Simon and Ian Bradley (eds.), *The Victorian public school: studies in the development of an educational institution* (Dublin, 1975), 111; K. Tolley, 'Science for ladies, Classics for gentlemen: a comparative analysis of scientific subjects in the curricula of boys' and girls' secondary schools in the United States, 1794–1850', *History of Education Quarterly*, 36 (1996), 129–53.

[55] E. D. Rudolph, 'How it developed that botany was the science thought most suitable for Victorian young ladies', *Children's Literature*, 2 (1973), 92–7; E. and S. Fitton, *Conversations on botany* (London, 1820), 179–80, quoted in Rudolph, 'How it developed', 94; C. Grasser, 'Jeune fille en fleur'.

[56] *Woman's worth*, 81–7.   [57] Rendall, *Origins,* 32.

However, tension and ambiguity continued to surround the relationship between women and learning. This was particularly clear in relation to Classics. Whilst girls' study of history and botany—not part of the dominant male curriculum—could be interpreted in a way that reinforced conventional notions of femininity, the question of whether girls should learn Latin—defined as *the* male subject—was more problematic. In the 1840s, Harriet Martineau argued, 'it had quite ceased to be a remarkable thing that a girl read the Latin classics for pleasure', and in the 1860s the SIC had few qualms about recommending that girls should be taught Latin.[58] Twelve schools in the sample (41%) offered Latin, and in seven it was included in the main curriculum. But girls wishing to take up classical languages often had more to contend with than this suggests. When Mary Russell Mitford wrote from school in 1802 announcing that 'I have just taken a lesson in Latin', her father responded by saying: 'Your mother and I have had much conversation concerning the utility of your learning Latin, and we both agree that it is perfectly unnecessary.'[59] Mary must have argued her case well because she continued her Latin lessons. Despite Martineau's optimistic assessment, this unease about women studying Classics was still prevalent in the 1860s when Dorothea Beale noted that 'many are the women who understand Greek and Latin and Mathematics, who keep it a profound secret'.[60] The classical curriculum was the centre-point of a notion of liberal education whose ideal was that of the independent gentleman.[61] To study Latin and Greek was to step outside a curriculum rationalized in accordance with a domestic conception of femininity and, ultimately, to challenge the prevailing ideal of womanhood.

Although treatises describing what girls should be taught at school abounded, and although counting subjects gives some indication of what was offered, it is more difficult to discover how they were taught. Sarah Ellis painted a vivid picture of dreary days at school: 'We all know too what it is to the learner to be dragged on day by day through the dull routine of exercises in which she feels no particular interest . . . The tones of the teacher's voice, though not always the most musical, might easily have been picked down in notes, they were so uniform in their cadences of interrogations, rejection and reproof.'[62] In the 1820s, J. R. Beard condemned the 'extracts, catechisms and the mummery which is practiced at our girls' schools under the pretence of imparting historical knowledge'.[63] History was the subject of the notorious 'Mangnall's Questions', in which chapters with subtitles like 'From the earliest times to the establishment of the imperial power

---

[58] H. Martineau, 'Middle-class education in England', *Cornhill Magazine*, 10 (1864), 553; 'Report', *SIC* i. 551.

[59] Mary Russell Mitford to her mother, 6 Aug. 1802; George Russell to Mary, 9 Aug. 1802, *The life of Mary Russell Mitford, related in a selection from her letters to her friends*, ed. A. G. L'Estrange (London, 1870), i. 14.

[60] Beale, 'Education of girls', 512.

[61] Sutherland, 'Secondary education'; Stray, *Classics*, chs. 1–4; Rothblatt, *Tradition*.

[62] Ellis, *Women*, 78.   [63] Beard, 'What should', 529.

in Rome, comprehending a sketch of general history' would be followed by long lists of questions such as: 'In what light were the Spartans considered?' The pupil was expected to respond: 'Entirely as a warlike nation; but they were forbidden to attack their neighbours without provocation.'[64] 'Mangnall', first published in 1800, was continuously re-edited until 1864; four of the girls whose reminiscences of school life are included in the biographical sample were taught from it. Other approaches do not seem much more inspiring. At Annie Keary's school in the 1840s, 'English, Grecian and Roman histories were read by turns, half an hour being allowed for each at a time; the pupils looked at the backs of the books, to be quite sure where they were'. Annie stood out from her fellow pupils because 'a thirst for any sort of knowledge outside the ordinary school routine was not a distinguishing feature of the place'.[65]

It is difficult not to feel that Beard's charges of 'mummery' were justified. But, as Fitch reported to the SIC, in some establishments history at least was well taught: 'I have found the classes reading Macaulay or Hume with much intelligence and relish, and making very clever abstracts or paraphrases of the most notable passages.'[66] Fearon was similarly impressed, recording that 'in several instances very creditable oral examinations were passed'.[67] Moreover, girls' schools did not have a monopoly on dullness and rote-learning. One man reminisced to Dorothea Beale how 'we committed daily to memory some page or half-page of the sacred, but unintelligible book [a Latin grammar], rules which no one seemed called upon to understand at the time'.[68] At the same time, Emily Jones remembered 'Mangnall' fondly, and gifted teachers could make the most of unprepossessing material. [69] In her Ambleside school in the 1850s, Anne Clough set the children to read pages of Mrs Markham's *English History*, but would enliven lessons with her own experiences and guide her pupils towards further reading.[70] Similarly, although contemporaries like Elizabeth Sewell could mock the 'ologies' [sic] offered in girls' schools and taught without understanding, some schoolmistresses were evidently developing lively teaching methods and fuelling their pupils' enthusiasm for the sciences.[71] Bessie Parkes fondly recalled lectures, with accompanying experiments, on steam engines and hydraulics given by Dr Field at Leam in the 1840s.[72] Whilst staying at Winnington Hall in 1862, Mrs Colenso was alarmed to discover that boys had been sent out to catch a rabbit, 'the skeleton of which is wanted for anatomical study by the young ladies!'[73]

---

[64] R. Mangnall, *Historical and miscellaneous questions* (London, 1856), 5.
[65] E. Keary, *Memoir*, 50–1.　　　[66] Fitch, 'West Riding', *SIC* ix. 291–2.
[67] Fearon, 'London', *SIC* vii. 406.
[68] Beale, 'Education of girls', 519; Roach, *Secondary education*, 70.
[69] Jones, *As I remember*, 7.
[70] Clough, *Memoir*, 91. The *History of England*, published by Elizabeth Penrose under the pseudonym of Mrs Markham, had reached its 12th edition by 1846.
[71] Sewell, *Principles*, i. 173.
[72] B. Parkes, Autobiographical material, undated, Girton College, GCPP Parkes 1/1–3.
[73] *Winnington Letters*, ed. Van Aikin Burd, 33.

Even if the teaching itself might leave something to be desired, many boarding-schools provided a space in which girls were given an opportunity to learn. The best schoolmistresses stimulated their pupils by example or by urging them to read widely. Anne White was inspired by her teacher, noting that 'it was very well I came. I am sure I am in the best way of learning a good deal . . . H. Brady told us the other day that the longer she lives, the more she is convinced that "knowledge is power".'[74] At Leam, Bessie Parkes felt that 'all might find an education of a very high order, whether a child's turn were practical or intellectual'. Pupils were encouraged to read widely and were given a free rein in the school library that, to her delight, included novels by Edgeworth and Scott. She remembered 'many happy hours, stretched out at full length', reading.[75] The Miss Fields who ran Bessie Parkes' school were Unitarians, and Hannah Brady was a Quaker. As such they have may have had more latitude to develop a demanding curriculum, and, interestingly, Bessie Parkes felt that not all her schoolfellows' parents would have approved of the Miss Fields' emphasis on learning independence.[76] However, they were not alone in stressing the value of knowledge. Anglican schoolmistresses were also offering their pupils a more robust vision of the value of instruction than that promoted at home.[77] Emily Jones felt that her year at the Anglican Miss Robinson's school had opened her horizons in a new way: 'I think that at school more tolerance and content were somehow infused with the general attitude. Never had I been so filled with confidence and approval.'[78] Within the parameters of the domestic model of schooling, Protestant schoolmistresses of all denominations, influenced by notions of self-improvement and human perfectibility, were able to develop courses of instruction that emphasized intellectual growth. If going to school meant girls might encounter the dynamic and potentially liberating forms of group socialization experienced by their brothers, these examples suggest that boarding-schools might also offer girls a space in which to discover and assert their intellectual autonomy.

Yet female instruction continued to suffer from low status. This was at least partly a function of the continued pre-eminence of Classics in boys' education.[79] The strength of feeling in support of Classics, the view that a non-classical education was merely utilitarian and lacked moral force, meant that any deviation from the classical model would lack social legitimacy and authority, and undermined the claims of boarding-schools to offer 'secondary education', since the only truly 'secondary' education was deemed to be a classical one.

---

[74] Clark and Sturge, *Mount School*, 47.

[75] Parkes, 'Autobiographical material', GCPP Parkes 1/1–3.

[76] Watts, 'Unitarian contribution'; K. Allen and A. Mackinnon, 'Allowed and expected to be educated and intelligent': the education of Quaker girls in nineteenth-century England', *History of Education*, 27 (1998), 391–402.

[77] Parkes, Autobiographical material, GCPP Parkes 1/1–3.   [78] Jones, *As I remember*, 43.

[79] Sutherland, 'Secondary education'; Roach, *Secondary education*, 72.

Without access to higher education, and often reliant on unimaginative and inaccurate textbooks, there was a limit to what even the most talented teacher could achieve. At the same time, the price of justifying the extension of women's education on the grounds of women's nature and role was that girls' studies were thus bound up with utilitarian notions of instruction. While this was the case, the female curriculum could never aspire to the prestige of a classical education, a fact that the mid-century reformers like Dorothea Beale recognized and challenged in asserting girls' unqualified right to education, which, as we have seen, she regarded as 'a *good in itself*'.[80] By the 1860s many schoolmistresses were looking to examinations as a way of asserting that right.

Emulation and Examinations

Pupils at Cheltenham Ladies' College were promoted from class to class according to their marks and to their results at half-yearly examinations. Although the methodical nature of this system was an innovation in girls' schools, various forms of examination and prize-giving had been part of female education since at least the end of the eighteenth century. In some establishments, medals were specially cast as prizes; a surviving example from Miss Herbert and Miss Moores' school in Bury, awarded to Eliza Wolfenden in 1828, reads: 'Continue in the things which thou hast learned.'[81] Academic work was also examined and rewarded at Miss Wooler's school. While a teacher there, Charlotte Brontë was forced to refuse an invitation because 'we are in the very thickest mêlée of the Repetitions'.[82] At the Friends' School, York, in the 1830s, the yearly examinations were an intimidating prospect. Anne White wrote to her parents in May 1835 that 'we feel rather frightened at the examinations'.[83] Later in the century some teachers were instituting written examinations. Anne Clough was remembered by one of her pupils as being 'very great on examinations, which went on for a fortnight before the holidays. We had a number of blank books given us for the different subjects, and she would call out the questions; we wrote each one on the top of a page and left the rest blank for the answer; two subjects were taken at the same time, but only every alternate girl took the same one, so that there could be no cribbing... Then marks were given, some for neatness though the answer might be wrong, and there were special examination prizes.'[84]

---

[80] Beale, 'Education of girls', 514.

[81] M. E. Grimshaw, *Silver medals, badges and trophies from schools in the British Isles, 1550–1850* (Cambridge, n.d.).

[82] Charlotte Brontë to Ellen Nussey, n.d., Shorter, *Brontës*, 121.

[83] Anne White to her parents, 7 May 1835, Clark and Sturge, *Mount School*, 45.

[84] Recollections of Sophie Bellasis, T. C. Down, 'Schooldays with Miss Clough', *Cornhill Magazine*, 3rd ser. 48 (1920), 676.

By the 1850s written examinations were increasingly the norm at Cambridge and were being introduced in the professions. They were also being seen as the means to raise standards in middle-class education and the College of Preceptors and University syndicates were developing a range of secondary examinations.[85] But although some girls' schools had introduced examinations early on, the SIC found that relatively few schools had adopted them. Of sixty-three schools in West Sussex, seventeen had examinations, but thirty-eight (60%) had none whatsoever. In addition, few girls' schools were sending their pupils to sit the College of Preceptors' examinations or the Cambridge Locals.[86] In London, only three of the sixty Grade I and II schools investigated by D. R. Fearon prepared pupils for the former.[87]

The SIC Report hints at one of the reasons why girls' schools held back from the examinations. Although it recommended examination as a means of raising standards in girls' education, it emphasized that 'the principle of emulation' should not be used, 'in its most stimulating form of individual competition'. Emulation was potentially dangerous for girls, whose 'excitable and sensitive constitutions' might cause them to overwork and damage their health.[88] The value of emulation in stimulating boys to strive for excellence was often underlined.[89] Competition amongst girls, however, threatened ideals of feminine modesty and endangered the notion of women's domestic sphere as a sanctuary from the competitive world of business.[90] The public nature of examinations like the University Locals was also a source of anxiety. H. A. Giffard found that one reason why girls' schools shunned the new examinations was fear of publicity.[91] The commissioners shared their apprehensions and recommended that 'the display of public exhibition be avoided'.[92] Emulation and examinations were a threat to ideals of femininity and domesticity on several levels.

But there was a further dimension to the reluctance to adopt public examinations. The anxiety expressed by a number of English schoolmistresses also reflected a concern about their pedagogical worth. Teachers like Hannah Pipe questioned any slavish adherence to examinations, which might force pupils 'to swallow that for which they had no appetite', maintaining the value of 'that free spontaneous growth of the mind' and more informal educational strategies.[93] The question of competition and emulation was also an ongoing concern of the London Association of Schoolmistresses. At their first meeting in 1866 the undesirable nature of competitive prizes was discussed and a later meeting

---

[85] C. Stray, 'The shift from oral to written examination: Cambridge and Oxford, 1700–1900', *Assessment in Education*, 8 (2001), 34–50; Sutherland, 'Examinations', 51–64; Roach, *Public examinations*.

[86] Giffard, 'Sussex', *SIC* vii. 212; Stanton, 'Devon', *SIC* vii. 75.

[87] Fearon, 'London', *SIC* vii. 554–66.   [88] 'Report', *SIC* i. 556.

[89] Cohen, 'Language'; Honey, *Tom Brown's universe*, 14.

[90] The same was true in the USA: N. Green, 'Female education and school competition: 1820–1850', *History of Education Quarterly*, 18 (1978), 129–42.

[91] Giffard, 'Sussex', *SIC* vii. 212.   [92] 'Report', *SIC* i. 556.   [93] Stoddart, *Life*, 175.

debated a paper by Miss Manning on emulation. She argued that it might be valuable if it were 'subordinated to higher motives', but that in small schools where the teaching was good, it would be better excluded.[94]

Despite these doubts, the first members of the LSM were recruited from amongst the schoolmistresses who had agreed to send their pupils to sit the Cambridge Locals in 1863, and by the end of the 1860s, even those who had been dubious were largely converted. In 1869, there were 953 female candidates for the College of Preceptors' examinations.[95] For Emily Davies, who organized the campaign for girls' admission to the Cambridge Locals, examinations were indispensable as a guarantee for teachers and would confer purpose, seriousness, and legitimacy on girls' studies.[96] Dorothea Beale insisted on their value for children: 'They give to them a sense of security, they show to themselves whether they really did know what they thought they did, and they teach them to feel that vague half-knowledge is worthless, since it will stand no fair test.'[97] By the end of the 1860s, these arguments were apparently appealing to a growing number of parents. Private schoolmistresses were highlighting examination success in order to attract pupils. Such developments led Frances Buss to note that 'without rushing to either extreme, it may be safe to commit ourselves to the very general proposition that for good or for evil, probably for both, methods and plans of examination do constitute one of the most powerful forces in our modern systems of education'.[98] Whilst suggesting that examinations were not a panacea, she recognized that they would in the future have a considerable effect on instruction in girls' schools.

LESSONS AND LEARNING IN FRANCE

The Location and Organization of Learning

Lessons and curricula were more formally structured in French establishments than in their English counterparts. Building on the Jesuit *Ratio Studiorum*, boys' *lycées* were divided up and organized in a ladder of promotion which led from the *sizième* to the *rhétorique*.[99] The *Légion d'Honneur* schools adopted an analogous

---

[94] Minutes 5 July 1866, Minute book of the London Association of Schoolmistresses, 1866–74, Girton College, GCPP Davies 9.

[95] Pupils' register, 1866 to 1875, University of London, Institute of Education, Records of the College of Preceptors, GB/366/DC/COP; A. Jacobs, 'The girls have done very decidedly better than the boys': girls and examinations, 1860–1902, *Journal of Educational Administration and History*, 33 (2001), 120–32.

[96] Davies, *Higher education*, 135–144; see also E. Wolstenholme, 'What better provision ought to be made for the education of girls of the upper and middle classes?', *Transactions of the National Association for the Promotion of Social Science*, (1865), 290.

[97] Beale, 'Education of girls', 523.

[98] F. Buss, 'On the influence upon girls' schools of internal examinations, with special reference to Cambridge Locals', reprinted from the 'London Student', May 1868, LSM pamphlets, NLC Archives, RS7iv, Place of the school in history.

[99] P. Albertini, *L'école en France, XIXe–XXe siècles* (Paris, 1998), 68–70.

system. At Ecouen, after an entry examination, which in 1857 consisted of a dictation and an arithmetic test, girls would be put into one of the seven classes (themselves each divided into two sections) corresponding to their ability and would move individually through the hierarchy.[100] Thérèse Martin remembered that 'the rule was to move successively through each section'. Sometimes, 'one might skip a section', but it was never possible to skip a whole class.[101] Private *pensions* adopted similar strategies. In the 1820s the Lille school run by Mmes Comère and Mairesse was divided into three classes, as was that of Mlles De Ridder in Roubaix in the 1840s.[102] In Bordeaux, their contemporary, Éléonore Ploux, separated her fifty-seven pupils into a hierarchy of eleven classes.[103] In Paris, a report for 1847 noted that at Mlle Guesnier's school 'studies are fairly well graduated for each class, following the age and strength of the pupils'.[104] Inspectors were expected to enquire as to how many classes there were in each school, how many divisions made up each class, and which subjects were taught in each division.[105]

By the end of the seventeenth century the term '*classe*' was already being associated with specialized teaching rooms when used in reference to the *collèges*.[106] This specialization was mirrored in establishments for girls in the nineteenth century. There were separate rooms for the *grande* and *petite classe* at the Couvent des Anglaises attended by George Sand from 1817 to 1820.[107] At Ecouen, each 'classe' had its own room, and there were specialized rooms for drawing, music, and dance lessons.[108] The 1821 regulations for the Seine instructed inspectors to oversee the *tenue des classes*, clearly anticipating that private girls' schools would also have more than one teaching room, and inspection reports from Paris are peppered with references to the size and cleanliness of classrooms.[109] At Mme Achet's school in Paris (Illustration 2 on page 35) there were three classrooms, three practice rooms for music, and a gymnasium. Éléonore Ploux's school also had several different *classes*. One was for mathematics, one for drawing, one was simply 'used as a class', and the last was an *étude* or study room.[110]

Not all institutions were so well endowed with individual classrooms. In the 1850s, at Sophie Thomas' Cambrai school, the pupils were divided into six classes

---

[100] Rogers, *Demoiselles*, 119.   [101] Martin, *Souvenirs*, 38.

[102] Bulletins de Amélie Canisse, Mmes Comère et Mairesse, Lille, 1821, 1823, AD Nord, 124 J 7. Distribution solonelle des prix, pensionnat des dames de Ridder, 1848, AM Roubaix, 1 T 19/4.

[103] Concours 1840–1851, AM Bordeaux, Fonds Ploux/8.

[104] Inspection pension Guesnier, 14 rue Charlot, 1847, AD Seine, VD⁶ 367–10.

[105] 'Feuille d'inspection des maisons d'éducation de demoiselles', 1844, AD Seine, VD⁶ 158–3.

[106] G. Dupont-Ferrier, *Du Collège de Clermont au Lycée Louis le Grand (1653–1920)*, 3 vols. (Paris, 1921–5), ii, fig. 71.

[107] Sand, *Histoire de ma vie*, 147.   [108] Martin, *Souvenirs*, 38.

[109] Règlement concernant les Maisons d'Éducation de filles dans le département de la Seine, 1 Dec. 1821, AN, F¹⁷ 12431.

[110] Inventaire après décès, François Ploux, 29 Apr. 1834, AD Gironde, 3ᴱ 41412.

but there were only two classrooms, so that three classes were taught in each.[111] Nonetheless, although not all schools could provide individual teaching rooms, schoolmistresses were expected to house their schools in specialized buildings if at all possible, and classrooms were clearly differentiated from other rooms. The room in which Césarie Farrenc was taught while at boarding-school in Marseilles in the 1810s—which contained a long table, writing desks, books, and exercise books—and the classroom at Mme Ploux's in the 1830s—which housed four tables and benches and two globes—were unlikely to be likened to a sitting-room.[112]

The widespread use of separate classrooms was probably related to the early adoption of forms of simultaneous instruction on the Continent. Class teaching was one of the key legacies of the Jesuit and Ursuline schools of the seventeenth century.[113] The seventeenth century had also seen the development of simultaneous methods for elementary instruction. Children progressed through a sequence of nine 'lessons', passing examinations at each stage. Those following a given 'lesson' would be taught as a group and were called on occasionally to answer questions or recite.[114] The question of how this, or a similar approach, came to be adopted in girls' boarding-schools needs more research; however, by the nineteenth century, most *pensions* were using some sort of simultaneous strategy. All the boarding-schools inspected in Douai in 1828 claimed to use a *méthode simultanée*, as did twenty-seven Bordeaux schools visited in 1849.[115]

The question of what teaching methods were used is complicated by schools' frequent recourse to visiting masters. In 1829, one inspectress reported that all the boarding-schools in the first *arrondissement* in Paris employed male professors, who taught 'not only literature and universal history, but also arithmetic, writing and the other sciences'.[116] In Strasbourg between 1800 and 1870, approximately 83% of those teaching in girls' schools were men.[117] However, assistant mistresses were often responsible for basic instruction in reading, writing, and arithmetic, and in sixteen of a survey of thirty-two Parisian schools visited by the inspectors in 1847–8, the director herself taught at least one subject.[118] At their school in Pont-Audemer, Eugénie and Aurélie Dubois were responsible for a large part of

[111] Rapport sur l'établissement de Sophie Thomas, institutrice libre à Cambrai, 14 Dec. 1854, AD Nord, 1 T 120/1.

[112] C. Farrenc [née Gensollen], *Ce que peut être une femme* (Paris, 1874), 148; Inventaire après décès de François Ploux, 29 Apr. 1834, AD Gironde, 3^E 41412.

[113] Rapley, 'Fénelon revisited', 306.

[114] Hamilton, *Theory*, 59–61. P. Giolotto, *Naissance de la pédagogie primaire (1815–1879)* (Grenôble, 1980), i. 129–39.

[115] État nominatif des institutrices primaires de la commune de Douai, 1828, AM Douai, 1 R 32.

[116] Rapport sur l'enseignement primaire des filles dans l'arrdt. de Bordeaux, 1849–50, AD Gironde, 6 T 12.

[117] Rapport de Mme la Marquise de MacMahon, 15 Nov. 1829, AD Seine, VD^6 158–3.

[118] M. Schvind, 'L'éducation des demoiselles de la bourgeoisie: l'exemple du Bas-Rhin (1800–1870)', Mémoire de Maîtrise (Strasbourg II, 1996), 54, cited in Rogers, *From the Salon*, 128, n. 79.

the teaching.[119] Moreover, as in England, visiting masters might spend only a few hours a week with their pupils. In 1841, at Mlle Viard's school in the eleventh *arrondissement*, pupils would usually spend only two and a half hours a day with visiting professors. The rest of their time was spent under the supervision of their schoolmistresses, who taught them French grammar, heard them say their lessons, and supervised them while they prepared the exercises set by the professors. In 1849, the three visiting masters employed at Mlle Viard's spent only seven hours per week between them at the school, teaching pupils writing, arithmetic, natural sciences, history, and literature.[120]

The distinction between the work of men and women teachers, however, was firmly established and was sometimes reflected in the allocation of space within the *pension*. This reflects the importance attributed to the *étude* in the nineteenth century. In the *lycées*, the *classe*, where boys would be guided in their exercises by a professor who would also lecture them on his subject, was clearly distinguished from the *étude*, the period devoted to written exercises and learning lessons. In the 1870s pupils would spend more than half their time in study under the supervision of *maîtres d'études* whose pay and status was inferior to that of the professors.[121] By the 1830s, the term *étude* was also being used to refer to rooms set aside for these supervised periods.[122] The distinction between lessons given by masters and study periods supervised by resident mistresses in girls' schools thus mirrored the situation in male establishments. In some cases, the specialization of space was also echoed. One of the rooms at Mme Ploux's was described as an *étude,* and in Paris in the 1840s the administrative authorities were encouraging schools to differentiate between the rooms in which pupils studied and the room in which they were taught.[123] At Mme Deslignières' Paris establishment in the 1850s, pupils spent the mornings at desks in their respective classrooms, but lessons with the masters took place in an annexe with rows of raised seats and a space at the front used for dancing.[124]

Although in boys' schools the status of the professor and those who supervised the *étude* differed, in female establishments that gap was widened by the distinction of sex. A survey of schools in the first *arrondissement* reveals that women teachers were responsible only for a limited range of subjects. Visiting mistresses in these schools were largely confined to the *arts d'agrément* (accomplishments), and even in these subjects they were outnumbered by men. Male

[119] Calculated from inspection records, 1847–8, AD Seine, VD[6] 158–3.

[120] Isambert-Jamati, *Solidarité*, 117–18.

[121] Règlement, Mlle Viard visé par la préfecture, 26 Aug. 1841, Inspection pension Viard, 6 and 19 May 1849, AD Seine, VD[6] 649–1.

[122] Prost, *L'enseignement*, 50–2; M.-M. Compère and P. Savoie, 'Temps scolaire', 282–3.

[123] Étude'–'*Lieu où l'on réunit les élèves pour leur faire étudier les leçons et composer les devoirs donné par le professeur',* Dictionnaire de l'Académie Française (1835), http://duras.uchicago.edu/cgi-bin/quick_look.new, last accessed 8 Nov. 2002. *Résultats de l'inspection des pensions de demoiselles*, 1846, AN, F[17] 12431.

[124] Brada, *Souvenirs*, 40–2, 59.

professors had a virtual monopoly on what the inspectors referred to as '*études classiques*'—arithmetic, history, geography, literature, and scientific subjects. In 1847, of the 496 teachers responsible for *études classiques* in Paris, 402 (81%) were men.[125] As we have seen, in the 1840s, this situation provoked a campaign for the exclusion of men from girls' schools and the development of a female professoriate. The response reveals an assumption of male intellectual superiority that goes some way towards explaining the predominance of male teachers in girls' schools. A woman's education, David Lévi-Alvarès argued, 'is only serious and complete if it has been undertaken by an enlightened man'. Unlike F. D. Maurice, he did not stress the complementarity of male and female intellect, but hinted at a strong sense of male superiority.[126] Similarly, Paul Buessard argued that the exclusion of male professors would result in the 'complete decadence of instruction' in girls' schools. Male teachers were better able to inspire young women and help them progress.[127] The implication was that though women were capable of elementary instruction, they could not aspire to higher-level teaching. These claims were perhaps to be expected from male professors who felt that their livelihood was being threatened. But even Marie Sincère, a supporter of the reform of girls' schooling, argued that 'the feminine mind feels a kind of repulsion for exact science' and that women's higher studies depended on the contribution of male professors.[128] As suggested above, one reason why the campaign to remove male professors never got off the ground was that the period was marked by an intense hostility to female learning and feminist ideas. The role played by male professors in girls' schools and debates on the subject in the 1840s suggest that such feelings were underpinned by a deep-seated belief in women's intellectual inferiority.

Emulation and Examinations

Despite this emphasis on women's intellectual weakness, girls at school were continually being examined as to their attainments and pitted against one another in these tests. The concept of *émulation* was a central feature of French pedagogy, operating in tandem with the classification system. An 'honourable rivalry', based on the assumption that competition was an essential spur to boys' progress, was a key part of the *Ratio Studiorum*.[129] Emulation was integral to instruction, even in the eighteenth-century *maisons d'éducation* for boys, which sought explicitly to distinguish themselves from the large religious colleges.[130] The same spirit

---

[125] The rest were either visiting mistresses or resident governesses, Préfet de la Seine au Ministre de l'Instruction Publique, 17 Nov. 1847, AD, F[17] 12432.

[126] D. Lévi-Alvarès, *Education secondaire et supérieure des jeunes filles* (Paris, 1847), 5–6.

[127] Paul Buessard au Comité Local du 4e arrdt., 12 Apr. 1847, AD Seine, VD[6] 706–1.

[128] Sincère, *Pensionnats*, 37–8.

[129] Janelle, *Catholic Reformation*, 153–4; Farrell, *Jesuit code*, 291–5.

[130] Grandière, 'L'éducation', 458.

of competition was evident in girls' schools.[131] Throughout the first part of the century, pedagogical tracts, prospectuses, and prize-day speeches were peppered with references to '*l'émulation salutaire*'. Emulation, Jeanne Campan maintained, 'is the main strength of public education'. Exercising a useful influence over young people's taste and habits, 'it in no way harms the generous feelings of the heart and of the soul'.[132] For Céline Fallet, the value of emulation was such that 'the schoolmistress must make her pupils' work a continual struggle, in which the prize belongs to the most hard-working and the most willing'.[133]

This competition was fostered by tests, marks, and prizes, meant as 'a useful encouragement, a powerful means of emulation'.[134] Caillot envisaged a system of weekly examinations, backed up by a '*Grand Examen*' at the end of each term.[135] A similar system was in place at Mlle Bourgeois' school in Cambrai in the 1850s, where the sixty pupils were subjected to weekly *interrogations* and termly examinations.[136] In some schools testing was based on written work. At Mlle Viard's in Paris in the 1840s, one good piece of homework was awarded one point, twenty-five points earned the pupil a '*carte de satisfaction*', four of these meant a '*carte de mérite*', and if a pupil earned four of the latter, she would be awarded a book.[137] In Bordeaux in 1851, all but one of the fifteen *pensions* visited by the inspector had some system of examination.[138] The culmination of such tests and examinations was usually the annual prize day. These were frequently elaborate ceremonies, often attended by local dignitaries and visitors. Maria Edgeworth attended the prize day held at Mme Campan's school in 1802, and noted the presence of the leading figures of French high society.[139] The girls were rewarded with prizes of books, or engravings like the one distributed at one Bordeaux school in the 1840s, itself depicting the prize-day ceremony (Illustration 6). Tests and prize days were a central feature of boarding-school education.

Although the conception of education as 'continual struggle' resonates with the ideals of abnegation expressed by some Catholic teachers, the idea of girls perpetually competing with one another is not easily reconciled with conventional notions of feminine modesty and docility. Nor does the display associated with prize days. Yet the notion that girls should be educated in a competitive environment raised

---

[131] Rapley, 'Fénelon revisited', 307.   [132] Campan, *De l'éducation*, i. 233.
[133] 'une lutte continuelle': Fallet, *Education*, 213.   [134] Lequien, *Discours*, 1.
[135] Caillot, *Plan d'éducation*.
[136] Pensions de l'arrdt. de Cambrai, 7 Dec. 1857, AD Nord, 1 T 120/2.
[137] Règlement, Mlle Viard, *c.*1842, AD Seine, VD⁶ 649–1.
[138] Pensions de demoiselles de l'arrdt. de Bordeaux, Inspecteur primaire Benoît, 16 Mar. 1851, AD Gironde, 6 T 12.
[139] C. Hill, *Maria Edgeworth and her circle in the days of Buonaparte and Bourbon* (London, 1909), 59; see also the description of an 'examen' in a Parisian boarding school, J. E. de Jouy, *L'hermite de la Chaussée d'Antin ou observations sur les mœurs et les usages français au commencement du XIXe siècle*, 5 vols. (Paris, 1812–14), i. 83–6.

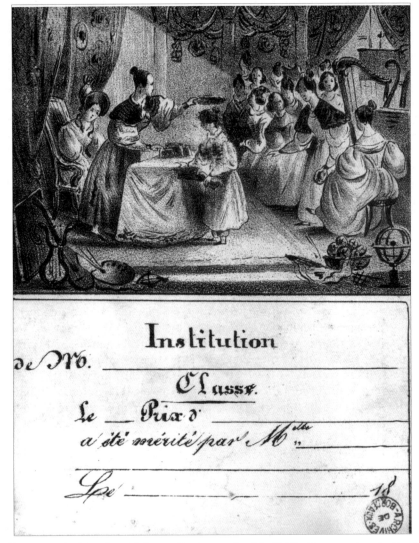

Illustration 6. Prize-day gift from a Bordeaux school (*c*.1840), Plaquette de prix, Fonds Ferrere/16, AM Bordeaux; © cliché, Archives Municipales de Bordeaux; photographe, Bernard Rakotomanga.

few serious objections. References to '*émulation salutaire*' imply that there were other less beneficial forms of emulation, and M. Lévi's assurance at a prize day in 1825 that parents need have no fear that their daughters would be puffed up with pride suggests a certain anxiety about what impact competitive prizes might have, although he spoke mainly to emphasize their value.[140] Paris rulings forbade public prize-givings, but this was mainly to prohibit the concerts and plays sometimes incorporated into the celebrations rather than to limit competitive learning.[141] The principle of emulation was not really in question.

Schoolgirls and their teachers seem to have taken school examinations seriously. In Le Mans in the 1850s, Adèle Riobé confided to her diary that she feared she would not be awarded any prizes. References to her marks in letters home suggest that her parents considered them important.[142] Good marks and prizes were not always liberally distributed. When asked about prize day at her school, Mme Babron, who kept a *pension* in Paris in the 1830s, replied that she was not sure if one would be held, since 'most of [my pupils] have not been awarded enough good marks to deserve a prize'.[143] Mme Estève also emphasized the value of examinations at her school in Paris in the 1850s. They were used to measure pupils' progress and to promote them to higher divisions, enabling them 'to benefit from the elementary and applied instruction indispensable to all these days'. Pupils could also take preparatory courses for the teaching diplomas that were increasingly popular in girls' schools, even amongst those not intending to teach.[144]

Taking the teaching examinations had become a common feature of middle-class girls' education. In 1845 a report from the Seine et Oise noted that 'most of the young women who are coming to the end of their education in the many boarding schools of Versailles and St Germain will take the exams, even if they have no intention of becoming teachers'.[145] In that year, there were 777 candidates for the Seine examinations, and inspectors were commenting on the schools that prepared pupils well. The institution headed by Mlle Overnay and Mlle Buttez was well known for its high-quality teaching, and 'quite a considerable number of the pupils of this school sit examinations either at the Hôtel de Ville or at the Sorbonne. Several have passed with distinction.'[146] Between 1855 and 1880, the Paris *Académie* delivered 24,171 diplomas to women between 1855 and 1880 (71% of all the *brevets* issued in Paris).[147] Large numbers of women were also taking the *brevet* elsewhere in France. Between 1851 and 1867, 463 female candidates obtained the *brevet* in Toulouse.[148] In

---

[140] M. Lévi, *Discours en vers, prononcé à la distribution des prix de l'institution de Mme Le Duc-Housset, le 23 août 1825* (Paris, 1825), 8.

[141] There were references to prize days in the Paris rulings of 1812, 1815, 1821, and 1837.

[142] Riobé, *Notice*, 37, 107–10.

[143] Mme Babron au Préfet de la Seine, 22 Aug. 1838, AD Seine, VD^6 650–1.

[144] Prospectus, Mme Estève, *c*.1852, AD Seine, VD^6 1191–4.

[145] Rapport de la Commission de pensions et institutions de demoiselles, Seine et Oise, 20 Nov. 1845, AD, F^{17} 12431.

[146] Inspection pension Overnay & Buttez, 1847, AD Seine, VD^6 367–10.

[147] Gréard, *L'enseignement secondaire*, 55.

[148] G. Bourgade, *Contribution à l'étude de l'éducaction féminine de 1830 à 1914* (Toulouse, 1979), 233.

Bordeaux there were 120 women taking the teaching examinations in 1860, rising to 183 in 1864.[149] Yet most candidates were not becoming teachers.

It is difficult to know precisely why the teaching examinations were so eagerly taken up. Gréard characterized it as a fashion—'*la mode des brevets*'—but this trivializes the interest the *brevets* provoked and underestimates the degree to which their adoption in schools built on a well-established pedagogical tradition.[150] In the 1840s, the *Revue de l'Enseignement des Femmes* emphasized their value as an insurance that women could fall back on. The *Revue* went on to say that 'thus, the diplomas have become for girls what the *baccalauréat* is for boys'.[151] This is an interesting comment on how male instruction might, like girls', be perceived as a kind of insurance, but also hints at a plausible explanation for the interest in the teaching examinations. Mlle Dziedzic, a Parisian schoolmistress in the 1870s, maintained that 'the *brevets* conferred by the *Académies* [are] the sanction of a solid and serious education'.[152] Significantly, though Bishop Dupanloup was to argue that young girls, being destined for private life, 'should not be taken to the lectures, to the examinations, to the diplomas, to the prize-givings which prepare men for public life', the publicity of the teaching examinations was precisely what was valued by schoolmistresses.[153] The teaching diplomas were being adopted as a prestigious school-leaving examination in establishments that had tested their pupils' attainments throughout their lives at school. Their success reflected both the degree to which girls' schools were regarded as public institutions and the continuing influence and long history of emulation as a pedagogical principle in France.

The Curriculum

In 1846 the prefect's report on boarding-schools in Paris noted that there had been an increase in the number of schools teaching scientific subjects since 1837, when 'elementary notions of physics' and natural history had been added to the subjects on which *maîtresses de pension* would be examined. Although, as he acknowledged, the teaching was fairly rudimentary, the sciences were taken up with considerable enthusiasm and the examinations were stimulating progress.[154] The administrative authorities in Paris clearly felt that the teaching examinations had an impact on schools, a view echoed by prefects in other departments.[155] An investigation of the subjects taught in 113 girls' schools in this period suggests

---

149 Brevets de Capacités—aspirantes, AD Gironde, Depot Vt III 3ᵉ E.
150 Gréard, *L'enseignement secondaire*, 55; Mayeur, *L'éducation*, 109; Rebecca Rogers challenges Gréard's interpretation on similar grounds, *From the Salon*, 183.
151 *REF* (Apr. 1845), 68.
152 Prospectus, Mme Dziedzic, Paris, 1876, AD Seine, VD⁶ 1191–4.
153 Dupanloup, *M. Duruy*, 27.
154 'Résultats de l'inspection des pensions de demoiselles, 1846', AD F¹⁷ 12431, 34, 38.
155 Réponses à l'enquête du Ministre suivant le règlement de la Seine de 1837, AD, F¹⁷ 12432.

that they were right (see Figure 6.2). The number of schools teaching subjects newly included on the examination programme in 1837, such as literature, astronomy, and English, appears to have increased after 1840.[156] The diplomas also contributed to the growing standardization of the curriculum. A study of forty-six girls' schools in Paris in the 1840s uncovers considerable homogeneity in the subjects taught.[157] The impact of examination programmes is also reflected in the decline in the number of schools teaching science after the passage of the *Loi Falloux* (1850), which dropped compulsory tests in scientific subjects. In the Nord, one schoolmistress subsequently noted that she would only teach natural history and physics if specially requested to do so by parents, because, although her *brevet supérieur* qualified her to teach those subjects, 'I understand that these sciences must not be preferred to useful subjects'.[158] Her attitude points to the reduced expectations and sceptical approach to female learning that coloured the provisions of the *Loi Falloux*.

But it is difficult to know whether changes to the examination programmes preceded or were in fact responding to changes to the curriculum in girls' schools. Schools were often more ambitious than the authorities. In 1832, when the programme was limited to reading and writing, religion, grammar, and arithmetic, Mme Nicolas' school in Avesnes offered a 'complete system of instruction' including religion, reading, writing, arithmetic, bookkeeping, French grammar, geography, use of the globes, history, and mythology.[159] Furthermore, as Figure 6.2 demonstrates, despite the more limited demands of the examination after 1850, girls' schools continued to teach a broad range of subjects. Although there was a decline in the teaching of science, the *Loi Falloux* does not seem to have had the negative impact on what was taught in schools that observers like Octave Gréard imagined.[160] The author of an 1845 article in the *Revue de l'Enseignement des Femmes* evidently felt that schoolmistresses were the prime movers in changes to the female curriculum; the development of instruction was due to 'the devotion of *Maîtresses d'institution* and the talent of professors'. But the article also recognized that the teaching examinations spurred on these schoolmistresses to extend girls' education further.[161] The incorporation of public examinations into school life both reflected and stimulated changes to the instruction offered to girls in schools. The *Revue* was recognizing the productive interaction between schools and the administrative authorities that contributed

[156] Following the same principle as Figure 6.1, Figure 6.2 shows the subjects taught in 113 private girls' schools in existence between 1820 and 1880, documenting the frequency with which each subject appeared on prospectuses and in inspection.

[157] Based on a study inspections of schools in the first *arrondissement*, 1845–9, AD Seine, VD[6] 158–3.

[158] Mlle Blanc au Maire d'Avesnes, 15 July 1852, AD Nord, 1 T 124/2.

[159] Prospectus, Mme Nicolas, Avesnes, 1832, AD Nord, 1 T 122/1. Arrêté du préfet du département du Nord, Extrait des registres des Actes de la Préfecture, 6 July 1830, AM Douai, 1 R 32.

[160] Gréard, *Enseignement secondaire*, 52–3.   [161] *REF* (Apr. 1845), 45.

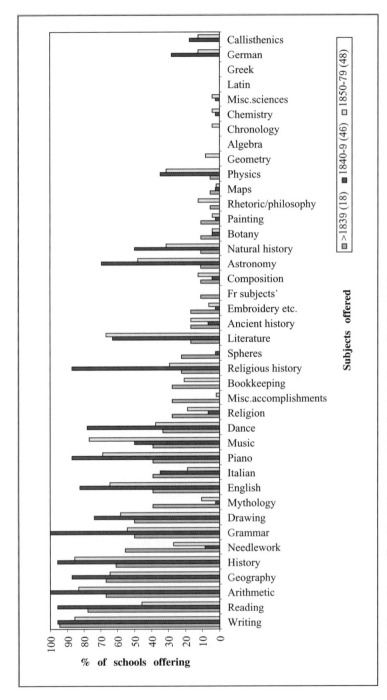

Figure 6.2. The subjects offered in 113 private girls' schools in France (1800–1880).

to the expansion of the female curriculum in the first half of the nineteenth century.

It is harder to assess what impact the examinations had on the quality of teaching in girls' schools. Only a few schoolgirl memoirs yield any information about how and how well girls were taught, suggesting that in most cases lessons proved eminently forgettable. At a convent school in Paris in the 1850s, Judith Gautier quickly reached the top of the class, having simply memorized the class textbook.[162] By contrast, at Mme Daubrée's school in the capital in the 1830s, Louise Ackermann was encouraged to read Byron, Shakespeare, Goethe, and Schiller. At home, her mother had been anxious to see her so often with a book, but reading was 'the activity and delight of my boarding-school life'.[163] At Mme Dupuy's Protestant boarding-school in the 1830s, Henriette Picanon remembered 'finding real pleasure' in her studies and in the '*émulation salutaire*' that inspired her and her schoolfellows. She recalled that her schoolmistress gave entertaining botany lessons, sending pupils out to collect flowers to study.[164] Mme Brada, at school in Paris in the 1850s, also enjoyed botany lessons. Professor LeMaoût, who used experiments to teach physics, would bring in flower specimens for his botany lessons: 'Nothing could have been more simple, more clear than these lessons, which furnished us with elementary notions of science, then judged fully sufficient.' The girls at her school, she felt, were made to feel that 'education was a serious business'.[165] The memories of Henriette Picanon and Mme Brada suggest that within limits some schools were providing stimulating instruction.

Responses to an inquiry in the late 1830s, however, tend to suggest that generally standards were not high. In eighteen departments, prefects felt that there was no need to establish a distinction between *pensions* and *institutions* because standards were so low that none of the boarding-schools in the region could aspire to the status of *institution*.[166] Nevertheless, the prefect of the Loire Inférieure felt that girls' education was keeping pace with the times in the larger towns; inspection reports from the Gironde and the Nord indicate that a considerable proportion of schools were offering good-quality instruction. Although in seven (29%) of twenty-four boarding-schools in Bordeaux in 1849–50 the instruction was considered weak, in twelve (50%) standards were good, and in two they were excellent.[167] In Paris in 1846, the prefect maintained that teaching in the 'higher' subjects was rarely very good. Too much time was devoted to the *arts d'agrément*, or accomplishments, though they were well taught. Scientific instruction, however, was improving, and his account of teaching in the basic subjects of the curriculum, reading, writing, grammar, arithmetic, history,

---

[162] Gautier, *Collier*, 225.   [163] Ackermann, *Œuvres*, p. v.   [164] Picanon, *Mon frère*, 35.
[165] Brada, *Souvenirs*, 87, 30.
[166] Réponses à l'enquête du Ministre suivant l de la Seine de 1837, AD, F^{17} 12432.
[167] Rapport sur l'enseignement primaire des filles dans l'arrdt. de Bordeaux, 1849–50, Inspection de M. Benoit, AD Gironde, 6 T 12.

and geography, was favourable. Overall the 1846 report gives the impression that, within limits, the teaching in Parisian girls' schools was reasonably successful.[168]

In 1864, when Victor Duruy investigated the condition of secondary schooling prior to establishing the *cours secondaires*, feelings were more mixed. In the Pyrénées Orientales, the inspector felt that instruction in girls' schools left much to be desired. The curriculum was usually limited to the compulsory subjects of the *brevet* to which was added piecemeal instruction in other subjects, usually given pompous titles.[169] Conversely, in the Seine Inférieure, the inspector recorded that curricula were extensive in the schools of Rouen, Dieppe, and Le Havre, and that schoolmistresses sent their pupils to be examined for the *brevet supérieur* with good results.[170] The verdict of the Eure et Loire inspector was similar, and, he observed, in the schools sending pupils to the examinations, 'pride is taken in joining useful and solid knowledge to the virtues of honourable women'.[171] The general impression is that although in some schools the instruction offered was pretentious, and although in many areas the standards aspired to were not high, they were usually met. Moreover, there were boarding-schools where the subjects of the *brevet supérieur* were well taught and the level of instruction was more elevated.

Compared to the reports of the SIC, the assessments of girls' schooling by inspectors and prefects in France seem relatively positive about the content and quality of girls' instruction. One explanation is that in boys' schools, though Classics continued to dominate the curriculum and retained considerable prestige, there was greater openness to other subjects. The Jesuit curriculum had incorporated history, geography, and scientific subjects, and the Revolutionary *écoles centrales* offered a curriculum less centred on Classics and incorporating scientific subjects. In the nineteenth-century *lycées*, Latin gradually regained its central place, but the sciences were retained in the higher classes and in the 1830s and 1840s history and geography were made a compulsory part of the curriculum.[172] The subjects of instruction in girls' schools, being recognized as part of the male curriculum, were more legitimate in the eyes of male observers. Undeniably, however, the positive assessments of instruction in girls' schools also reflect the inspectors' limited conception of what female education should encompass. In four departments, the inspectors were strongly opposed to the creation of a new secondary diploma. In nine others, they felt something like

---

[168] 'Résultat de l'inspection des pensions de demoiselles, 1846', AD, F^{17} 12431, 31–40.

[169] Rapport de l'inspecteur d'Académie sur le département des Pyrénéées Orientales, 6 Aug. 1864, AD, F^{17} 6846.

[170] Rapport de l'inspecteur d'Académie sur le département de la Seine Inférieure, 23 Aug. 1864, AD, F^{17} 6844.

[171] Rapport de l'inspecteur d'Académie sur le département du Pas de Calais, June 1864, AD, F^{17} 6845. Rapport de l'inspecteur d'Académie sur le département de l'Eure et Loire, 10 Aug. 1864, AD, F^{17} 6847.

[172] Prost, *L'énseignement*, 55–8; Compère and Savoie, 'Temps scolaire', 283–4.

the inspector of the Landes, who argued that the *brevet supérieur* marked the upper limits of what a woman should know.[173] Within those limits, girls' schools largely seemed to be achieving their objectives.

The extension of female education had not been the primary objective of the ministers and prefects who had drawn up the qualifications required for teachers in girls' schools. Their first consideration had been to ensure that teachers were of good morals.[174] But many also hoped that the teaching examinations would contribute to improving female instruction since, as the essay awarded first prize by the *Société pour l'Instruction Élémentaire* in 1838 argued, 'a woman without instruction and judgment will be the bane and ruin of her house'.[175] Such statements picked up on a long-standing theme in French girls' education, most famously and influentially articulated by Bishop Fénelon in *De l'éducation des filles*. Challenging the tendency to neglect girls' education and the view that all instruction made women pedantic and pretentious, he argued that they should be given an education which would prepare them for their role as 'the soul of the home'.[176] That education should consist of reading and writing, religion (not theology), arithmetic, and some basic legal knowledge. Latin, as the language of the church, could be allowed.[177]

Fénelon's treatise had considerable influence on girls' education in the nineteenth century. At least twenty-nine new editions were published between 1810 and 1870, and those calling for the extension of female instruction, whatever their political background, often cited it. In 1864, the prefect of the Eure et Loire, supporting the creation of a secondary *brevet* because he felt the education offered in convents was insufficient, quoted Fénelon to justify his case.[178] Bishop Dupanloup likewise cited Fénelon when maintaining the importance of women's education.[179] Ernest Legouvé, who gave the first course of lectures designed for women at the Collège de France, argued that, like Fénelon, he believed that 'woman being different from man, must be brought up differently, but at the same time she must be taught history, letters and even some of the sciences, in a serious way, but in a different way from that in which they are taught to men'. Girls' education should be based on a programme that would 'shed some light on everything'.[180] As one commentator noted in a new edition of *De l'éducation*

[173] Rapport de l'inspecteur d'Académie sur le département des Landes, 24 Aug. 1864, AD, F[17] 6844.

[174] Écoles de degré supérieur et pensionnats de filles, Barthez, conseiller de préfecture délégué, pour le préfet en congé, 30 Dec. 1820, *Actes Administratifs de la Gironde*, 165.

[175] Charpentier, *Des moyens*, 19.

[176] Fénelon, François Salignac de La Mothe, *De l'éducation des filles* (1687), ed. C. Defodon, 3rd edn. (Paris, 1882), 5.

[177] Ibid. 122.

[178] Rapport de l'inspecteur d'académie sur le département de l'Eure et Loire, 10 Aug. 1864, AD, F[17] 4867.

[179] Dupanloup, *M. Duruy*, 5.

[180] E. Legouvé, *La femme en France au XIXe siècle* (Paris, 1873), 34.

des filles in 1882, even if what girls were expected to learn had changed and
expanded since the seventeenth century, Fénelon's arguments were still relevant
to the France of the nineteenth century.[181]

Yet although Fénelon's treatise might be interpreted as justifying the importance of girls' education, the notion that women were weak and that, as a
result, their instruction must be contained within strict limits, was integral to *De
l'éducation des filles*.[182] Latin could be taught, but only to girls who would 'hide
what they had learned and would seek in it only their own edification'. 'You
should restrain their minds within the usual bounds and teach them that their
sex must have a reticence with regard to knowledge, almost as sensitive as that
which inspires the horror of vice.'[183] Care must be taken not to let girls' curiosity
run away with them or to let them become 'savantes ridicules', an allusion to
Molière's plays, *Les précieuses ridicules* (1659) and *Les femmes savantes* (1672),
which satirized those who pursued knowledge to the point of pedantry. In the
nineteenth century it was not only Fénelon's arguments in favour of providing
a solid education for girls that were reiterated: the notion that there were and
should be limits to female instruction was echoed by the same authors who
called for girls' education to be reformed, and Molière's plays were cited almost
as frequently as Fénelon's treatise to warn of the dangers of female education.
Women's domestic role required that they should receive an education which
'shed light on everything', but they should never be allowed to become *femmes
savantes*. The influence of this idea emerges clearly from the inspection reports
and prefectoral rulings. The prefect of the Loire Inférieure argued in 1837 that
'woman' should receive an instruction analogous to that of men, but emphasized
that 'there is no need for her to study the great theories of mathematics in depth,
nor for her to plunge in to the smoke of a chemistry laboratory'.[184] Examination
programmes set limits to the depth of girls' studies. According to the 1837 Seine
ruling, they should learn only 'elements of literature', 'elementary notions of
physics and natural history'. The *Loi Falloux* limited the study of history and
geography to 'elements' and advocated only applied arithmetic.[185]

Extensive reading was also considered suspect for women. Fénelon had advised
careful selection of the books given to girls. His collaborator at Saint-Cyr,
Mme de Maintenon, recommended that the sisters there should 'teach your
demoiselles to be extremely sober with regard to reading and always to prefer
needlework, housekeeping and the duties of their state'.[186] Her advice was
echoed by the *Journal des demoiselles*, which in 1883 advised girls against reading,

[181] C. Defodon, 'Introduction', in Fénelon, *De l'éducation*, p. xiii.
[182] Rapley, 'Fénelon revisited', 306–8; M. Alcover, 'The indecency of knowledge', *Rice University
Studies*, 64 (1978), 31–7.
[183] Fénelon, *De l'éducation*, 71.
[184] Réponses à l'enquête du Ministre suivant le règlement de la Seine de 1837, AD, F[17] 12432.
[185] Loi sur l'enseignement, 15 mars 1850, *Lois et actes*, 109–27.
[186] Maintenon, *Entretiens*, 21.

a self-indulgent use of time that would be better spent in domestic duties.[187] The numerous prohibitions against day girls bringing books to school and the close surveillance of school books by the *dames inspectrices* shows how such prescriptions translated into school practice. Louise Ackermann's experience of wide reading in poetry and literature seems to have been very much the exception to the rule. At Mme Allix-Mollard's school in the first *arrondissement* in the 1830s, the only books permitted were textbooks. Although there was a whole library at a neighbouring school, in 1840 the inspectress made sure that it was 'purified'.[188] Bishop Dupanloup, who in the 1870s sought to improve and extend the education offered to Catholic women, argued that women should read, but 'only what is pure and exquisite, and they must take care to re-read . . . always to read attentively, and as much as possible pen in hand . . . never to leave a book without having finished, and never to finish a book without summarizing it in writing'.[189] He particularly recommended the literature of the seventeenth century, especially Bossuet, Bourdaloue, Pascal, Fénelon, and Mme de Maintenon: choices reflecting the conservatism of his approach to women's education and which were echoed in pedagogical texts and school libraries. Dupanloup's prescriptions reflect the view that girls' education must be solid, serious, and intellectual, but also the sense that, for women, instruction was seen as the foundation of moral improvement, rather than intellectual growth.

In both England and France, in the period before 1867, girls' schools developed relatively broad curricula, encompassing history, geography, literature, modern languages, and scientific subjects. Contrary to what the critics of the 1860s suggested, in neither country does girls' schooling seem to have been exclusively concerned with training in the accomplishments, though on both sides of the Channel music, dance, and drawing were an important part of the female curriculum. It is difficult to gauge the quality of the instruction offered to girls. Pupils' memoirs uncover a wide spectrum of experiences, ranging from the excessive amounts of memory work and chaotic schoolrooms described by Frances Cobbe and Judith Gautier to the vigorous intellectual atmosphere encountered by Bessie Parkes and Louise Ackermann. But it seems fair to suggest that the criticisms of observers like the SIC and Jules Simon tell us more about their own assumptions than they do about the instruction available in girls' schools.

However, the organization and structure of learning were very different in France and England. French girls' schools, building on a Jesuit and *Ancien Régime* model of the school, were organized into hierarchies of classes, sometimes housed in individual classrooms. In England, schoolmistresses often continued

---

[187] 'Le monologue', *Journal des Demoiselles* (May 1883), 120, quoted in Cosnier, *Le silence,* 241.
[188] Inspection pension Allix-Mollard, 1838, AD Seine, VD⁶ 158–3; Procès verbaux du comité de surveillance du 1er arrdt., 2 May 1840, AD Seine, VD⁶ 158–3.
[189] Dupanloup, *Femme studieuse,* 44.

to use an individual method of instruction late into the century, seeking to preserve the advantages of pedagogic strategies that permitted a child-centred approach to teaching. This was also often reflected in a sceptical attitude to emulation and competition. While some schools did have systems of internal examinations and prize-giving ceremonies, they were not the organizing principle of school education as they were on the Continent. In France, again building on the Catholic educational tradition, schoolmistresses embraced the notion of emulation and rapidly incorporated public examinations into the school programme.

Schoolgirl memoirs and inspection reports sometimes give a favourable impression of the instruction offered in French girls' schools. There were, however, considerable restrictions on women's access to knowledge, reflecting a hostility to female intellectual activity that seems to have been related to Catholic understandings of femininity which emphasized innocence and piety. In both countries, schools employed male visiting professors, but in England schoolmistresses taught a broader range of subjects while in France the assumed superiority of the male professors was further underlined by the hierarchical structure of the school. In the 1860s, whereas the SIC affirmed the intellectual equality of the sexes, argued that 'the main and leading elements of instruction should be the same in the two cases', and recommended that more women should have access to higher instruction, the inspectors who responded to Duruy's inquiry were insisting upon the limits that should be put on girls' education. At the inaugural session of the *Cours Duruy* in Tours in 1869, rather than extolling the new horizons his course would open out for them, M. de Tastes told his future pupils that 'these studies, in developing your youthful intelligence, can only add to the feelings of modesty which are the gracious attribute of your age and sex, since the more you are taught, the more you will see how much you are still ignorant of'.[190] It is not surprising that Geneviève Breton, who followed the *Cours Duruy* in Paris, wrote in her diary that 'a woman hides her knowledge as a man hides his ignorance'.[191]

Yet while ideas of feminine domesticity played out in different ways on either side of the Channel, posing different challenges to schoolmistresses and their pupils, in both countries the period 1800 to 1867 saw a considerable expansion and development of the female curriculum. In both England and France, some lay schoolmistresses were developing curricula that emphasized the importance of a scientific approach to girls' instruction and, in the process, undermining ideas about women's intellectual inferiority. At the same time, pupils and parents were increasingly inclined to attach importance to girls' success in their studies, implying an unspoken challenge to the view that the value of female education lay solely in the uses girls would have for it as wives and mothers, and a recognition that it could be a source of fulfilment and an important element of a girl's personal

---

[190] Discours inaugural de M de Tastes, Tours, 5 décembre 1867, quoted in Cosnier, *Le silence*, 76.
[191] Journal entry, 22 Dec. 1869, G. Breton, *Journal 1867–1875* (Paris, 1985), 69.

growth. Moreover, the increasing use of diplomas and school examinations as school-leaving exams offered an alternative to a conception of feminine growth and development whose end point was socially defined by entry to the marriage market, or marriage itself. Together, these developments combined to expand, and ultimately to undermine, ideals of domestic womanhood.

7

Crossing the Channel

In 1847, Dorothea Beale, then 16, was sent with her two sisters to a school in Paris. The establishment was run by a Mlle Bray. This was the same schoolmistress who had run into trouble with the authorities in the Seine in 1841 for refusing to place a sign at the entrance to the school she had taken over from her mother, because 'in her own country, this was not done'. Despite Mlle Bray's attempts to preserve the English character of her school, the young Dorothea Beale was evidently struck by its foreignness. Looking back on her experiences at school in Paris, she commented: 'The mechanical order, the system of the French school was worth seeing, worth living in, only not for long.'[1]

The Beales were not unusual in sending their daughters to school in France. In 1847–8, foreign pupils—most of them English—made up 9% of the 1,382 girls in the thirty-four boarding-schools of the first *arrondissement* of Paris.[2] Teachers were also crossing the Channel for their education, and there was movement in both directions: throughout the period, English schoolmistresses were opening schools in France, and French teachers were establishing themselves in England. Others travelled in search of work as school assistants and governesses. By the mid-nineteenth century, so many English women were seeking positions in France that a guide for English schoolmistresses published in 1866 warned that of the estimated 400 English teachers currently in Paris, three-quarters were unable to find work.[3] In Britain scholastic agents advertised that they were particularly adept in placing foreign governesses. There may have been some truth to this: in 1861, the census enumerators recorded 885 French teachers and governesses in England and Wales.[4]

The first half of the nineteenth century, moreover, saw research into foreign education systems becoming a feature of educational policy-making, with both the French and the British dispatching observers to the other side of the Channel.[5]

---

[1] D. Beale, MS Autobiography, quoted in Raikes, *Dorothea Beale,* 13. See also the comments in Beale, 'Girls' schools', 544.

[2] Feuilles d'Inspection, 1846–7, AD Seine, VD[6] 158–3.   [3] Mair, *Educator's guide,* 108.

[4] For example, the 'Oxford and Cambridge Select English and Foreign Governess Scholastic and Tutorial Agency', 19 Cockspur St., London, conducted by Mme Hulbert, Prospectus, JJ Coll., Education/45. 'Census 1861—Summary Tables', *Parliamentary Papers* (1863), Vol. 58, Pt. 1. 90.

[5] C. de Bellaigue, '"Educational homes" and "barrack-like schools": cross-Channel perspectives on secondary education for boys in mid-nineteenth century England and France', *Oxford Studies*

At the same time, perceived differences between the situation of women in France and England were attracting the attention of many contemporary observers; at mid-century, comparisons between the two countries played a part in the arguments of those who sought to extend opportunities for female employment. English commentators contrasted the activity and involvement with commerce of middle-class French women and the enforced idleness of English women.[6] In France, C. de Sault argued that the French should spend less time thinking about the philosophical question of 'woman' and more time making small and pragmatic changes, like their English neighbours.[7] In this context, it might be expected that pupils' and schoolmistresses' journeys across the Channel would have contributed to the dissemination of pedagogical ideas—that French practices would influence English schoolmistresses, and that their French counterparts would be affected by what they discovered in England.

However, as Dorothea Beale's remarks suggest, impressions of education abroad were not always favourable, and the effect of schoolgirls' and teachers' experiences abroad was complex. In the memoirs and correspondence of those who travelled for their education, the different traditions and practices which pupils and teachers discovered when crossing the Channel were commented on, but not necessarily viewed as worthy of imitation. Despite the volume of traffic between the respective countries in this period, schoolmistresses in the respective countries do not seem to have been much influenced by their counterparts abroad. The differing educational traditions of the two countries, differing ideas about the role and nature of women, and deeply engrained conceptions of Frenchness or Englishness limited the depth and impact of these educational exchanges. There were those for whom travelling abroad served primarily to reinforce existing attitudes. Examining the circumstances in which women and girls were sent across the Channel and their experiences abroad throws into relief the intersections between gender, education, and notions of national identity that shaped and informed the experiences of pupils and schoolmistresses in the period 1800 to 1867.

ENGLISH WOMEN IN FRANCE

A French education

The phenomenon of English girls travelling to France for their education had a long history. From the seventeenth century the daughters of the Catholic nobility were being sent to convent schools in Belgium or France for their education.

in Comparative Education, 14 Solidus 2 (2004), 89–108; K. Ochs and D. Phillips, 'Comparative Studies and "cross-national attraction" in education', *Educational Studies,* 28 (2002), 325–39.

  [6] Parkes, *Essays,* 147; J. Boucherett, *Hints on self-help: a book for young women* (London, 1863), 34.
  [7] C. de Sault (pseud. of Claire de Charnacé), 'Les femmes', 300.

Some were sent to establishments opened by English sisters whose orders had been expelled from Britain during the Reformation. The English Canonesses of the Holy Sepulchre, for example, attached a small school for English girls to the convent they founded in Liège in 1616.[8] By the end of the eighteenth century, the practice was also being adopted by Protestant families, prompting concerns about the 'fashion for foreign education'. Most of these travelling schoolgirls were sent to France. In 1861, *Crockford's* drew parents' attention to 641 'foreign schools' for girls, 607 (94.7%) of which were in France; prospectuses for French schools were also translated and disseminated in Britain.[9]

It is difficult to discover precisely how many English girls were in fact educated abroad. As noted above, in the late 1840s, English girls made up about 9% of boarders at schools in the first *arrondissement* of Paris. Although many, like the Beale sisters, must have returned home during the troubles of 1848–51, by 1854 the schools had recovered, with the *dames déléguées* reporting that of the 13,500 pupils in *pensionnats* around the capital, 359 (2.7%) were British.[10] Outside the capital, English pupils tended to be concentrated in the north-west, particularly Calais, Dieppe, and Boulogne. Some travelled further south: *Crockford's* listed twenty-two schools in the Gironde, and six in the Pyrénées. In Bordeaux, in 1851, Mélanie Durand opened a boarding-school specifically intended for English pupils. That such a school was considered potentially profitable suggests that demand among English families was considerable.[11] This interest in French schooling may help to explain why, in 1861, women and girls outnumbered boys and men among the English community in France, representing 56% of the 25,711 British residents of France in that year.[12] English girls were also sent to schools in Belgium, a phenomenon documented in the novels Charlotte Brontë based on her own experience as a teacher in Brussels—*Villette* (1853), and *The Professor* (1857). Like Brontë's fictional schools, the Belgian establishments attended by English pupils tended to be modelled on French institutions. A French woman in fact headed the *pensionnat* where Brontë herself taught. The English girls who made up part of the 4,092-strong British population of Belgium in 1861 were being sent to Brussels in search of a *French* education.

There were a number of reasons why parents, and Protestant parents in particular, would consider sending their daughters to French schools. Of the fifty-six women in the biographical sample of English pupils, five (9%), including

---

[8] S. Smith, *History of the New Hall Community of Canonesses Regular of the Holy Sepulchre* (Roehampton, 1899), 48–67, cited in M. Whitehead, 'Jesuit secondary education revolutionized: the Académie Anglaise, Liège, 1773–1794', *Paedagogica Historica*, 40/1–2 (2004), 33–44.

[9] Pendered, *Remarks*, 40; *Crockford's*, 'Foreign schools', 188–96. See, for example, the prospectus from Mme Aubert's school preserved in the Special Collections of the Institute of Education, Prospectus AR Eb.1 AUB.

[10] Cited in R. Rogers, 'French education for British girls in the nineteenth century', *Women's History Network Magazine*, 24 (2002), 22.

[11] Déclaration d'ouverture, Mélanie Durand, 25 Oct. 1851, AD Gironde, 48 T 1.

[12] *Statistique de la France: résultats généraux du dénombrement de 1861* (Strasbourg, 1864), 76.

Dorothea Beale, spent time at school in France. For Beale, as for some other English *pensionnaires*, attending a French school was part of being 'educated for a governess'. For some parents, the chief attraction may have been the relative cheapness of a boarding-school education in France. Although James Grant claimed in 1844 that the average cost of educating a girl in Paris, which he estimated at 1,500F p.a. (£62.50), was roughly equivalent to the price of an English education, this was based on a fairly conservative estimate of English prices, and did not take into account the inevitable 'extras' not included in the English fee.[13] If they took the full range of subjects, pupils at Rachel Martineau's school in Liverpool in the 1830s paid at least £84 p.a.[14] Sending a daughter to France for her education might take some pressure off the family purse. Above all, however, girls were sent to France to 'finish' their education. For Fanny Kemble, Emmeline Pankhurst, and Margaret Nevinson, whose last years as schoolgirls were spent in France, receiving a French education was the final stage in their progress towards becoming, as Emmeline Pankhurst put it, 'a finished young lady'.[15]

As seen above, French was one of the subjects most commonly offered in girls' boarding-schools in England, and considerable time and effort was devoted to it. By the end of the eighteenth century, an 'accomplished woman' was expected to know French, just as a man who had received a liberal education was expected to know Latin.[16] French continued to be of central importance in the female curriculum in the nineteenth century. In the 1870s, even the staunchly patriotic Charlotte Yonge would claim that 'French is a necessity. To speak it with perfect ease and a Parisian accent is a useful and graceful accomplishment.'[17] Such arguments highlight the social value of French, which, like Latin for boys, served as a sign of membership of the educated classes. They also reveal the way in which French was conflated with femininity in this period. By the nineteenth century the vigorously masculine training and classical education offered in public schools was replacing the Grand Tour as an ideal in middle- and upper-class boys' education, and French manners and politeness were decried as effeminate in men. For girls, however, exposure to French society and knowledge of the language was still valued. Indeed, partly because of the association of Frenchness with politeness, it was seen as characteristically feminine. For young women, having received a French education signified social status and cultural sophistication.[18] The girl who spent a year or so in France before entering society had both 'finished' her education and acquired the 'finish' and polish offered by education there.

French 'finish' and 'polish', however, also had negative connotations. Parents were warned that, by sending their daughters to France, they would also acquire

[13] J. Grant, *Paris and its people* (London, 1844), 296.
[14] Prospectus, Miss Martineau, Liverpool, 1838, HMCO, MS Radice 8, Hutton family letters.
[15] Pankhurst, *My own story*, 11.   [16] Barbauld, *A legacy*, 27.
[17] C. Yonge, *Womankind* (London, 1876) 159–61.   [18] Cohen, 'Manliness', 44–61.

the superficiality, frivolity, and hypocrisy that were considered part of the French national character. Hannah More was critical of 'that levity of manners, that contempt of the Sabbath, that fatal familiarity with loose principles, and those relaxed notions of conjugal fidelity' brought from France to England by fashionable women who had lived too long in France.[19] Such concerns for the English girls exposed to these dangers was reiterated throughout the century, and the harmful effects of a French education personified in fiction by characters like the flirtatious and flighty Ginevra Fanshawe in *Villette*, or the superficial Cynthia Kirkpatrick in *Wives and Daughters* (1865) by Elizabeth Gaskell. The frivolity of these characters, their interest in appearance and fashion, and their lack of proper concern for the domestic virtues exemplified, in Gaskell's novel, by the modest and home-loving Molly Gibson, all refer back to the French education they had received.

For Brontë, however, worse than Ginevra's flirtatiousness was her irreligion: 'they call me a Protestant, you know, but really I am not sure whether I am one or not. I don't well know the difference between Romanism and Protestantism.'[20] This impiety, and the possibility of conversion to Catholicism, was Hannah More's principal objection to the employment of French governesses. 'Piety and principle', she argued, should not be 'offered up as victims to sounds and accents'.[21] Similar concerns were expressed about the situation of Protestant girls sent to school in Catholic France. In 1821, the alleged kidnapping and conversion to Catholicism of Emily Loveday, the daughter of an Englishman living in France, attracted widespread attention in both France and England, and seemed to give credence to such fears.[22] Novels like Rachel McCrindell's *The schoolgirl in France*, published in 1840, drew inspiration from cases like Emily Loveday's and sought to remind parents of the dangers of a French education. The novel tells the story of two English girls' struggle to resist their teachers' efforts to convert them while at school in France. It was based, McCrindell claimed, on her own experience in witnessing all too often 'the foundation of a Protestant education sapped and undermined . . . and the deluded parents left to mourn their alienated child a prey to the seductions of Popery, or the not less probable danger of unsettled principles and practical infidelity'.[23] With such tales in mind, the *Morning Advertiser* warned families that they should even be

---

[19] More, *Strictures*, i. 104; on anti-French feeling see L. Colley, *Britons forging the nation, 1707–1837* (New Haven, 1992), 17–18, 251–6; S. Cottrell, 'The Devil on two sticks: Franco-phobia in 1803', in R. Samuel (ed.), *Patriotism: the making and unmaking of British national identity* (London, 1989), 259–74.

[20] C. Brontë, *Villette*, (London, 1979) 63.   [21] More, *Strictures*, i. 106.

[22] *Pétition à la Chambre des Pairs par M. Douglas Loveday, anglais et Protestant, se plaignant du rapt de séducation opéré sur ses deux filles et sur sa nièce dans une maison d'éducation où il les avait placées à Paris* (Paris, 1821); C. Ford, 'Private lives and public order in Restoration France: the seduction of Emily Loveday', *American Historical Review*, 99/1 (1994), 21–43.

[23] R. McCrindell, *The schoolgirl in France*, 4th edn. (New York, 1846), Preface.

circumspect about governesses who had acquired their French accent in France; they might secretly have been converted to Catholicism.[24]

One option for parents who wished their daughters to receive the benefits of education in France, but were concerned about the influence of Catholic schoolmistresses, was to send them to a Protestant establishment. This was common enough for an article of 1858 to mock the parents swayed by advertisements for establishments like the 'Protestant Collegiate School for Young Ladies by Madame Pourpre', which offered both French and religion. One better were the French schools run by Protestant Englishwomen that claimed to offer 'education in France, and at a first-rate finishing school', but '*en famille*, with English comforts and maternal care'. As the author put it, 'France *pur et simple* we know has its drawbacks. France teaches manners, but England is the school for morals'; the English schoolmistress in France offered the ideal combination of both.[25] In practice, as we have seen, it was not so simple. English schoolmistresses in France had to negotiate between the demands of English parents, and pressures to conform to French models of schooling. Mlle Bray presented her school as an English institution, and to the extent that she did not conform to French rulings, the administration shared this view. Yet, to Dorothea Beale, Mlle Bray's school was a foreign and 'French' establishment. In the 1860s, difficulties like those encountered by Mlle Bray were common enough for Robert Mair to warn prospective buyers of French establishments that they might find themselves on the wrong side of the law.[26] Despite these tensions, English-run schools in France were fairly numerous. In the 1840s, the first *arrondissement* in Paris was home not only to Mlle Bray's establishment (opened before 1819) but also to that of the Demoiselles Martin (established in 1837) and to that of Mme Shanahan, an Irish Catholic (although she was described as 'anglaise' by the inspectors),. The latter seem to have found a balance between parental and prefectoral demands. Both the inspectors and British visitors were pleased with the school, which, in the words of one 'English visitor', combined 'the strictest regard to religious education, based on Evangelical principles, with the highest order of secular instruction'.[27]

It is not clear how Mlle Bray's mother or the Demoiselles Martin came to establish their schools in France, but the relative cheapness of life on the Continent—which attracted many British families—may well have influenced their decision.[28] This was certainly the case for Elizabeth Lachlan's teacher. In 1802, on returning to Miss Shepherd's London school after the vacation,

---

[24] Cited in F. C. Green, *A comparative view of French and British civilisation, 1850–70* (London, 1965), 51.

[25] 'Girls' schools', article cutting marked 'Nov. 1858' in JJ Coll., Education/49.

[26] Mair, *Educator's guide*, 41.

[27] Bulletins d'Inspection, 1838–41, Feuilles d'Inspection, 1846–7, AD Seine, VD[6] 158–3; 'An English visitor', quoted by Rogers, 'French education', 22.

[28] P. Gerbod, *Voyages aux pays des mangeurs de grenouilles* (Paris, 1991), 88.

Lachlan learnt that 'my governess had, during the holidays, taken advantage of the peace, and rambled over to France . . . The country was tempting, provisions were cheap, the natives were courteous. The thought struck her of establishing herself with all her school in that country . . . in less than three months all was ready for her departure from England.'[29] With rents and salaries lower in France, a schoolmistress could live very comfortably. Fanny Kemble, a pupil at Frances Rowden's school in Paris in the 1820s, recalled that after a year or so in Paris, her schoolmistress was able to move to 'a much finer [house], at the very top of the Champs Elysées, a large, substantial, stone mansion, within lofty iron gates and high walls of inclosure [sic]'.[30] Such descriptions, and the longevity of schools like Mlle Bray's (in existence at least from 1829 to 1841), suggest that the combination of English demand for a 'safe' form of French education and cheaper living costs meant that establishing a school in France could be a profitable move.

Teaching in France could also be financially beneficial in other ways. The primacy of French in the female curriculum meant that the ability to speak and write it was regarded as a considerable advantage in an English governess or schoolmistress. Like English schoolmistresses in France, a teacher who had a good knowledge of French could offer the benefits of a French education, while mitigating its dangers. As a *Guide for governesses* published in 1875 put it, 'a well-trained, highly educated, good principled English gentlewoman will always prove the best governess and the one most fitted to retain the bloom of innocence and purity in [a girl's] heart, while she educates her mind'. The same guide estimated that a governess with 'French acquired in France' could expect to earn at least forty guineas p.a. (£42), a substantial sum in a period when they might otherwise be paid as little as £26 p.a.[31] Thus, the Brontë sisters' stint in Brussels was prompted by Charlotte's recognition of the monetary value of 'French acquired in France'. In September 1841, she wrote to Aunt Branwell that she had been advised to delay the opening of the school she and her sisters were planning by six months and 'by all means to contrive, by hook or by crook, to spend the intervening time in some school on the continent. They say . . . that without some such step towards attaining superiority we shall probably have a very hard struggle and fail in the end.'[32] By the time the Brontës were travelling, the journey between London and Calais took only nine hours and a ticket could be had for just over ten shillings. Once in Brussels, the sisters paid £50 each for their board and extra French lessons.[33] Considering the difference in earnings that 'French acquired in France' could make, this was a reasonable investment.

---

[29] Lachlan, *Jehovh-jireh*, 20.   [30] Kemble, *Records*, 115.

[31] C. Stevens, *Guide for governesses (English and Foreign) Nursery and Finishing* (York, 1875), 29, 22.

[32] C. Brontë to E. Branwell, Rawdon, 29 Sept. 1841, in Shorter, *Brontës*, i. 219.

[33] Gerbod, *Voyages*, 111; C. Brontë to E. Nussey, Haworth, 20 Jan. 1842, Shorter, *Brontës*, i. 227.

Certainly, in Carlisle in the 1850s, Mary Smith found it difficult to obtain pupils because she could not offer French.[34]

A period in France was not only valuable in financial terms, it was prized as training by those who sought to equip themselves for their work as teachers. For example, in 1822, Rebecca Franklin and Eliza Dyer travelled to France to prepare themselves for teaching. Franklin would return to join with her sister in opening the school in Coventry where George Eliot was a pupil. Dyer, the daughter of a London schoolmistress, came home to assist her mother before opening her own establishment. Sending the girls to France was part of a clear family strategy—as Mrs Dyer explained, 'I feel it a duty to qualify [Eliza] as speedily as possible to occupy a useful station in my own school, and this it appears to me will best be accomplished by sending her to France.'[35] Similarly, in 1829, when Mary Carpenter and her sister Anna decided to carry out their father's project of a school for girls, they spent a summer in Paris 'by way of further qualifying themselves for this fresh enterprise'.[36] Some future teachers, like Dorothea Beale, were sent to Paris as pupils; however, it was more common for them to travel as governesses or school assistants. At least eight (10.8%) of the seventy-four schoolmistresses in the biographical sample of English schoolmistresses spent time in France perfecting their language skills and working as assistant teachers. In 1847, school inspectors found fourteen English women working in boarding-schools of the first *arrondissement* in Paris alone, and, as noted above, in the 1860s the number of English teachers in Paris was so large that it was feared that many would not find work.[37] By the 1870s, a period in France was expected of those intending to teach: 'The proper training for a finishing governess, is for her to be educated at a good school in the south of England, remaining there a year or two as governess pupil, and from there, going (if possible as a pupil, but if not, as governess pupil,) to Paris for a year to acquire fluency in speaking French; from France she should proceed to Hanover for a year, to perfect herself in German and music.'[38]

The formality hints at the degree to which strategies for acquiring French in France had become institutionalized as more and more young women found it necessary to offer some kind of qualification for teaching work. Before the development of secondary training colleges in the 1870s, and before public examinations and university degrees were opened to women, offering 'French acquired in France' was one of the few ways in which English schoolmistresses could demonstrate that they were qualified for their work, or hope to gain an edge over their competitors.

[34] Smith, *Autobiography*, 169.

[35] Agnes Dyer to Mrs John Saffery, Battersea, 5 Jan. 1822, Angus Library, Regent's Park College, Dyer papers, R16/12; Haight, *George Eliot*, 10; R. Aldrich, *School, state and society in Victorian Britain* (Theydon Bois, 1995), 22–3.

[36] Carpenter, *Mary Carpenter*, 22.   [37] Feuilles d'inspection, 1847–8, AD Seine, VD[6] 158–3.

[38] Stevens, *Guide*, 10.

Experiences in France

On arriving in France, what reaction did English schoolgirls and schoolmistresses have to their new surroundings? Few of those who crossed the Channel left detailed descriptions of life abroad—however, the writings of some of the teachers and pupils in the biographical samples offer glimpses of their experiences. Several were struck by the grandeur of the buildings in which their schools were housed. Fanny Kemble's description of the 'fine' house into which Frances Rowden transferred her Parisian school in the 1820s echoes Elizabeth Lachlan's memories of the building into which Miss Shepherd's school moved in 1802: she describes a large château, owned by aristocrats who had suffered during the Revolution, which boasted twenty rooms 'en enfilade'. Like Lachlan, Margaret Nevinson remembered the school she attended near Paris from 1874 to 1875 as being housed in a château; she also remarked on it size—forty boarders, and another twenty day girls—and on the new classrooms, built as a wing to the 'great house'. Louisa Lumsden recalled how the French school near Brussels—the Château de Koekelberg—which she had attended in the 1850s had a separate salon, a room for dancing with a platform for spectators, an 'English' classroom, and a 'French' classroom, as well as dormitories of six beds, side by side.[39] That these English schoolgirls should comment on the size, specialized rooms, and grand style of the buildings in which their French schools were housed is not surprising. Their descriptions hint at the contrast between the imposing surroundings of French schools, and the more homely character of English establishments. At the same time, however, these schoolgirls were echoing contemporary travel literature that placed great emphasis on the architectural splendour of the capital and of French châteaux.[40] It is difficult to know how much such accounts coloured the experiences and reminiscences of schoolgirls like Elizabeth Lachlan. There were significant contrasts in location and physical organization between English and French schools, but in discovering and remarking on these differences, English pupils and teachers may well have been influenced by their preconceptions about French architectural style.

Yet while Parisian streets and French palaces impressed many travellers, they were also struck by the Spartan interiors, or even the squalor they found hidden behind these imposing façades. The same theme appears in the recollections of some English schoolgirls. Mary Browne, who attended a Mme Crosnier's school in Paris in 1821, was scathing about the dirty conditions. The tables in the

---

[39] Lachlan, *Jehovh-Jireh*, 25–6; Lumsden, *Yellow leaves*, 6–7; Pankhurst, *My own story*, 10; Charlotte Brontë's friend Mary Taylor also attended the Château de Koekelberg in the 1840s; Charlotte described it as 'a first rate establishment', but it was too expensive for the Brontë family: Charlotte Brontë to Elizabeth Branwell, Rawdon, 29 Sept. 1841, Shorter, *Brontës*, i. 219.

[40] C. Hancock, 'Your city does not speak my language: cross-channel views of Paris and London in the early nineteenth century', *Planning Perspectives*, 12 (1997), 1–18; C. Hancock, *Paris et Londres au XIXe siècle: représentations dans les guides et récits de voyage* (Paris, 2003), 133–42.

schoolroom were 'black with ink stains and dirt', the maps looked 'as if they have been nibbled by mice on the walls'.[41] Little seemed to have changed in the second half of the century. Margaret Nevinson's school may have been housed in a château, but the sanitation was 'medieval', and the windows were constantly kept closed. Sarah Fitton's fictional account of life as a teacher in France (which is probably based on her own experience) echoes these descriptions. On her arrival, the heroine of *How I became a governess* (1861) is struck by the strangeness of the Empire furniture in Mme de Beaumonde's school—it was 'cold and lifeless'. Her room in the attic was no better: cold and bare, and furnished only with an iron bedstead, a rush chair, a washing-stand with a jug of dirty water, and a few pegs for her clothes. The deficiencies of the classrooms and dormitories were further accentuated by the comforts of the school proprietor's apartments. Mme de Beaumonde's room was 'luxurious'.[42]

Such descriptions of the physical conditions of life at school in France echoed another recurring idea in English travel writing on France in this period: the notion that the apparent contrast between the splendid exterior and the bare and comfortless interior of homes in France reflected French national character. In this analysis, the French attention to exteriors and ornament indicated their superficial and deceitful nature. The appeal and attractiveness of French architecture, and, by implication, of the French, was based on a shallow showiness, not on interior comfort, or on virtue and morality.[43] Highlighting the contrast between the schoolmistress's apartments and those inhabited by the pupils was another variation on this theme, underlining the hypocrisy of the French schoolmistresses who professed to care so well for their charges. While discovering the contrasts between the physical conditions of life at school in France and England, these schoolgirls and teachers were also responding to and contributing to, and reinforcing, English notions of the French national character.

Accounts of encounters with French teachers and pupils pointed to differences between Continental practices and what was common at home, while reflecting contemporary ideas of Frenchness. Charlotte Brontë began by noticing the similarity between Mme Héger and her English schoolmistress: 'Mme Héger, the head, is a lady of precisely the same cast of mind, degree of cultivation, and quality of intellect as Miss Catherine Wooler.' There was a significant difference between them, however, because the former had not been disappointed and 'soured'. 'In other words, she is a married instead of a maiden lady.'[44] It clearly emerges from Brontë's letters that she believed Mme Héger wielded considerable authority as both a married woman and a schoolmistress, and that she was struck by this as something unusual and foreign. Brontë did not explore the contrasts further in

---

[41] M. Browne, *The diary of a girl in France,* ed. H. N. Shore (London, 1905), 94–5.

[42] Nevinson, *Life's fitful fever,* 37; S. Fitton, *How I became a governess* (London, 1861), 36.

[43] Hancock, 'Your city'.

[44] C. Brontë to E. Nussey, Brussels, May 1842, in Shorter, *Brontës,* i. 237.

her fiction: Mlle Reuter in *The Professor* is unmarried and Mme Beck in *Villette* is a widow. She did, however, emphasize the theme of authority, evoking Mlle Reuter and Mme Beck's management of their schools with images of monarchy and government. Brontë's relationship with the Hégers was complex (most scholars believe that she had a romantic attachment to M. Héger), and may well have influenced her assessment. Her analysis must therefore be treated with caution, as must the fictionalized portraits of Mme Héger. Yet depictions of school life in France by Brontë's less well-known contemporaries are also peopled with imposing schoolmistresses. They, and Charlotte Brontë, were echoing the language used by Mme Campan, and picking up on the authoritative persona cultivated, as we have seen, by many French teachers. But they were also responding to the common notion that a married woman was a powerful figure in French society.[45]

Brontë also described the real Mme Héger as 'always cool and reasoning', and later as 'a politic, plausible and interested person', descriptions which again may reflect her personal dislike, but which also resonate with contemporary stereotypes about French coldness and hypocrisy.[46] For example, Sarah Bache noted that on receiving news of her father's death, Miss Le Frebone, the French assistant at Bache's Edgbaston school in the 1820s, appeared unmoved.[47] Other accounts hinted at the deceitfulness of the French. Mary Browne clearly felt that the 'genteel' Mme Crosnier, who, she discovered, exerted very little effort in teaching her pupils, had duped her parents. Brontë described Mlle Blanche, another teacher at Mme Héger's school, as having a character 'so false and so contemptible I can't force myself to associate with her'. Mary Taylor's description of one teacher at the Château de Koekelberg suggests that such deceitfulness might be contagious: Miss Evans was 'a well-educated Englishwoman who has been eight years in France, whom I should like very well if she were not so outrageously civil, that I every now and then suspect her of hypocrisy'.[48] When English authors could assert that, although 'it is not right to condemn a whole nation, but it is notorious that the French standard of truth, is very unlike the English, especially in Roman Catholics', it is not surprising that English schoolmistresses and pupils might be especially prone to detecting hypocrisy and deceit in their French teachers.[49]

This critical attitude towards French schoolmistresses, however, was not universal. Fanny Kemble was very fond of the principal teacher at Frances Rowden's school. Mlle Descuillès was 'a handsome woman of about thirty . . . active, energetic, intelligent and good-tempered'. Kemble recalled with pleasure the

[45] Other examples of this type include 'Mme d'Elfort' in McCrindell, *Schoolgirl*, 'Mlle Dantin' in *Nathalie*, by Julia Kavanagh (London, 1850), and Sarah Fitton's 'Mme de Beaumonde'.

[46] C. Brontë to B. Brontë, Brussels, 1 May 1843; C. Brontë to E. Nussey, Brussels, 13 Oct. 1843, in Shorter, *Brontës*, i. 265–6 and 271–3.

[47] Matthews, *Sarah Bache*, 79.

[48] Browne, *Diary*, 75, 94–9; C. Brontë to E. Brontë, 2 Sept. 1843, and M. Taylor to E. Nussey, Brussels, 1842, in Shorter, *Brontës*, i. 270–1, 234.

[49] Yonge, *Womankind*, 159–61.

amateur theatricals that Mlle Descuillès and her pupils engaged in.[50] Emmeline Pankhurst also admired her schoolmistress. She was perhaps fortunate in that the Neuilly school she attended in the 1870s was the establishment run by Joséphine Marchef-Girard, a teacher committed to providing her pupils with a stimulating environment in which to learn. Pankhurst found that the 'highest ideals of honour' were held to in the school, and that pupils were 'kept to the strictest principles of truth-telling and candour'. Flourishing in this environment, she felt 'understood' by her schoolmistress, and had real affection for her. Indeed, the impression one gets from her memoirs is that her years at school in Paris were formative. She returned home, having been inspired both by Mlle Marchef-Girard and by her friendship with Noémie Rochefort, whom she describes as the daughter of a Republican journalist, which 'strengthened all the liberal ideas I had previously acquired'.[51]

Emmeline Pankhurst liked the French pupils she encountered, unlike many of the other women who crossed the Channel. Charlotte Brontë described the girls at Mme Héger's as having a 'cold, selfish, animal and inferior' character. She was not especially complimentary about the English girls she had taught at Miss Wooler's school in Yorkshire (she described them as asses), but it is significant that, in Brussels, Brontë clearly attributed her pupils' defects to the Belgian national character; *Villette* is full of references to the 'phlegmatic' 'Flemish' pupils of Mme Beck's school.[52] Mary Browne was similarly unimpressed by the girls she met at school in Paris, but in her case this undermined rather than reinforced her conception of the French national character, since she had previously believed the French to be especially polite. The pupils at Mme Crosnier's, however, were dirty and rude, they had inelegant manners and they were vulgar.[53] On the other hand, for Margaret Nevinson, the idea that the French were frivolous and excessively interested in fashion seemed amply supported by her experience of French schoolgirls. She had little sympathy with her fellow pupils' 'obsession' with clothes, and lamented that the forthcoming marriage of one of the pupils was the only subject of interest during the spring term.[54] On the whole, the schoolgirls in the sample found little to commend in their French and Belgian counterparts, and much which resonated with contemporary stereotypes of French frivolity or Belgian phlegm.

Opinions of the instruction girls received at school in France varied. The practical character of the teaching at Joséphine Marchef-Girard's school impressed

[50] Kemble, *Record,* 85.

[51] Pankhurst, *My own story,* 10–11. Noémi Rochefort was probably the daughter of Henri Rochefort, a radical Republican and later extreme Nationalist. When, in 1873, he was threatened with deportation, Victor Hugo wrote to protest, emphasizing that he was 'père de famille' and would be leaving behind a 17-year-old daughter. I am grateful to Robert Tombs for drawing my attention to Rochefort.

[52] C. Brontë to E. Nussey, Brussels, 1842 in Shorter, *Brontës,* i. 239. Extract from C. Brontë's 'Roe Head Journal', Feb. 1836, quoted in Gordon, *Charlotte Brontë,* 55.

[53] Browne, *Diary,* 59, 89–90.   [54] Nevinson, *Life's fitful fever,* 37.

Emmeline Pankhurst. She noted that it included chemistry and bookkeeping, and attributed this to her schoolmistress's foresight and vision (in fact, as we have seen, both were fairly common subjects in French schools). Fanny Kemble thought the sanitized literature that the girls at Frances Rowden's school were given to read was 'rubbish if not poison', and she made fun of the visiting masters. But she was clearly inspired by Mlle Descuillès' teaching and made the most of an opportunity to study Latin. On the other hand, Dorothea Beale found the rote learning, which took up much of her time at Mlle Bray's school, boring and uninspiring; Margaret Nevinson was dismayed by the francocentric nature of the curriculum at her school: 'little or no concern was shown for anything outside France, no Classics, nor foreign languages were studied, but we learnt in great detail French literature, French grammar, French history, French geography'.[55]

The reminiscences of most English pupils and teachers, however, focus on the 'system' of education in France, rather than the content of the curriculum. Dorothea Beale's experience, as the quotation with which the chapter begins suggests, was not entirely positive. Although Beale later valued the insight into the French approach to education that her stay at Mlle Bray's school had provided, as a child she 'felt oppressed with the routine life; I, who had been able to moon, grub alone for hours, to live in a world of dreams and thoughts of my own, was now put into a cage and had to walk around like a squirrel. I thought was killed.' Margaret Nevinson also suffered from the constraint she felt characterized her schoolmistress's approach to education and complained of 'the monotony of school life', with much of the girls' recreation time spent in detention for lessons they had not learned. Rachel McCrindell described the pupils in her fictional French convent as 'watched as prisoners of state'. Long hours spent in lessons and constant supervision are recurring themes in both reminiscences and fictional accounts by English women of life in French boarding-schools for girls.[56]

Depictions of the closely supervised monotony of life at school resonated with a constellation of ideas about the differences between French and English women and about differences between education in France and England. English observers frequently commented on the degree to which girls and young women in France were constrained and supervised. It was commonly said 'that young French women are from infancy upwards subject to an espionage and surveillance that only ends at the altar...that a French girl must only walk with her "chaperone"; never dream, nor appear to dream, of marriage or love until her parents have chosen her a husband; unmindful often of her feelings, because she is not supposed to have any, or at least they are so tutored, subdued, and tamed down, that they are never suffered to appear'.[57] This was contrasted

[55] Pankhurst, *My own story*, 10–11; Kemble, *Record*, 85–99; Beale, MS Autobiography, quoted in Raikes, *Dorothea Beale*, 13; Nevinson, *Life's fitful fever*, 33.
[56] Beale, ibid. 13. Nevinson, ibid. 33; McCrindell, *Schoolgirl*, 22.
[57] Marandon, *L'image*, 280–3; C. Smith, *Anne Cave* (London, 1864), ii. 209.

with the degree of liberty wisely allowed to young English women, who thus learned self-control without their natural feelings and frankness being impaired, and whose freedom of choice and fidelity in marriage was contrasted with the materialism and immoral behaviour seen in the French tradition of marriages of convenience. 'Marriage here is a matter of traffic,' commented the American educationist Emma Willard, echoing sentiments expressed less pithily by many English observers, 'girls are watched. Love is an affair of their mothers, not of theirs. They are bargained away, often sent from their boarding schools to be married to men whom they have never seen; and they go to the altar, delighted that they are now to be no longer guarded, but henceforth free to frequent the haunts of amusement and receive uncensured the attentions of men.'[58]

The emphasis in English schoolgirl reminiscences on the systematic character and the monotony of school life in France was also echoed in assessments of education on the other side of the Channel. While Matthew Arnold, visiting French *lycées* for boys on behalf of the SIC, approved of many aspects of secondary education in France, he found the Lycée Saint Louis in Paris 'hopelessly prison-like'. Arnold speculated that English boys would chafe under the 'constraint and rule' of organized games in French schools, linking differences between French and English schools to differences between the French and English national character.[59] Oscar Browning went further, concluding that there were two approaches to education:

the one pays especial regard to the individual; it considers its great aim the development of character; it rejoices in diversity, and cheerfully sacrifices method and order to the vigour of spontaneous enterprise... the other makes discipline and obedience the test of efficiency... it delights in programmes, and is great on paper... it is naturally a favourite with those governments who fear the force of free intellect... The one method is English, and the other is French; liberty is just as impossible with the one as it is certain to spring up and grow out of the other.[60]

Reacting to what they discovered in France (and, as we have seen, surveillance *was* a feature of school life there), these observers, and the schoolgirls and teachers who crossed the Channel, were also responding to the comparison frequently made at the time, between the liberty and freedom deemed characteristic of English political and social life, and the despotism and constraint of life in France.

Interestingly, this difference is something French schoolmistresses also gave credence to. Those who received English pupils sought to adapt to the different needs of their foreign charges. Jeanne Campan described her English pupils in words strikingly similar to Dorothea Beale's. 'I always found', she wrote, 'that

---

[58] Letter from Emma Willard to her pupils, 1 Dec. 1830; Willard, *Journal*, 63.
[59] M. Arnold, 'Schools and universities on the Continent', in R. H. Super (ed.) *The Complete Prose Works of Matthew Arnold* (Ann Arbor, 1962), iv. 89.
[60] O. Browning, 'Schools and universities on the continent', *Quarterly Review*, 125 (Oct. 1868).

they seemed like fully grown birds put into a cage.' In 1819, she advised a fellow teacher to allow more liberty to foreign pupils, because they were, she said, 'less docile than French girls'. Looking back on her life at Mme Deslignières school in Paris in the 1850s, Mme Brada remembered how the thirty or so English girls were also allowed to leave the school when they wanted. By contrast, the French pupils could only receive visits, and then only from their parents, and then only under supervision in the *parloir*.[61]

Exchanges

Given the contrasts which travelling English schoolmistresses and pupils observed between schools in France and England, and given the tendency to relate such contrasts to national differences in the condition of women, and to deep-seated differences in national character, it is perhaps not surprising that the traffic of teachers and pupils across the Channel does not seem to have encouraged the importing of pedagogical practices and ideas from France. At the beginning of the eighteenth century, French treatises on female education had been relatively widely read in Britain. Works like the Marquise de Lambert's *Avis d'une mère à son fils et à sa fille* (1728), which appeared in English editions in 1729, 1737, and 1749, proved popular with a growing middle-class audience attracted by their focus on intellectual instruction combined with moral rigour and piety. Later in the century Rousseau had had considerable influence on English pedagogues, and the translation of Mme de Genlis' *Adèle et Théodore* (1783) went through four editions before the end of 1796.[62] Between 1800 and 1870, however, there seems to have been much less interest in contemporary French pedagogical writing. There were no English translations of the educational works of Mme Campan, Mme de Rémusat, Mme Guizot, or Mme Necker de Saussure. Although there was some interest in the pedagogical theories of Jacotot, *The Monthly Repository* dismissed his ideas by commenting that his injunction to 'Know one thing and relate everything to it' corresponded to how bigots explained and understood the world.[63] Similarly, although reports on education abroad were being commissioned as part of the policy-making process, and although there was ostensibly considerable interest in the patterns of educational provision and schooling in France, in the case of middle-class education at least, the reports

---

[61] Campan, *De l'éducation*, ii. 34; Brada, *Souvenirs*, 41.

[62] W. A. C. Stewart, *Progressives and radicals in English education, 1750–1970* (London, 1972), 12–20; J. Carré, 'Les traductions anglaises d'ouvrages français sur le comportement et l'éducation des femmes au XVIIIe siècle', in A. Montandon (ed.), *Le même et l'autre: regards européens* (Clermont-Ferrand, 1997), 87–101; J. Birkett, 'Mme de Genlis et l'éducation des filles: pédagogie et romance', in G. Leduc (ed.), *L'éducation des femmes en Europe et en Amérique de la Révolution à 1848* (Paris, 1997); G. Dow, 'Reviewing Madame de Genlis: gouverneur, mere de l'Église, hypocrite', D.Phil. thesis (Oxford, 2004), 87–93.

[63] Admittedly, these texts may have been read in French, but the fact that there were no English editions nevertheless seems indicative of limited interest; 'Jacotot', *Monthly Repository* (1831), 257.

produced by Matthew Arnold and other comparativists were more likely to be taken as underlining the superiority of English public schools than as offering ideas and practices to be emulated.[64]

Significantly, the one aspect of French education that English schoolmistresses and educationists did seek to take back to Britain, despite the general lack of interest in French pedagogy, was the French emphasis on training, examination, and certification. Although she had taken no formal examination, Charlotte Brontë returned to England with 'a kind of diploma certifying my abilities as a teacher' given to her by M. Héger which she was quick to deploy when seeking pupils for the school she and her sisters had planned. In the 1840s, the schoolmistress Frances Goodacre recommended in the *Educational Times* that the College of Preceptors establish a system of certification like that she had observed in Paris. In 1875, the *Guide for governesses* noted that 'diplôméed foreign governesses' had an advantage in obtaining positions in England, and indeed in 1865 the SIC noted that English schoolmistresses were travelling to France in order to obtain the certificates and diplomas available there.[65] In the 1860s, Harriet Martineau argued that as a result of such examinations, 'the education given in French boarding-schools is immeasurably superior to anything that can be had in the same class in England'. There, she felt, 'the intellect is more effectively trained and something of a masculine robustness is given to the powers'.[66]

Yet, like others, Martineau still had misgivings about France and the French. English observers regarded competition between schoolgirls and prize days—and the display and vanity associated with them—as particularly French. They were unconvinced of the benefits either of emulation or of the publicity associated with it. Looking back on the grand prize-day ceremony she attended whilst a pupil at Mme Faudier's school in Boulogne, Fanny Kemble commented that she doubted its good effects but had 'no doubt at all that abundant seeds of vanity, self-love and love of display were sown by it'. Similarly, Harriet Martineau felt that 'we should not like to see our boarding-schools thrown open on examination days, for the public, or an invited crowd, to enter and see the pupils exhibit their attainments'. She cautioned against the public nature of French certificates and praised Elizabeth Garrett for obtaining her medical degree 'quietly'. Likewise, the SIC advised that while examinations could usefully be adopted to improve female education, 'public exhibition' must be avoided.[67]

On balance, it would seem that ideas about the character and condition of women in France, and prejudice against French education, militated against

---

[64] Bellaigue, '"Educational homes"'; Ochs and Phillips, 'Comparative studies'.

[65] Charlotte Brontë to Ellen Nussey, Haworth, 23 Jan. 1844, in Shorter, *Brontës*, i. 276–7; Frances Goodacre, Letter to the Council of the College of Preceptors, *Educational Times* (1 Dec. 1847), 47; Stevens, *Guide for governesses*, 16; Bompas, 'Glamorgan', *SIC* vii. 41.

[66] Martineau, 'Middle-class education', 553.

[67] Kemble, *Record,* 50; Martineau, 'Middle-class education', 561.

the importing of ideas and practices from across the Channel. Even in the 1780s, when Mme de Genlis was widely read, some reviewers warned of the backwardness of French views on education, noted that 'some of the descriptions of female manners in France will be thought by many to be, in a moral light, injudicious', and were anxious that English girls should be supervised in their reading of such texts.[68] The views expressed in an 1844 review of Mme Necker de Saussure's *L'éducation progressive* (1836–8) suggest that little had changed by the mid-nineteenth century. The author commended the book, but noted that its advice was intended for a country where 'woman is a far more artificial character than in our own . . . retarded in her march towards perfection by institutions, habits and manners by no means favourable to the development of her best energies'.[69] The interaction of mutually reinforcing notions of gender and national character tended not only to colour the experiences of the English schoolgirls and schoolmistresses who travelled to France, but also to obstruct the exchange of pedagogical ideas and practices across the Channel. If anything, half a century of educational travel by English pupils and teachers only reinforced prejudices against French pedagogy.

FRENCH WOMEN IN ENGLAND

An English education

If considerable numbers of English schoolmistresses and pupils were profiting from the newly peaceable relationship between Britain and France to travel to France, traffic in the opposite direction was much lighter. French governesses, school assistants, and schoolmistresses did cross the Channel, as will be demonstrated below, but French pupils who crossed the Channel were few and far between. None of the women in the French biographical sample of schoolgirls was sent to England for her schooling (as compared to 9% of the English schoolgirl sample). Taking her daughters to board at Mrs Mayer's London school in 1822, Elizabeth Wedgwood was pleased to discover that they would be sharing a room with 'a pretty French girl . . . who cant [*sic*] speak a word of English', but this situation was not repeated in the establishments headed by the schoolmistresses in the English biographical sample, nor are prospectuses for English schools translated into French to be found in the archives in France.[70] The 1861 census counted only 168 female scholars of French origin, and many of these may have been day scholars living with their expatriate French families

    [68] *Monthly Review*, 70 (1784), 338–45, quoted in Dow, 'Madame de Genlis', 91.
    [69] Review of A. Necker de Saussure, '*L'éducation progressive*', *Scholastic Quarterly Review*, 3 (July 1844), 311.
    [70] Elizabeth Wedgwood, Murdochs, to Sarah Elizabeth Wedgwood, 28 Jan. 1822, KUL, Wedgwood papers, M/W 105.

rather than girls sent across the Channel for an English education. It was apparently much less common for French schoolgirls to travel to England than for their English counterparts to go to France.

Various factors explain this disparity. In the nineteenth century, the French travelled less than the British generally, and there was much more traffic in the direction of France than vice versa. Until the 1850s, when their number began to rise, fewer than 8,000 French tourists travelled to Britain each year—a marked contrast to the 20,000 British visitors who passed through Calais in 1830.[71] The high costs of travel and schooling in England, as compared to those in France, must have played a part in discouraging many parents from sending their daughters across the Channel. As noted above, for those with an English income, French school fees could be very attractive. Travelling in the other direction, however, would entail a substantial increase in the cost of schooling. Yet even the very wealthy were not sending their daughters to school in England. Two other considerations, with deep roots in French cultural attitudes and ideas about female education, were of greater significance than cost in explaining the small number of French schoolgirls in England.

First, English language and literature did not occupy the central place in the female curriculum in France that French did in the English curriculum. Whereas French was offered in twenty-five (86.2%) of the twenty-nine English schools analysed in Chapter 6, only seventy-six (67.3%) of the 113 French schools offered English. Moreover, over two-thirds of the schools that did offer English were located in the capital and may have been among those schools that sought specifically to cater for English pupils. Provincial schools, like the one attended by Margaret Nevinson in the 1870s, were more likely to concentrate on 'French literature, French grammar, French history, French geography'. Although, as in England, modern languages were deemed appropriate for female study, learning English, or Italian, or German was not considered more than a pleasant accomplishment. Thus whereas Anna Laetitia Barbauld would argue that French should occupy the same place in the female curriculum as Latin in boys' studies, her contemporary Jeanne Campan did not even mention the study of modern languages in her treatise on female education, and none was taught during her time at Ecouen.[72] The eighteenth century had seen an increasing interest in the study of English, yet, as Paul Gerbod notes, in the nineteenth century, 'knowledge of foreign languages was not a socio-cultural imperative. Public opinion, rooted in nationalist prejudice, remained persuaded of the fact that the French language was the most beautiful in the world, and that its universal currency was still a reality.' In the case of English, moreover, this sense of superiority was reinforced by the idea that it was nothing but 'a language

---

[71] Gerbod, *Voyages*, 108.

[72] L. Aikin (ed.), *A legacy for young ladies, consisting of miscellaneous pieces in prose and verse by the late Mrs Barbauld* (Boston, 1826); Campan, *De l'éducation;* Martin, *Souvenirs,* 48.

of shopkeepers'.[73] Whereas for English girls the ability to speak French was a marker of sophistication and status, for French girls, mastery of the maternal language and literature was more important.

More influential even than French cultural confidence was the emphasis on preservation of innocence which shaped notions of the education appropriate for middle-class girls in nineteenth-century France. The freedoms enjoyed by English girls surprised and sometimes scandalized French mothers. The regrettable 'liberty of English manners' with respect to young women was almost axiomatic.[74] For the author of a review of one book on London life, the ideal of self-government, seen by French observers as the cornerstone of English education, was to be deplored as undermining girls' femininity. The freedom it allowed them meant that English girls manifested the modesty and decorum appropriate to a young woman only in the presence of older relations.[75] In a context where a popular 'Reader' for schoolgirls could argue that 'a pupil who is keen to see everything, to know everything and to hear everything will expose herself to a thousand threats to her morals and to her religion', it was not likely that parents would rush to send their daughters abroad.[76]

Although French schoolgirls were not a significant presence in English schools, older French women did cross the Channel, and a few remained long enough to open their own establishments. Throughout the eighteenth and nineteenth centuries, religious and political exiles from France were a prominent group among French residents in England. Teaching was an important source of income for many of them, and both schoolmistresses and tutors were able to profit from the demand among English families for a French education.[77] This demand may also have encouraged other French women to establish themselves in England. The Mme Antoinette Amelin who headed a school in Bristol in the first half of the century certainly believed that her French origins would attract pupils; her school's prospectus emphasized that she was Parisian.[78]

Nevertheless, as might be expected, French schools in England did not always meet with approval. At the beginning of the eighteenth century, *The Spectator* complained of the 'foreign fopperies' being taught at the girls' boarding-schools established by Huguenot refugees in Bloomsbury, and in the 1780s the *Bath*

[73] P. Gerbod, 'La langue anglaise en France, 1800–1871', *Revue Historique*, 275 Solidus 1 (1986), 111, 120; Gerbod, *Voyages,* 108; Fougeret de Montauban, *Préservatif contre l'Anglomanie* (Minorca, 1757), 34, quoted in L. Gallet-Blanchard, 'L'enseignement de la langue anglaise en France au 18e siècle', *Franco-British Studies*, 12 (1991), 54.

[74] Green, *Comparative view,* 74; J. Marchef-Girard, *Femmes,* 405; P. de Noirfontaine, *Une joie de ma vie* (Le Havre, 1866), 89; G. Houbre, 'Demoiselles Catholiques'.

[75] A. Rondelet, '*Londres. Pour ceux qui n'y vont pas*', *Journal des Demoiselles,* 1 (1833), 5.

[76] *Guide de la pieuse pensionnaire, à l'usage des pensions et de toutes les maisons religieuses d'éducation,* 2nd edn. (Tours, 1850)—a further twenty-one editions appeared by 1905.

[77] K. Carpenter, *Refugees of the French Revolution: émigrés in London, 1789–1802* (New York, 1999), 100–13.

[78] Prospectus for Park Street boarding-school, Bristol, n.d., JJ Coll., Education/1; Whittaker, *Directory,* 1–27.

Journal complained that French émigré teachers were undermining British culture.[79] Nor was Frenchness necessarily a guarantee of success. Jeanne Deroin, the French feminist and socialist who emigrated to London in 1852 in order to avoid arrest and persecution under the Napoleonic regime, had only limited success with the school she opened in West London. In 1866, her poverty was such that she was excused from payment of local taxes.[80]

French schoolmistresses do not seem to have been as eager to open their schools in England as their English counterparts were to establish themselves in France. In 1861, the census recorded only twenty-nine French women as established in their own schools in the whole of England and Wales. Unfortunately the French census does not provide figures for comparison, but the frequency with which English schoolmistresses established in France appear in the archives does suggest that they were a much larger group. In part, this is explained by the differences in the cost of living; for English teachers, opening a school in France was attractive financially; French schoolmistresses might have been deterred by the higher rents they would face on the other side of the Channel. The proliferation of convent schools in England in the nineteenth century may also explain the relative scarcity of lay French schoolmistresses.[81] In France, as we have seen, it was difficult for private individuals to compete with teaching sisters supported by the social and financial resources of their congregation and of the church. In England, however, French lay schoolmistresses faced additional pressure because they competed for a fairly limited market. Whereas English schoolmistresses in France were responding to a well-established demand for 'French education' from English families, and might also hope to attract local pupils, French schoolmistresses and religious establishments in England had little to offer French families. Indeed, aside from one or two philanthropic institutions established for émigré children, the schools established by both lay and religious women of French origin in England tended to attract English, rather than French, pupils, offering families the benefits of a French education without the discomfort and expense of having to cross the Channel.[82]

Another route was to employ a French governess, or to select one of the many schools whose prospectuses advertised that French was taught by 'a native of France'. As noted above, anti-Catholic and anti-French sentiment meant that even English governesses who had spent time in France might be viewed with suspicion. Some schoolmistresses sought to offset such anxieties by

[79] Cited in Bryant, *London experience*, 145; *Bath Journal*, 5 Sept. 1796, quoted in Carpenter, *Refugees*, 107.

[80] P. Pilbeam, 'Jeanne Deroin: French feminist and socialist in exile', in S. Freitag (ed.), *Exiles from European revolutions: refugees in mid-Victorian England* (New York, 2003), 275–94; V. Baker, 'Jeanne Deroin: the years in exile', *Proceedings of the Western Society for French History*, 25 (1998), 145–8. I am grateful to Karen Offen for this reference.

[81] S. O'Brien, 'French nuns', 142–81; G. McAdam, 'Willing women and the rise of convents in nineteenth-century England', *Women's History Review*, 8, 3 (1999), 411–43.

[82] O'Brien, 'French nuns', 175–9; Kollar, 'Foreign and Catholic', 335–50.

recruiting Protestant teachers. In the 1860s, mention of French being taught by 'a Parisienne Protestant' was so common that Robert Mair suggested there could be no Protestant women left in France, and expressed concern about the false position of Catholic teachers who had to pretend to be Protestant in order to find positions in England.[83] Nevertheless, just as some parents were prepared to take the risk of sending their daughters to convent schools, many must have been prepared to run the risk of entrusting their daughters to French and Catholic teachers: the 1861 Census found 489 French governesses, and 396 language, music, and general teachers working in England and Wales. At least seven of the seventy-four teachers in the English biographical sample of schoolmistresses employed, or worked alongside, a French assistant. In some cases, anxieties about Catholic or French influences may have been offset by the advantages perceived in employing a 'diplôméed foreign governess'.[84]

While it seems clear French teachers were in demand in England as governesses and teaching assistants, gaps in the sources mean we know relatively little of the reasons that prompted French women to respond. For Louise and Noémi Reclus, the daughters of the Orthez schoolmistress Zéline Reclus, who worked as assistants in schools in London and Edinburgh from 1857 to 1858, the attraction was primarily financial. Writing to a friend in 1857, Noémi commented that although much was to be asked of her sister, who was on the point of becoming an assistant in the London school of a Miss Taylor, the salary of 1,000F was very attractive.[85] Similar concerns lay behind the fictional 'institutrice' whose memoirs were the subject of an 1859 novel by Mme Bourdon, the author of numerous moral tales for Catholic girls. Having spent her last francs, Bourdon's heroine returns to the convent school where she had once taught and the Mother Superior finds her a position in an English Catholic family.[86] Yet, although becoming an assistant in England could be lucrative, comparing the numbers of women teachers who crossed the Channel in the French and English biographical samples suggests that there were more women travelling from England to France than vice versa. Only seventeen (3.76%) of the 452 French teachers in the combined biographical and *déclarations* samples travelled to England, compared to eight (10.8%) of the seventy-four schoolmistresses in the English sample.[87]

Why was this? The fact that English teachers were so numerous in France may have meant that 'English acquired in England' was a less worthwhile investment for French women than 'French acquired in France' was for their English counterparts, particularly given the lesser importance of English in the French curriculum. Even in the case of those schoolmistresses who had crossed the

[83] Mair, *Educator's guide*, 66.   [84] Stevens, *Guide*, 16.

[85] Noémi Reclus, à Orthez, à Zoë Tuyes, Dec. 1857, in Carrive (ed.), 'Lettres', 143 (1997), 225.

[86] Bourdon, *Souvenirs*, 78

[87] The difference was statistically significant ($P < 0.05$, chi2 = 35.04, df = 1).

Channel, the fact that they had spent time in England passes without comment on their *déclarations d'ouverture* or on surviving prospectuses. And although in 1884 when applying to the *Ministre de l'Instruction Publique* for a position, Marie Matrat would emphasize that 'I have a good knowledge of English and I am very familiar with the English school system', the Vice-Rector of Paris was less convinced of the value of such skills. Commenting on Mlle Matrat in 1878, he noted only that she had good manners, adding as an afterthought that she 'has quite a good knowledge of English'.[88]

In explaining the limited attraction of a period in England to French schoolmistresses, however, two other factors are of greater importance. First, as we have seen, the careers of French schoolmistresses were subject to a relatively clear pattern of qualification, promotion, and advance, regulated by the state. Schoolmistresses were required to obtain a diploma certifying to their ability to teach certain subjects, and specialized courses emerged to prepare them for these examinations. English only appeared on the diploma programme as an examination subject in 1837, and even then it was optional. In this context, unlike their English counterparts, French schoolmistresses had no need to spend time on the other side of the Channel 'by way of further qualifying themselves' for teaching. It is significant, then, that *l'institutrice* in Bourdon's novel is required to obtain her diploma *before* she can travel. For French women, qualification as a schoolmistress preceded the journey to England. It was not itself an important part of the process of professional training.

Second, as we have seen above, French educators and commentators were often disapproving of English approaches to women's education, while at the same time emphasizing that the focus of the education of Catholic girls should be the preservation of innocence. Mastery of foreign languages, travel abroad, and to a Protestant country, had little place in this conception of women's education. In this context, it seems especially significant that—despite Robert Mair's sarcasm about 'Parisiennes Protestants'—nine (56.3%) of the French schoolmistresses in the biographical and *déclarations* sample who did travel to England—including Louise and Noémi Reclus—were in fact Protestant.[89] It seems plausible to suggest that this reflected the influence of supply from France as well as demand from England.

Experiences in England

The French schoolgirls and teachers who crossed the Channel have left little record of their time in England. The letters of Louise and Noémi Reclus, to which

[88] Mlle Matrat au Ministre de l'Instruction Publique, 30 juin 1884; Vice-Recteur de l'Académie de Paris au Ministre, 17 Sept. 1878, AN, F[17] 21940.

[89] Those in the biographical and *déclarations* sample who crossed the Channel were significantly more likely to be Protestant than Catholic.

can be added a few brief references in contemporary novels and the responses of Parisians to the English schools in their midst, give only the briefest hint of how French women reacted to school life in England, and, in Noémi's case, Scotland. What little can be learned reveals that responses were mixed.

In 1858, as noted above, Noémi Reclus took up a position as teacher in a school in Edinburgh. The Miss Geddes were, she wrote to her friend Zoë, everything she had hoped for: 'If you only knew how gentle they are in their manner, their look and tone of voice', and though such gentleness was accompanied by firm principles and seriousness, 'truly, I respect them, I may even dare to love them'.[90] Her words echo those chosen by George Sand to describe the Demoiselles Martin, to whose Parisian school she sent her daughter Solange in the 1840s. They were 'two good English sisters, truly maternal towards their young pupils', of whom there were only eight.[91] Like their counterparts in England, the Martins and other Parisian schoolmistresses limited the numbers of pupils they would accept, and, like the Miss Geddes in Edinburgh, in their gentleness, they seemed unusual to French observers.

Sand was also impressed with the homeliness of the Martins' establishment, describing it as a 'charming little school' with a 'cheerful garden'. The *dame inspectrice* who had visited the school in 1838 concurred—it was a 'pretty house'.[92] Such descriptions contrast with the aspirations to grandeur of other Parisian establishments. They echo the account given of 'Mrs Halet's school' in Regent's Park, described in the 'memoirs' of 'Adèle Boury'. These were almost certainly a hoax by the publisher Catherinet de Villmarest, but the detailed descriptions of schools in France and England suggest that it was well researched. At Mrs Halet's establishment, 'Adèle' discovered a pretty garden, and dormitories that were divided up into individual cubicles for the pupils—a marked contrast to the large, characterless French dormitories.[93] Mrs Halet and her daughters undertook all the teaching themselves and shared the pupils' dormitories—both phenomena thought worthy of comment by 'Boury' and the *inspectrices* who visited the Demoiselles Martin. Such descriptions, underlining the domestic character of English establishments, clearly reflect some of the contrasts discovered between schools in England and France. At the same time, they picked up on two common themes in French writing about the English in the first half of the nineteenth century: the idea that, in the words of Mme Roland, English women lived 'the life of the interior', focusing their attentions on their maternal and domestic duties, and the idea that the English were obsessed with having 'a comfortable home'. Depending on the views of the writer, these domestic inclinations were either viewed negatively, as legitimizing a self-centred materialism (in the eyes of Adolphe de Custine, for example), or positively

---

[90] Noémi Reclus, à Orthez, à Zoë Tuyes, Sept. 1858 in Carrive (ed.), 'Lettres', 671.
[91] Sand, *Histoire*, 309.   [92] Inspection, pension Martin, 1838, AD Seine, VD⁶ 158–3.
[93] *Mémoires de Adèle Boury* (Paris, 1833) 30.

as a source of moral strength and national success (as they were by François Guizot).[94]

Louise Reclus would probably have had more sympathy with the former assessment. While Noémi appreciated the lack of ceremony and homeliness at the Miss Geddes', at Miss Taylor's establishment, Louise experienced the other side of the coin. The London schoolmistress was very protective of her status. She 'constantly feared that one should take her for a simple boarding schoolmistress', to such an extent that she made it difficult for her assistants and pupils to know what to call her. Perhaps in order to assert her distance from the French teacher, Miss Taylor ensured that Louise was 'constantly made to feel that she was an inferior creature'.[95] In her desire to present herself as something other than 'a simple boarding school mistress', Miss Taylor resembled other English teachers, like the Miss Sewells, who 'were indignant if [their establishment] was called a school, and were referred to as 'Aunt' by their pupils.[96] It was a marked contrast to the Reclus' schoolmistress mother Zéline, who was a public figure in Orthez and was awarded a medal by the *Ministre de l'Instruction Publique* on her retirement. Tiring of Miss Taylor's treatment, Louise eventually resigned and took a position as governess in an aristocratic Irish family. Writing to Zoë from Ireland, she contrasted the bourgeois mothers who made her wait to see them and spoke to her with hauteur with the graciousness of the aristocracy, who 'though no doubt think that I am [an inferior creature]', did not make her feel it.[97]

Noémi was fonder of her employers than Louise was of Miss Taylor; she had, however, more trouble with her pupils. At the end of a long day, she wrote of being exhausted and depressed by the effort it took to keep them under control. She described her work as 'telling off, screeching, making myself unbearable to myself and to others', and considered resigning.[98] Noémi soldiered on, but, faced with a similar situation, Miss G., the German woman who also taught French at Louisa Carbutt's school in Knutsford in the 1860s, resigned. She 'had really suffered from the independence of the English girls; she called their perhaps too outspoken words to their elders "rudeness"'.[99] While Noémi Reclus attributed her own problem to lack of authority, she seems to have shared the belief that British girls were allowed more freedom than their French counterparts. In 1857, she commented on the liberty allowed to one of her pupils, the youngest daughter of a Mr Murdoch, then living in Pau. Fanny, she wrote, with some admiration, 'takes such pleasure in trotting on horseback, fishing and whistling—which she

[94] Adolphe de Custine, *Courses en Angleterre* (Paris, 1830); F. Guizot, *Mémoires pour servir à l'histoire de mon temps* (Paris, 1862), extracts in J. Gury, *Le voyage outre-manche: anthologie de voyageurs français de Voltaire à Mac Orlan* (Paris, 1999) 771, 768.

[95] Louise Reclus, en Irlande, à Zoë Tuyes, *c.*1859–60, in Carrive (ed.), 'Lettres', 701–2.

[96] See Ch. 1, 'A domestic model of schooling'.

[97] Louise Reclus, en Irlande, à Zoë Tuyes, *c.*1859–60, in Carrive, (ed.), 'Lettres', 701.

[98] Noémi Reclus, London, à Zoë Tuyes, 1858, in Carrive (ed.), 'Lettres', 672.

[99] Herford, *In Memoriam*, 59.

does admirably—while being utterly jovial and ignoring convention, which she disdains to a supreme degree'.[100] As we have seen, the belief that British girls were accustomed to more liberty than their French counterparts was widespread, and meant that special provision was sometimes made for those accommodated in French schools.

For the author of an article on the historian Agnes Strickland, the liberty allowed to English girls extended to intellectual freedom, the results of which it was hoped would be emulated in France. The author commended the 'generous independence' given to English women, and the fact that 'many English women know Latin and Greek, and are no more pedantic for all that'. Calling into question French anxieties about *femmes savantes*, the author added that 'pedantry and pride come from scarcity'.[101] Appearing in the *Journal des Demoiselles*, this article was partly intended to encourage young French women to extend their own instruction; however, the idea that English women were well read, even in Classics, was reiterated by a number of French observers.[102] Neither Noémi or Louise commented on the quality of the teaching offered in English schools, and they do not appear to have been impressed by the level of instruction of English or Scottish women in general. Nor were the English schools in Paris regarded as particularly impressive by the inspectors. Indeed, Mme Shanahan's school was criticized for the weakness of the teaching, although no more so than many other establishments visited by the *dames déléguées*.[103] What did attract attention was the way in which pupils were taught. At Mlle Bray's, the inspectress noted in 1847, reading and writing—for which a Mr Jump was responsible—were taught according to the 'système anglais', and Louise's departure from Miss Taylor's was hastened by her frustration with 'son système'.[104] Unfortunately, what this 'système' was is not specified. Evidence from other quarters, however, points to the paradox that whereas French pupils and teachers crossing the Channel were fewer in number than their English counterparts, there was more interest in France in English 'systèmes' than vice versa.

Exchanges

In the 1810s, the system of monitorial instruction being developed by Andrew Bell and Joseph Lancaster was attracting considerable attention in France.[105] In

---

[100] Noémi Reclus, Pau, à Zoë Tuyes, 1857, in Carrive (ed.), 'Lettres', 215–16.

[101] Miss Agnes Strickland', *Journal des Demoiselles*, 42 (1874) 10, 293.

[102] E. Jones, *Les voyageurs français en Angleterre de 1815 à 1830* (Paris, 1930), 300.

[103] Inspections, pension Shanahan, 1846–7, 1847–8, 1848–9, AD Seine, VD⁶ 158–3.

[104] Inspection, pension Bray, 1847–8, AD Seine VD⁶ 158–3; Louise Reclus, en Irlande à Zoë Tuyes, *c*.1858, in Carrive (ed.), 'Lettres', 701.

[105] On the monitorial system see C. Kaestle, *Joseph Lancaster and the monitorial school movement* (New York, 1973), and A. Digby and P. Searby, *Children, school and scoiety in nineteenth-century England* (London, 1981).

1815 a group of former émigrés—the Abbé Gaultier, the Comte de Laborde, the Comte de Lasteyrie, and the Baron de Gérando, all of whom had encountered the monitorial method in England—combined to found the *Société pour l'Instruction Élémentaire* (SIE). Its object was to encourage the adoption of the monitorial method—known in France as *enseignement mutuel*—by training teachers, by founding schools, and by publishing the *Journal d'Éducation*.[106] A number of French schoolmistresses were enthusiastic supporters. Writing to her former pupil and fellow schoolmistress Fanny Kastner in 1819, Mme Campan observed that she had heard promising things of the system, which Fanny was apparently thinking of introducing in her school.[107] Jeanne Sauvan, then a schoolmistress in Chaillot, became Secretary of the Ladies' Committee of the SIE, and head of the society's *École Normale* for women in the 1830s.[108] Mme Dupuy, who later had a boarding-school for Protestant girls in Sainte-Foy, was also an enthusiast. In 1817 she attended a course of lectures on monitorial instruction given by a M. Martin, 'who had studied in England', in Bordeaux.[109] Her example was followed by Mme Deslignières in Paris, who is recorded as having obtained a 'Diplôme de Premier Ordre' in *enseignement mutuel* in 1843, and may thus have been a pupil of Jeanne Sauvan's.[110]

It is difficult to see how exactly the monitorial method can have been used by women like Mme Dupuy and Mme Deslignières. The system—whereby one child was taught and then transmitted what they had learned to their juniors—was intended to provide instruction for hundreds of children without requiring too many expensive teachers. Moreover, in the British context it was emphatically aimed at working-class children. Mme Deslignières' school often catered for over 100 pupils: however, her pupil Mme Brada's memoirs describe a strict hierarchy of class groups, each taught by a combination of assistants and visiting masters, rather than anything resembling mutual instruction.[111] It may be that by undergoing training in the monitorial method, schoolmistresses like Mme Deslignières were simply seeking to extend their expertise, or at least the number of qualifications they could boast. And it is not clear whether these schoolmistresses attributed significance to the English origins of the system.

The system's critics were most definitely aware of its origins. In the 1820s, the ultras would criticize those who adopted the alien new English method; it was characterized as 'foreign', 'the work of regicides', 'the dangerous offspring

[106] On the SIE see R. Tronchot, 'Du nouveau sur l'enseignement mutuel en France de 1815 à 1833', *Information Historique*, 4 (1974), 183–4; P. Gerbod, 'La Société pour l'Instruction Elémentaire et la diffusion du modèle éducatif britannique en France de 1815 à 1848', *Information Historique*, 57 (1995), 32–6; M. Raveaud, 'L'enfant, l'écolier et le citoyen: apprendre à appartenir et à participer à l'école en France et en Angleterre', Thèse de Doctorat (Paris VII, 2002) 7–10.

[107] Jeanne Campan, Mantes sur Seine, à Fanny Kastner, 6 Jan. 1819, AN, 137 AP 28, Dossier 11.

[108] Gossot, *Sauvan*, 144 and Appendix, 'Notice à la Séance du 9 Jan 1868 de la SIE'.

[109] Comité cantonnal Protestant de Bordeaux au Baron Cuvier, 1 Apr. 1828, AN, F^{17} 12505.

[110] Inspection, pension Deslignières, 27 Apr. 1872, AD Seine, VD^6 1731–10.

[111] Brada, *Souvenirs*.

of Quakers'.[112] Instead, they championed the simultaneous system used by the Frères des Écoles Chrétiennes. As well as being Catholic and French in origin, it was better suited, they argued, to ensuring that children absorbed correct principles. Struggles between the liberal supporters of *l'enseignement mutuel* and its opponents would continue into the 1850s.[113] In light of this, it seems significant that, in 1819, Jeanne Campan was lamenting that deciding whether to adopt the method had become a question of party, that Mme Dupuy was Protestant, and that Mme Deslignières was amongst those who received a large number of English pupils.

If certain sections of the French educational establishment were receptive to practical innovations from the other side of the Channel, it is also clear that British educational literature was relatively widely read in France, particularly at the end of the eighteenth century. Isabelle Havelange found that of 100 pedagogical texts published in France between 1750 and 1830, nine were by English authors, and three were by Scots.[114] James Fordyce's *Sermons for young women*, first published in 1766 in English, appeared in French translation in 1778, 1779, and 1781. Nine French editions of Anna Laetitia Barbauld's *Hymns in prose and verse for children* were published between 1818 and 1859. The works of Hester Chapone, Sarah Trimmer, Jane Marcet, and John Gregory also appeared in translation. In the 1840s, the *Revue de l'Enseignement des Femmes* published reviews of works by Hester Chapone, Thomas Day, and Maria Edgeworth.[115] The latter was the most widely translated British author. French editions of her tales and stories for children were published at regular intervals throughout the first half of the nineteenth century, and there were at least three French editions of the *Essays on practical education*, written with her father, which first appeared in English in 1798. Edgeworth's popularity may partly have been explained by the fact that she was a frequent visitor to France. In 1801 she even visited Mme Campan's school, describing its proprietor as 'mistress of the first boarding school here, who educated Mme Louis Buonaparte, and who professes to keep her pupils entirely separate from servants, according to "Practical Education", and who paid us many compliments'.[116]

The degree to which Jeanne Campan really sought to implement Edgeworth's ideas is unclear; there was not much scope for the practical instruction advocated by Edgeworth in the curriculum at Ecouen. However, she was clearly interested in English approaches to education. Before opening her establishment in St Germain-en-Laye, as well as reading Edgeworth (who was *anglaise* in Mme Campan's eyes) and following the progress of monitorial instruction, she had sent for information on English and Swiss boarding-schools. Drawing a contrast

[112] Tronchot, 'Du nouveau', 183–4.
[113] Raveaud, 'L'enfant', 10–12; Gildea, *Education*, 53–4; M. Sacquin, *Entre Bossuet et Maurras: l'anti Protestantisme en France, de 1814 à 1870* (Paris, 1998), 164–7.
[114] Havelange, 'La littérature', 30   [115] *REF* 2 (Feb. 1845), 28; 4 (Feb. 1846) 36.
[116] Letter, quoted in Hill, *Maria Edgeworth*, 33.

with France, whose long history of convent schooling she documented in *De l'éducation*, she noted that in England lay establishments had existed since the Reformation. The English example, and her knowledge of it, was being used here to underline her claims to authority and to legitimize her projects for secular instruction. Her chief import, she claimed, was the adoption of prize days.[117] This is revealing, since, as we have seen, it could not be said that emulation and competition were the leading principles of English girls' education. Prize days were held in many English schools, but, as noted above, contemporaries like Harriet Martineau viewed them as particularly French, an example of the French love of display. That Campan should seize on the practice of prize ceremonies as the most useful practice to borrow from English schools says more about the degree to which her ideas of schooling were shaped by the French context than about the influence of English practices on French schoolmistresses.

Also significant in assessing the influence of English pedagogy on French schools is the record of what Jeanne Campan did not borrow. First, she noted that it would not have been possible for her to establish a small school of the type common in England where 'the schoolmistress can think of herself as the mother of a large family'.[118] Although she claimed that such a pattern was impossible in France, because low school fees meant that a teacher could not survive with so few pupils, Campan showed little interest in the familial and domestic ideals enshrined in such establishments. Arguing for the benefits of emulation, *De l'éducation* is essentially a manual for the development of a large-scale, institutional model of school instruction for girls. Nor was Mme Campan convinced by what she perceived as an example of the liberty allowed to English girls. She condemned the English practice of holding school balls, to which young men would be invited, on Saturdays. Such occasions, she felt, might just be acceptable in England, where as a result of custom and climate, ' "*the great boys*" and "*the young misses*" of the English' remained children for two or three years longer than their French counterparts. In France, however, such occasions would be too dangerous, a point she underlined by describing a society of young Swiss girls, whose members met daily and without chaperones to play cards, and even act in plays, with a host of young men. 'The fine line between liberty and licence was never crossed . . . evidence of the innocent simplicity of Swiss manners.'[119] Clearly, in Jeanne Campan's eyes, French girls were lacking in the innocence such pastimes would require. This view both reflects the French sense of female adolescence as sexualized and dangerous, and Campan's belief that such differences were the result of cultural and geographic influences (climate and custom) rather than innate national or sexual difference. Other commentators were less sophisticated. For Mme Simons-Candeille, observing the difference between French and English marital mores—the former being more susceptible to infidelity—'it seems, in truth, that in France, women are more the "daughters

---

[117] Campan, *De l'éducation,* i. 335.   [118] Ibid. i. 313.   [119] Ibid. i. 334, ii. 218.

of Eve" than English women'.[120] Such ideas strengthened the position of those who emphasized the importance of surveillance and containment in the education of French girls.

Thus, although French schoolmistresses expressed more interest in British pedagogical practices than their English counterparts did in education on the Continent, genuine exchange was limited. Through the aegis of the SIE, British educationists had considerable influence in France; the society kept up a regular correspondence with Henry Dunn of the BFSS, and two members of the SIE even travelled to London to strengthen this relationship. However, as we have seen, from the 1820s there was considerable resistance from some quarters to the introduction of the English method. By the 1840s, even within the SIE and liberal circles, criticisms of the 'anarchy' of English education were being voiced, and the strong ties with British educators were relaxed.[121]

At the same time, although there was an audience in France for the pedagogical literature of authors like Maria Edgeworth, even in the 1840s most of what was translated and reviewed dated from the late eighteenth century, and came from authors who were heavily influenced by Rousseau and what were perceived in England as 'French' educational practices. There were no translations of the treatises on female education by Bessie Parkes or Emily Shirreff, or even of Mrs Barbauld's views on girls' schooling, although some of her other works were appreciated. In 1847, the *Revue de l'Enseignement des Femmes* recorded the establishment of the GBI and plans for Queen's College, commenting that the English were ahead of the French in their efforts to improve teachers' lives, but this does not seem to have been followed with any similar initiative in France.[122] Nor does it seem that the links between the SIE and BFSS stimulated direct exchanges between schoolmistresses in the two countries. The 1860s saw two major investigations into English education, those of Marguerin and Motheré (1864) and Demogeot and Montucci (1868). However, in neither case were the investigators asked to report on girls' schooling. Despite this, Marguerin and his colleague argued that developments in England highlighted the need to reform girls' education in France. They emphasized, however, that 'what is done in England, and even more so in America, cannot be simply imported to France'. Nothing came of their plans for a superior professional school for women.[123] While French observers, including prominent schoolmistresses like Jeanne Campan and Mme Deslignières, may have drawn some inspiration from English pedagogical practices, there was never any danger that the convent model of schooling would succumb to schools established along English lines.

[120] Mme Simons-Candeille, *Souvenirs de Brighton, de Londres et de Paris: et quelques fragments de littérature légère* (Paris, 1818), 82.

[121] Gerbod, 'Société', 35.   [122] *REF* 9 (1847), 147.

[123] E. Marguerin and J. Motheré, *De l'enseignement des classes moyennes et des classes ouvrières en Angleterre* (Paris, 1864), 231.

Throughout the first half of the nineteenth century, English and French schoolgirls and women teachers travelled back and forth across the Channel in search of 'finish', of experience and qualifications, of a more comfortable life. In England, the importance of French in the female curriculum and the need to seek out opportunities for professional training and certification encouraged parents and teachers to invest in travel to France. By mid-century, schoolmistresses like Dorothea Beale were seeking to promote the study of German, which could be taught in a manner analogous to the 'thorough' methods used to teach Latin. It would provide a better training for girls' minds than French, which could not be freed from the taint of frivolity, even immorality, it had acquired in the eighteenth century. Yet parents continued to send their daughters to France in considerable numbers. And, judging by *Crockford's*, which did not distinguish the Parisian schools we know to have been Protestant establishments from the mass of Catholic schools, English parents were not always as concerned as Rachel McCrindell about the seductions of popery. At the same time, despite the development of a more formalized system of training in the second half of the century, the 1891 census recorded 39,867 British men and women living in France, of whom a large proportion were teachers.[124]

Such statistics suggest that French was still an essential part of the female curriculum, complicating our understanding of nineteenth-century notions of Englishness, and of the influence of ideals of domesticity in this period. Critics of the fashion for foreign education, like Hannah More, were developing a domestic model of womanhood that they presented as distinctively English and Protestant. A gendered notion of national character portrayed English women as particularly home-loving. In the words of W. H. Bainbridge: 'it is a proud distinction to the women of England that they are fitted for home. I know of no other country where that place is rendered so sacred by woman's presence—no land where it is filled with such blessed affections.'[125] Yet the centrality of French in the female curriculum points to the continuing influence of a conception of femininity centred on sociability, politeness, fashion, culture, and display.

In France, studying English was a much less important part of the female curriculum, and had none of the associations with femininity that French had in England. On the whole, English models of womanhood were not to be emulated. For the more conservative the freedom allowed to young English women undermined the principles of modesty, reserve, and restraint that they believed should be at the heart of girls' education. At the other end of the scale, the extreme view was that English women were ill-dressed prudes, subordinated to their husbands to a degree that was shocking to observers like Flora Tristan. But even for those with a more sympathetic view of the English, French cultural confidence, and the certainty that France led the way in civilization meant that

---

[124] *Statistique de la France: dénombrement des étrangers en France, 1891* (Paris, 1896).
[125] Bainbridge, *Lecture*, 26.

there was little incentive to encourage the study of English.[126] French women, seen as the exemplars of this unique civilization, and as those who would 'civilize the human race', had little need to study abroad. Such ideas meant that English schoolgirls and schoolmistresses might be welcomed in France. Thus, in 1846, the *Ministre de l'Instruction Publique* suggested that allowances should be made for English schoolmistresses in Paris, because 'it seems important, at a time when relations between peoples are multiplying, to encourage a establishment which will offer English families the means, in Paris, to provide a complete and distinguished education'. He was in no doubt about the superiority of French female education.[127]

The correspondence and memoirs of the schoolgirls and schoolmistresses who crossed the Channel in both directions reflect the powerful influence of contemporary notions of Englishness and Frenchness, as does the response to the pedagogical ideas and practices that were carried across. French and English women travellers participated in the construction of these ideas and viewed what they discovered in foreign schools through the lens of ideas about national character. Such notions meant that, although among educationists on both sides of the Channel there was some interest in the pedagogical theories and practices being developed by their foreign counterparts, the depth of the exchange, even for a schoolmistress as ready to borrow as Jeanne Campan, was limited. Yet, for some women, the crossing of the Channel was an opportunity to experiment and explore beyond the bounds of ordinary experience. Amélie Weiler saw a position in England as the key to independence from her father and Emmeline Pankhurst evidently regarded her period at school in France as central to her political education. Although Charlotte Brontë returned to England with her ideas about Belgian 'phlegm' and the treachery of Catholics reinforced, her experiences in Brussels were crucial for her development as a writer. Noémi Reclus looked forward to her journey to Scotland as likely to provide 'some much-needed intellectual development'. But it was second best: 'Don't you think that we are very narrow here . . . I would like to go to the tropics, to see creation in all its grandeur and learn!! And I am a woman!!!'[128] Her exclamation is a reminder that, although both French and English women were routinely crossing national frontiers in this period, the boundaries of gender were more difficult to transgress.

---

[126] E. Weber, 'Of stereotypes and of the French', *Journal of Contemporary History*, 25 (1990), 178.
[127] Ministre de l'Instruction Publique au Préfet de la Seine Inférieure, Paris, 26 Dec. 1846, AN, F[17] 12432.
[128] Noémi Reclus, à Zoë Tuyes, Orthez, beg. 1858, Carrive (ed.), 'Lettres', 233.

Conclusion

In both England and France private lay boarding-schools for girls played a more significant part in the development of women's education between 1800 and 1867 than has usually been recognized. Over half a century before the establishment of government-sponsored forms of female secondary education, the schools that emerged on both sides of the Channel were providing formal secondary instruction for a large proportion of middle-class girls and reinforcing the notion that female education was important and necessary.

As this book has shown, the received picture of schoolmistresses in the first part of the century as inexperienced and untrained amateurs needs substantial modification. Nineteenth-century images of the 'reduced gentlewoman' schoolmistress and stereotypes of the self-interested profit-seeking school proprietor point to the tensions and anxieties surrounding the work of schoolmistresses, but they conceal the complex and diverse circumstances of the women who became teachers. On both sides of the Channel, establishing a school was often part of a long-term strategy to provide for daughters in families where status was important but resources were lacking. School-keeping might be a family business; and, far from being excluded from economic activity, women teachers were entrepreneurs who often revealed a sophisticated understanding of business and legal practice. Destined to be teachers from a young age, girls were 'educated for a governess' just as their brothers were trained for the professions. Many future teachers actively sought out opportunities to gain experience and pedagogical expertise, and when formal qualifications were offered, these women presented themselves as candidates with alacrity. While economic need was often a factor in influencing women to take up teaching, many schoolmistresses were deeply committed to their work and developed a conception of their role that emphasized its importance and their sense of expertise. Building on this heritage of feminine professional commitment, schoolmistresses in the middle years of the century in both England and France deliberately set out to develop teaching as a professional career for women. They made important contributions to the development of teacher training, established teaching associations, and campaigned for the expansion and improvement of girls' secondary instruction and for the extension of government support for female education.

At the same time, in England as in France, increasing numbers of parents were sending their daughters to school, revealing the mounting importance attached to school instruction. Attempts to explain this phenomenon have tended to focus on the way female education was used as a means of social advance, and stress the aspirations of middle-class parents who sought to emulate those further up the social scale. In fact, parental motivations were often more complex than notions of emulation suggest. At the same time, 'education' was increasingly being equated with school instruction and it was coming to be expected that a period at school would form part of a middle-class girl's educational itinerary. Moreover, parents, pupils, and teachers were increasingly insisting upon the value of intellectual instruction and prizing examination success as well as social accomplishments. Although modern languages, music, and drawing were an important part of the curriculum in many schools, they were often taught with a rigour that belied critics' stress on the superficiality of female education. In both England and France, girls' schools were developing broad courses of instruction that anticipated the 'modern' curricula introduced in boys' schools in the second part of the century.

Notions of feminine domesticity shaped the development of boarding-schools for girls on both sides of the Channel. The idea that women's sphere was the home, their nature maternal and their virtues domestic was reiterated throughout the period. The instruction offered to girls was defined by the notion that a woman's role was to be a wife and mother, and the same ideals of domestic womanhood informed the experiences of their teachers. Especially in England, but also in France, teaching, as an extension of the maternal role, was one of very few occupations middle-class women could take up without loss of status. This in itself helped fuel the expansion of girls' schooling as growing numbers of women turned to teaching to provide for themselves. But domestic ideals also generated support for the extension of women's education in that they elevated the role of women and underlined the importance of offering girls a serious education to prepare them for home duties. At the same time, notions of domestic womanhood could be an inspiration for schoolmistresses, reinforcing their sense that their work was valuable and indeed essential.

Yet the position of women teachers in relation to the conventions of feminine domesticity was ambivalent. The role of schoolmistresses who operated as commercial entrepreneurs and were often unmarried and childless ran counter to visions of the angel in the house who devoted herself to motherhood. Women teachers sought to reconcile their work with conventional notions of femininity but their position in relation to the ideal was always ambiguous. Notions of domesticity, moreover, did not constitute a monolithic ideology and might be challenged or expanded in practice. Some schoolmistresses drew on the rhetoric of domestic womanhood to argue for extending the boundaries of women's sphere. Implicit in the support of women teachers for teacher training was a challenge to the conception of women as naturally maternal.

By claiming the status of professionals and asserting their expertise they contributed to expanding the range of opportunities available to women, undermining the idea that women could only fulfil their natural destiny within the

home. At the same time, by underlining the importance of intellectual development, they encouraged their pupils' sense of independence and autonomy. Even
if schoolmistresses preached the virtues of domesticity, the collective sociability
of school life could destabilize conventional understandings of femininity. At
school, girls challenged and worked around visions of domestic womanhood.
The extension of girls' schooling, the expansion of the curriculum, and the
sense that a girl's school years were a period of transition undermined the view
that girls made the transition to maturity only through marriage. By giving
institutional expression to the idea that young women developed emotionally
and intellectually between the ages of about 12 and 16, and by marking that
transition through examinations—certificates of personal achievement—girls'
boarding-schools posed a significant challenge to the idea that women were
'relative creatures'.

Despite the parallels in the ideas informing girls' education in England and
France, there were significant contrasts between the schools established in the
two countries, as the schoolgirls and teachers who crossed the Channel were
quick to observe. These contrasts reflected differences in the situation of women
on either side of the Channel. Nineteenth-century commentators like Blanqui
attributed the different position of women in the two countries to patterns of
sociability, which they related to political organization. More recently, Mona
Ozouf has suggested that such contrasts amounted to a national difference in
the conception of femininity. The women who travelled abroad as teachers and
pupils tended to explain such differences with reference to notions of Englishness
or Frenchness.

Examining the situation of women in England and France through the prism
of girls' boarding-schools suggests that while differences in gender ideals are
important considerations in explaining the contrasting experiences of women in
the two countries, other major differences need to be taken into account—in
the role of the state, economic conditions, the legal status of women, but also
differences between Catholic and Protestant thought and practice. It was the
complex interaction of these factors with differing conceptions of gender that
produced contrasts between the lives of women in the two countries.

The institutional models of female schooling adopted on either side of the
Channel were dramatically different. Schools in England tended to be small
and domestic in setting and atmosphere, reflecting the strength of a domestic
tradition of schooling, and the resistance to state intervention in middle-class
education. In England, even for boys, a formal institutional pattern of secondary
education developed comparatively late, and it still retained some elements
of earlier domestic arrangements, as Demogeot and Montucci observed when
they contrasted the family-like atmosphere of English boys' schools with the
regimented character of French *lycées*. Such contrasts point to the absence, in
England, of the networks of institutions established by religious orders that
were so influential in France, and on which the nineteenth-century *lycées* were

superimposed. They highlight the influence in England of a Protestant conception of education that fostered self-reliance and the cultivation of personal judgement, and saw in the school 'a little world'. But the domestic model of female schooling also reveals the compelling influence of ideals of domesticity that emphasized the distinction between a male public sphere of work and a female sphere centred on the family. Reflecting the influence of Evangelical ideas that made the home the source of morality and piety, the home was constructed as a private sanctuary divorced from outside influences, and the essence of middle-class masculinity was perceived as a man's ability to operate successfully in the public sphere, supporting his wife and daughters through his work. Such feelings intensified anti-Catholic resistance to feminine institutions that smacked of the convent. As noted above, in practice the reality often fell short of the theory. Indeed, women commonly opened schools precisely because this domestic ideal could not be attained and they were obliged to provide for themselves. Such ideals nonetheless had a powerful impact on the experiences of middle-class women. Seeking to reconcile their situation with the conventions of feminine domesticity, and to respond to the understanding that female virtue developed only in a domestic setting, schoolmistresses sought to accentuate the familial character of their schools and prized privacy and autonomy.

In France, by contrast, girls' boarding-schools were large, hierarchical establishments. The system of education developed by the Jesuits in the early modern period had established the outline of a highly formalized and hierarchical institutional model of schooling. In the seventeenth century, religious orders of women drew on this pattern to establish large convent boarding-schools that were rigidly structured and housed in specially adapted buildings. They underlined the importance of enclosure and articulated the views expressed by Catholic authors who conceived of the school as a protective enclave that would preserve pupils from the corrupting influence of the world, and of education as a means to preserve innocence. The precedents these religious institutions established provided a model for the lay institutions that developed in their wake in the early nineteenth century. Although Revolutionary plans to create a system of secondary instruction for girls came to nothing, they helped establish the principle that female education was a matter of state concern. In the first part of the nineteenth century, prefects set out rulings for the administration of girls' schooling which testified to the enduring hold of that principle, and which reinforced the public presence of the boarding-schools established by lay women. These schools offered an education that responded to increasingly influential notions of domesticity; but in their institutional structure and public character they reflected the influence of Catholic educational practice and thought and contrasted strongly with the domestic model of schooling that was developing in England.

The notion that girls' education was a public matter also shaped the careers of French schoolmistresses. After 1810 in Paris (and after 1820 in other regions), prospective schoolmistresses were required to obtain a diploma certifying their ability and official authorization to open a school. Prefectoral regulations advanced the notion of teaching as a career with a fairly fixed itinerary of promotion. By becoming teachers, women could move up the social scale in a context where service to the state established the middle-class status of many families. In England, by contrast, entry into teaching was not formally regulated, although many women did seek training. There, teaching tended to be a means to protect against downward mobility in a period where middle-class standing often depended on more unstable sources of income and status.

These differences help explain the contrast in the proportions of French and English schoolmistresses who married, a contrast which reveals a divergent approach to the work of married women in England and France. For French schoolmistresses, marriage could mean the creation of a fruitful professional partnership and mark the beginning of a new stage in their careers. English schoolmistresses were less likely to marry than their French counterparts, and, if they did so, rarely continued to teach once married. In England, middle-class status depended on at least the appearance of conformity to an ideal of domesticity based on the assumption that husbands could provide for their wives, and there was often intense pressure for married women not to work. This pressure was reflected in the serious legal disabilities faced by married women in the management of their property. The effect was to make teaching an alternative to marriage (though not necessarily an unattractive one) and to encourage schoolmistresses to withdraw if they married. On the Continent, opposition to married women's work was less intense, partly as a result of the longevity of family enterprise and the more secure position of a middle class buttressed by the state. At the same time, although the legal status of women in France was definitely subordinate, married French women often had more control over their property than their English counterparts. And while the Napoleonic Codes formalized the notion of women's dependence and subordination, they also underlined the contractual character of marriage. As Emma Willard commented when she visited France in 1833, French women played a more important part in business than their English or American counterparts: 'the laws are different, a married woman here not being a nullity'.[1] This contrasting approach to married women's work in England and France emerges very clearly from developments at the end of the nineteenth century, and in the beginning of the twentieth century. In France, governments hoped to encourage male schoolmasters to marry their colleagues and idealized the partnership of schoolmaster and schoolmistress that this could establish. In England, a marriage bar sought to exclude married women from teaching.[2]

---

[1] Willard, *Journal*, 237.
[2] L. P. Moch, 'Government policy and women's experience: the case of teachers in France', *Feminist Studies*, 14 (1988), 301–24; Copelman, *London's women teachers*, 176.

Examining the development of teaching as a profession reveals that contrasts between the domestic and convent models of schooling and between the experiences of teachers were reinforced by national differences in the conception of domestic womanhood which further comparative investigation of the prescriptive literature could usefully illuminate. In France, the Revolution and Restoration had seen the elaboration of a conception of the domestic sphere as complementary to, rather than isolated from, the political world. Such ideas had contributed to the politicization of motherhood, imbuing it with a public character. Domesticity was itself political, part of the political project of revolution and reconstruction, and adopted and adapted by successive regimes. In this context, women were represented as 'the wives and mothers of citizens', and as the 'mothers of the nation'. The emphasis on complementarity further strengthened the position of married schoolmistresses in France, and this publicly oriented understanding of domesticity was reflected in French conceptions of the role of the schoolmistress. Schoolmistresses in France drew both on the socially legitimate precedents set by women religious and on politicized ideals of motherhood to develop an authoritative public persona. In England, the domestic sphere and motherhood were perceived and presented as intensely private. Although English women used the rhetoric of domesticity to expand that sphere, they did not have access to the powerful models of public female authority on which French schoolmistresses were able to draw. As a result, the conception of their role articulated by English schoolmistresses emphasized personal influence and intimacy, and many struggled with the contradictions between this private persona and their semi-public role.

The contrast between Catholic and Protestant conceptions of the school, and the influence of Catholic models of sisterhood on the experiences of French schoolmistresses, underlines the impact of confessional differences on women's experiences in the two countries. Highlighted by Alexis de Tocqueville in the 1840s, the question of religious difference has also interested historians. Natalie Davis emphasizes the complex effect of religious affiliation on the situation of women, suggesting that the break with priestly order implied by the Protestant Reformation generated opportunities for women to develop an autonomous intellectual life. Catholic women, however, had more opportunities for organization outside the home under the aegis of the church.[3] Examining the experiences of schoolmistresses reflects analogous contrasts. In the nineteenth century, Catholic women in France developed vital forms of female association, and lay schoolmistresses inherited considerable power and authority from the examples set by women religious. However, the influence of Catholic educational thought might often be conservative. While many schoolmistresses in France were inspired by their Catholic faith, seeing it as underlining the importance

---

[3] A. de Tocqueville, *Democracy in America*, trans. H. C. Mansfield and D. Winthrop (London, 2000), 563; N. Z. Davis, *Society and culture in Early Modern France*, 4th edn. (Stanford, 1975), 65–97.

of their work, the emphasis placed on abnegation as a feminine virtue could contain impulses for change and for intellectual development. In this tradition, knowledgeable women were seen as having deviated from the true path of femininity, which was to cherish moral virtues: they were *savantes ridicules*. By contrast, some Anglican and Nonconformist teachers in England were able to draw inspiration from the Protestant emphasis on self-improvement and perfectibility to develop demanding programmes of instruction and call for the reform of girls' education. At the same time, as the religious orders of women expanded in France, the ambiguities of the relationship between lay schoolmistresses and religious models of vocation and mission were accentuated, undermining the professional identity of lay women teachers. Especially after 1848, hostility to feminist campaigns and to women intellectuals influenced by Catholic suspicion of female learning seems to have obstructed the mobilization of lay schoolmistresses for professional development in France.

Yet this kind of mobilization would have run counter to the state-centred model of professionalization dominant in France that contrasted strongly with patterns of professional development in England. Independent association was not integral to the process of achieving professional status in France. As a result, French schoolmistresses focused their efforts on incorporation into the national system of educational administration. Government attempts to develop a corps of certified schoolmistresses and the creation by the state of a female inspectorate demonstrated that female education was a matter of public importance and promoted the conception of women teachers as professional educators. In England, by contrast, patterns of professionalization were characterized by the formation of independent professional networks. The models of feminine activity developed by Protestant charitable associations provided a precedent for the formation of schoolmistresses' associations. These articulated a notion of professional service that married well with the notions of religious and moral mission that had inspired many women teachers, and schoolmistresses mobilized to campaign for the development of the teaching profession and government support. In both France and England, however, obtaining public recognition also entailed compromise. The authority allowed to French female inspectors was restricted and government support for the extension of female instruction had distinct limits. In England, adopting the dominant pattern of practice-based professional training following a general liberal education meant that the long-standing support of women teachers for vocational training was eroded.

Contrasts between the experiences of girls at school and the instruction they received there further underline the impact of religion on women's lives and the distinctions between the experiences of French and English women. School life in France was strictly regulated, building on the traditions established by convent schools in the eighteenth century. Pupils might bend or break rules, but daily life was characterized by continual supervision and a sense of physical seclusion. This surveillance reflected a widespread suspicion of feminine autonomy and an enduring anxiety about female sexuality that was influenced by Catholic conceptions of female susceptibility. Emerging notions of feminine adolescence heightened such fears. In England, life at school seems to have been less rigorously regulated and controlled; pupils sometimes recalled their period at school as one of freedom and discovery. The prevalence of Evangelical conceptions of women's moral superiority tended to allay fears of female susceptibility, and the idea that adolescence marked a separate stage in girls' development, though gaining currency, was less fully developed than in France. For Catholics, First Communion helped define this period of transition. Possibly one reason why English observers were less attuned to the notion of a liminal state between childhood and adulthood was that, in England, the Protestant confirmation ceremony was not of the same social and cultural importance as First Communion.

The organization and structure of learning at schools in France and England also differed, diverging in ways that reflect the effect of contrasts between the convent and domestic models of schooling. Girls at school in France tended to be clearly divided into a hierarchy of classes inspired by Jesuit patterns of instruction, and examinations and the notion of competitive emulation were integral to teaching. Preparation for taking the teaching diplomas was readily absorbed into the pattern of school instruction. In England, by contrast, both boys' and girls' schools were informally organized, and it was not until the middle of the nineteenth century that more rigid forms of classification were introduced. In girls' schools this informality, which accorded well with the notion of the school as family, was often prized and accentuated in ways that permitted schoolmistresses to develop child-centred pedagogical strategies. Interest in approaches focusing on the individual child often engendered a suspicion of rigid systems of examination in England, although by mid-century many schoolmistresses were recognizing the value of external examinations as a way of attesting to the quality of the instruction they offered.

Although the content of the curriculum in France and England was broadly similar, attitudes to female intellectual development often differed. This divergence is reflected in the greater number of male professors employed in French girls' schools and in the higher status accorded them. In England, schoolmistresses and their assistants often took on most of the teaching, delegating only the 'accomplishments' to visiting masters. While there were limits to what they could achieve without access to higher education and with only limited resources, the instruction some offered seems to have been of a fairly high standard. Anxiety about the unfeminine nature of certain subjects did sometimes put limits on the instruction girls were offered, and contemporary commentators tended to emphasize the difference in male and female intellects. But the notion that women were fundamentally intellectually inferior seems to have had little sway, and was decisively rebutted by the SIC. In France, male professors played a more significant part in instruction and their intellectual superiority was often stressed.

At the same time, while the teaching examinations offered a public endorsement of female instruction, there was resistance to proposals for extending the limited demands made of candidates. The contrast again highlights the impact of religion on women's experiences. While the Protestant notion of the 'priesthood of all believers' undermined claims that women were of inferior intelligence, the authority attributed to male clerics in the Catholic church could strengthen those claims. In Protestant circles, notions of self-improvement could foster a positive understanding of women's intelligence, while Catholic authors tended to insist upon the moral value of learning for women and to present reading as a devotional activity. The instruction girls received at school on either side of the Channel differed less in content than in scope.

There were thus significant contrasts between the experiences of pupils and their teachers in France and England, contrasts that point to distinctions between the experiences of English and French women more generally. Pupils at school in England had more freedom than their French counterparts and might be encouraged to develop their intellectual knowledge in ways which were more often closed to French girls; women in France, on the other hand, were more often able to claim a public role and less subject to stringent legal constraints than their English counterparts. These differences seem to support both Blanqui's view that 'the ideal for a woman was to become an adult in France, having been a girl in England', and Mona Ozouf's contention that patterns of gender relations differed on either side of the Channel. Such differences contributed to shaping the gendered notions of national character that hindered the exchange of pedagogical ideas and practices across the Channel.

In both countries, notions of domestic femininity shaped women's lives behind and beyond the school walls, but such ideas resonated differently in distinct social, political, cultural, religious, and economic contexts. At the same time, in different ways, women in the two countries were able to carve out roles for themselves that expanded, challenged, and modified contemporary gender ideals. However, differences between women's experiences in England and France cannot simply be attributed to differences in these ideals, nor explained by reference to conceptions of singularity. Gender was a powerful factor, but so were religious differences, differences in the economic and class structure of the two countries, and differences in notions of the state, patterns of professionalization and the legal status of women. None of these forces can be taken as paramount. It is by exploring the interplay of gender with religion, with nation, with class, with the state, the economy, the legal system, with cultural influences and representations, that we can come a little closer to understanding the experiences of women and men in the nineteenth century.

Select Bibliography

MANUSCRIPT SOURCES

England

British and Foreign School Society Archive, Brunel University:
    319: Middle class schools: women.
    437–49: Applications and testimonials to Borough Road College (women), 1817–58.
    814: Home and Colonial Training School Society Reports, 1836–1900.

College of Preceptors Archive, Institute of Education Archives, University of London:
    GB/366/DC/COP

Girton College, Cambridge:
    GCPP Davies 9: Papers of the London Association of Schoolmistresses, 1866–88.
    GCPP Parkes 1: MS writings, 1843–83.
    GCPP Parkes 6: Major correspondents, 1846–72.

Harris Manchester College, Oxford: MSS J. Martineau 1, 2, 3, 8.

Keele University Library, Special Collections and Archives: Wedgwood Papers, E13, E50, E55.

King's College, Cambridge: Papers of E. M. Forster, GBR/0272/EMF/21/1.

Lilly Library, Indiana University, Bloomington: Gill MSS.

London Metropolitan Archives:
    Governess papers, I: 1846–7
    E4: GBI Ladies' Accounts

North London Collegiate School Archives:
    Frances Mary Buss and Family, History of the school, B1.
    Place of the School in History, Rs7iv.
    Register of applications for admission to North London Collegiate School, 1871, 1881.

Regent's Park College, Oxford, Angus Library, Acc. 142 Ryland/ Saffery.

Tudor Hall School, Banbury, Prospectuses and miscellaneous papers on the history of the school.

University of Sheffield, Special Collections Department, Elizabeth Firth Manuscripts, MS 58/A–B.

Whitelands College, London, Archives, Register of Mistresses, 3 vols., 1842–9

France

Archives Nationales: Sous-série F^{17}: Instruction publique 2680, 6843–9, 9763–71, 12431, 12432, 12433, 12448, 20215–22999.

Archives Départementales:
    Gironde: principally séries T (Instruction publique) and Depot Vt III 3e E: Brevets de Capacité.
    Nord: principally séries T (Instruction publique) and J (Archives privées).
    Seine: principally séries VD (Fonds des mairies), $D^2 T^1$ (Personnel enseignant dans les écoles privées de jeunes filles 1836–49), DT Supplément (*Déclarations* d'ouverture), séries Q (Enregistrement), D10 (Faillites), and séries U (Justice).

Archives Municipales de Bordeaux: Fonds Ploux, Fonds Ferrere.

Archives Municipales de Douai: series R (Instruction publique).

PRINTED PRIMARY SOURCES

When these works are comparative or European in perspective, they are classified by language. For instance, C. Campbell-Orr (ed.), *Wollstonecraft's daughters: womanhood in England and France, 1780–1920* (Manchester: Manchester University Press, 1996), is to be found in the sources on England.

England

Advice to governesses (London, 1827).

Aikin, Lucy, *Epistles on women* (London, 1818).

Austen, Jane, *Emma* (London: Penguin Books, 1996).

Bainbridge, William Henry, *A lecture to promote the establishment of a governesses' institution in Liverpool* (London, 1849).

Barbauld, Anna Laetitia, *A legacy for young ladies, consisting of miscellaneous pieces in prose and verse by the late Mrs Barbauld*, ed. Lucy Aikin (Boston, 1826).

Beale, Dorothea, 'On the education of girls, by a Utopian', *Fraser's Magazine*, 74 (Oct. 1866), 509–24.

——— *Reports issued by the Schools Inquiry Commission on the education of girls* (London, 1869).

——— 'Girls' schools past and present', *Nineteenth Century*, 25 (1888), 541–54.

Beale, D. and Soulsby, L., *Work and play in girls' schools* (London, 1898).

Beard, John Relly, 'What should a woman learn?', *Monthly Repository*, 5 (Aug. 1831), 526–31.

Bennet, George (ed.) *The Christian governess: a memoir and selection from the correspondence of Miss Sarah Bennet* (London, 1862).

Bennet, Georgiana, *Remarks on female education* (London, 1842).

Boucherett, Jessie, 'The condition of women in France', *Contemporary Review*, 5 (1867), 98–113.

Broadhurst, Frances, *A word in favour of female schools* (London, 1826).

Brontë, Anne. *Agnes Grey*, 2nd edn. (Edinburgh, 1850).

Brontë, Charlotte, *Jane Eyre* (Oxford: Oxford University Press, 1992).

——— *Villette* (London: Penguin Books, 1979).

Browne, Mary, *The diary of a girl in France*, ed. H. N. Shore (London: John Murray, 1905).

Butler, Josephine, *An autobiographical memoir* (Bristol: J. W. Arrowsmith, 1909).

Chirol, John Louis, *An enquiry into the best system of female education, or boarding school and home education attentively considered* (London, 1809).

Clough, Anne Jemima, 'Hints on the organization of girls' schools', *Macmillan's Magazine*, 14 (Oct. 1866), 434–9.

Clough, Blanche Athena, *A memoir of Anne Jemima Clough* (London, 1897).

Cobbe, Frances Power, *Female education and how it would be affected by university examinations*, 2nd edn. (London, 1862).

——— *Life of Frances Power Cobbe by herself* (London, 1894).

The complete governess: a course of mental instruction for ladies, by an experienced teacher (London, 1826).

Crockford's Scholastic Directory for 1861 (London, 1861).

Davies, Emily, *The higher education of women*, 2nd edn. (London, 1988).

Down, T. C., 'Schooldays with Miss Clough', *Cornhill Magazine*, 3rd series, 48 (1920), 674–8.

Eastlake, Elizabeth, 'Vanity Fair, Jane Eyre and the Governesses Benevolent Institution', *Quarterly Review*, 84 (Dec. 1848), 153–85.

Edgeworth, Maria, *Letters to literary ladies* (London: Everyman, 1993).

Ellis, Mildred, 'Education of Young Ladies', *Central Society for Education, First Publication* (1838).

Ellis, Sarah, *The women of England: their social duties and domestic habits* (London, 1839).

——— *The home life and letters of Mrs Ellis, compiled by her nieces* (London, 1893).

Eliot, George, 'Woman in France: Mme de Sablé', *Westminster Review*, 91 (1854), 448–73.

Fawcett, Millicent Garrett, *What I remember* (London: F. Unwin, 1924).

Fitton, Sarah, *How I became a governess* (London, 1861).

Fraser, Mary Crawford, *A diplomatist's wife in many lands*, 2 vols. (London: Hutchinson & Co., 1911).

Gardiner, Everilda Anne, *Recollections of a beloved mother* (London, 1842).

Elizabeth Gaskell: a portrait in Letters, ed. J. A. V. Chapple (Manchester: Manchester University Press, 1980).

The letters of Elizabeth Gaskell, ed. J. A. V. Chapple and A. Pollard (Manchester: Manchester University Press, 1997).

The Governess, a repertory of female education, 1855–6.

Governesses' Benevolent Institution (GBI), *Reports of the committee of management, 1843–1853* (London, 1844–54).

Haldane, Mary Elizabeth, *Mary Elizabeth Haldane, a record of a hundred years, 1825–1925* (London: Hodder & Stoughton, 1925).

Harrison, Jane Elizabeth, *Reminiscences of a student's life* (London: Hogarth Press, 1925).

Havergal, Maria, *Memorials of Frances Ridley Havergal* (London, 1880).

Herford, William Henry, *In Memoriam: Louisa Carbutt and Brooke House, 1860–1870* (Manchester: Manchester University Press, 1907).

Hints to a young governess on beginning a school (London, 1857).

'An inquiry into the state of girls' fashionable schools', *Fraser's Magazine*, 31 (1845), 703–12.

Jolly, Sarah, *Thoughts on the vocation and profession of the teacher* (London, 1854).

Jones, Emily, *As I remember: an autobiographical ramble* (London: A. & C. Black, 1922).

Memorial of Agnes Elizabeth Jones (1832–1868) (London, 1871).

Kavanagh, Julia, *Nathalie*, 3 vols. (London, 1850).

Keary, Eliza, *Memoir of Annie Keary* (London, 1882).

Kemble, Frances Ann, *Records of a girlhood: an autobiography*, 3 vols. (London, 1878).

Lachlan, Elizabeth, *Jehovh-Jireh, or the provisions of a faithful God* (London, 1850).

A Legacy of affection, advice and instruction from a retired governess to the present pupils of an establishment near London for female education (London, 1827).

Lumsden, Louisa, *Yellow leaves: memories of a long life* (Edinburgh: Blackwood & Sons, 1933).

McCrindell, Rachel, *The schoolgirl in France*, 4th edn. (New York, 1846).

Mair, Robert H., *The educator's guide for teachers, parents and guardians* (London, 1866).

Elizabeth Malleson: autobiographical notes and letters, ed. Hope Malleson (London: privately printed, 1926).

Martineau, Harriet, 'Female industry', *Edinburgh Review*, 222 (1859), 293–337.

—— 'Middle class education in England', *Cornhill Magazine*, 10 (1864), 549–68.

—— 'On female education', *Monthly Repository*, 18 (1823), 77–81.

——*Autobiography* (London: Virago, 1983).

Harriet Martineau: selected letters, ed. Valerie Sanders (Oxford: Clarendon Press, 1990).

Harriet Martineau's letters to Fanny Wedgwood, ed. Elizabeth Arbuckle (Stanford: Stanford University Press, 1983).

Maurice, Mary, *Governess life: its trials, duties and encouragements* (London, 1836).

——*Mothers and governesses* (London, 1847)

The life of Mary Russell Mitford, related in a selection from her letters to her friends, ed. A. G. L'Estrange, 3 vols. (London, 1870).

More, Hannah, *Strictures on the modern system of female education with a view of the principles and conduct prevalent among women of rank and fortune*, 2 vols. (London, 1826).

Nevinson, Margaret Wynne, *Life's fitful fever: a volume of memories* (London: A. & C. Black, 1920).

Pankhurst, Emmeline, *My own story* (London: Eveleigh Nash, 1914).

Parkes, Bessie Rayner, *Essays on women's work* (London, 1865).

Parliamentary papers XXVIII: Reports of the Schools Inquiry Commission (London, 1868).

Pendered, Anne Eliza, *Remarks on female education, adapted particularly to the regulation of schools* (London, 1823)

Pitman, Emma, *My governess life* (London, 1883).

Reeve, Clara, *Plans of education, with remarks on the system of other writers* (London, 1792).

Ridout, S. F., *Letters to a young governess on the principles of education* (London, 1838).

Robinson, Clare, *Notes and letters* (Frome: Limpsfield & Co., 1906).

Ruskin, John, *The Winnington Letters: John Ruskin's correspondence with Margaret Alexis Bell and the children at Winnington Hall*, ed. John Van Aikin Burd (London: George Allen & Unwin, 1969).

Sewell, Elizabeth, *Principles of education drawn from nature and revelation and applied to female education in the upper classes*, 2 vols. (London, 1865).

—— 'The reign of pedantry in girls' schools', *Nineteenth Century*, 23 (1888), 216–38.

——*Autobiography of Elizabeth Missing Sewell* (London: Longmans, Green & Co., 1907).

The life of Mrs Sherwood (chiefly autobiographical), ed. Sophia Kelly (London, 1854)

Shirreff, Emily, *Intellectual education and its influence on the character and happiness of women* (London, 1858)

Shorter, Clement (ed.), *The Brontës: life and letters*, 2 vols., 2nd edn. (New York: Haskell House Publishers, 1969).

The memoirs of Susan Sibbald (1783–1812), ed. Francis Paget-Hett (London: J. Lane, 1926).

Smith, Charlotte, *Anne Cave*, 2 vols. (London, 1864).

Smith, Mary, *Autobiography of Mary Smith, schoolmistress and non-conformist*, 2 vols. (London, 1892).

The letters of S.S.S and L.H.M.S: Mrs and Miss Soulsby, ed. E.A, B.H.S., and P.H. (London: privately printed, 1929).

Squier, J. O., *The character and mission of women* (London, 1837).

Stevens, C., *Guide for governesses (English and Foreign) Nursery and Finishing* (York, 1875).

Stoddart, Anna, *Life and letters of Hannah E. Pipe* (London, 1908).

Taylor, Ann, *Hints on the education of girls* (London, 1814).

Transactions of the National Association for the Promotion of Social Science, 1859–65.

Ward, Mrs Humphry, *A writer's recollections*, 2 vols. (London: William Collins, 1918).

Webb, Beatrice, *My apprenticeship*, 2nd edn. (Cambridge: Cambridge University Press, 1979).

Whittaker, G. B., *Boarding schools and London masters' directory* (London, 1828).

Willard, Emma, *Journals and letters from France and Great Britain* (New York, 1833).

Wilson, Sheridan, *Agnes Moreville* (London, 1845).

Woman's worth, or hints to raise the female character (London, 1844).

A word to a young governess by an old one (London, 1860).

Yonge, Charlotte, *Womankind* (London, 1876).

France

A.M. (Madame), *Les Promenades du pensionnat: ouvrage moral, instructif et amusant, dédié aux jeunes demoiselles* (Paris, 1825).

Ackermann, Louise, *Œuvres de Louise Ackermann. Ma vie, premières poésies* (Paris, 1885).

Adam, Juliette, *Mme Adam (Juliette Lamber). Le roman de mon enfance et de ma jeunesse* (Paris: A. Lemerre, 1902).

Allix, Mlles, *Trois allocutions adressées aux familles par Mlles Allix, lors des distribution de prix qui ont eu lieu à leur institution, les trois premières années de sa fondatoin, les 17 août 1843, 16 août 1844, 19 août 1845, Institution Allix, Fontenay-le-Comte (Vendée), 2 rue des Capucins* (Paris, 1845).

Armaillé, Comtesse d', *Quand on savait vivre heureux (1830–1860), souvenirs de jeunesse* (Paris, 1931).

Audouard, Olympe, *Voyage à travers mes souvenirs* (Paris, 1884).

Bachellery, Joséphine, *Discours prononcé par Mme Bachellery, le jour de la distribution des prix, donné le 25 août 1842, en son institution, Passage Sandrié, 2* (Paris, 1842).

———— *Discours prononcé par Mme Bachellery, le jour de la distribution des prix, donnés le 21 août 1843 en son Institution, Passage Sandrié 2, à Paris* (Paris, 1843).

———— *Lettres sur l'éducation des femmes* (Paris, 1848).

———— *Discours prononcé par Mme Bachellery, le jour de la distribution des prix, en son institution, Grande Rue Neuve, Cote St André (Isère)* (Lyon, 1857).

———— *Discours prononcé par Mme Bachellery, le jour de la distribution des prix, donné le 21 août 1858, en son institution, Grande Rue Neuve, Cote St André (Isère)* (Lyon, 1858).

Badère, Clémence, *Mes mémoires* (Paris, 1886).

Barrau, Caroline, *La femme et l'éducation* (Paris, 1870).

Bastard de Saulieu (Madame), *Dernière année du pensionnat* (Paris, 1826).

Bonnefonds, Elisabeth de, *Mes souvenirs* (Paris, 1869).

Bourdon, Mathilde, *Souvenirs d'une institutrice* (Paris, 1859).

Mémoires de Adèle Boury (Paris, 1833).

Brada, Mme (pseud. of Henrietta Consuela de Puliga), *Souvenirs d'une petite du Second Empire* (Paris, 1921).

Breton, Geneviève, *Journal 1867–1875* (Paris: Ramsay, 1985).

Bronville, Laure, *Mémoire en défense et expertise pour Mlle Laure Bronville (Pensionnat, demi-pension et externat de demoiselles) contre la ville de Paris* (Paris, 1865).

Buisson, Ferdinand (ed.), *Nouveau dictionnaire de pédagogie et d'instruction primaire*, 2nd edn., 2 vols. (Paris, 1914).

Caillard, Marie, *Entretiens familiers d'une institutrice avec ses élèves* (Paris, 1863).

Caillot, Antoine, *Tableau des exercices et de l'enseignement en usage dans un pensionnat de jeunes demoiselles dirigé par une sage institutrice*, 2 vols. (Paris, 1816).

Camecasse, Valentine, *Souvenirs de Mme Camecasse, Douai au XIXe siècle, salons parlementaires sous la IIIe République* (Paris, 1924).

Campan, Jeanne, *De l'éducation, suivi de conseils aux jeunes filles*, 3 vols. (Paris, 1824).

Capelle, Marie, *Mémoires de Marie Capelle, Veuve Lafarge, écrits par elle-même*, 4 vols. (Paris, 1841–2).

Carroy (Madame), *Étude et récréation ou l'intérieur d'un pensionnat: ouvrage divisé en trente journées, contenant plusieurs histoires morale et instructives, dédié aux jeunes demoiselles* (Paris, 1825).

Charpentier, Léopold, *Des moyens d'améliorer et de généraliser l'éducation des jeunes filles* (Paris, 1838).

Conseils d'une maîtresse de pension à ses élèves, sur la politesse et sur la manière de se conduire dans le monde, 4th edn. (Lyon, 1841).

Daubié, Julie-Victoire, *La femme pauvre au XIXe siècle*, 3rd edn., 2 vols. (Paris: Côté-femmes, 1992).

Dauriat, Louise, *Mémoire adressé à Messieurs les membres du Conseil Général du Département de la Seine* (Paris, 1846).

Delacoste, Amicie, *Souvenirs de la Marquise Delacoste* (Lille, 1886).

Demogeot, Joseph and Montucci, Henry, *De l'enseignement secondaire en Angleterre et en Écosse* (Paris, 1868).

Desplechin, Mme, *Essai sur l'éducation par Mme D____, Institutrice* (Paris, 1825).

Dupanloup, Félix-Antoine, *Femmes savantes et femmes studieuses* (Paris, 1867).

____ *La femme studieuse*, 3rd edn. (Paris, 1875).

____ *M. Duruy et l'éducation des filles. Lettre de Mgr. L'Evêque d'Orléans à un des ses collègues* (Paris, 1867).

Dupuy, Mme, 'Pension normale de jeunes filles Protestantes', *Archives du Christianisme*, 11 (1828), 378.

Esquiros, Adèle, *Histoire d'une sous-maîtresse* (Paris, 1861).

Examen de conscience d'une pensionnaire, à l'usage des maisons d'éducation (Paris, 1825).

Fallet, Céline, *Education des jeunes filles. Conseils aux mères et aux institutrices* (Paris, 1854).

Farrenc, Césarée, *Ce que peut être une femme* (Paris, 1874).

Fénelon, François Salignac de la Mothe, *De l'éducation des filles*, ed. C. Defodon, 3rd edn. (Paris, 1882).

Gautier, Judith, *Le collier des jours, souvenirs de ma vie* (Paris, 1904).

Genlis, Stéphanie-Félicité Du Crest, de, *Discours sur la suppression des couvents des religieuses et sur l'éducation publique des femmes* (Paris, 1790).

Goblet, François, *Dictionnaire administratif et topographique de la ville de Paris* (Paris, 1808).

Gossot, Emile, *Un pensionnat d'autrefois. Souvenirs d'une pensionnaire* (Tours: A. Mame et fils, 1900).

Goy, P., *L'éducation des filles. Discours prononcé dans l'École Normale de Sainte Foy, le 6 juillet 1868* (Paris, 1868).

Le Groing la Maisonneuve, Antoinette, *Essai sur le genre d'instruction qui paraît le plus analogue à la destination des femmes* (Paris, an VII).

Guide de la pieuse pensionnaire, à l'usage des pensions et de toutes les maisons religieuses d'éducation, 2nd edn. (Tours, 1850)

Guizot, Pauline, *Education domestique ou Lettres de famille sur l'éducation*, 2 vols. (Paris, 1826).

Jubé de la Perelle, Camille, *Des établissements d'éducation de la première enfance et des établissments d'éducation des filles* (Paris, 1849).

Kilian, Etienne, *De l'instruction des filles à ses divers degrés, institutions et pensions, enseignement primaire, supérieure et élémentaire* (Paris, 1842).

Leblois, L., *La mission de la femme et en particulier son rôle dans l'éducation religieuse de l'enfance*, 3rd edn. (Paris, 1870).

Lebrun, Isidore, *Vues sur l'organization de l'Instruction Publique et sur l'éducation des filles* (Paris, 1816).

Legouvé, Ernest, *La femme en France au XIXe siècle*, 2nd edn. (Paris, 1873)

Lemonnier, Charles, *Elisa Lemonnier, fondatrice de la société pour l'enseignement professionnel des femmes* (Saint-Germain, 1866).

Léon, Henri, *Les indiscrétions de Jehan Bomoloque à l'endroit des maîtresses de pensions* (Paris, 1855).

Lévi, M., *Discours en vers, prononcé à la distribution des prix de l'institution de Mme Le Duc-Housset, le 23 août 1825, par M.Lévi, Professeur* (Paris, 1825).

Lévi-Alvarès, David, *Education secondaire et supérieure des jeunes filles* (Paris, 1847).

―――― *Instruction publique et privée. Manuel de la méthode de M. D. Lévi* (Paris, 1835–6).

―――― *Éducation des femmes. David Lévi-Alvarès, 1794–1870*, ed. T. Lévi-Alvarès, 2 vols. (Paris: L. Cerf, 1909).

Lequien, Mlle, *Institution des jeunes demoiselles dirigée par Mlle Lequien. Discours prononcé à la distribution des prix, le 28 août 1838, Poissy* (Paris, 1838).

Une belle âme. Notice et souvenirs intimes de Mlle Adeline Lombrail (Lille, 1913).

Louis, Mme (Veuve), *Mémoires, écrits par elle-même* (Bordeaux, 1844).

Loveday, Douglas, *Petition à la Chambre des Pairs par Douglas Loveday se plaignant du rapt de séduction opéré sur ses deux filles et sur sa nièce dans une maison d'éducation, où il les avait placées à Paris* (Paris, 1821).

Maintenon, Françoise de, *Entretiens sur l'éducation des filles*, ed. Th. Lavallée (Paris, 1854).

Marchef-Girard, Joséphine, *Les femmes, leur passé, le présent, leur avenir* (Paris, 1860).

Marguerin, E. and Motheré, J., *De l'enseignement des classes moyennes et des classes ouvrières en Angleterre* (Paris, 1864).

Martin, Louis-Aimé, *De l'éducation des mères de famille, ou de la civilisation du genre humain par les femmes* (Paris, 1834).

Martin, Thérèse Mélanie, *Souvenirs d'une ancienne élève de la Maison d'Education de la Légion d'Honneur d'Ecouen* (Saint Dizier, 1924).

Méliot, Agathe, *Derniers conseils, conversations entre une institutrice et ses élèves sur divers sujets de morale et d'instruction* (Paris, 1841).

Michel, Louise, *Je vous écris de ma nuit: correspondence générale, 1850–1904*, ed. Xavière Gauthier (Paris: Éditions de Paris, 1999).

Un ménage d'artistes sous le Premier Empire, Journal inédit de Mme Moitte, femme de Jean-Guillaume Moitte, statuaire, membre de l'academie des Beaux-Arts, 1805–7, ed. P. Cottin (Paris: Plon, 1932).

Necker de Saussure, Albertine, *L'éducation progressivem ou, étude du cours de la vie.* Vol. III: *Étude de la vie des femmes* (Paris, 1838).

Le petit manuel de la pieuse pensionnaire, ou recueil de réflexions, prières et pratiques de piété à l'usage de la jeunesse Chrétienne, (Paris, 1836).

Picanon, Mme (Henriette Berthoud), *Mon frère et moi. Souvenirs de jeunesse, accompagnés de poèsies d'Eugène Berthoud* (Paris, 1876).

Elizabeth de Prades. Sa vie. Son journal. Ses funérailles, ed. Henri Calbiat (Tours, 1890).

Puech, Hermance, *Nôtre ange-gardien. Souvenirs intimes* (Paris, 1891).

Rémusat, Claire de, *Essai sur l'éducation des femmes* (Paris, 1826).

Renan, Ernest, *Ma sœur Henriette* (Paris, 1896).

Renneville, Sophie de, *Lettres d'Octavie, jeune pensionnaire de la Maison St Clair, ou essai sur l'éducation de demoiselles* (Paris, 1806).

Revue de l'enseignement des femmes, January 1845–January 1848.

Riobé, Charles, *Notice sur ma fille* (Le Mans, 1863).

Rivail, H. L. D., *Projet de réforme concernant les examens et les maisons d'éducation des jeunes personnes, suivi d'une proposition touchant à l'adoption des ouvrages classiques par l'Université au sujet du nouveau projet de loi sur l'enseignement* (Paris, 1847).

Le Roy, Mélanie, *Veillées des pensionnaires ou les récréations d'une retraite* (Paris, 1830).

Sand, George, *Correspondance de George Sand*, ed. G. Lubin, 25 vols. (Paris: Garnier, 1964–91).

———— *Histoire de ma vie* (Paris: Stock, 1996).

Sault, C. de (pseud. of Claire de Charnacé), 'Les femmes dans la société anglaise', *Revue Européenne*, 8 (1860), 299–31.

Sauvan, Jeanne Lucile, *Cours normal des institutrices primaires* (Paris, 1840).

Shaw, Mathilde, *Illustres et inconnus, souvenirs de ma vie* (Paris, 1906).

Simons-Candeille, Mme, *Souvenirs de Brighton, de Londres et de Paris: et quelques fragmens de littérature légère* (Paris, 1818).

Sincère, Marie (pseud. of Marie Romieu), *Les pensionnats de jeunes filles* (Paris, 1853).

———— *La femme au XIXe siècle* (Paris, 1858).

Stern, Daniel (pseud. of Marie d'Agoult), *Mes souvenirs 1806–33* (Paris, 1877).

Tristan, Flora, *Promenades dans Londres, ou l'aristocratie et les prolétaires anglais*, ed. François Bédarida (Paris: François Maspero, 1978).

Villars, Fanny, *Deux ans dans la vie d'une jeune fille* (Paris, 1868).

Weiler, Amelie, *Journal d'une jeune fille mal dans son siècle, 1840–1859*, ed. Nicolas Stoskopf (Strasbourg: La Nuée bleue, 1994).

SECONDARY LITERATURE

England

Aldrich, R., *School, and society in Victorian Britain: Joseph Payne and the new world of education* (Epping: College of Preceptors, 1995).

Allen, K. and Mackinnon, A., '"Allowed and expected to be educated and intelligent": the education of Quaker girls in nineteenth century England', *History of Education*, 27 (Dec. 1998), 391–402.

Anderson, K., 'Frances Mary Buss, the founder as headmistress, 1850–1894,' in *The North London Collegiate School, 1850–1950* (Oxford: Oxford University Press, 1950), 37–9.

Auerbach, N., *Communities of women: an idea in fiction* (Cambridge, Mass.: Harvard University Press, 1978).

Bamford, T. W., *The rise of the public schools* (London: Nelson, 1967).

Banks, O., *Biographical dictionary of British feminists, 1800–1930* (Brighton: Wheatsheaf, 1985).

Bellaigue, C. de, 'The development of teaching as a profession for women before 1870', *Historical Journal*, 44 (2001), 963–88.

—— ' "Educational homes" and "barrack-like schools": cross-Channel perspectives on secondary education for boys in mid-nineteenth century England and France', *Oxford Studies in Comparative Education*, 14/2 (2004).

Binfield, C., *Belmont's Portias: Victorian non-conformist education for girls* (London: Dr William's Trust, 1981).

Bryant, M., *The unexpected revolution: a study in the history of the education of women and girls in the nineteenth century* (London: University of London, 1979).

—— *The London experience of secondary education* (London: Athlone Press, 1986).

Burstall, S., *The story of Manchester High School for Girls* (Manchester: Manchester University Press, 1911).

Burstyn, J., *Victorian education and the ideal of womanhood* (London: Croom Helm, 1980).

Caine, B., *Destined to be wives: the sisters of Beatrice Webb*, 2nd edn. (Oxford: Oxford University Press, 1986).

Campbell-Orr, C. (ed.), *Wollstonecraft's daughters: womanhood in England and France, 1780–1920* (Manchester: Manchester University Press, 1996).

Carpenter, J. E., *The life and work of Mary Carpenter* (London, 1879).

Casteras, S., *Images of Victorian womanhood in English Art* (London: Associated University Presses, 1987).

Chambers-Schiller, L. V., *Liberty a better husband: single women in America: the generations of 1780–1840* (London: Yale University Press, 1984).

Charlton, K., *Women, religion and education in Early Modern England* (London: Routledge, 1999).

Cholmondely, E., *The story of Charlotte Mason, 1842–1923* (London: Dent, 1960).

Clark, T. and Sturge, W. H., *The Mount School, York; 1785–1814, 1831–1931* (London: J. M. Dent, 1931).

Cohen, M., ' "A habit of healthy idleness": boys' underachievement in historical perspective', in D. Epstein and J. Elwood (eds.), *Failing boys? Issues in gender and achievement* (Buckingham: Open University Press, 1998), 19–32.

—— 'Manliness, effeminacy and the French: gender and the construction of national character in eighteenth century England', in M. Cohen and T. Hitchcock (eds.), *English masculinities, 1660–1800* (Harlow: Longman, 1999) 44–61.

—— 'Gender and the public/private debate on education in the long eighteenth century', in R. Aldrich (ed.), *Public or private education? Lessons from history* (London: Woburn Press, 2004).

—— 'Language and meaning in a documentary source: girls' curriculum from the late eighteenth century to the Schools Inquiry Commission, 1868', *History of Education*, 34 (2005), 77–93.

Copelman, D. M., *London's women teachers: gender, class and feminism, 1870–1930* (London: Routledge, 1996).

Corfield, P., *Power and the professions in Britain*, 1700–1850 (London: Routledge, 1995).

Crawford, E., *Enterprising women: the Garretts and their circle* (London: Francis Boutle Publishers, 2002).

Davidoff, L. and Hall, C., *Family fortunes: men and women of the English middle class, 1780–1850*, rev. edn. (London: Routledge, 2002).

Davies, K., *Polam Hall: story of a school* (Darlington: Prudhoe, 1981).

De Zouche, D. E., *Roedean School, 1885–1955* (Brighton: privately printed, 1955).

Dyhouse, C., *Girls growing up in late Victorian and Edwardian England* (London: Routledge, 1981).

Firth, C. B., *Constance Louisa Maynard, Mistress of Westfield College* (London: Allen & Unwin, 1949).

Fletcher, S., *Feminists and bureaucrats: a study in the development of girls' education in the nineteenth century* (Cambridge: Cambridge University Press, 1980).

Freedman, E., 'Separatism as strategy: female institution building and American feminists, 1870–1930', *Feminist Studies*, 3 (1979), 512–29.

Gardner, P., *The lost elementary schools of Victorian England* (London: Croom Helm, 1984).

Gareth Evans, W., *Education and female emancipation: the Welsh experience, 1846–1914* (Cardiff: University of Wales Press, 1990).

Gerbod, P., 'L'enseignement de la langue française en Grande Bretagne au XIXe siècle', *Documents pour l'histoire du français langue étrangère ou seconde*, 2 (1988), 8–12.

Gerin, W., *Emily Brontë: a biography* (Oxford: Clarendon Press, 1971).

Glenday, N. and Price, M., *Reluctant revolutionaries: a century of Head Mistresses, 1884–1974* (London: Pitman, 1974).

Goldman, H., *Emma Paterson* (London: Lawrence & Wishart, 1974).

Goldman, L., *Science, reform and politics in Victorian Britain* (Cambridge: Cambridge University Press, 2002).

Goodman, J. and Martin, J., *Women and education, 1800–1980* (Basingstoke: Palgrave Macmillan, 2004).

Gordon, L., *Charlotte Brontë: a passionate life* (London: Vintage, 1995).

Gordon, S. C., 'Studies at Queen's College, Harley Street, 1848–1868', *British Journal of Educational Studies*, 3 (1955), 144–55.

Gorham, D., *The Victorian girl and the feminine ideal* (London: Croom Helm, 1982).

Green, N., 'Female education and school competition: 1820–1850', *History of Education Quarterly*, 18 (1978), 29–42.

Haight, G., *George Eliot: a biography* (Oxford: Clarendon Press, 1968).

Harvie, C., *The lights of liberalism: university liberals and the challenge of democracy, 1860–1886* (London: Allen Lane, 1976).

Hicks, P., *A quest of ladies: the story of a Warwickshire school* (Birmingham: Frank Jukes, 1949).

Higgs, E., 'Women, occupations and work in nineteenth-century censuses', *History Workshop Journal*, 23 (1987), 59–80.

Hill, B., 'A refuge from men: the idea of a Protestant nunnery', *Past and Present*, 117 (1987), 107–31.

Hilton, M. and Hirsch, P. (eds.), *Practical visionaries: women, education and social progress, 1790–1930* (London: Routledge, 2000).

Hirsch, P. and McBeth, M., *Teacher training at Cambridge: the initiatives of Oscar Browning and Elizabeth Hughes,* (London: Woburn Press, 2004).

Honey, J. R. de S., *Tom Brown's universe: the development of the public school in the nineteenth century* (London: Millington, 1977).

Howarth, J., 'Public schools, safety-nets and educational ladders: the classification of girls' secondary schools, 1880–1914', *Oxford Review of Education*, 11 (1985), 59–71.

Hughes, K., *The Victorian governess* (London: Hambledon Press, 1993).

Hunt, F. (ed.), *Lessons for life: the schooling of girls and women, 1850–1950* (Oxford: Basil Blackwell, 1987).

Jacobs, A., ' "The girls have done very decidedly better than the boys": girls and examinations, 1860–1902', *Journal of Educational Administration and History*, 33 (2001), 120–32.

James, M. E., *Alice Ottley: first Head-Mistress of the Worcester High School for Girls* (London: Longmans, 1914).

Kamm, J., *How different from us: a biography of Miss Buss and Miss Beale* (London: Bodley Head 1958).

—— *Hope deferred: girls' education in English history* (London: Methuen, 1965).

—— *Indicative past: a hundred years of the Girls' Public Day School Trust* (London: Allen & Unwin, 1971).

Kaye, E., *A history of Queen's College, London, 1848–1972* (London: Chatto & Windus, 1972).

Kollar, R., 'Foreign and Catholic: a plea to Protestant parents on the dangers of convent education in Victorian England', *History of Education*, 31 (2002), 335–50.

Koven, S. and Michel, S., 'Womanly duties: maternalist politics and the origins of welfare states in France, Germany, Great Britain and the United States, 1880–1920', *American Historical Review,* 95 (1990), 1077–1108.

Leach, C., 'Religion and rationality: Quaker women and science education, 1790–1850', *History of Education,* 35/1 (2006), 69–90.

McDermid, J. *The schooling of working-class girls in Victorian Scotland: gender, education and identity* (London: Routledge, 2005).

—— 'Handmaiden to a patriarchal tradition? The schoolmistress in Victorian Scotland', *Études Écossaises*, 9 (2003–4), 43–57.

MacLachlan, Herbert, *Records of a family, 1800–1933: pioneers in education, social service and liberal religion* (Manchester: Manchester University Press, 1935).

Manton, J., *Elizabeth Garrett Anderson* (London: Butler & Tanner, 1965).

—— *Mary Carpenter and the Ragged Schools* (London, 1976).

Marcus, S., *Apartment stories: city and home in nineteenth-century Paris and London* (Berkeley: University of California Press, 1999).

Matthews, A. W., *The life of Sarah Bache* (London: privately published, 1900).

Miller, P. J., 'Women's education, self-improvement and social mobility: a late eighteenth century debate', *British Journal of Educational Studies*, 20 (Oct. 1972), 302–14.

Mozeley, G. (ed.), *Letters to Jane from Jamaica, 1786–1796* (London, 1938).

Newsome, D., *Godliness and good learning: four studies on a Victorian ideal* (London: John Murray, 1961).

O'Brien, S., 'French nuns in nineteenth century England', *Past and Present*, 154 (1997), 142–81.

Ochs, K. and Phillips, D., 'Comparative studies and "cross-national attraction" in education', *Educational Studies,* 28 (2002), 325–39.

O'Connor, A. V., 'Influences affecting girls' secondary education in Ireland, 1860–1910', *Archivium Hibernicum*, 41 (1986), 83–98.

Pedersen, J. S., 'School-mistresses and Headmistresses: elites and education in nineteenth century England', *Journal of British Studies*, 15/1 (1975), 135–62.

—— *The reform of girls' secondary education in Victorian England: a study of elites and educational change* (New York: Garland, 1987).

Peterson, M. J., 'The Victorian governess: status incongruence,' in M. Vicinus (ed.), *Suffer and be still: women in the Victorian age*, 2nd edn. (London: Virago, 1980), 3–20.

—— *Family, love and work in the lives of Victorian gentlewomen* (Bloomington: Indiana University Press, 1989).

Pollock, L., *Forgotten children: parent–child relations from 1500–1900*, 6th edn. (Cambridge: Cambridge University Press, 1996).

Pope, R. D., 'Ladies' educational organizations in England, 1865–1875', *Paedagogica Historica*, 16 (1976), 336–60.

Poovey, M., *Uneven developments: the ideological work of gender in mid-Victorian England* (Chicago: University of Chicago Press, 1988).

Raikes, E., *Dorothea Beale of Cheltenham* (London: Archibald Constable, 1908).

Reeves, M., *Pursuing the muses: female education and non-conformist culture, 1700–1900* (Leicester: Leicester University Press, 1997).

Rendall, J., *The origins of modern feminism: women in Britain, France, and the United States, 1780–1860* (Basingstoke: Macmillan, 1985).

Ridley, A. E., *Frances Mary Buss and her work for education* (London, 1895).

Roach, J., *Public examinations in England, 1850–1900* (Cambridge: Cambridge University Press, 1971).

—— *A history of secondary education in England, 1800–1870* (London: Longman, 1986).

Rossiter, M., *Women scientists in America: struggles and strategies to 1940* (Baltimore: Johns Hopkins Press, 1982).

Rothblatt, S., *Tradition and change in English Liberal education* (London: Faber & Faber, 1976).

—— *The revolution of the dons*, 2nd edn. (Cambridge: Cambridge University Press, 1981).

—— and Wittrock, B. (eds.), *The European and American university since 1800* (Cambridge: Cambridge University Press, 1993).

Seaborne, M., *The English school, its architecture and organization, 1370–1870* (London: Routledge & Kegan Paul, 1971).

Sharp, E., *Hertha Ayrton, 1854–1923: a memoir* (London: Edward Arnold, 1926).

Skedd, S., 'The education of women in Hanoverian Britain, c.1760–1820', D.Phil. thesis (Oxford, 1996).

—— 'Women teachers and the expansion of girls' schooling in England, c.1760–1820,' in H. Barker and E. Chalus (eds.), *Gender in eighteenth century England* (London: Longman, 1997), 101–26.

Stewart, W. A. C., *Progressives and radicals in English education, 1750–1970* (London: Macmillan, 1972).

Stoddart, A., *The life and letters of Hannah E. Pipe* (Edinburgh: Blackwood & Sons, 1908).

Stray, C., *Classics transformed: schools, universities, and society in England, 1830–1960* (Oxford: Clarendon Press, 1998).

—— (ed.), *Teaching and learning in nineteenth century Cambridge* (Cambridge: Cambridge University Press, 2001).

Sutherland, G., ' "Secondary education", the education of the middle classes', in G. Sutherland (ed.), *Education in Britain* (Dublin: Irish University Press, 1977).

Sutherland, G., *Ability, merit and measurement: mental testing and English education, 1800–1940* (Oxford: Clarendon Press, 1984).

—— 'The movement for the higher education of women: its social and intellectual context in England, c.1840–80', in P. J. Waller (ed.), *Politics and social change in modern Britain* (Brighton: Harvester Press, 1987), 91–116.

—— 'Examinations and the construction of professional identity: a case-study of England 1800–1950', *Assessment in Education*, 8 (2001), 51–64.

—— *Faith, duty and the power of mind: the Cloughs and their circle, 1820–1960* (Cambridge: Cambridge University Press, 2006).

Sutherland, J., *Mrs Humphry Ward: eminent Victorian, pre-eminent Edwardian* (Oxford: Oxford University Press, 1991).

Theobald, M., 'The sin of Laura: the meaning of culture in the education of nineteenth century women', *Journal of the Canadian Historical Association*, 1 (1990), 257–73.

Todd, M., *The life of Sophia Jex-Blake* (London: Macmillan, 1918).

Tolley, K., 'Science for ladies, Classics for gentlemen: a comparative analysis of scientific subjects in the curricula of boys' and girls' secondary schools in the United States, 1794–1850', *History of Education Quarterly*, 36 (1996), 129–53.

Tombs, R. and I., *That sweet enemy: the French and the British from the Sun King to the present* (London: Heinemann, 2006).

Uglow, Jenny, *Elizabeth Gaskell: a life* (London: Faber & Faber, 1985).

Vicinus, Martha, *Independent women: work and community for single women, 1850–1920* (London: Virago, 1985).

Vickery, Amanda, 'Golden Age to separate spheres? A review of the categories and chronology of English women's history', *Historical Journal*, 36 (1993), 383–414.

Wadsö-Lecaros, C., *The Victorian governess novel* (Lund: Lund University Press, 2001).

Watts, R., 'The Unitarian contribution to the development of female education 1790–1850', *History of Education*, 9 (1980), 273–86.

—— 'The Unitarian contribution to education in England from the late eighteenth century to 1853', Ph.D. thesis (Birmingham, 1987).

—— *Gender, power and the Unitarians in England, 1760–1860* (London: Longman, 1998).

West, K., *Chapter of governesses: a study of the governess in English fiction, 1800–1949* (London, 1949).

Whyte, W., 'Building a public school community, 1860–1910', *History of Education*, 32 (2003), 601–26.

Widdowson, F., *Going up into the next class: women and teacher training, 1840–1914* (London: Women's Research and Resources Centre, 1980).

Wilson, E. C., *Catherine Isabella Dodd, 1860–1932* (London: Sidgwick & Jackson, 1936).

Wilson, K., *Island Race: Englishness, empire and gender in the eighteenth century* (London: Routledge, 2003).

France

Abensour, L., *Le féminisme sous le règne de Louis Philippe et en 1848* (Paris, 1913).

Adams, C., 'Constructing mothers and families: the Society for Maternal Charity of Bordeaux, 1805–1860', *French Historical Studies*, 22 (1999), 65–86.

Ainval, C. d', *Le Couvent des Oiseaux: ces jeunes filles de bonne famille* (Paris: Perrin, 1991).

Albistur, M. and Armogathe, D. *Histoire du féminisme français du moyen âge à nos jours* (Paris: Éditions des femmes, 1977).

Alcover, M., 'The indecency of knowledge', *Rice University Studies*, 64 (1978), 25–41.

Ambrière, F., *Le siècle des Valmore: Marceline Desbordes-Valmore et les siens*, 2 vols. (Paris: Seuil, 1987).

Arnold, O., *Le corps et l'âme: la vie des religieuses au XIXe siècle* (Paris: Seuil, 1984).

Avanzani, G. (ed.), *Histoire de la pédagogie du XVIIe siècle à nos jours* (Toulouse: Privat, 1981).

Bardet, J.-P., Luc, J.-N., Robin-Romero, I. and Rollet, C. (eds.), *Lorsque l'enfant grandit: entre dépendance et autonomie* (Paris: Presses de l'Université de Paris-Sorbonne, 2003).

Bergman-Carton, J., *The woman of ideas in French art, 1830–1848* (London: Yale University Press, 1995).

Bertholet, D., *Les Français par eux-mêmes, 1815–1885* (Paris: Olivier Orban, 1991).

Birkett, J., 'Mme de Genlis et l'éducation des filles: pédagogie et romance', in G. Leduc (ed.), *L'éducation des femmes en Europe et en Amérique de la Révolution à 1848* (Paris: l'Harmattan, 1997), 433–41.

Bloch, J., 'Knowledge as a source of virtue: changes and contrasts in ideas concerning the education of boys and girls in eighteenth century France', *British Journal for Eighteenth Century Studies*, 8 (1985), 83–92.

Bourdelais, P. 'La femme seule', *Annales de Démographie Historique,* Section C (1981), 207–317.

Bourgade, G., *Contribution à l'étude de l'éducation féminine de 1830 à 1914* (Toulouse: Privat, 1979).

Cadier-Rey, G., 'Les Protestants, Orthez et l'enseignement: de la loi Guizot à la loi Ferry', *Bulletin de la société pour l'histoire du Protestantisme français*, 142 (1996), 738–52.

Cahour, J., *Les écoles et pensionnats privés au XIXe siècle* (Laval: Impr. Goupil, 1924).

Caplat, G. (ed.), *Les inspecteurs généraux de l'instruction publique: dictionnaire biographique, 1802–1914* (Paris: CNRS-INRP, 1986).

Caron, J.-C., *A l'école de la violence* (Paris: Aubier, 1999).

Carrive, L. (ed.), 'Lettres écrites par les filles du pasteur Reclus à Zoë Tuyes, 1856–1863', *Bulletin de la société pour l'histoire du Protestantisme français*, 143 (1997), 189–244, 663–70.

Chartier, R., Julia, D. and Compère, M.-M., *L'éducation en France du XVIe au XVIIIe siècle* (Paris: Société d'édition d'enseignement supérieur, 1976).

Clark, E., ' "By all the conduct of their lives": a laywomen's confraternity in New Orleans, 1730–1744', *William and Mary Quarterly*, 3rd ser. 54/4 (1997), 769–94.

Clark, L., *Schooling the daughters of Marianne: textbooks and the socialization of girls in modern French history* (Albany, NY: State University of New York Press, 1984).

—— *The rise of professional women in France* (Cambridge: Cambridge University Press, 2000).

Compère, M.-M., *Histoire de l'éducation en Europe: essai comparatif sur la façon dont elle s'écrit* (Paris: INRP, 1995).

—— 'Les pensions à Paris (1789–1820)', *Revue du Nord*, 78 (1996), 823–31.

—— and Savoie, P., 'Temps scolaire et condition des enseignants du secondaire en France depuis deux siècles', in M. M. Compère and P. Savoie (eds.), *Histoire du temps scolaire en Europe* (Paris: INRP, 1997), 267–312.

Constant, P., *Un monde à l'usage des demoiselles* (Paris: Gallimard, 1987).

Corbin, A., Lalouette, J. and Riot-Sarcey, M. (eds.), *Femmes dans la cité, 1815–1871* (Grâne: Créaphis, 1997).

Corrado-Pope, B., 'Maternal education in France, 1815–1848', *Proceedings of the Western Society for French History* (1975), 368–73.

Cosnier, C., *Le silence des filles: de l'aiguille à la plume* (Paris: Fayard, 2001).

Curtis, S. A., *Educating the faithful: religion, schooling and society in nineteenth-century France* (Dekalb, Ill.: Northern Illinois University Press, 2000).

Desan, Suzanne, *The family on trial in Revolutionary France* (Berkeley: University of California Press, 2004).

Dow, G., 'Reviewing Madame de Genlis: gouverneur, mere de l'Église, hypocrite', D.Phil. thesis (Oxford, 2004).

Duprat, C., *Usages et pratiques de la philanthropie: pauvreté, action sociale et lien sociale à Paris, au cours du premier XIXe siècle*, 2 vols. (Paris: Asssociation pour l'étude de l'histoire de la Sécurité Sociale, 1997)

Encrevé, A., *Protestants français au milieu du XIXe siècle: les réformés de 1848 à 1870* (Geneva: Labor-Fidès, 1986).

Farge, A. and Klapisch, C. (eds.), *Madame ou mademoiselle: itinéraires de la solitude féminine* (Paris: Montalba, 1984).

Ford, C., 'Private lives and public order in Restoration France: the seduction of Emily Loveday', *American Historical Review*, 99 (1994), 21–43.

_____ *Divided houses: religion and gender in modern France* (Ithaca: Cornell University Press, 2005).

Fraisse, G., *Muse de la raison: la démocratie exclusive et la différence des sexes* (Aix-en-Provence: Alinéa, 1989).

Fraisse, G. and Perrot, M. (eds.), *Histoire des femmes en occident: le XIXe siècle*, Vol. 4 of G. Duby and M. Perrot (eds.), *Histoire des femmes en occident* (Paris: Seuil, 1991).

Fumat, Y., 'La socialisation des filles au XIXe siècle', *Revue française de pédagogie*, 52 (1980), 36–46.

Gaignault, A.-C., 'L'éducation des jeunes filles au XIXe siècle à travers le "Journal des Jeunes Personnes", 1833–1848', *Mémoire de Maîtrise* (Paris IV, 1999).

Geison, G. L. (ed.), *Professions and the French state, 1700–1900* (Philadelphia: University of Pennsylvania Press, 1984).

Gemie, S., '"A danger to society?" Teachers and authority in France, 1833–1850', *French History*, 2 (1988), 264–87.

_____ *Women and schooling in France, 1815–1914* (Keele: Keele University Press, 1995).

Gerbod, Paul, *La condition universitaire en France au XIXe siècle* (Paris: Publications de la Faculté des Lettres et des Sciences Humaines de Paris, 1965).

_____ 'La langue anglaise en France, 1800–1871', *Revue Historique*, 275 (1986), 109–27.

_____ *Voyages aux pays des mangeurs de grenouilles* (Paris: l'Harmattan, 1991).

Gildea, R., *Education in provincial France 1800–1914: a study of three departments* (Oxford: Clarendon Press, 1983).

Gossot, E., *Mlle Sauvan, première inspectrice des écoles de Paris* (Paris: Hachette, 1880).

Grandière, M., 'L'éducation en France à la fin du XVIIIe siècle: quelques aspects d'un nouveau cadre éducatif, les "maisons d'éducation", 1760–1790', *Revue d'histoire moderne et contemporaine*, 33 (1986), 440–62.

Gréard, O., *L'enseignement secondaire des filles,* 3rd edn. (Paris: Delalain, 1883).

Groult, B., *Pauline Roland et comment la liberté vient aux femmes* (Paris: Laffont, 1991).

Harrigan, P., *Mobility, elites and education in French society of the Second Empire* (Waterloo: Wilfrid Laurier University Press, 1980).

Havelange, I., 'La littérature à l'usage des demoiselles (1750–1830)', Thèse de 3ᵉ cycle (Paris, École des Hautes Études en Sciences Sociales, 1984).

Hecquet, M. (ed.) *L'éducation des filles au temps de George Sand* (Artois: Presses Université, 1998).

Hirtz, C., 'L' ENS de Fontenay: les Protestants aux sources de la laïcité française', *Bulletin de la société pour l'histoire du Protestantisme français,* 135 (1989), 281–90.

Horvath, S., 'Victor Duruy and the controversy over secondary education for girls', *French Historical Studies,* 9 (1975), 83–104.

Houbre, G., 'Les influences religieuses sur l'éducation sentimentale des jeunes filles dans la première moitié du XIXe siècle (France et pays anglo-saxons ou germaniques),' in *Foi, fidélité, amitié en Europe à la période moderne; mélanges offerts à Robert Sauzet,* 2 vols. (Tours, 1995), ii. 341–54.

—— *La discipline de l'amour: l'éducation sentimentale des filles et des garçons à l'âge du romantisme* (Paris: Plon, 1997).

—— 'Demoiselles Catholiques et misses Protestantes: deux modèles éducatifs antagonistes au XIXe siècle', *Bulletin de la société pour l'histoire du Protestantisme français,* 146 (2000), 49–68.

Hufton, O., 'Women without men: widows and spinsters in Britain and France in the eighteenth century', *Journal of Family History,* 9 (1984), 355–76.

—— *Women and the limits of citizenship in the French Revolution* (Toronto: University of Toronto Press, 1990).

—— *The prospect before her: a history of women in Western Europe, 1500–1800* (London: Harper Collins, 1995).

Isambert-Jamati, V., *Solidarité fraternelle et réussite sociale: la correspondance familiale des Dubois-Goblot, 1841–1882* (Paris: l'Harmattan, 1995).

Julia, D., *Les trois couleurs du tableau noir: la Révolution* (Paris: Belin, 1981).

—— 'Le choix des professeurs en France: vocation ou concours, 1780–1850', *Paedagogica historica,* 30 (1994), 175–205.

Langlois, C., 'Les effectifs des congrégations féminines au XIXe siècle: de l'enquête statistique à l'histoire quantitative', *Revue de l'histoire de l'église de France,* 60 (1974), 44–53.

—— 'Le Catholicisme au féminin', *Archives des sciences sociales des religions,* 57 (1984), 29–53.

—— *Le Catholicisme au féminin: les congrégations féminines à supérieure générale au XIXe siècle* (Paris: Ed. du Cerf, 1984).

Lejeune, P., *Le moi des demoiselles: enquête sur le journal de jeune fille* (Paris: Seuil, 1993).

Lejeune-Resnick, E. 'L'éducation domestique (1830–1856): méthode pédagogique ou mission sociale?' *1848 Révolutions et mutations au XIXe siècle,* 8 (1992), 49–55.

Lemonnier, C., *Élisa Lemonnier, fondatrice de la société pour l'enseignement professionnel des femmes* (Saint-Germain, 1866).

Lévy, M.-F., *De mère en fille: l'éducation des françaises (1850–1880)* (Paris: Calman-Lévy, 1984).

Lewis, H. D., 'The legal status of women in nineteenth century France', *Journal of European Studies*, 10/3 (1980), 178–88.

Lougee, C., 'Noblesse, domesticity and social reform: the education of girls by Fénelon and Saint-Cyr', *History of Education Quarterly*, 14 (1974), 87–113.

Luc, J.-N., *L'invention du jeune enfant au XIXe siècle: de la salle d'asile à l'école maternelle* (Paris: Belin, 1997).

McMillan, James, *France and women, 1789–1914* (London, 2000).

Marchand, P., 'Un modèle éducatif à la veille de la révolution: les maisons d'éducation particulière', *Revue d'histoire moderne et contemporaine*, 22 (1975) 549–67.

Margadant, J. B., *Madame le Professeur: women educators in the Third Republic* (Princeton: Princeton University Press, 1990).

——— *The new biography: performing femininity in nineteenth-century France* (Berkeley: University of California Press, 2000).

Mayeur, F., *L'enseignement secondaire des jeunes filles sous la Troisième République* (Paris: Presses de la FNSP, 1977).

——— *L'éducation des filles au XIXe siècle* (Paris: Hachette, 1979).

——— 'Les Protestants dans l'Instruction publique au début de la Troisième République', in A. Encrevé and M. Richaud (eds.), *Les Protestants dans les débuts de la Troisième République* (Paris: Société de l'histoire du Protestantisme français, 1979), 37–57.

——— 'La formation des institutrices avant la loi Paul Bert: les cours normaux', *Revue d'histoire de l'Église de France*, 81 (1995), 121–30.

Mills, H., 'Negotiating the divide: women, philanthropy and the "public sphere" in nineteenth century France', in F. Tallet and N. Atkin (eds.), *Religion, society and politics in France since 1789* (London: Hambledon, 1991), 29–54.

——— 'Women and Catholicism in provincial France, 1800–1850: Franche-Comté in national context', D.Phil. thesis (Oxford, 1994).

Moch, L. P., 'Government policy and women's experience: the case of teachers in France', *Feminist Studies*, 14 (1988), 304–24.

Offen, K.,'The second sex and the Baccalauréat in Republican France, 1880–1924', *French Historical Studies*, 13 (1983), 252–86.

——— 'Defining feminism: a comparative historical approach', *Signs*, 14 (1988), 119–57.

Ozouf, M., *Les mots des femmes: essai sur la singularité française* (Paris: Fayard, 1995).

Pellissier, C., *La vie privée des notables lyonnais (XIXe siècle)* (Lyon: Ed. lyonnaises d'art et d'histoire, 1996).

Perrot, M. (ed.), *Histoire de la vie privée: de la Révolution à la Grande Guerre*, Vol. 4 of P. Ariès and G. Duby (eds.), *Histoire de la vie privée* (Paris: Seuil, 1986).

Poinsot, E. (pseudonym of Georges d'Heylli), *La fille de George Sand* (Paris: Impr. A. Davy, 1900).

Prost, A., *Histoire de l'enseignement en France 1800–1867* (Paris: Armand Colin, 1968).

Quartararo, A. T., *Women teachers and popular education in nineteenth century France* (Newark: University of Delaware Press, 1995).

Rapley, E.,'Fénelon revisited: a review of girls' education in eighteenth century France', *Social History/Histoire sociale,* 20 (1987), 299–318.

——— *Les Devotes: women and the church in seventeenth century France* (Montreal: McGill-Queen's University Press, 1990).

Raveaud, M., 'L'enfant, l'écolier et le citoyen: apprendre à appartenir et à participer à l'école en France et en Angleterre', Thèse de Doctorat (Paris VII, 2002), 7–10.

Riot-Sarcey, M., *De la liberté des femmes: lettres de dames au "Globe"* (Paris: Côté-Femmes, 1992).

—— *La démocratie à l'épreuve des femmes: trois figures critiques du pouvoir, 1830–1848* (Paris: Albin Michel, 1994).

Rogers, R., *Les demoiselles de la Légion d'Honneur* (Paris: Plon, 1992).

—— 'Competing visions of girls' secondary education in post-revolutionary France', *History of Education Quarterly*, 34 (1994), 147–70.

—— 'Boarding schools, women teachers and domesticity: reforming girls' secondary education in the first half of the 19th century', *French Historical Studies*, 19 (1995), 153–83.

—— 'Schools, discipline and community: diary writing and schoolgirl culture in the late nineteenth century', *Women's History Review*, 4/4 (1995), 525–54.

—— 'Le Professeur a-t-il un sexe? Les débats autour de la présence d'hommes dans l'enseignement féminin, 1840–1880', *Clio—histoire, femmes et société*, 4 (1996), 221–39.

—— 'Retrograde or modern? Unveiling the teaching nun in nineteenth century France', *Social History*, 23 (1998), 146–65.

—— 'Professional opportunities for middle class women in Paris', in M. Hietala and L. Nilsson (eds.), *Women in towns: the social position of urban women in historical context* (Stockholm: Stockholms universitet, 1999), 110–25.

—— 'French education for British girls in the nineteenth century', *Women's History Network Magazine*, 24 (2002), 21–9.

—— *From the Salon to the schoolroom: educating bourgeois girls in nineteenth century France* (Philadelphia: Penn State University Press, 2005).

Savoie, P., *Les enseignants du secondaire, XIXe–XXe siècles: le corps, le métier, les carrières* (Paris: INRP, 2000).

Secondy, Louis, 'L'éducation des filles en milieu Catholique au XIXe siècle', *Cahiers d'Histoire*, 26 (1981), 337–52.

Smith, B., *Ladies of the leisure class: the bourgeoises of Northern France in the nineteenth century* (Princeton: Princeton University Press, 1981).

Sonnet, M., *L'éducation des filles au temps des Lumières* (Paris: Ed. du Cerf, 1987).

—— 'Education', in N. Zemon-Davis and A. Farge (eds.), *Histoire des femmes, XVIe–XVIIIe siècles* (Paris: Seuil, 1991).

Thiercé, A., *Histoire de l'adolescence, 1850–1914* (Paris: Belin, 1999).

Timmermans, L., *L'accès des femmes à la culture, 1598–1715* (Paris: Champion, 1993).

Troubat, J., 'Le pensionnat des jeunes demoiselles de la rue de Monceau, vu par Balzac', *Revue de l'Econome*, 18 (1952), 321–7.

Yalom, Marilyn, 'Women's autobiography in French, 1793–1939: a selective bibliography', *French Literature Series*, 12 (1985), 197–205.

Index

Index